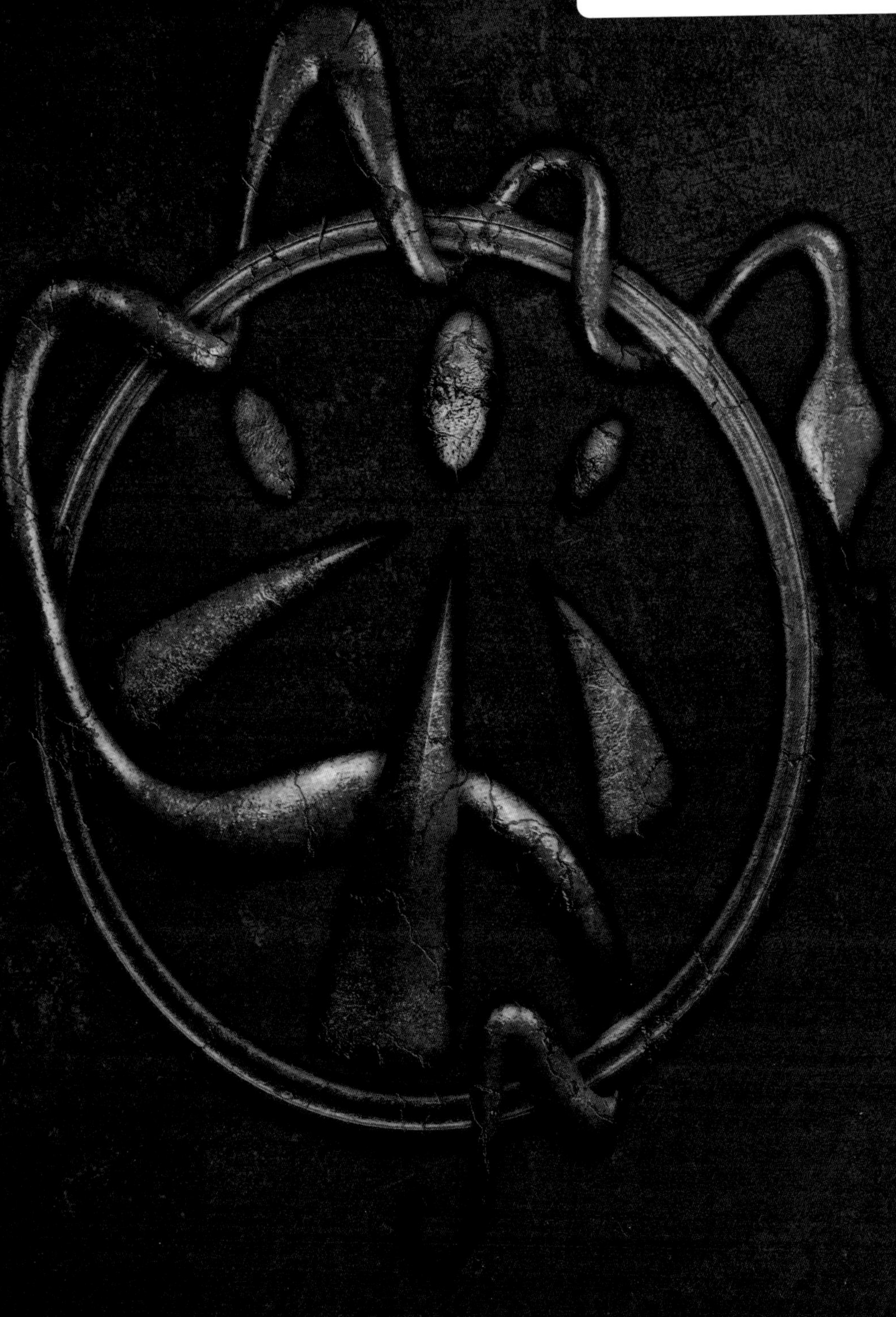

BLACK CARAVAN

Co-Publisher
JOSEPH SCHMALKE

Co-Publisher
RICH WOODALL

Editor
SHAWN FRENCH

Hype Man
STEVE ZAPP

SCOUT COMICS AND ENTERTAINMENT, INC

Chief Executive Officer
BRENDAN DENEEN

Co-Publishers
DAVID BYRNE &
CHARLIE STICKNEY

Chief Strategy Officer
TENNESSEE EDWARDS

Chief Media Officer
DON HANDFIELD

President
JAMES HAICK III

WRITER
David A. Byrne

ARTIST
Francesca Fantini

LETTERER
Joel Rodriguez

BLACK
CARAVAN

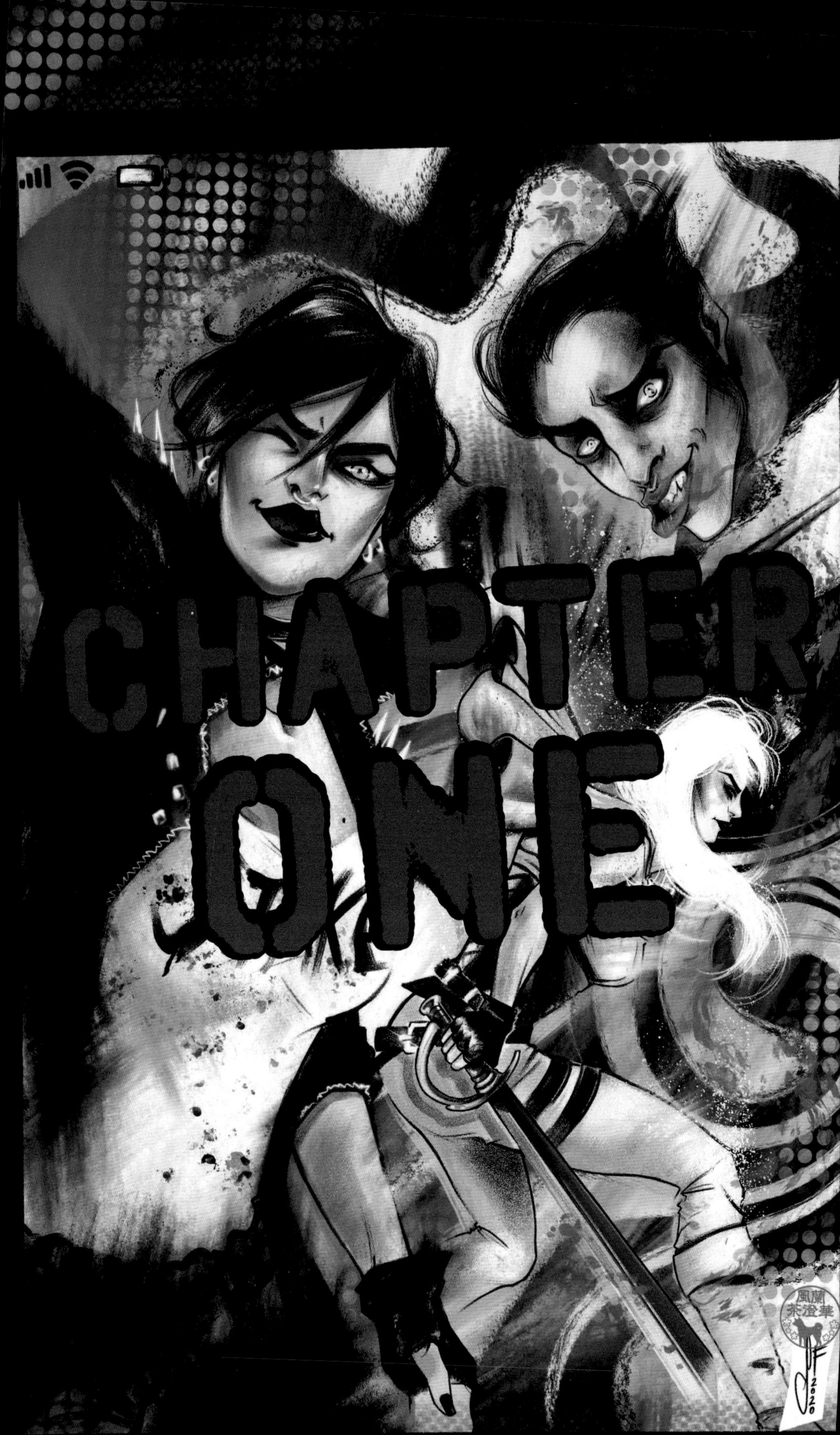
CHAPTER
ONE

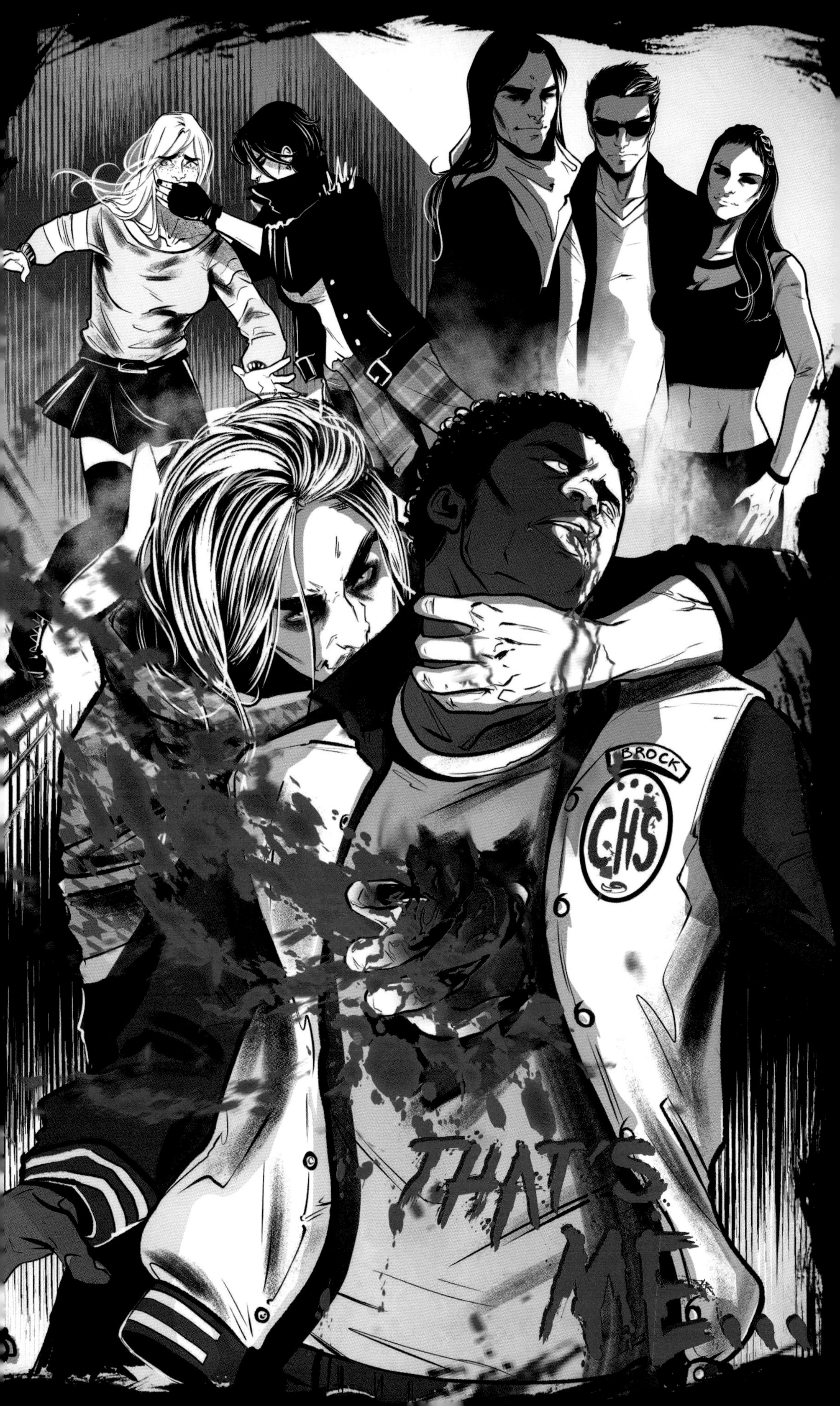
BROCK
CHS
THAT'S ME...

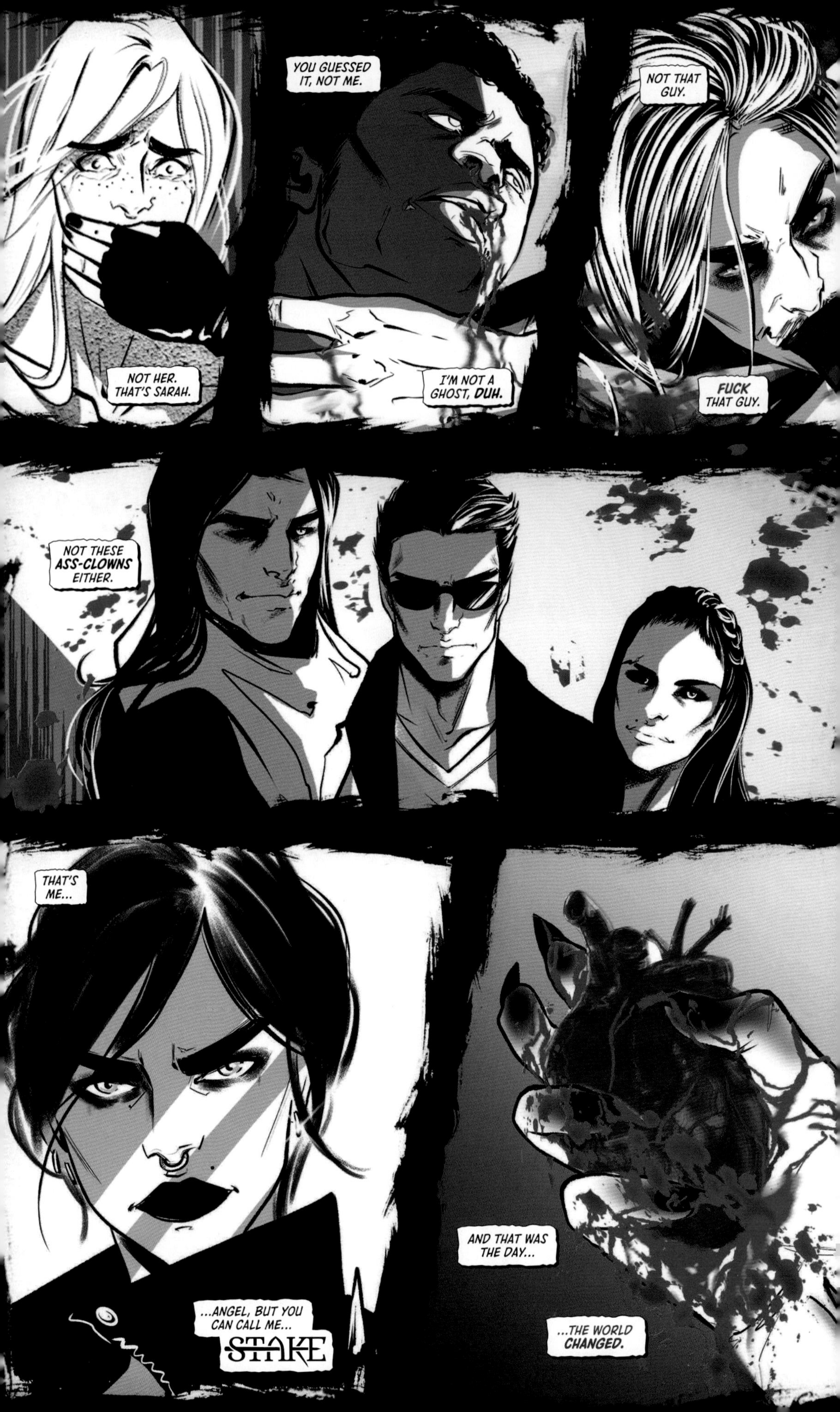

NOT HER. THAT'S SARAH.
YOU GUESSED IT, NOT ME.
I'M NOT A GHOST, **DUH.**
NOT THAT GUY.
FUCK THAT GUY.
NOT THESE **ASS-CLOWNS** EITHER.
THAT'S ME...
...ANGEL, BUT YOU CAN CALL ME...
STAKE
AND THAT WAS THE DAY...
...THE WORLD **CHANGED.**

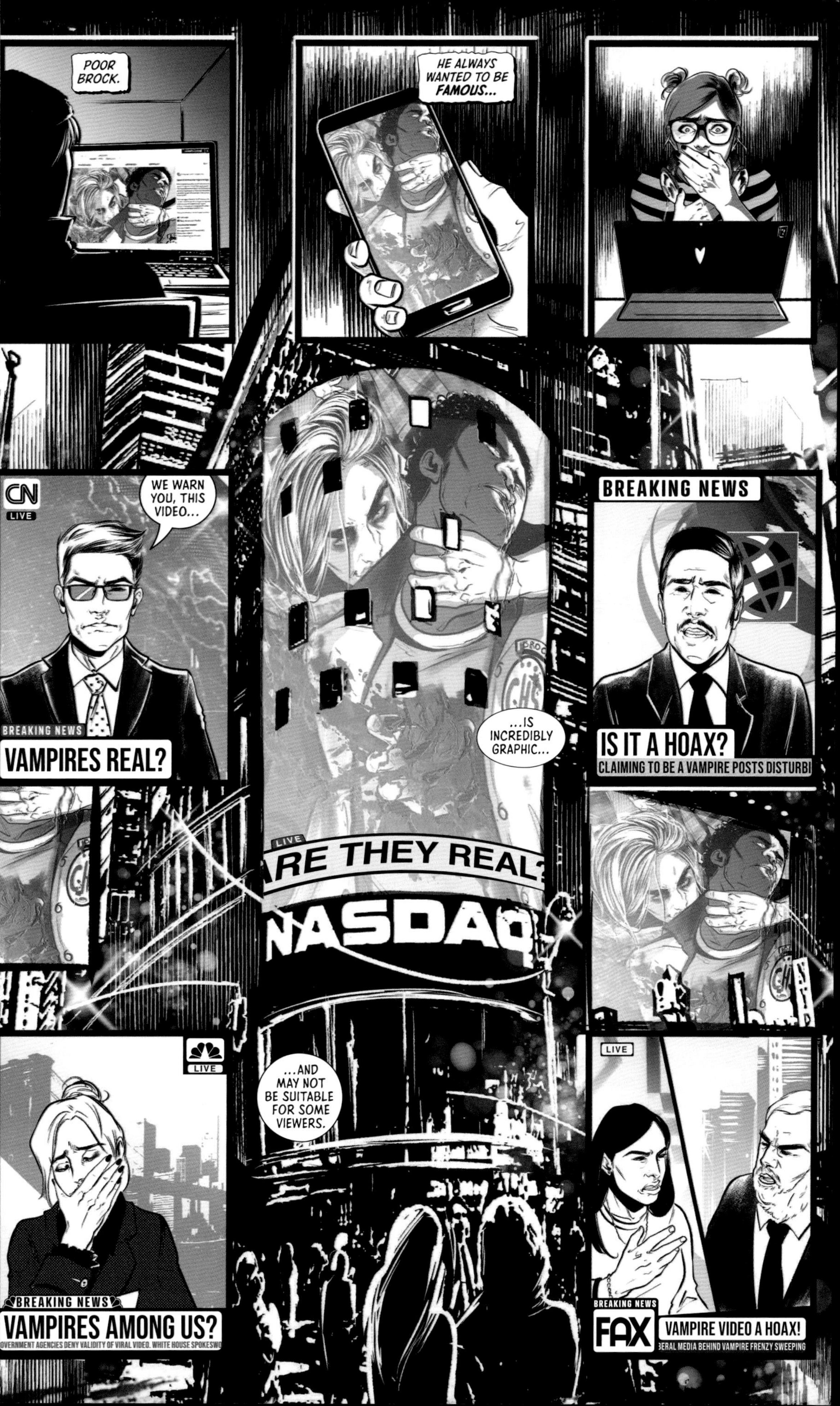
POOR BROCK.
HE ALWAYS WANTED TO BE FAMOUS...
CN
LIVE
WE WARN YOU, THIS VIDEO...
BREAKING NEWS
VAMPIRES REAL?
LIVE
ARE THEY REAL?
NASDAQ
...IS INCREDIBLY GRAPHIC...
BREAKING NEWS
IS IT A HOAX?
CLAIMING TO BE A VAMPIRE POSTS DISTURBI
LIVE
...AND MAY NOT BE SUITABLE FOR SOME VIEWERS.
BREAKING NEWS
VAMPIRES AMONG US?
OVERNMENT AGENCIES DENY VALIDITY OF VIRAL VIDEO. WHITE HOUSE SPOKESWO
LIVE
BREAKING NEWS
FAX
VAMPIRE VIDEO A HOAX!
BERAL MEDIA BEHIND VAMPIRE FRENZY SWEEPING

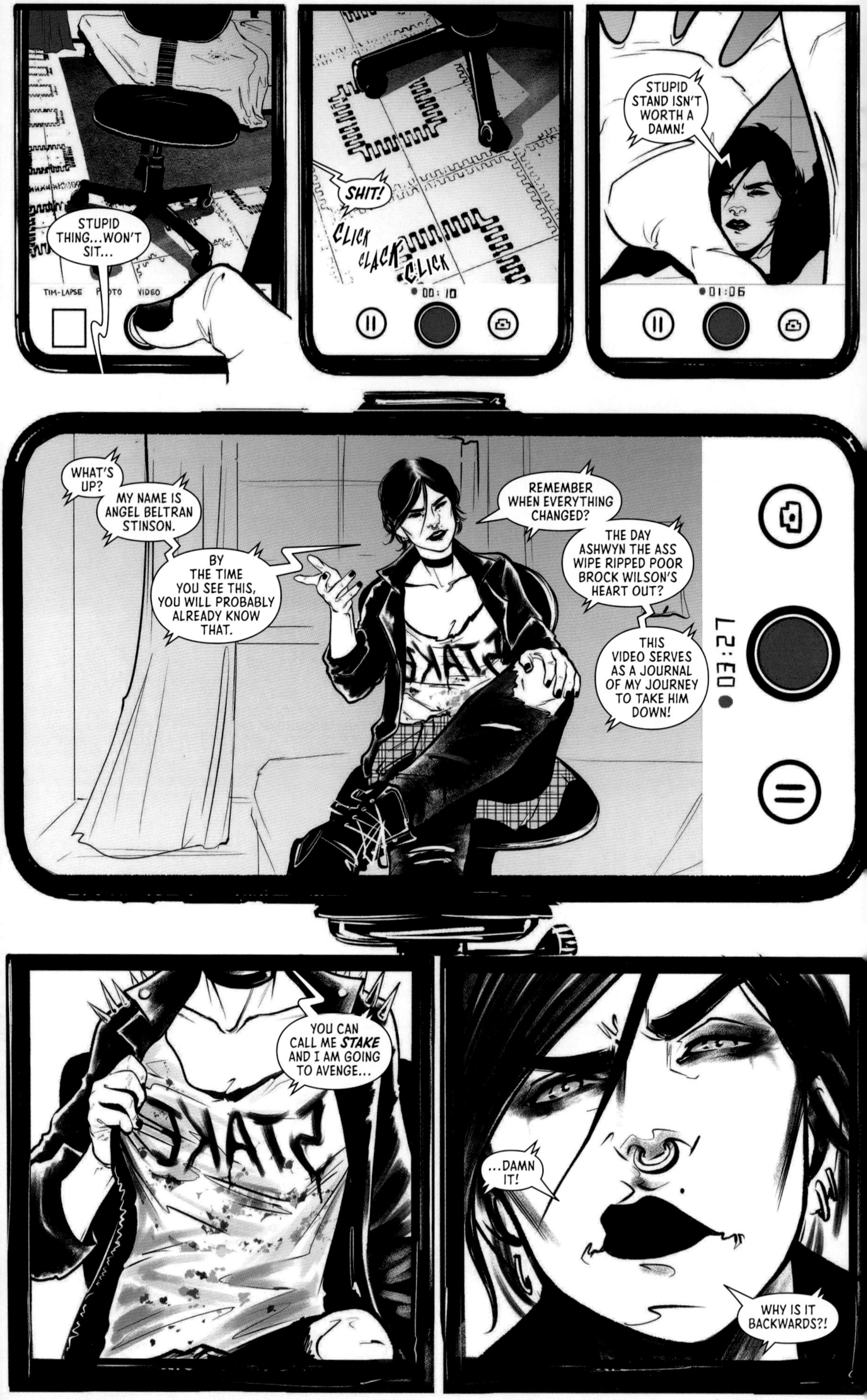
TIM-LAPSE
PHOTO
VIDEO
STUPID THING...WON'T SIT...
SHIT!
CLICK CLACK CLICK
00:10
STUPID STAND ISN'T WORTH A DAMN!
01:06
WHAT'S UP?
MY NAME IS ANGEL BELTRAN STINSON.
BY THE TIME YOU SEE THIS, YOU WILL PROBABLY ALREADY KNOW THAT.
REMEMBER WHEN EVERYTHING CHANGED?
THE DAY ASHWYN THE ASS WIPE RIPPED POOR BROCK WILSON'S HEART OUT?
THIS VIDEO SERVES AS A JOURNAL OF MY JOURNEY TO TAKE HIM DOWN!
03:27
YOU CAN CALL ME *STAKE* AND I AM GOING TO AVENGE...
...DAMN IT!
WHY IS IT BACKWARDS?!

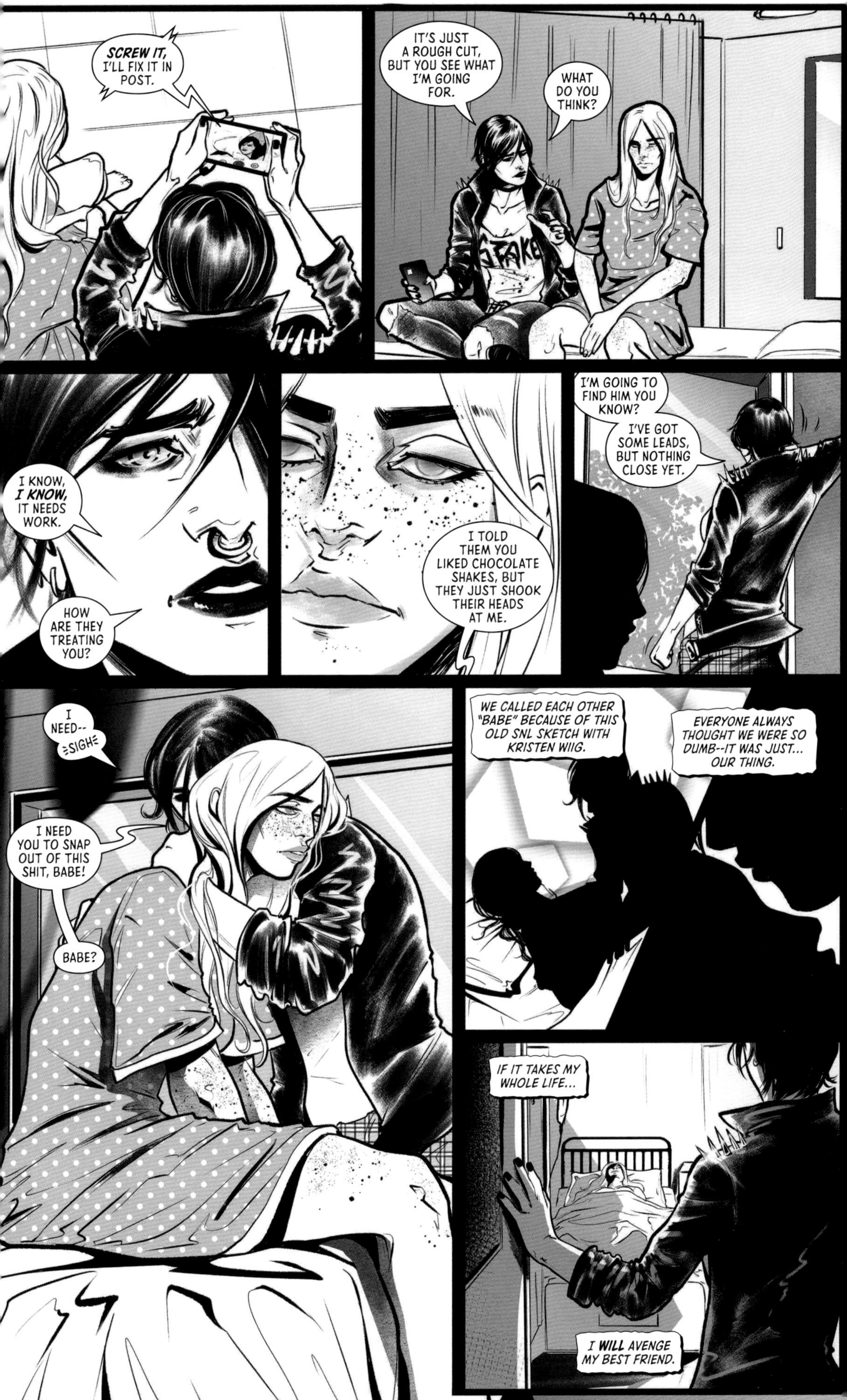

SCREW IT, I'LL FIX IT IN POST.
IT'S JUST A ROUGH CUT, BUT YOU SEE WHAT I'M GOING FOR.
WHAT DO YOU THINK?
I KNOW, I KNOW, IT NEEDS WORK.
HOW ARE THEY TREATING YOU?
I TOLD THEM YOU LIKED CHOCOLATE SHAKES, BUT THEY JUST SHOOK THEIR HEADS AT ME.
I'M GOING TO FIND HIM YOU KNOW?
I'VE GOT SOME LEADS, BUT NOTHING CLOSE YET.
I NEED-- SIGH
I NEED YOU TO SNAP OUT OF THIS SHIT, BABE!
BABE?
WE CALLED EACH OTHER "BABE" BECAUSE OF THIS OLD SNL SKETCH WITH KRISTEN WIIG.
EVERYONE ALWAYS THOUGHT WE WERE SO DUMB--IT WAS JUST... OUR THING.
IF IT TAKES MY WHOLE LIFE...
I WILL AVENGE MY BEST FRIEND.

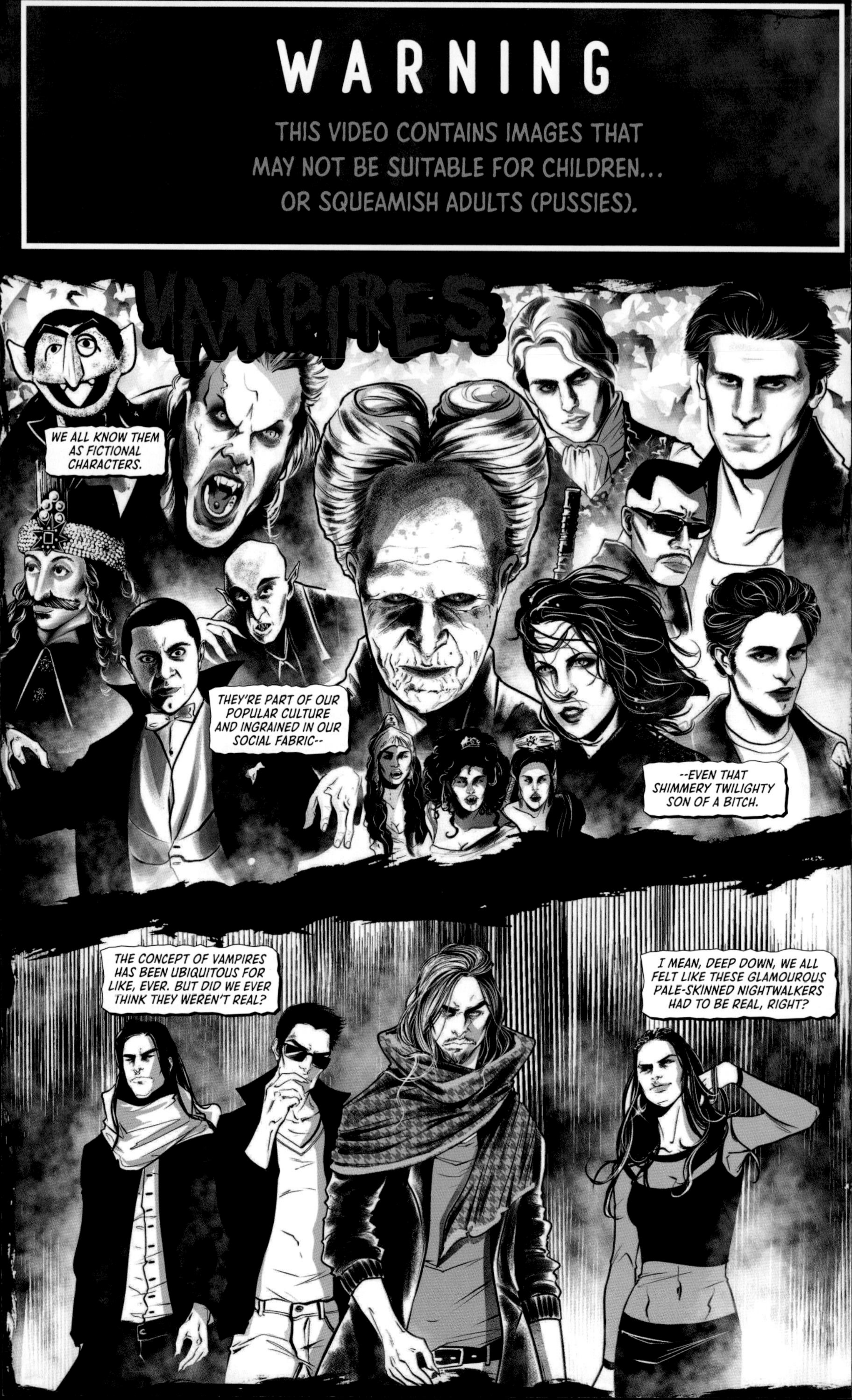
WARNING
THIS VIDEO CONTAINS IMAGES THAT MAY NOT BE SUITABLE FOR CHILDREN... OR SQUEAMISH ADULTS (PUSSIES).
VAMPIRES.
WE ALL KNOW THEM AS FICTIONAL CHARACTERS.
THEY'RE PART OF OUR POPULAR CULTURE AND INGRAINED IN OUR SOCIAL FABRIC--
--EVEN THAT SHIMMERY TWILIGHTY SON OF A BITCH.
THE CONCEPT OF VAMPIRES HAS BEEN UBIQUITOUS FOR LIKE, EVER. BUT DID WE EVER THINK THEY WEREN'T REAL?
I MEAN, DEEP DOWN, WE ALL FELT LIKE THESE GLAMOUROUS PALE-SKINNED NIGHTWALKERS HAD TO BE REAL, RIGHT?

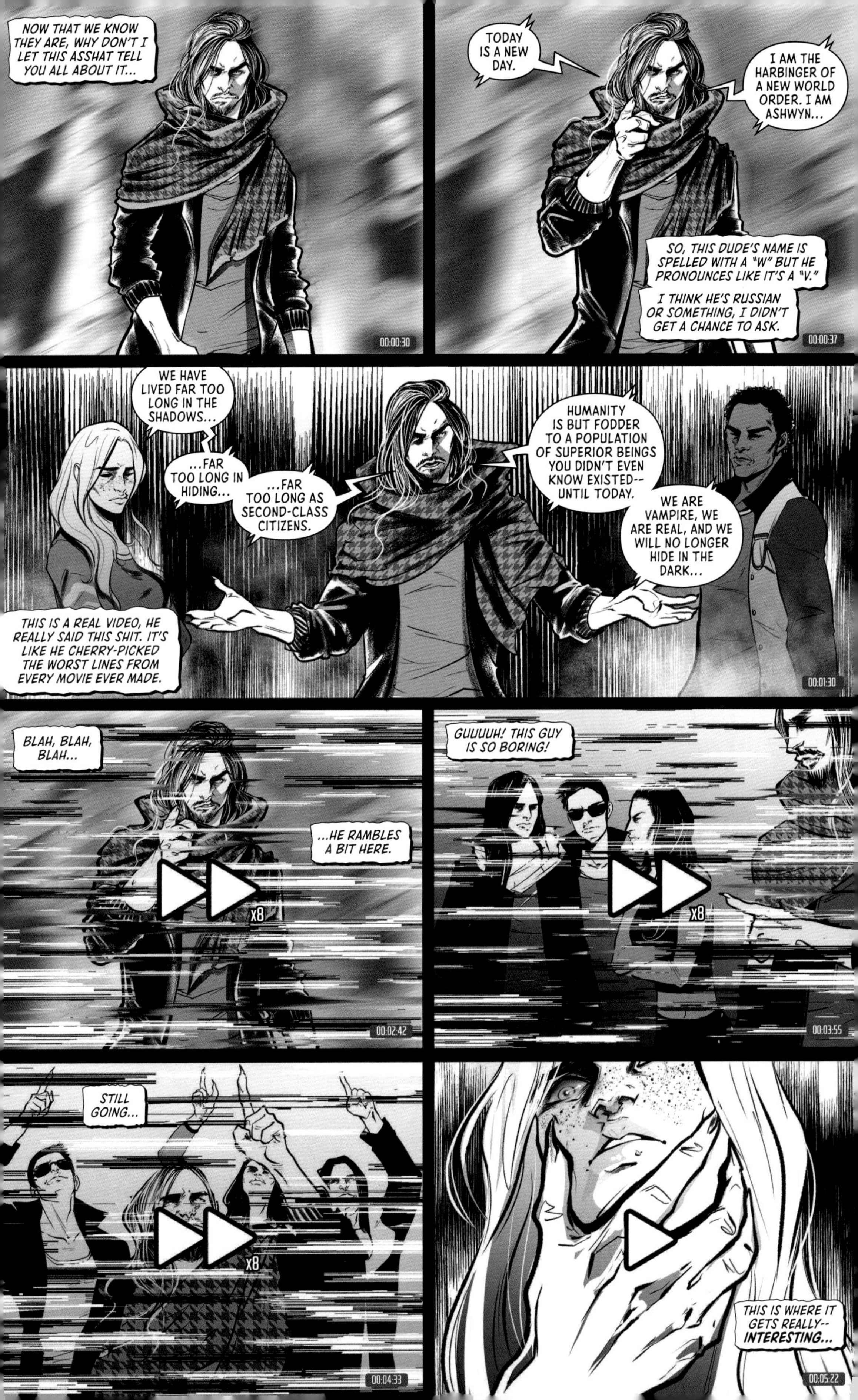
NOW THAT WE KNOW THEY ARE, WHY DON'T I LET THIS ASSHAT TELL YOU ALL ABOUT IT...
00:00:30
TODAY IS A NEW DAY.
I AM THE HARBINGER OF A NEW WORLD ORDER. I AM ASHWYN...
SO, THIS DUDE'S NAME IS SPELLED WITH A "W" BUT HE PRONOUNCES LIKE IT'S A "V."
I THINK HE'S RUSSIAN OR SOMETHING, I DIDN'T GET A CHANCE TO ASK.
00:00:37
WE HAVE LIVED FAR TOO LONG IN THE SHADOWS...
...FAR TOO LONG IN HIDING...
...FAR TOO LONG AS SECOND-CLASS CITIZENS.
HUMANITY IS BUT FODDER TO A POPULATION OF SUPERIOR BEINGS YOU DIDN'T EVEN KNOW EXISTED--UNTIL TODAY.
WE ARE VAMPIRE, WE ARE REAL, AND WE WILL NO LONGER HIDE IN THE DARK...
THIS IS A REAL VIDEO, HE REALLY SAID THIS SHIT. IT'S LIKE HE CHERRY-PICKED THE WORST LINES FROM EVERY MOVIE EVER MADE.
00:01:30
BLAH, BLAH, BLAH...
...HE RAMBLES A BIT HERE.
X8
00:02:42
GUUUUH! THIS GUY IS SO BORING!
X8
00:03:55
STILL GOING...
X8
00:04:33
THIS IS WHERE IT GETS REALLY--INTERESTING...
00:05:22

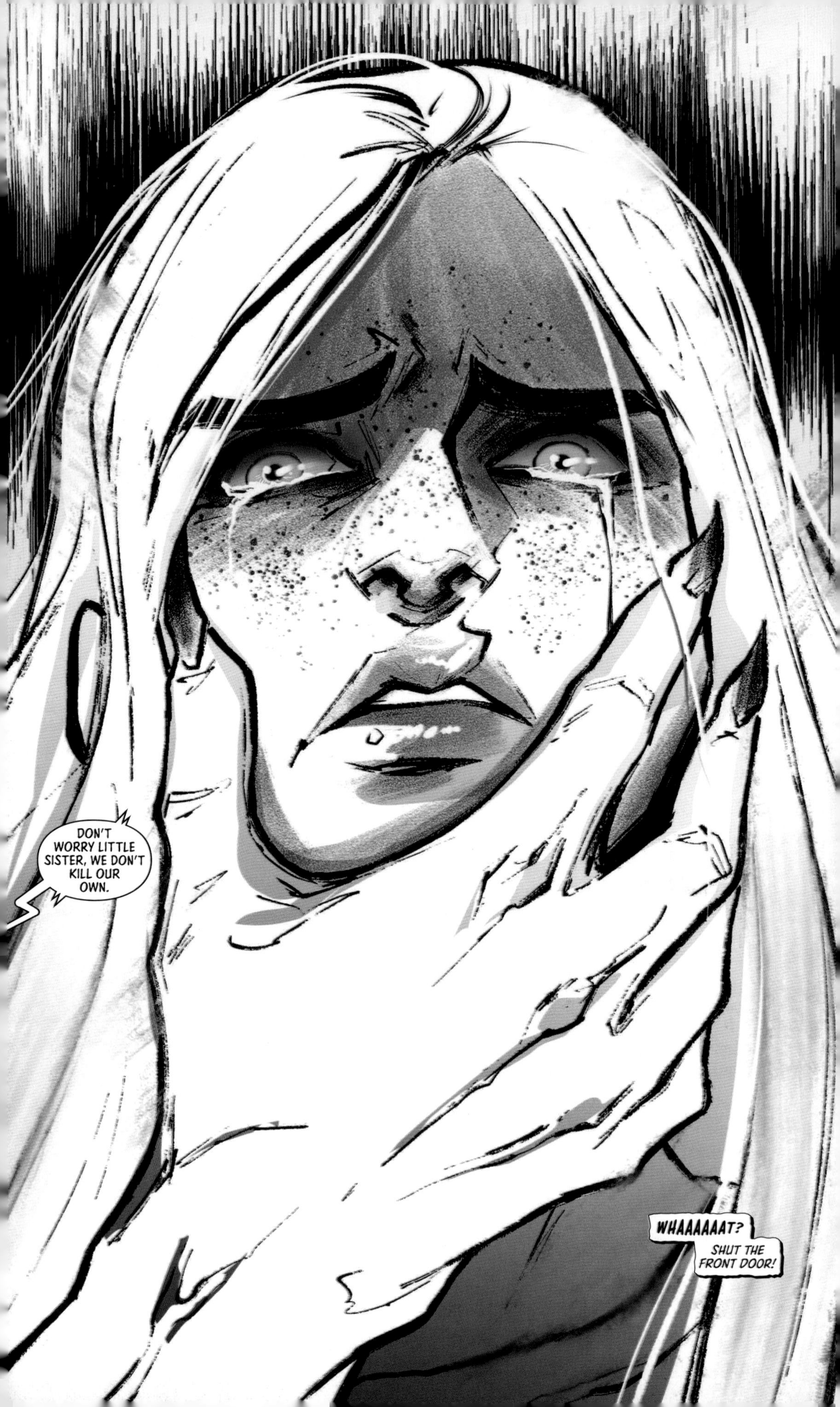
DON'T WORRY LITTLE SISTER, WE DON'T KILL OUR OWN.
WHAAAAAAT?
SHUT THE FRONT DOOR!

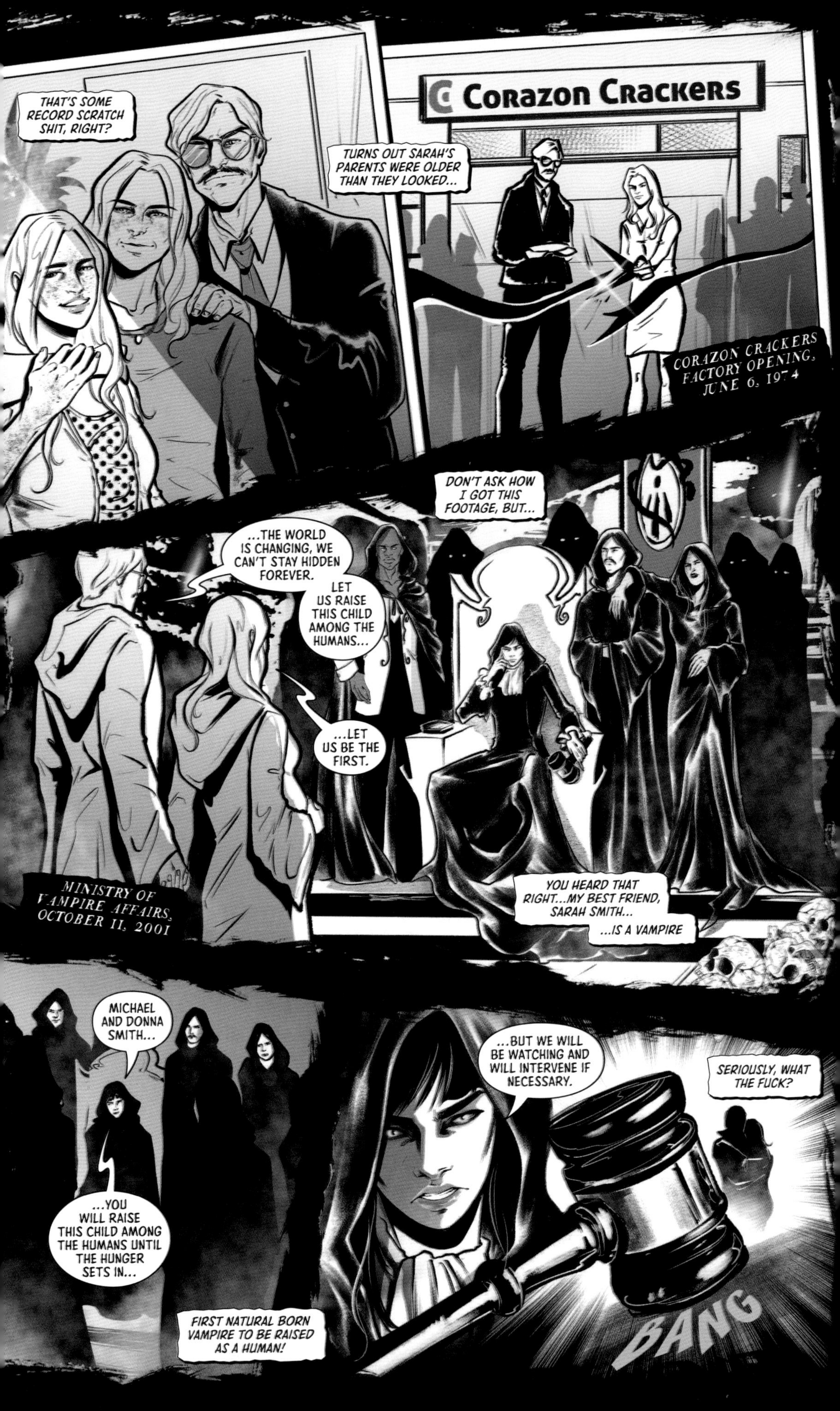

THAT'S SOME RECORD SCRATCH SHIT, RIGHT?
TURNS OUT SARAH'S PARENTS WERE OLDER THAN THEY LOOKED...
Corazon Crackers
CORAZON CRACKERS FACTORY OPENING, JUNE 6, 1974
DON'T ASK HOW I GOT THIS FOOTAGE, BUT...
...THE WORLD IS CHANGING, WE CAN'T STAY HIDDEN FOREVER.
LET US RAISE THIS CHILD AMONG THE HUMANS...
...LET US BE THE FIRST.
MINISTRY OF VAMPIRE AFFAIRS, OCTOBER 11, 2001
YOU HEARD THAT RIGHT...MY BEST FRIEND, SARAH SMITH...
...IS A VAMPIRE
MICHAEL AND DONNA SMITH...
...YOU WILL RAISE THIS CHILD AMONG THE HUMANS UNTIL THE HUNGER SETS IN...
FIRST NATURAL BORN VAMPIRE TO BE RAISED AS A HUMAN!
...BUT WE WILL BE WATCHING AND WILL INTERVENE IF NECESSARY.
SERIOUSLY, WHAT THE FUCK?
BANG

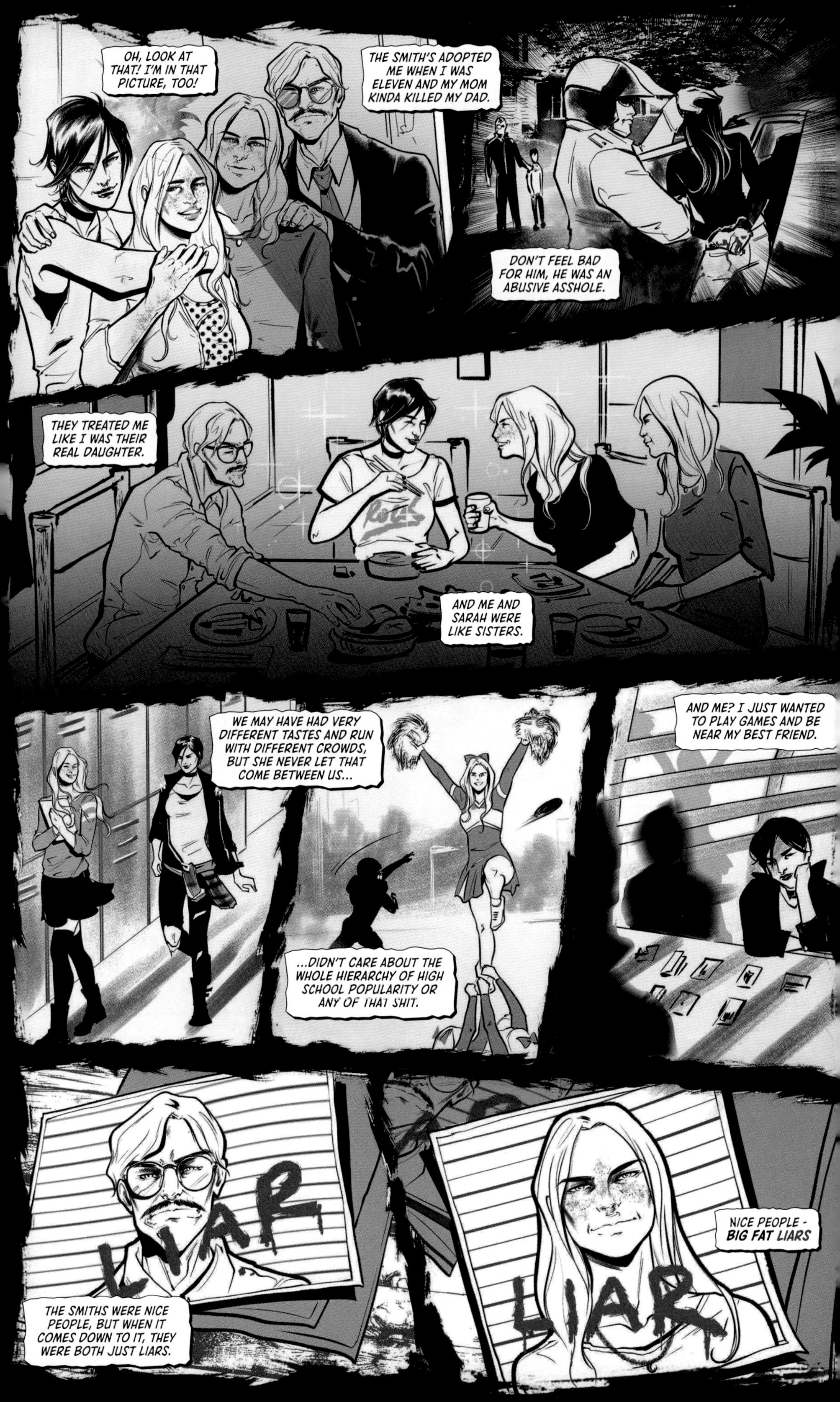

OH, LOOK AT THAT! I'M IN THAT PICTURE, TOO!
THE SMITH'S ADOPTED ME WHEN I WAS ELEVEN AND MY MOM KINDA KILLED MY DAD.
DON'T FEEL BAD FOR HIM, HE WAS AN ABUSIVE ASSHOLE.
THEY TREATED ME LIKE I WAS THEIR REAL DAUGHTER.
AND ME AND SARAH WERE LIKE SISTERS.
WE MAY HAVE HAD VERY DIFFERENT TASTES AND RUN WITH DIFFERENT CROWDS, BUT SHE NEVER LET THAT COME BETWEEN US...
...DIDN'T CARE ABOUT THE WHOLE HIERARCHY OF HIGH SCHOOL POPULARITY OR ANY OF THAT SHIT.
AND ME? I JUST WANTED TO PLAY GAMES AND BE NEAR MY BEST FRIEND.
LIAR
THE SMITHS WERE NICE PEOPLE, BUT WHEN IT COMES DOWN TO IT, THEY WERE BOTH JUST LIARS.
LIAR
NICE PEOPLE - **BIG FAT LIARS**

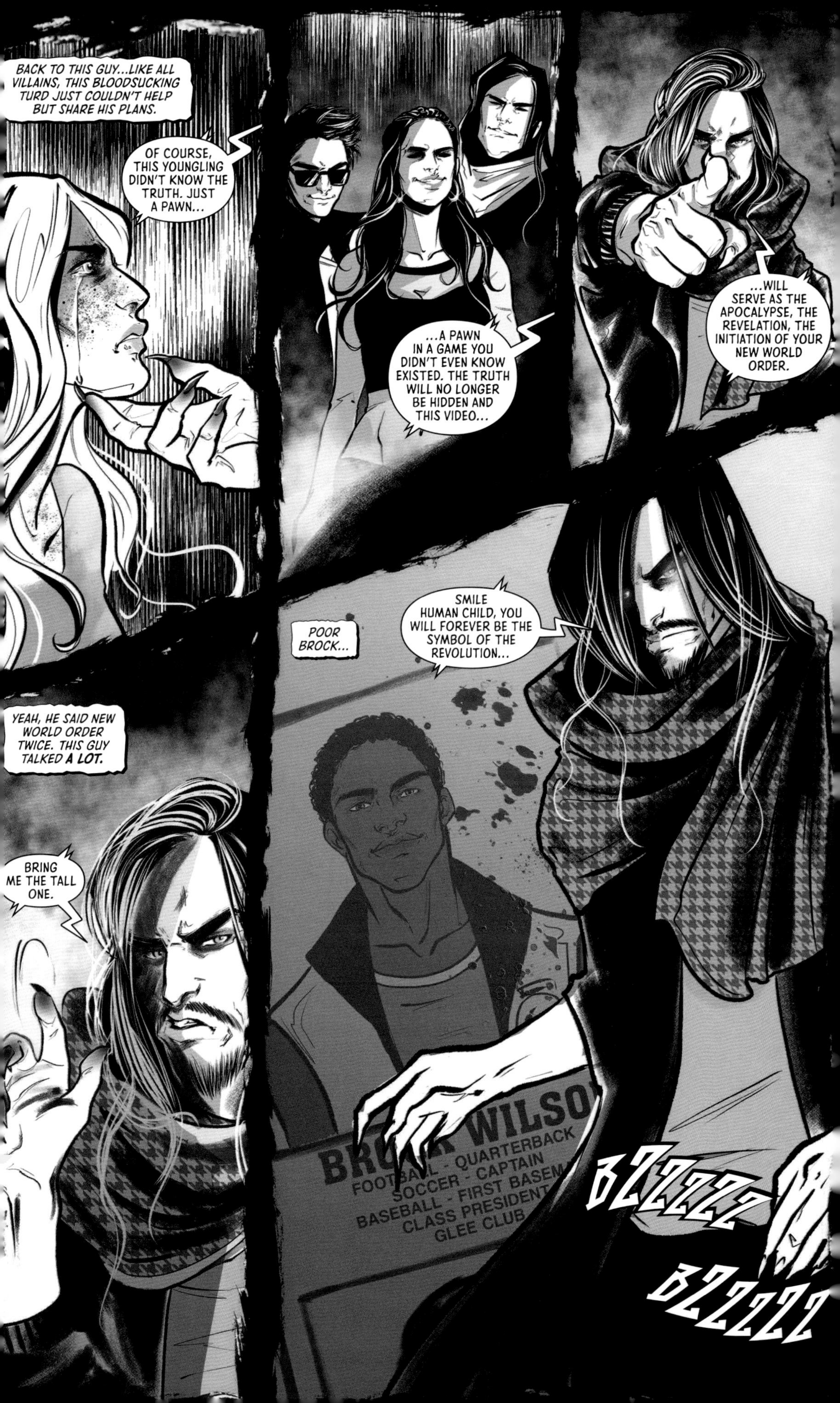
BACK TO THIS GUY...LIKE ALL VILLAINS, THIS BLOODSUCKING TURD JUST COULDN'T HELP BUT SHARE HIS PLANS.
OF COURSE, THIS YOUNGLING DIDN'T KNOW THE TRUTH. JUST A PAWN...
...A PAWN IN A GAME YOU DIDN'T EVEN KNOW EXISTED. THE TRUTH WILL NO LONGER BE HIDDEN AND THIS VIDEO...
...WILL SERVE AS THE APOCALYPSE, THE REVELATION, THE INITIATION OF YOUR NEW WORLD ORDER.
YEAH, HE SAID NEW WORLD ORDER TWICE. THIS GUY TALKED **A LOT.**
BRING ME THE TALL ONE.
POOR BROCK...
SMILE HUMAN CHILD, YOU WILL FOREVER BE THE SYMBOL OF THE REVOLUTION...
FOOTBALL - QUARTERBACK
SOCCER - CAPTAIN
BASEBALL - FIRST BASEM
CLASS PRESIDENT
GLEE CLUB
BZZZZZ
BZZZZZ

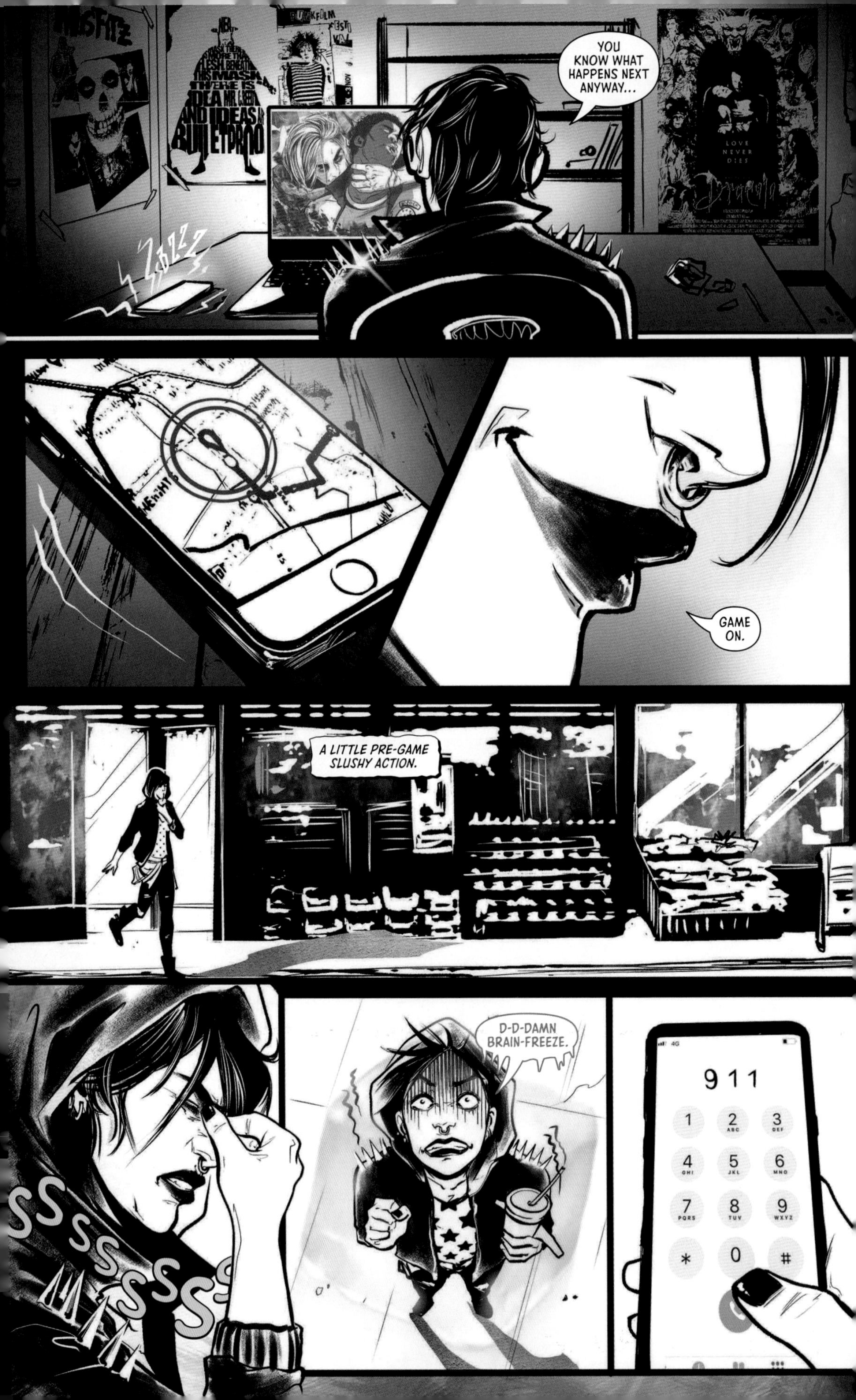

YOU KNOW WHAT HAPPENS NEXT ANYWAY...
GAME ON.
A LITTLE PRE-GAME SLUSHY ACTION.
D-D-DAMN BRAIN-FREEZE.
911

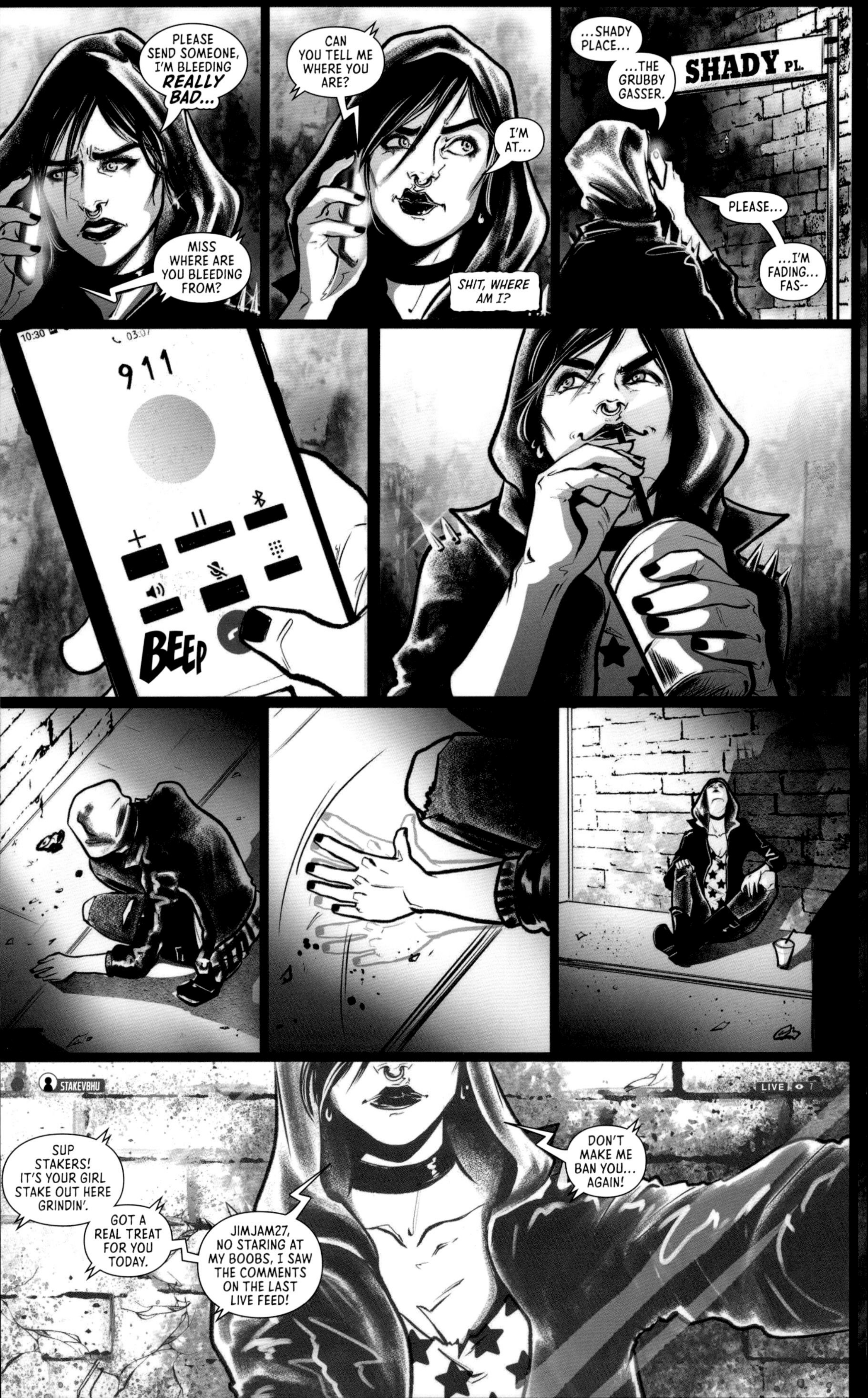
PLEASE SEND SOMEONE, I'M BLEEDING REALLY BAD...
MISS WHERE ARE YOU BLEEDING FROM?
CAN YOU TELL ME WHERE YOU ARE?
I'M AT...
SHIT, WHERE AM I?
...SHADY PLACE...
...THE GRUBBY GASSER.
SHADY PL.
PLEASE...
...I'M FADING... FAS--
10:30
911
BEEP
STAKEVBHU
LIVE
SUP STAKERS! IT'S YOUR GIRL STAKE OUT HERE GRINDIN'.
GOT A REAL TREAT FOR YOU TODAY.
JIMJAM27, NO STARING AT MY BOOBS, I SAW THE COMMENTS ON THE LAST LIVE FEED!
DON'T MAKE ME BAN YOU... AGAIN!

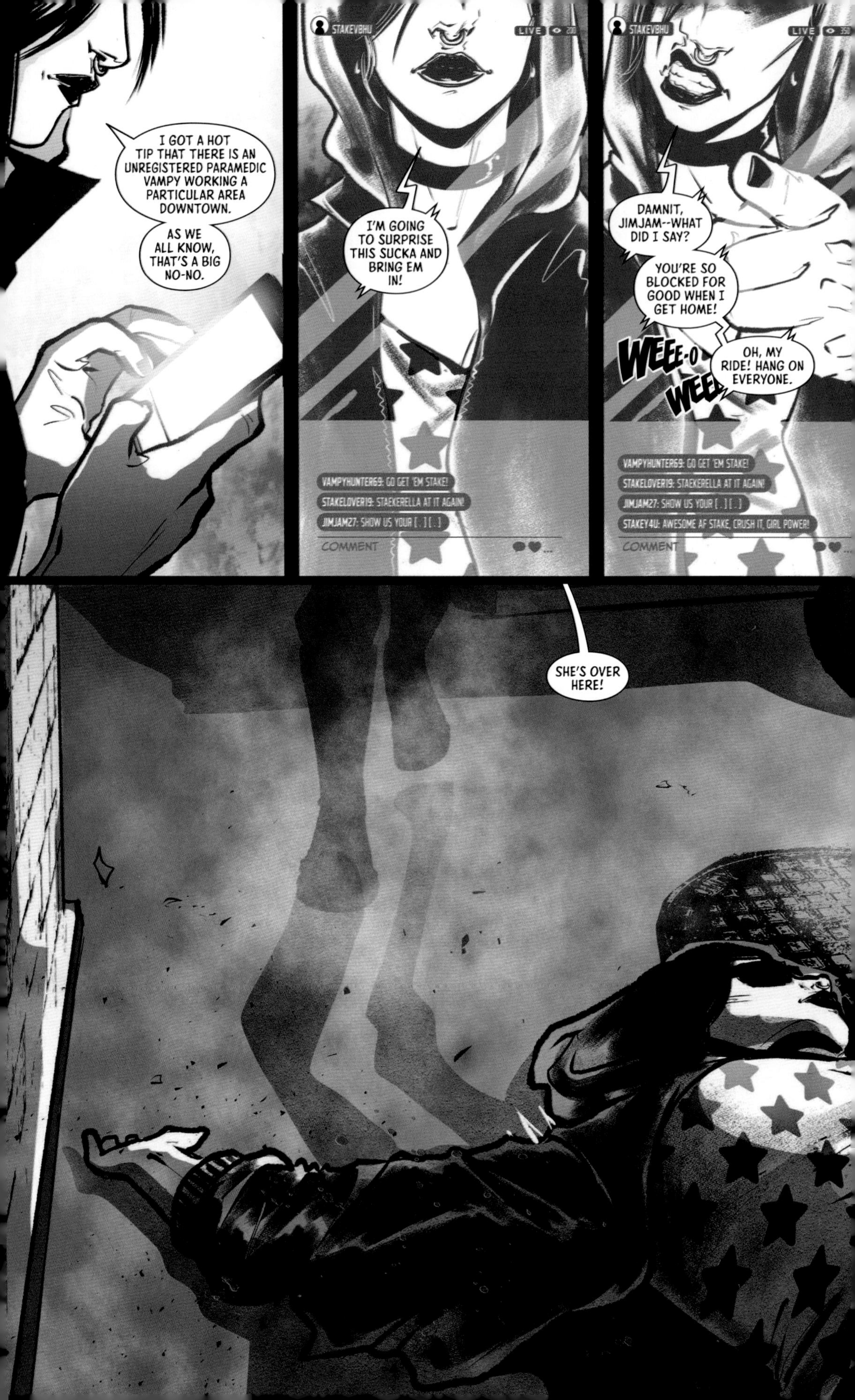
I GOT A HOT TIP THAT THERE IS AN UNREGISTERED PARAMEDIC VAMPY WORKING A PARTICULAR AREA DOWNTOWN.
AS WE ALL KNOW, THAT'S A BIG NO-NO.
STAKEVBHU
LIVE 200
I'M GOING TO SURPRISE THIS SUCKA AND BRING EM IN!
VAMPYHUNTER69: GO GET 'EM STAKE!
STAKELOVER19: STAEKERELLA AT IT AGAIN!
JIMJAM27: SHOW US YOUR [.] [.]
COMMENT
STAKEVBHU
LIVE 350
DAMNIT, JIMJAM--WHAT DID I SAY?
YOU'RE SO BLOCKED FOR GOOD WHEN I GET HOME!
WEEE-O
WEE
OH, MY RIDE! HANG ON EVERYONE.
VAMPYHUNTER69: GO GET 'EM STAKE!
STAKELOVER19: STAEKERELLA AT IT AGAIN!
JIMJAM27: SHOW US YOUR [.] [.]
STAKEY4U: AWESOME AF STAKE, CRUSH IT, GIRL POWER!
COMMENT
SHE'S OVER HERE!

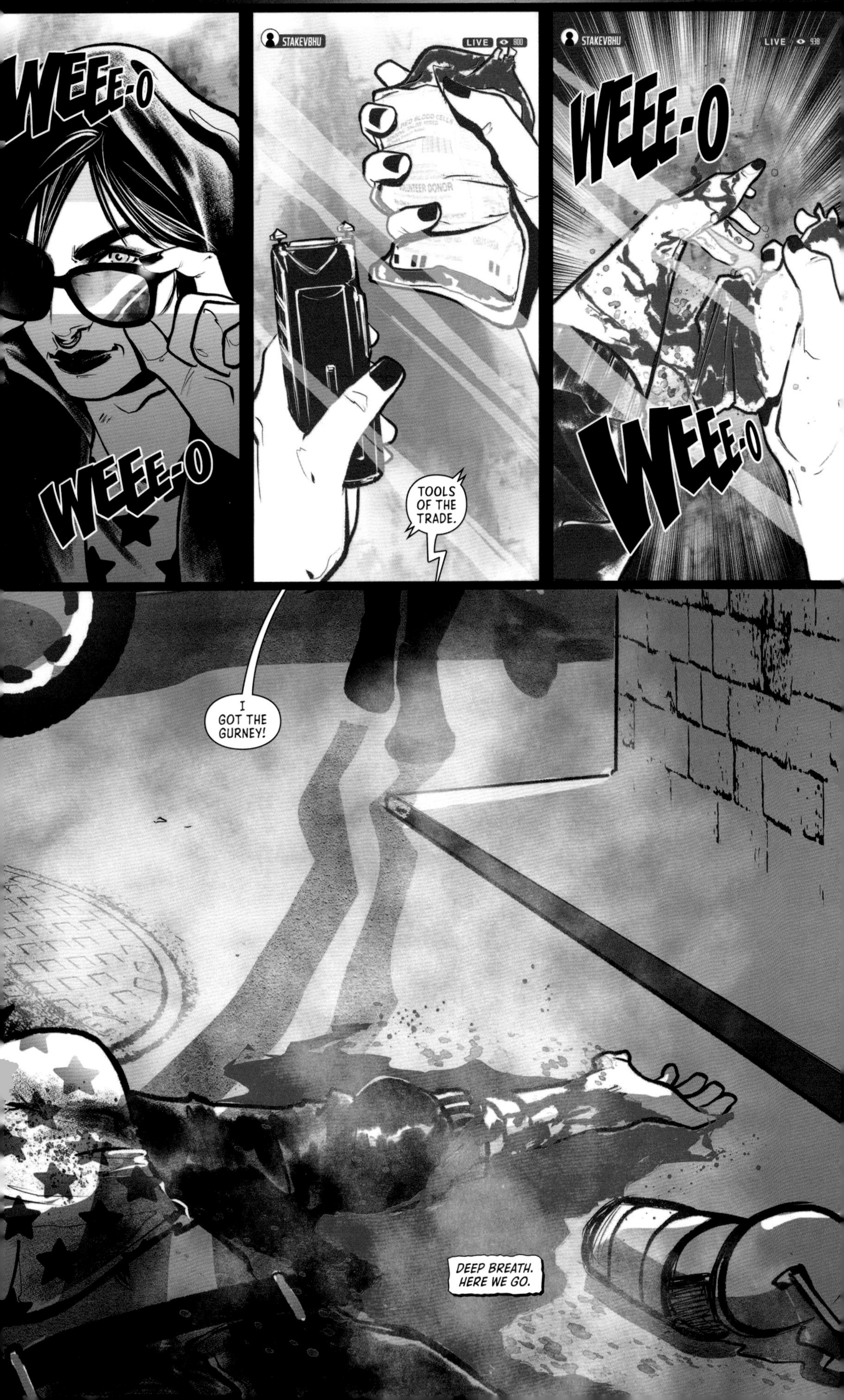
WEEE-O
WEEE-O
STAKEVBHU
LIVE 800
TOOLS OF THE TRADE.
STAKEVBHU
LIVE 938
WEEE-O
WEEE-O
I GOT THE GURNEY!
DEEP BREATH. HERE WE GO.

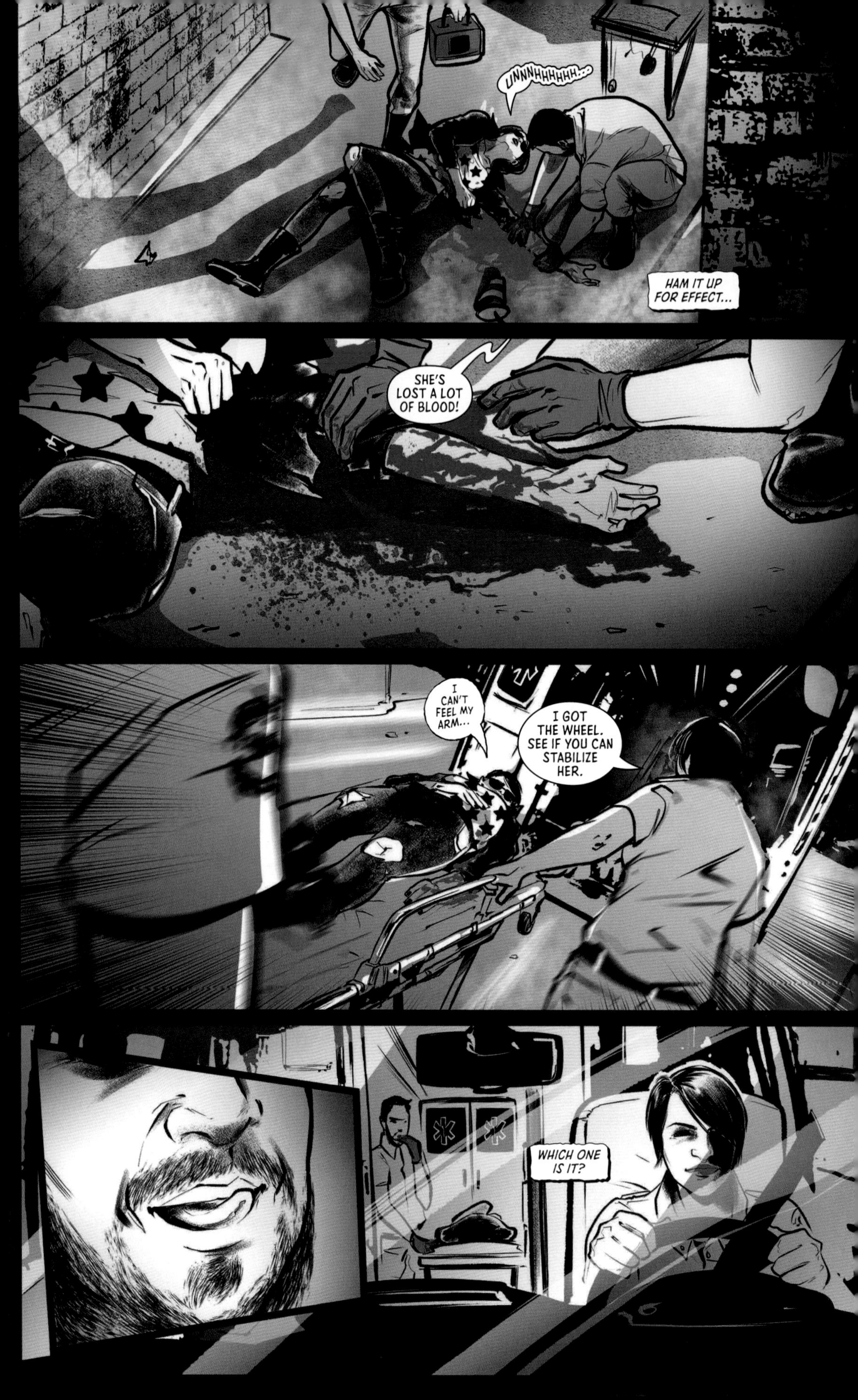
UNNNHHHHHH...
HAM IT UP FOR EFFECT...
SHE'S LOST A LOT OF BLOOD!
I CAN'T FEEL MY ARM...
I GOT THE WHEEL. SEE IF YOU CAN STABILIZE HER.
WHICH ONE IS IT?

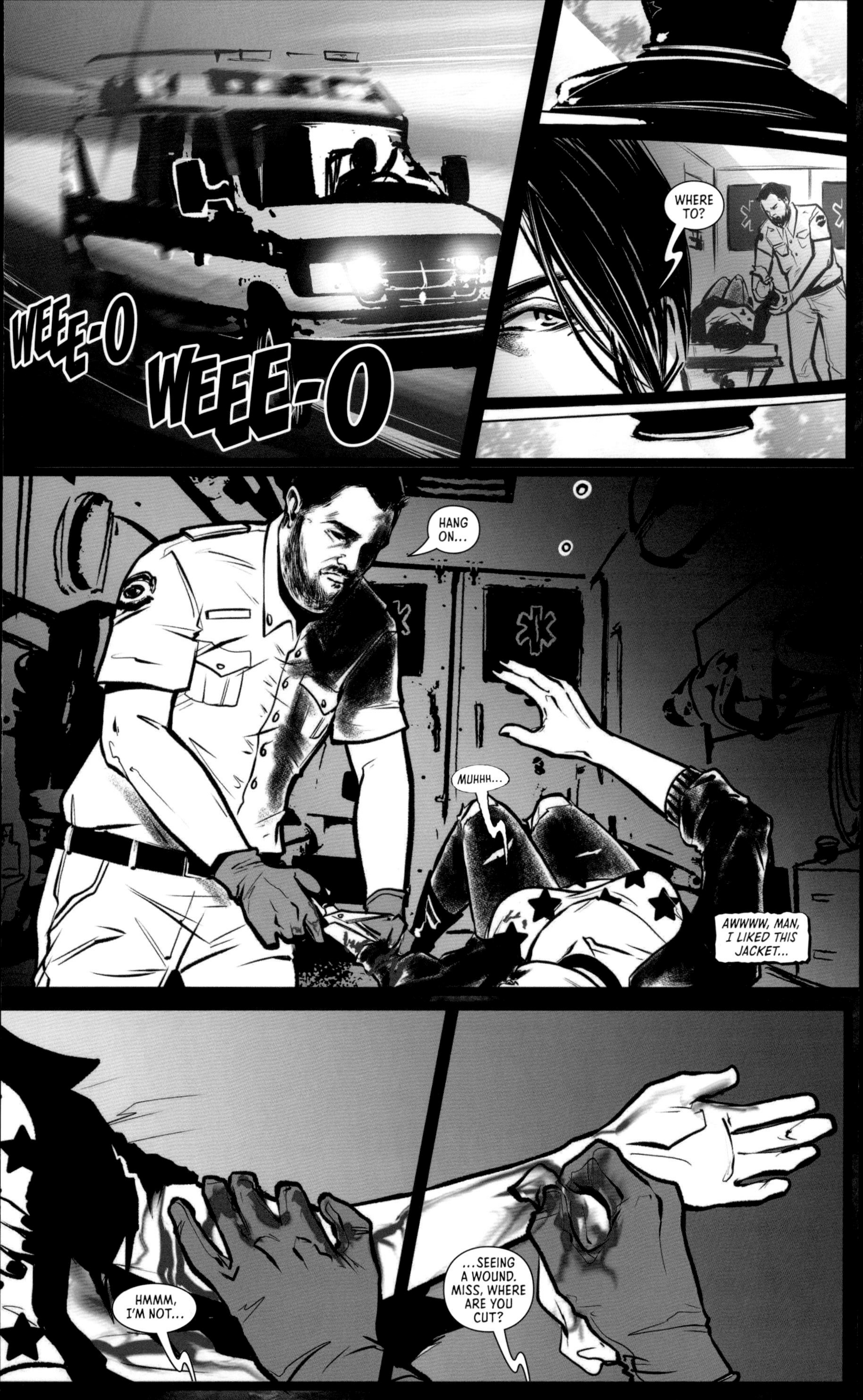
WEEE-O
WEEE-O
WHERE TO?
HANG ON...
MUHHH...
AWWWW, MAN, I LIKED THIS JACKET...
HMMM, I'M NOT...
...SEEING A WOUND. MISS, WHERE ARE YOU CUT?

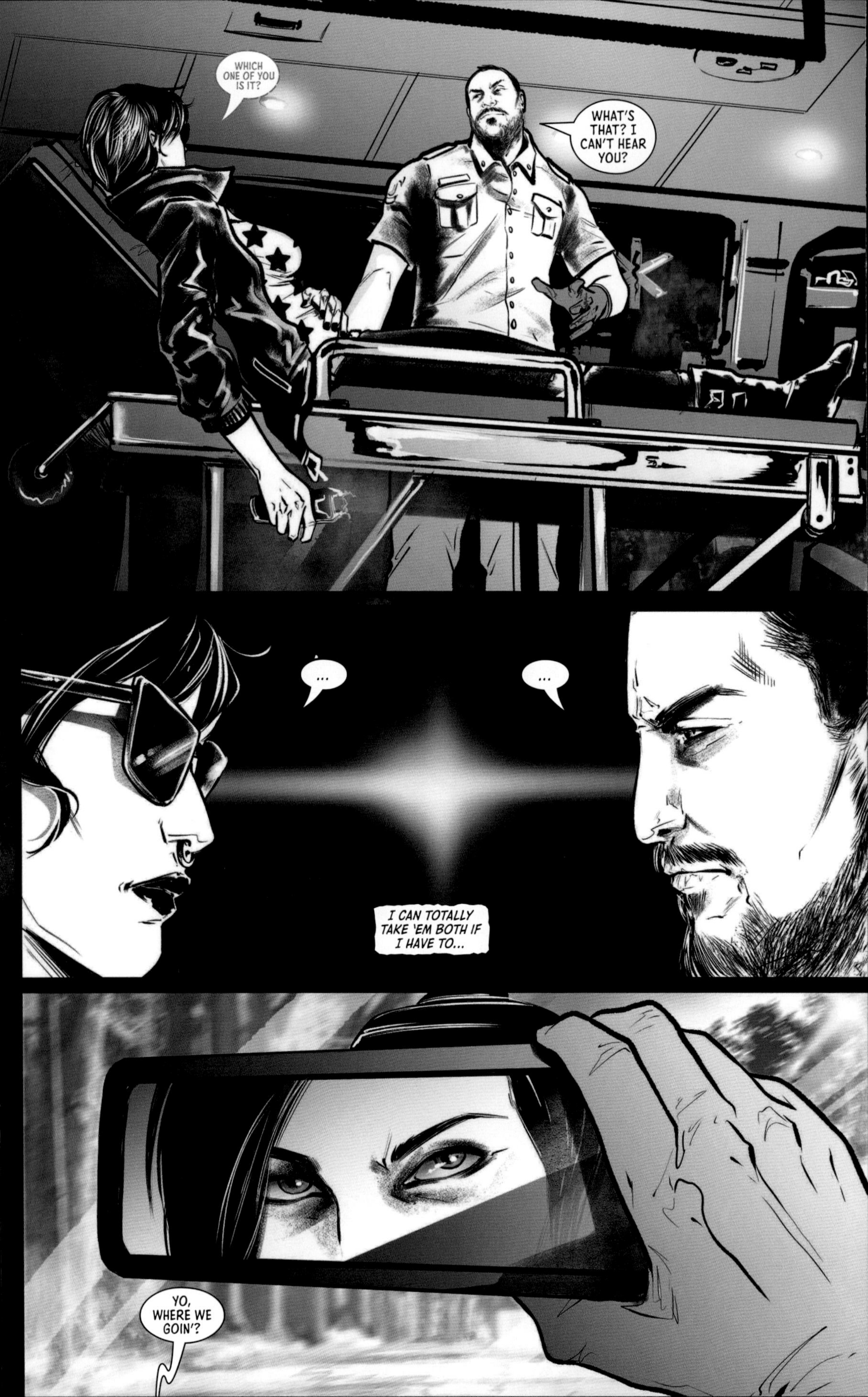
WHICH ONE OF YOU IS IT?
WHAT'S THAT? I CAN'T HEAR YOU?
...
...
I CAN TOTALLY TAKE 'EM BOTH IF I HAVE TO...
YO, WHERE WE GOIN'?

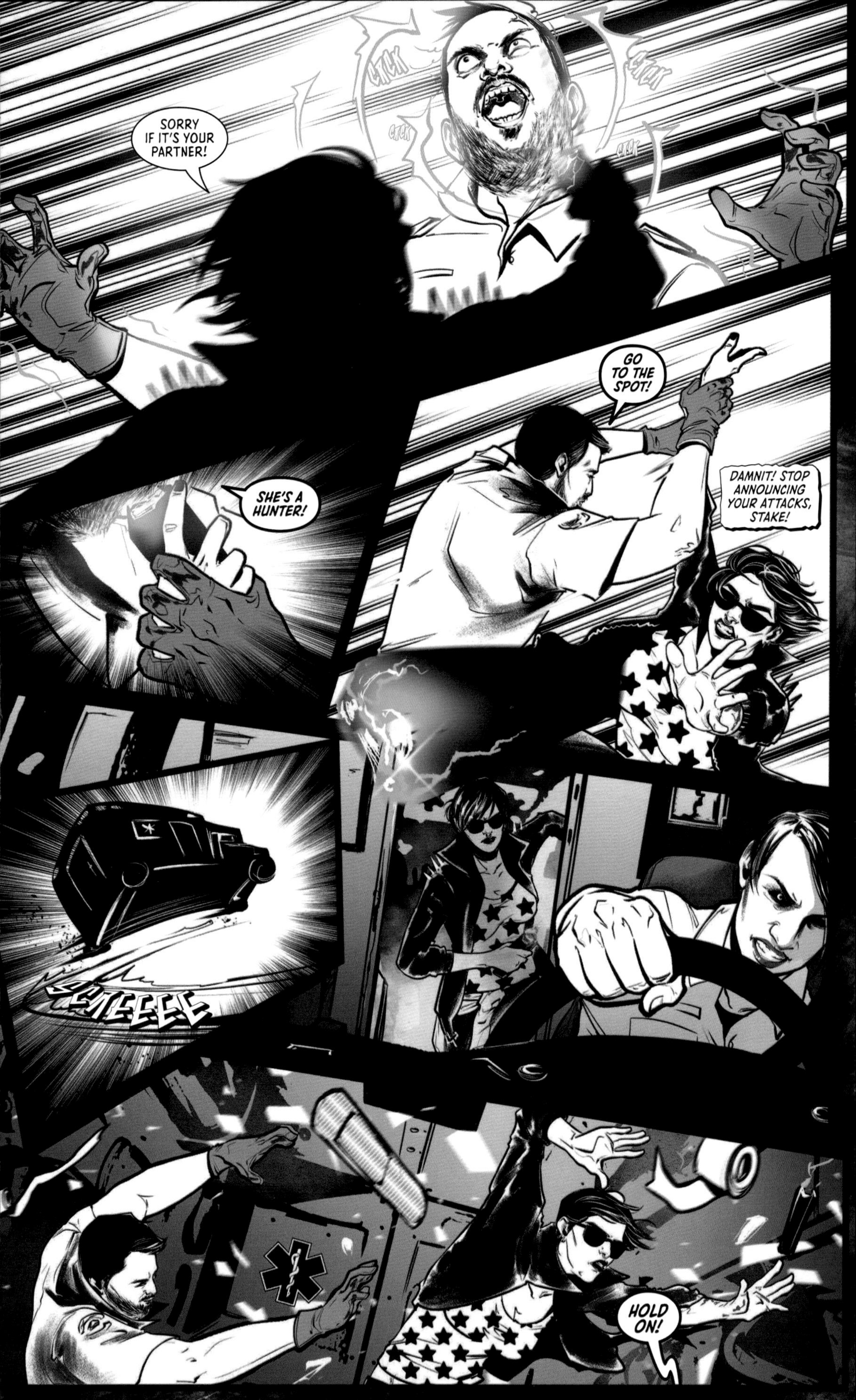
CRCK
CRCK
CRCK
CRCK
SORRY IF IT'S YOUR PARTNER!
GO TO THE SPOT!
SHE'S A HUNTER!
DAMNIT! STOP ANNOUNCING YOUR ATTACKS, STAKE!
SCREEEEE
HOLD ON!

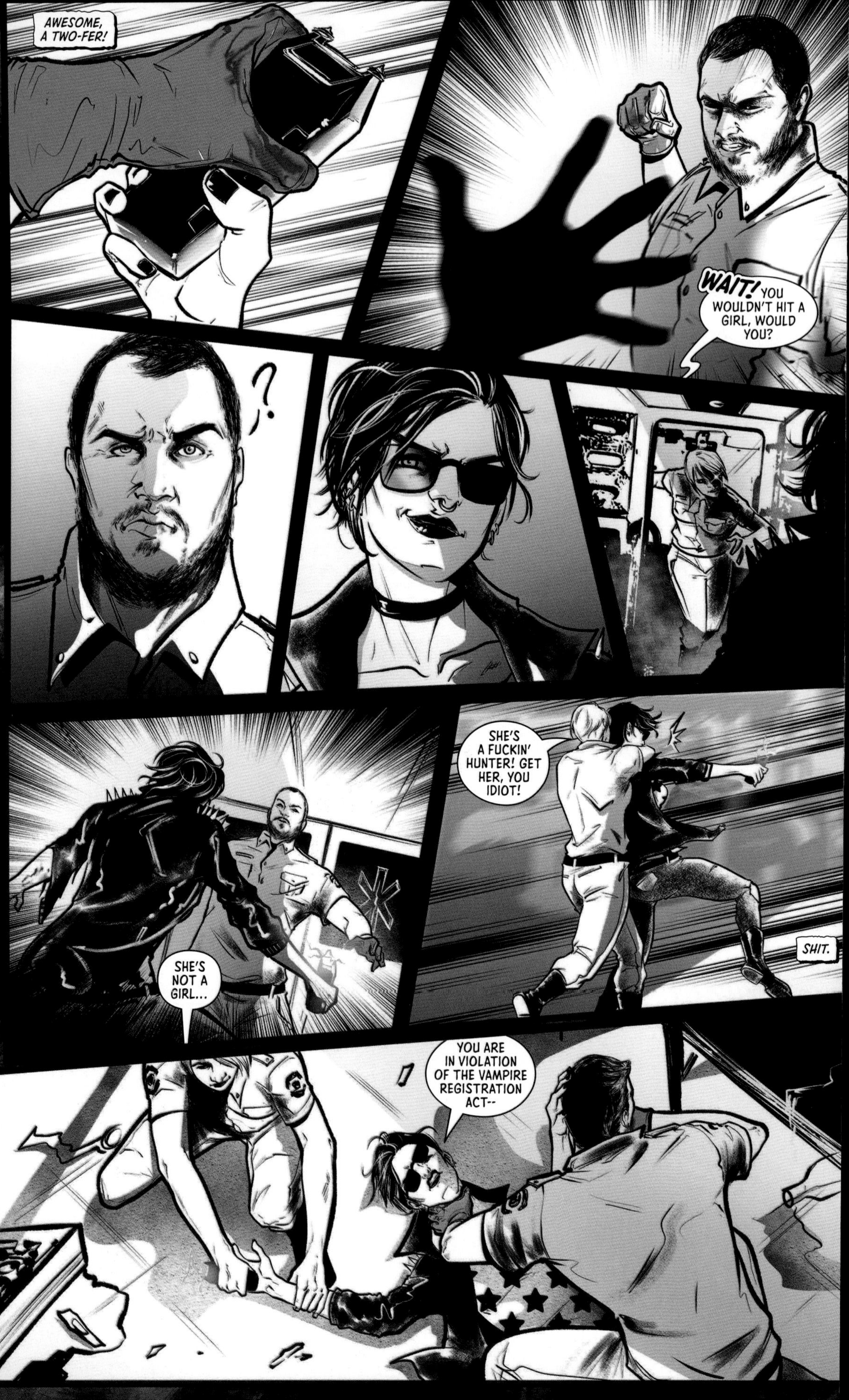
AWESOME, A TWO-FER!
WAIT! YOU WOULDN'T HIT A GIRL, WOULD YOU?
?
SHE'S NOT A GIRL...
SHE'S A FUCKIN' HUNTER! GET HER, YOU IDIOT!
SHIT.
YOU ARE IN VIOLATION OF THE VAMPIRE REGISTRATION ACT--

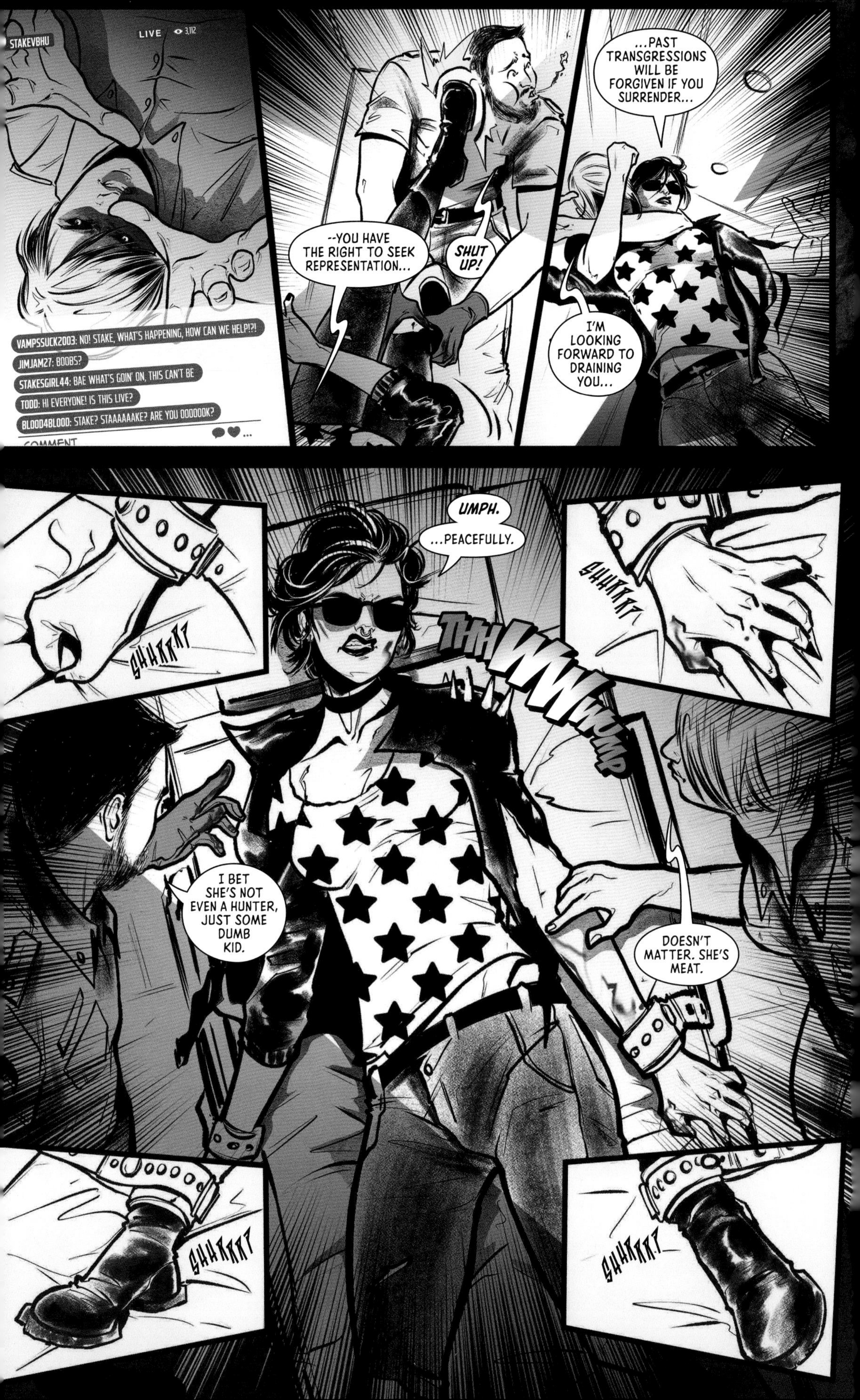
STAKEVBHU
LIVE 3,112
VAMPSSUCK2003: NO! STAKE, WHAT'S HAPPENING, HOW CAN WE HELP!?!
JIMJAM27: BOOBS?
STAKESGIRL44: BAE WHAT'S GOIN' ON, THIS CAN'T BE
TODD: HI EVERYONE! IS THIS LIVE?
BLOOD4BLOOD: STAKE? STAAAAAAKE? ARE YOU OOOOOOK?
--YOU HAVE THE RIGHT TO SEEK REPRESENTATION...
SHUT UP!
...PAST TRANSGRESSIONS WILL BE FORGIVEN IF YOU SURRENDER...
I'M LOOKING FORWARD TO DRAINING YOU...
UMPH.
...PEACEFULLY.
SHHRRRT
SHHRRRT
THHWWWWUMP
I BET SHE'S NOT EVEN A HUNTER, JUST SOME DUMB KID.
DOESN'T MATTER. SHE'S MEAT.
SHHRRRT
SHHRRRT

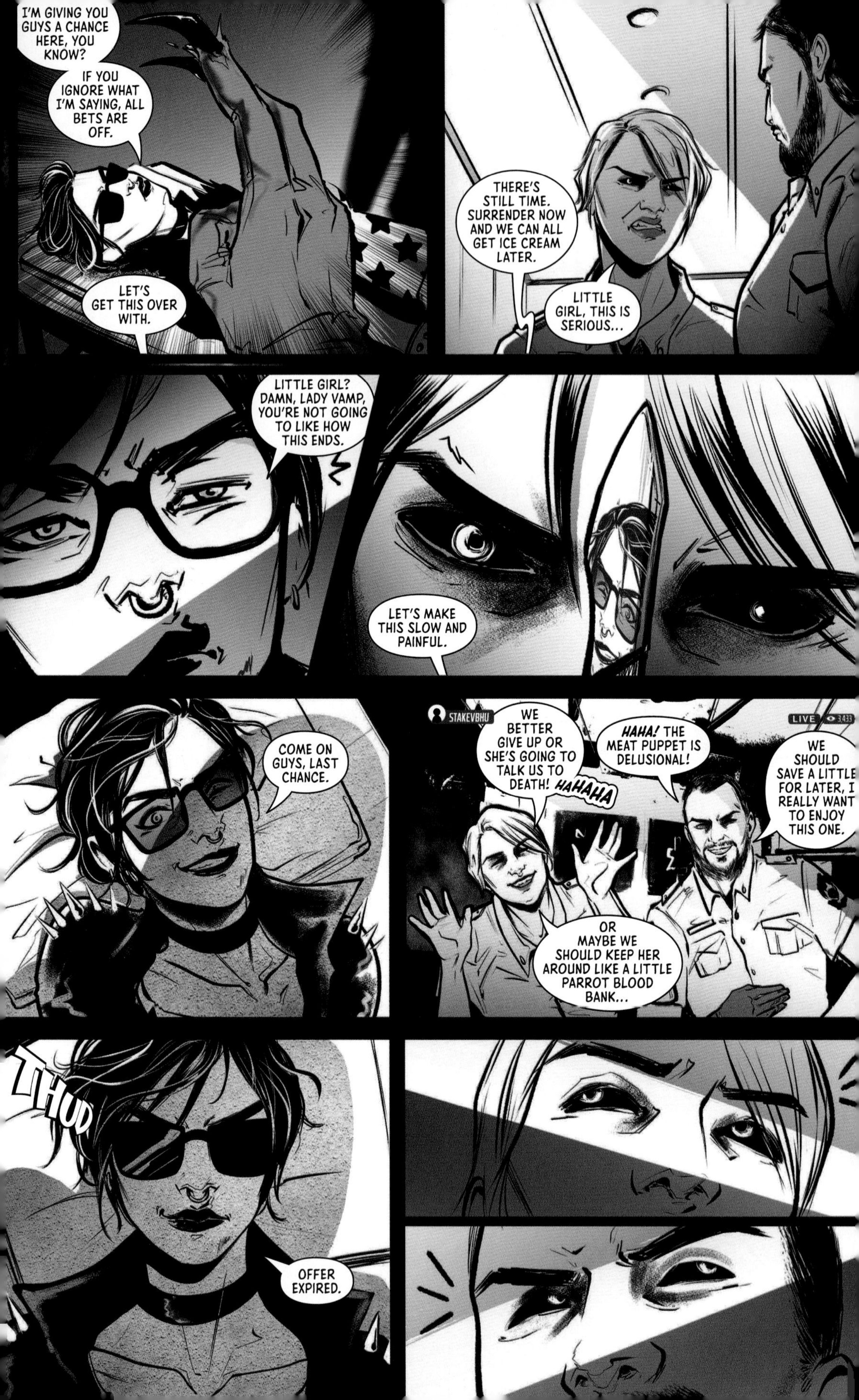
I'M GIVING YOU GUYS A CHANCE HERE, YOU KNOW?
IF YOU IGNORE WHAT I'M SAYING, ALL BETS ARE OFF.
LET'S GET THIS OVER WITH.
THERE'S STILL TIME. SURRENDER NOW AND WE CAN ALL GET ICE CREAM LATER.
LITTLE GIRL, THIS IS SERIOUS...
LITTLE GIRL? DAMN, LADY VAMP, YOU'RE NOT GOING TO LIKE HOW THIS ENDS.
LET'S MAKE THIS SLOW AND PAINFUL.
COME ON GUYS, LAST CHANCE.
STAKEVBHU
LIVE
WE BETTER GIVE UP OR SHE'S GOING TO TALK US TO DEATH!
HAHAHA
HAHA! THE MEAT PUPPET IS DELUSIONAL!
WE SHOULD SAVE A LITTLE FOR LATER, I REALLY WANT TO ENJOY THIS ONE.
OR MAYBE WE SHOULD KEEP HER AROUND LIKE A LITTLE PARROT BLOOD BANK...
THUD
OFFER EXPIRED.

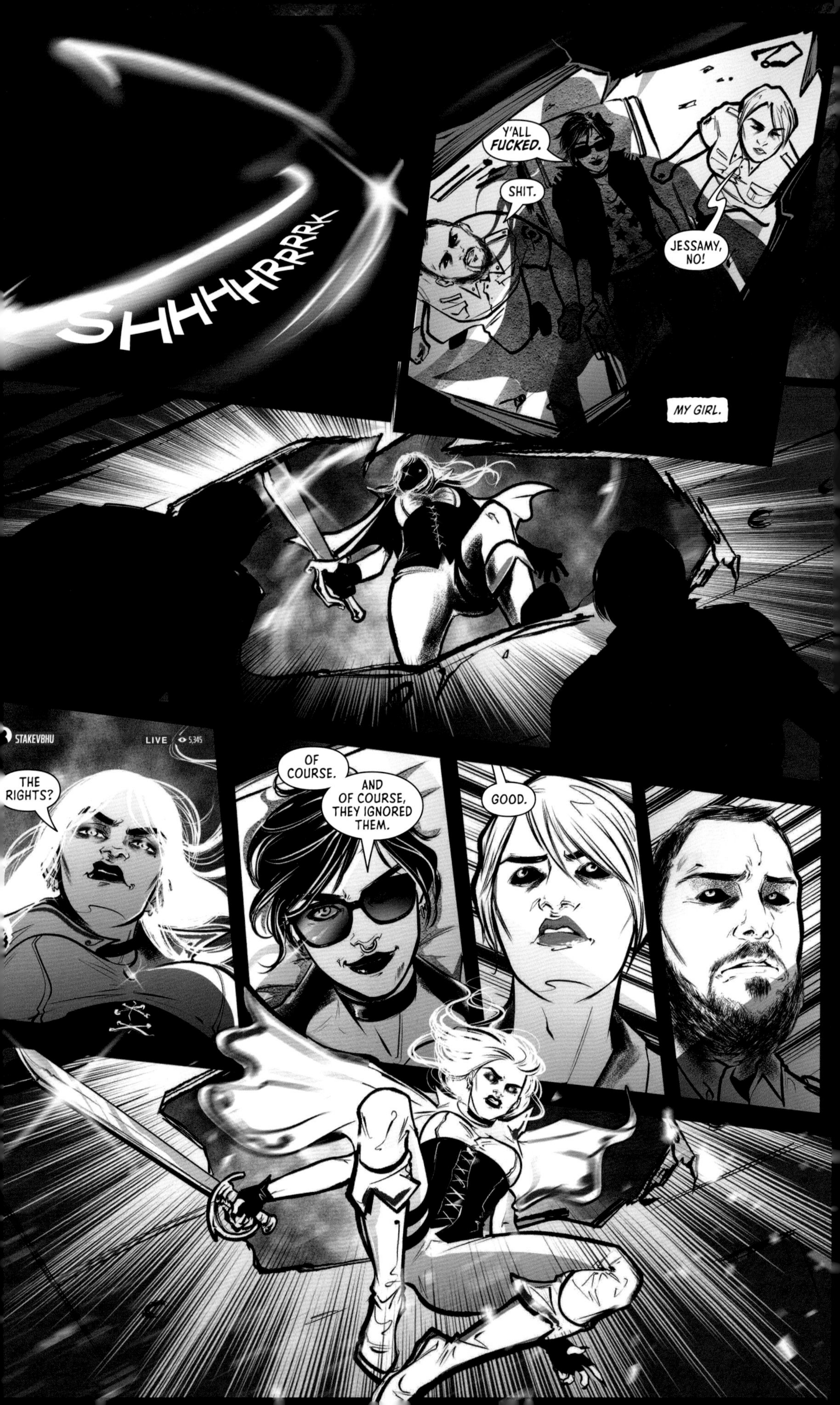
SHHHHRRRRK
Y'ALL FUCKED.
SHIT.
JESSAMY, NO!
MY GIRL.
STAKEVBHU
LIVE 5,345
THE RIGHTS?
OF COURSE.
AND OF COURSE, THEY IGNORED THEM.
GOOD.

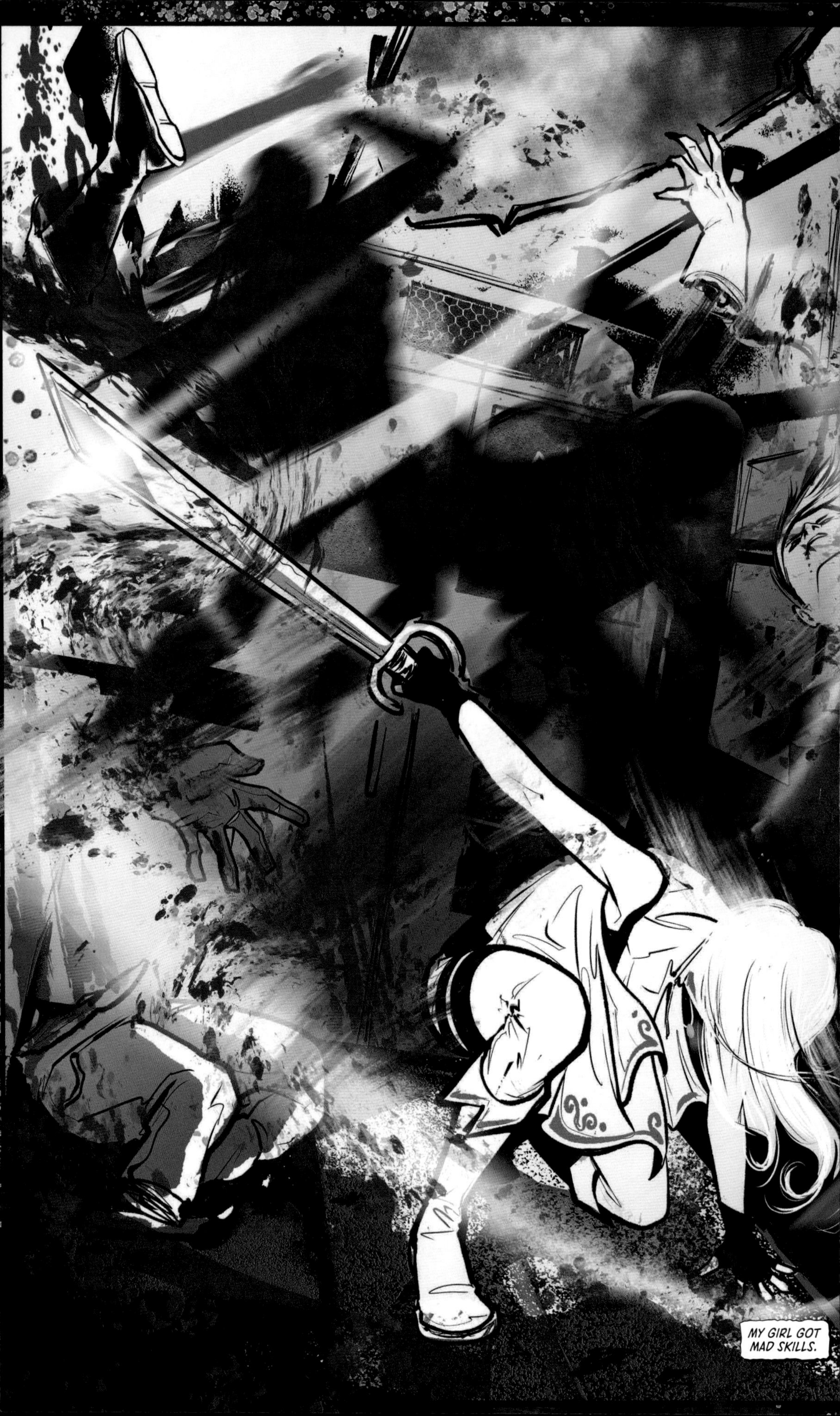
MY GIRL GOT MAD SKILLS.

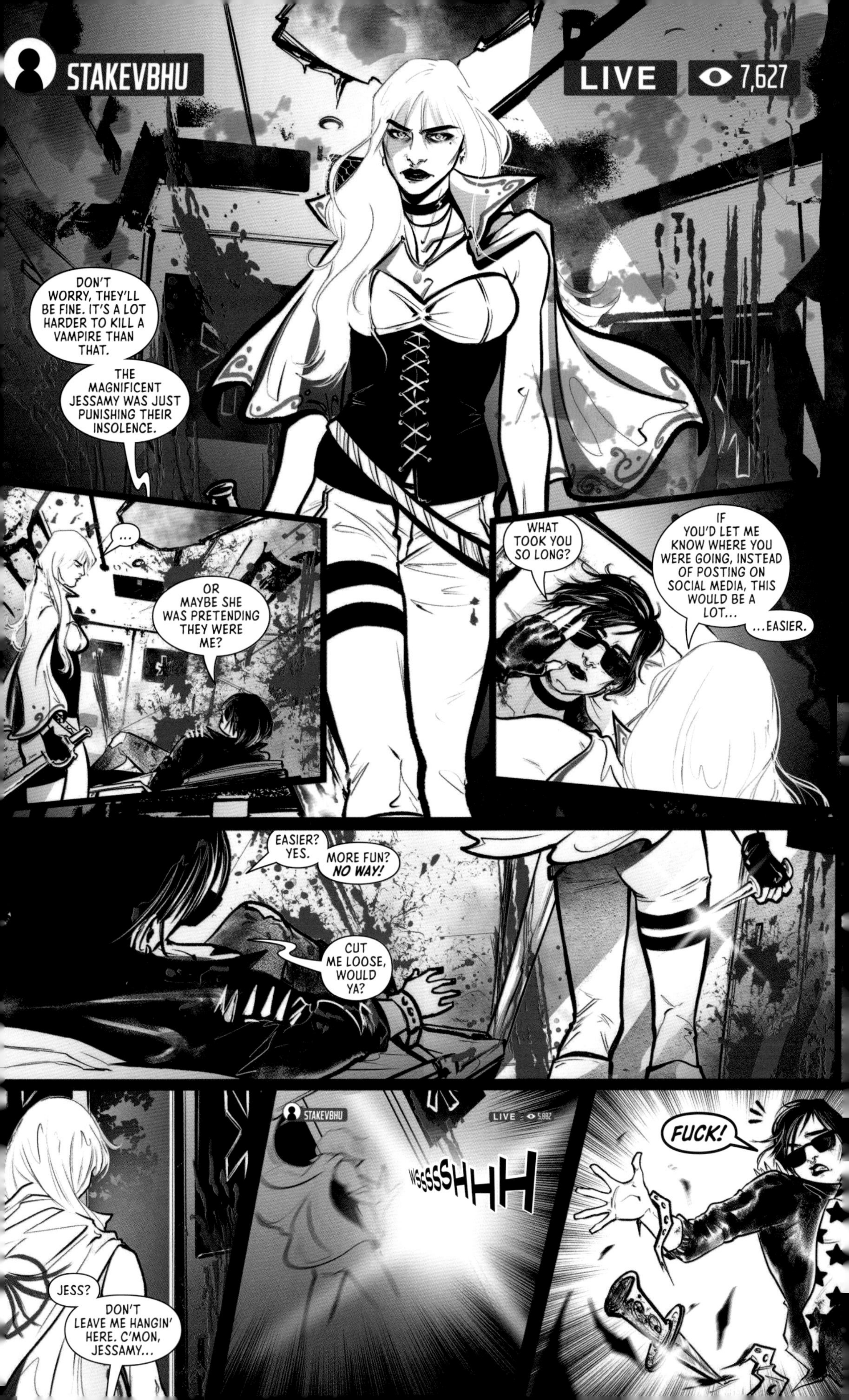
STAKEVBHU
LIVE
7,627
DON'T WORRY, THEY'LL BE FINE. IT'S A LOT HARDER TO KILL A VAMPIRE THAN THAT.
THE MAGNIFICENT JESSAMY WAS JUST PUNISHING THEIR INSOLENCE.
...
OR MAYBE SHE WAS PRETENDING THEY WERE ME?
WHAT TOOK YOU SO LONG?
IF YOU'D LET ME KNOW WHERE YOU WERE GOING, INSTEAD OF POSTING ON SOCIAL MEDIA, THIS WOULD BE A LOT...
...EASIER.
EASIER? YES.
MORE FUN? NO WAY!
CUT ME LOOSE, WOULD YA?
JESS?
DON'T LEAVE ME HANGIN' HERE. C'MON, JESSAMY...
STAKEVBHU
LIVE
WSSSSSHHH
FUCK!

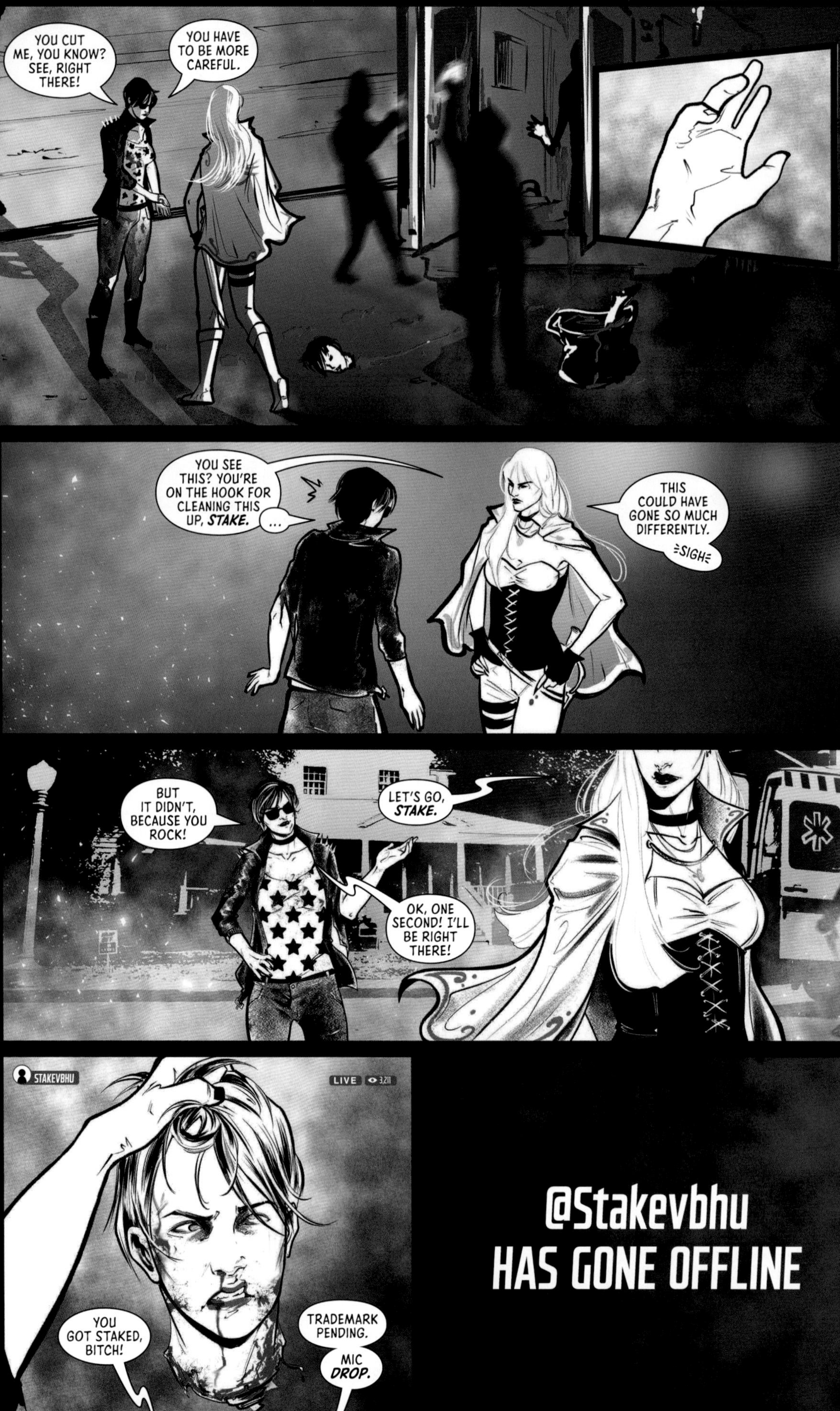

YOU CUT ME, YOU KNOW? SEE, RIGHT THERE!
YOU HAVE TO BE MORE CAREFUL.
YOU SEE THIS? YOU'RE ON THE HOOK FOR CLEANING THIS UP, STAKE.
...
THIS COULD HAVE GONE SO MUCH DIFFERENTLY.
SIGH
BUT IT DIDN'T, BECAUSE YOU ROCK!
LET'S GO, STAKE.
OK, ONE SECOND! I'LL BE RIGHT THERE!
STAKEVBHU
LIVE
3,211
YOU GOT STAKED, BITCH!
TRADEMARK PENDING.
MIC DROP.
@Stakevbhu
HAS GONE OFFLINE

End Chapter One

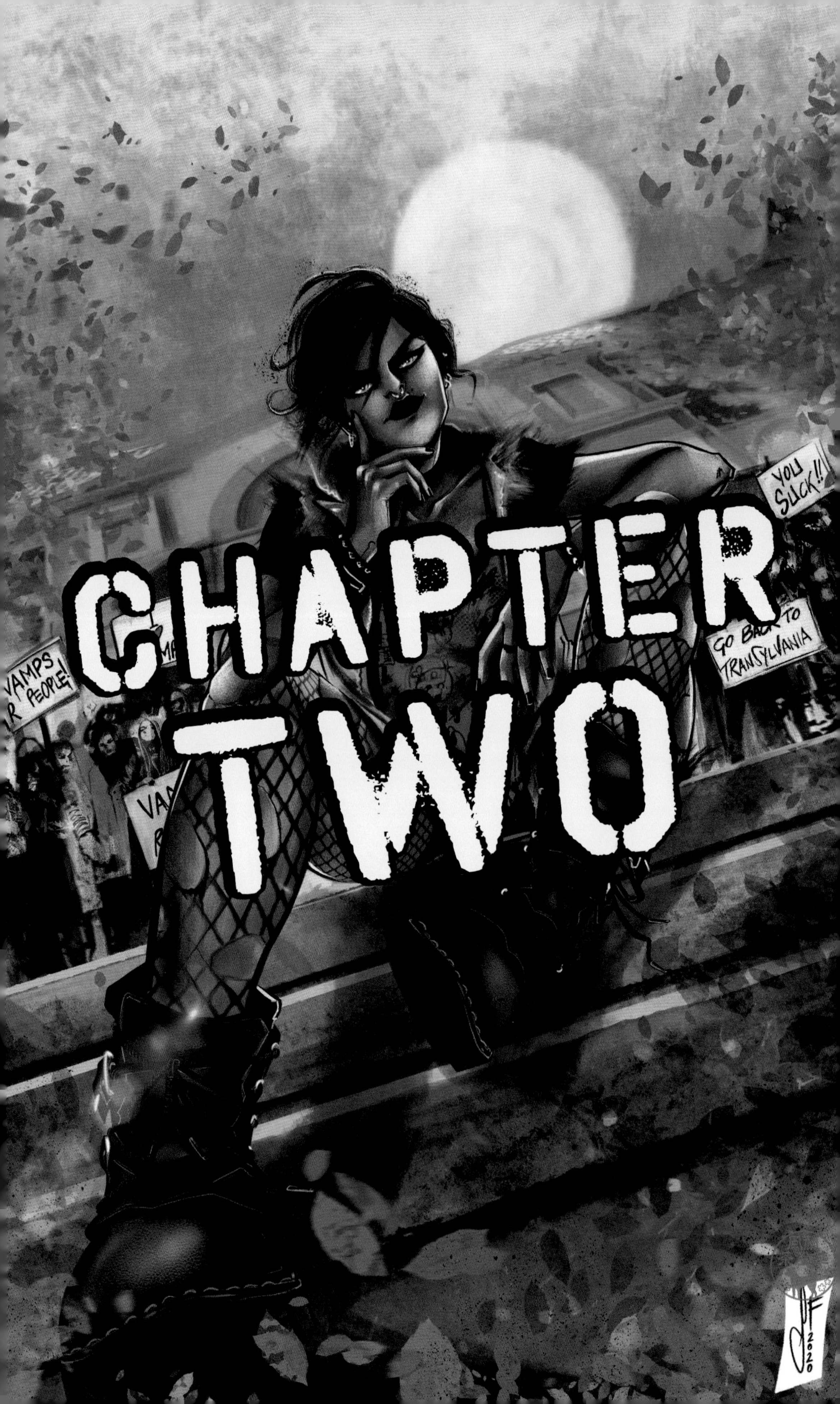

CHAPTER
TWO
YOU SUCK!!
GO BACK TO TRANSYLVANIA
VAMPS

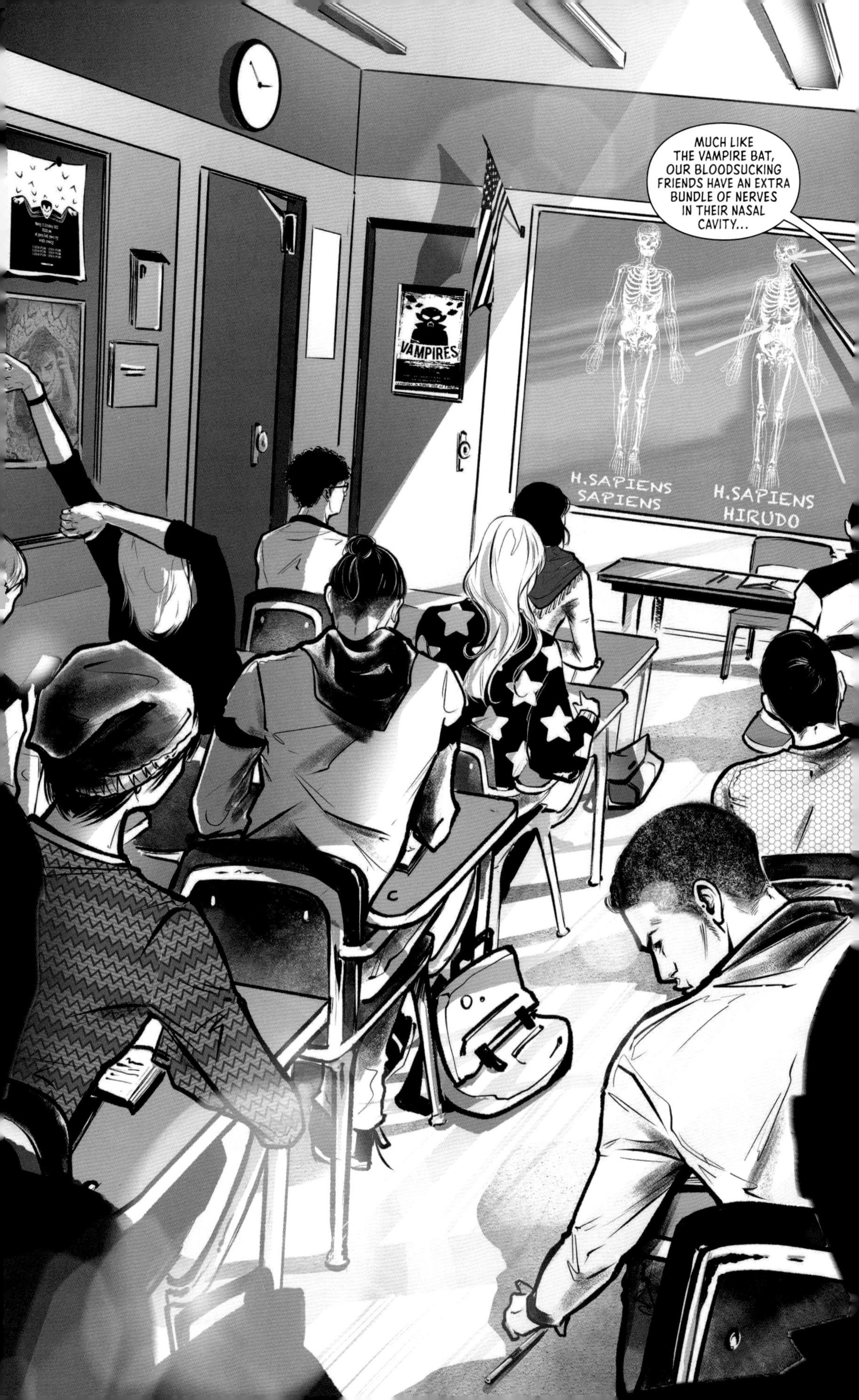
MUCH LIKE THE VAMPIRE BAT, OUR BLOODSUCKING FRIENDS HAVE AN EXTRA BUNDLE OF NERVES IN THEIR NASAL CAVITY...
VAMPIRES
H.SAPIENS SAPIENS
H.SAPIENS HIRUDO

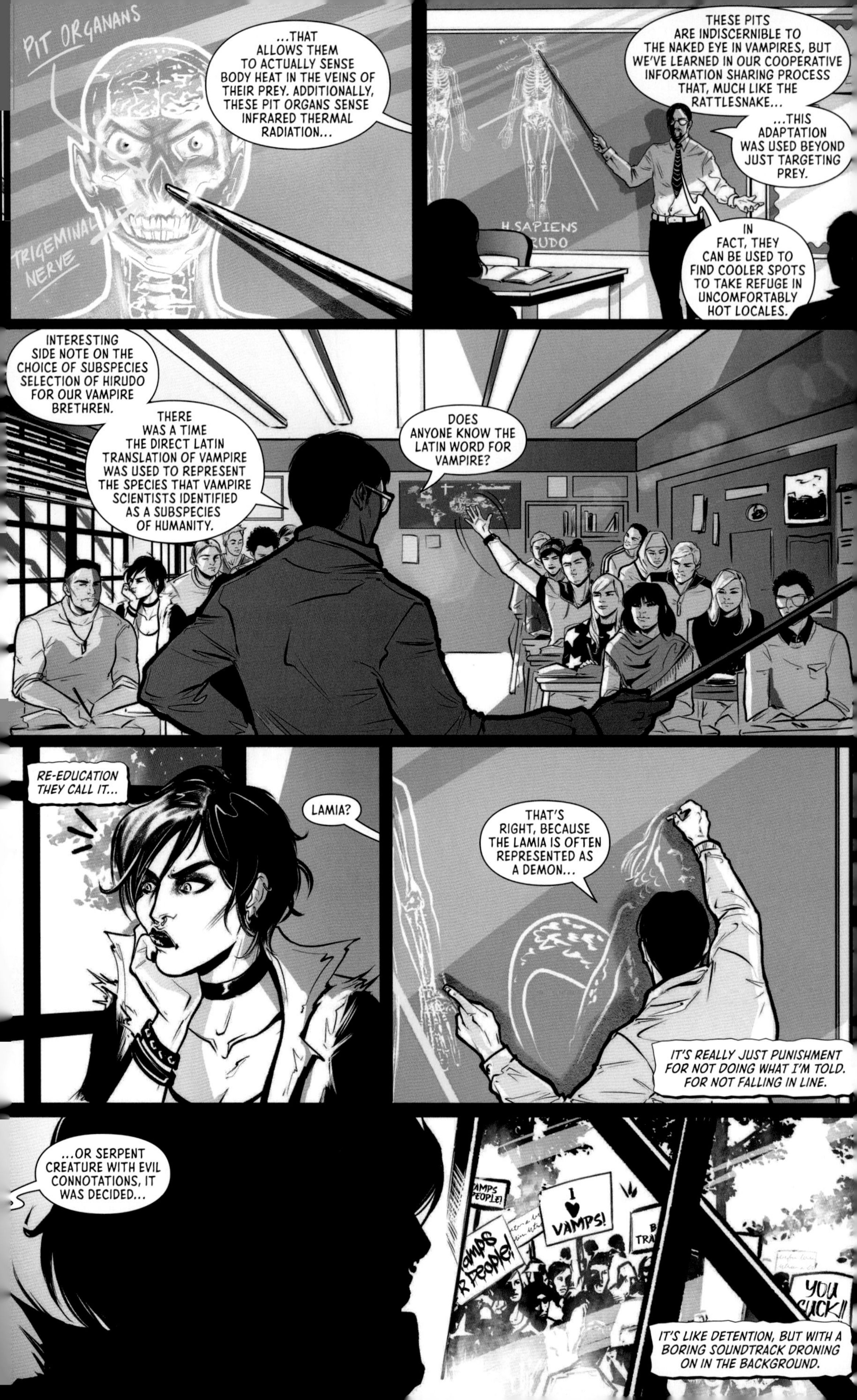
PIT ORGANANS
TRIGEMINAL NERVE
...THAT ALLOWS THEM TO ACTUALLY SENSE BODY HEAT IN THE VEINS OF THEIR PREY. ADDITIONALLY, THESE PIT ORGANS SENSE INFRARED THERMAL RADIATION...
H.SAPIENS
RUDO
THESE PITS ARE INDISCERNIBLE TO THE NAKED EYE IN VAMPIRES, BUT WE'VE LEARNED IN OUR COOPERATIVE INFORMATION SHARING PROCESS THAT, MUCH LIKE THE RATTLESNAKE...
...THIS ADAPTATION WAS USED BEYOND JUST TARGETING PREY.
IN FACT, THEY CAN BE USED TO FIND COOLER SPOTS TO TAKE REFUGE IN UNCOMFORTABLY HOT LOCALES.
INTERESTING SIDE NOTE ON THE CHOICE OF SUBSPECIES SELECTION OF HIRUDO FOR OUR VAMPIRE BRETHREN.
THERE WAS A TIME THE DIRECT LATIN TRANSLATION OF VAMPIRE WAS USED TO REPRESENT THE SPECIES THAT VAMPIRE SCIENTISTS IDENTIFIED AS A SUBSPECIES OF HUMANITY.
DOES ANYONE KNOW THE LATIN WORD FOR VAMPIRE?
RE-EDUCATION THEY CALL IT...
LAMIA?
THAT'S RIGHT, BECAUSE THE LAMIA IS OFTEN REPRESENTED AS A DEMON...
IT'S REALLY JUST PUNISHMENT FOR NOT DOING WHAT I'M TOLD. FOR NOT FALLING IN LINE.
...OR SERPENT CREATURE WITH EVIL CONNOTATIONS, IT WAS DECIDED...
I ♥ VAMPS!
YOU SUCK!!
IT'S LIKE DETENTION, BUT WITH A BORING SOUNDTRACK DRONING ON IN THE BACKGROUND.

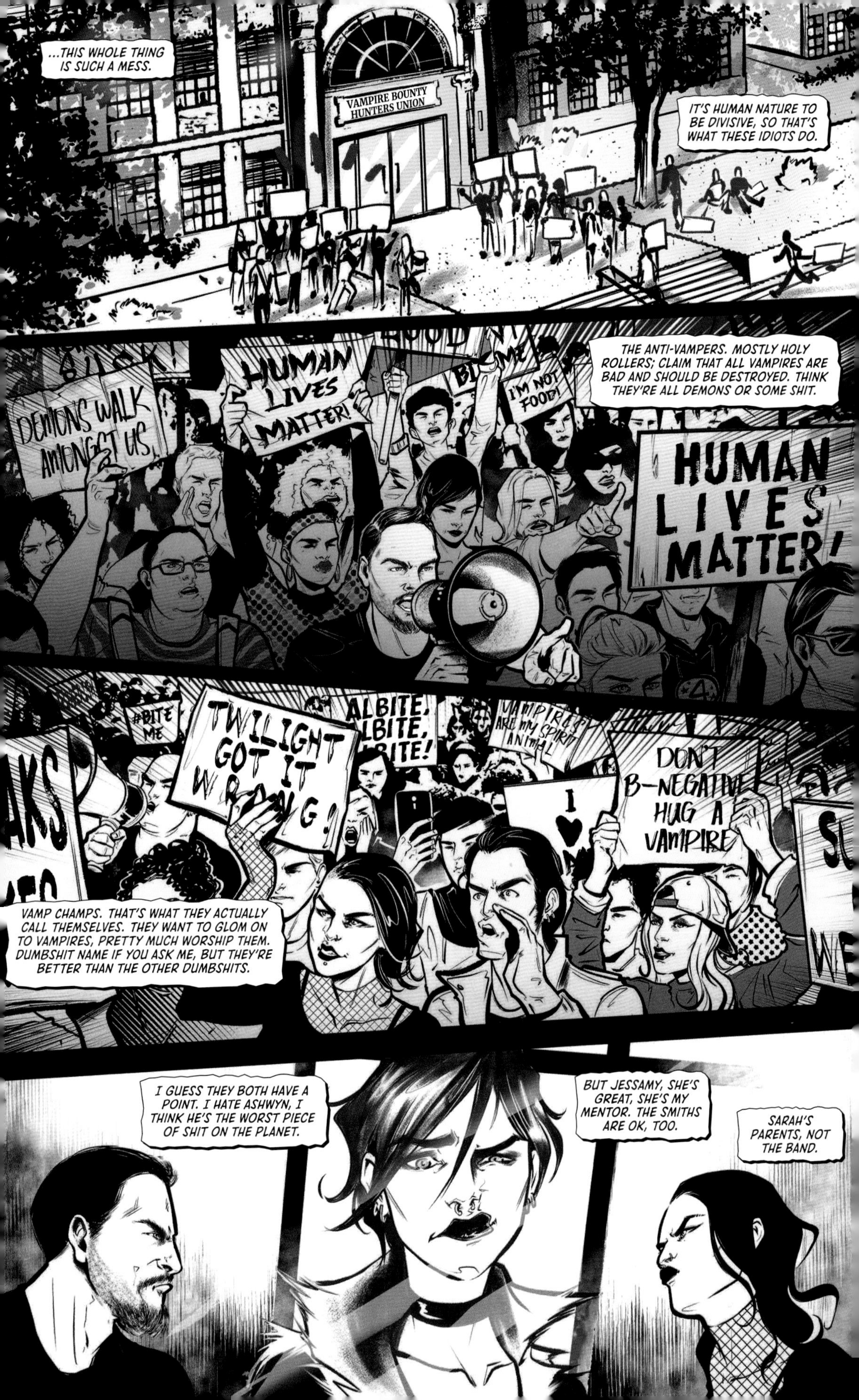

...THIS WHOLE THING IS SUCH A MESS.
VAMPIRE BOUNTY HUNTERS UNION
IT'S HUMAN NATURE TO BE DIVISIVE, SO THAT'S WHAT THESE IDIOTS DO.
THE ANTI-VAMPERS. MOSTLY HOLY ROLLERS; CLAIM THAT ALL VAMPIRES ARE BAD AND SHOULD BE DESTROYED. THINK THEY'RE ALL DEMONS OR SOME SHIT.
DEMONS WALK AMONGST US
HUMAN LIVES MATTER!
I'M NOT FOOD!
HUMAN LIVES MATTER!
#BITE ME
TWILIGHT GOT IT WRONG!
VAMPIRES ARE MY SPIRIT ANIMAL
DON'T B-NEGATIVE HUG A VAMPIRE
VAMP CHAMPS. THAT'S WHAT THEY ACTUALLY CALL THEMSELVES. THEY WANT TO GLOM ON TO VAMPIRES, PRETTY MUCH WORSHIP THEM. DUMBSHIT NAME IF YOU ASK ME, BUT THEY'RE BETTER THAN THE OTHER DUMBSHITS.
I GUESS THEY BOTH HAVE A POINT. I HATE ASHWYN, I THINK HE'S THE WORST PIECE OF SHIT ON THE PLANET.
BUT JESSAMY, SHE'S GREAT, SHE'S MY MENTOR. THE SMITHS ARE OK, TOO.
SARAH'S PARENTS, NOT THE BAND.

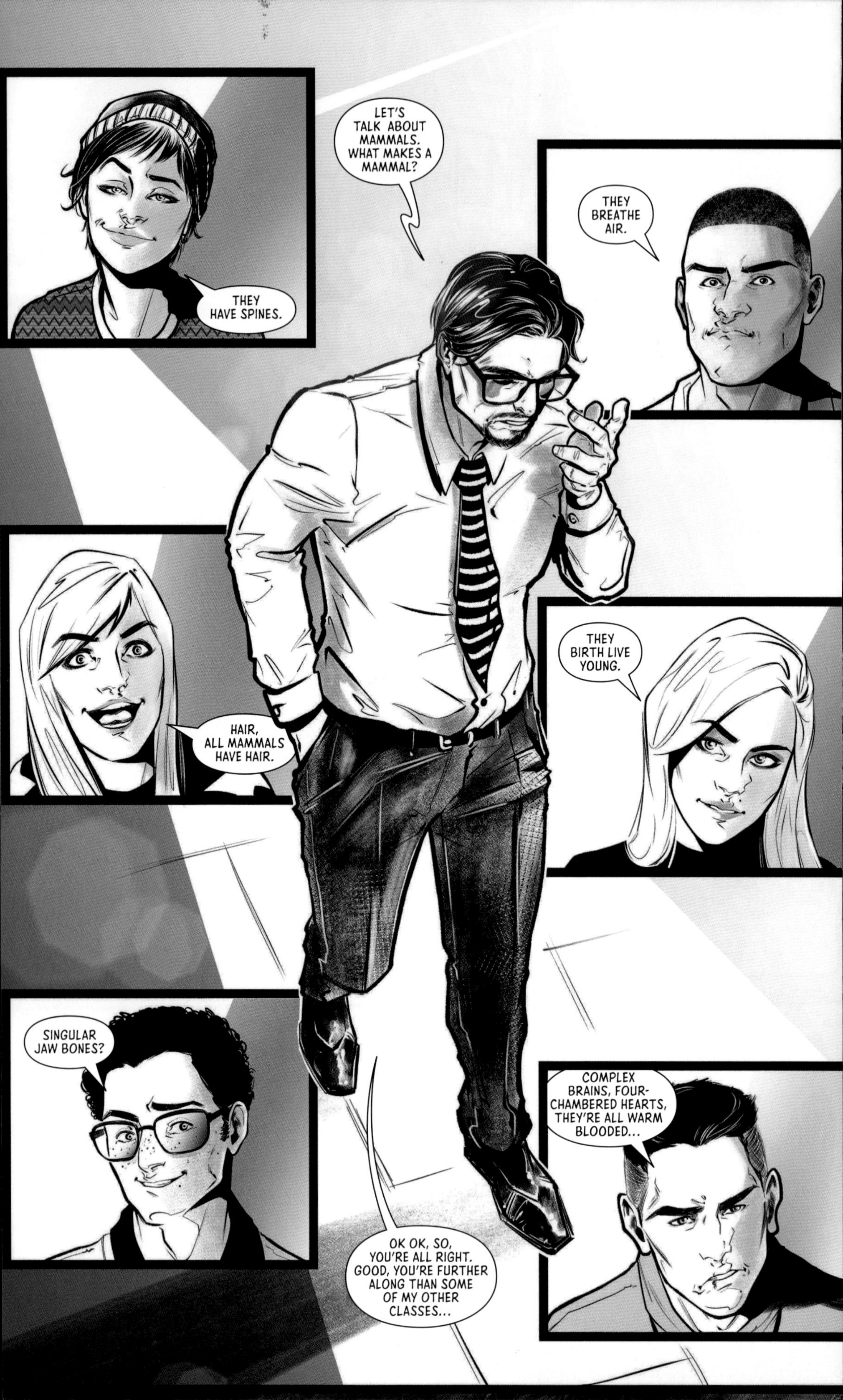
LET'S TALK ABOUT MAMMALS. WHAT MAKES A MAMMAL?
THEY HAVE SPINES.
THEY BREATHE AIR.
HAIR, ALL MAMMALS HAVE HAIR.
THEY BIRTH LIVE YOUNG.
SINGULAR JAW BONES?
COMPLEX BRAINS, FOUR-CHAMBERED HEARTS, THEY'RE ALL WARM BLOODED...
OK OK, SO, YOU'RE ALL RIGHT. GOOD, YOU'RE FURTHER ALONG THAN SOME OF MY OTHER CLASSES...

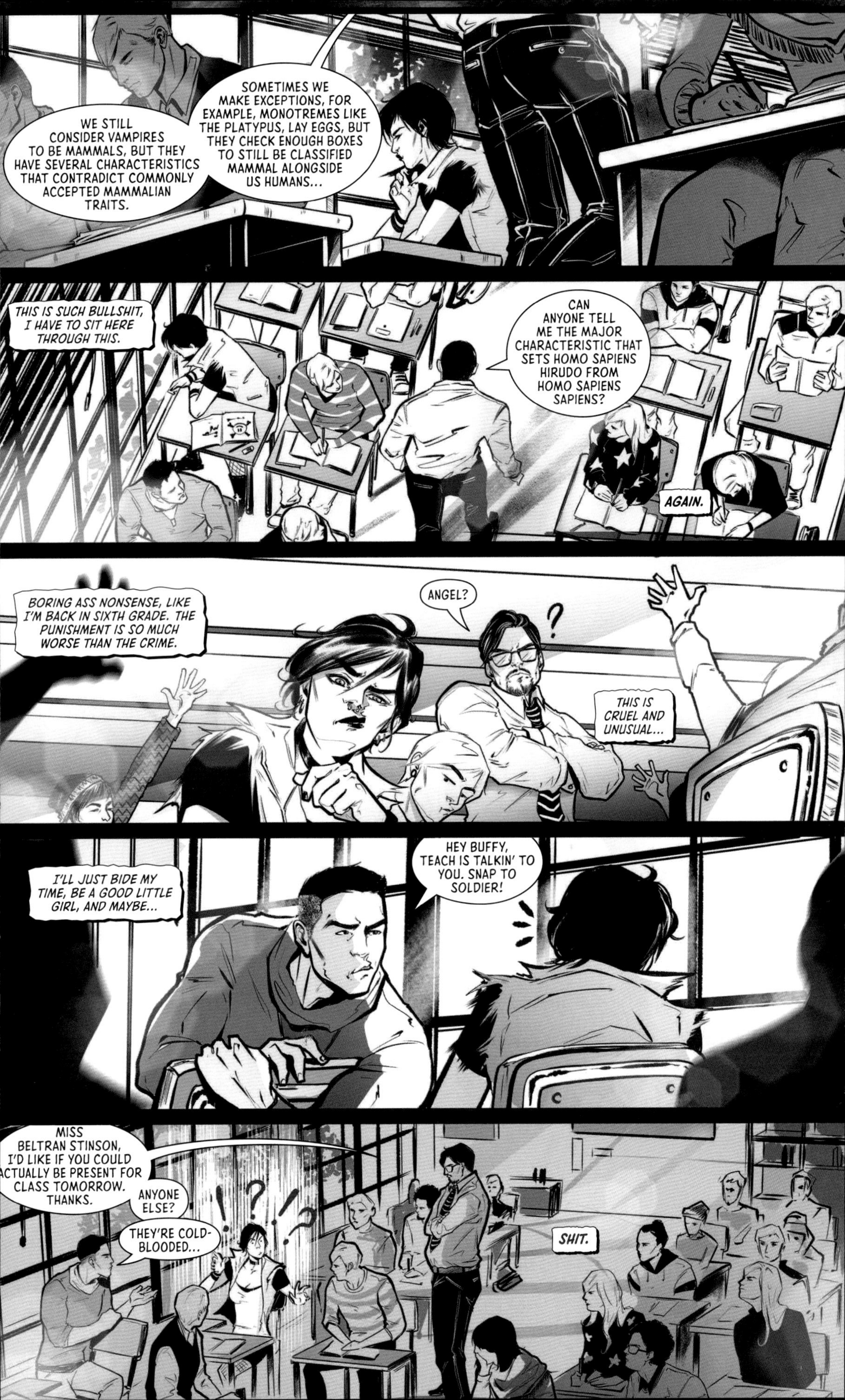
WE STILL CONSIDER VAMPIRES TO BE MAMMALS, BUT THEY HAVE SEVERAL CHARACTERISTICS THAT CONTRADICT COMMONLY ACCEPTED MAMMALIAN TRAITS.
SOMETIMES WE MAKE EXCEPTIONS, FOR EXAMPLE, MONOTREMES LIKE THE PLATYPUS, LAY EGGS, BUT THEY CHECK ENOUGH BOXES TO STILL BE CLASSIFIED MAMMAL ALONGSIDE US HUMANS...
THIS IS SUCH BULLSHIT, I HAVE TO SIT HERE THROUGH THIS.
CAN ANYONE TELL ME THE MAJOR CHARACTERISTIC THAT SETS HOMO SAPIENS HIRUDO FROM HOMO SAPIENS SAPIENS?
AGAIN.
BORING ASS NONSENSE, LIKE I'M BACK IN SIXTH GRADE. THE PUNISHMENT IS SO MUCH WORSE THAN THE CRIME.
ANGEL?
?
THIS IS CRUEL AND UNUSUAL...
I'LL JUST BIDE MY TIME, BE A GOOD LITTLE GIRL, AND MAYBE...
HEY BUFFY, TEACH IS TALKIN' TO YOU. SNAP TO SOLDIER!
MISS BELTRAN STINSON, I'D LIKE IF YOU COULD ACTUALLY BE PRESENT FOR CLASS TOMORROW. THANKS.
ANYONE ELSE?
THEY'RE COLD-BLOODED...
SHIT.

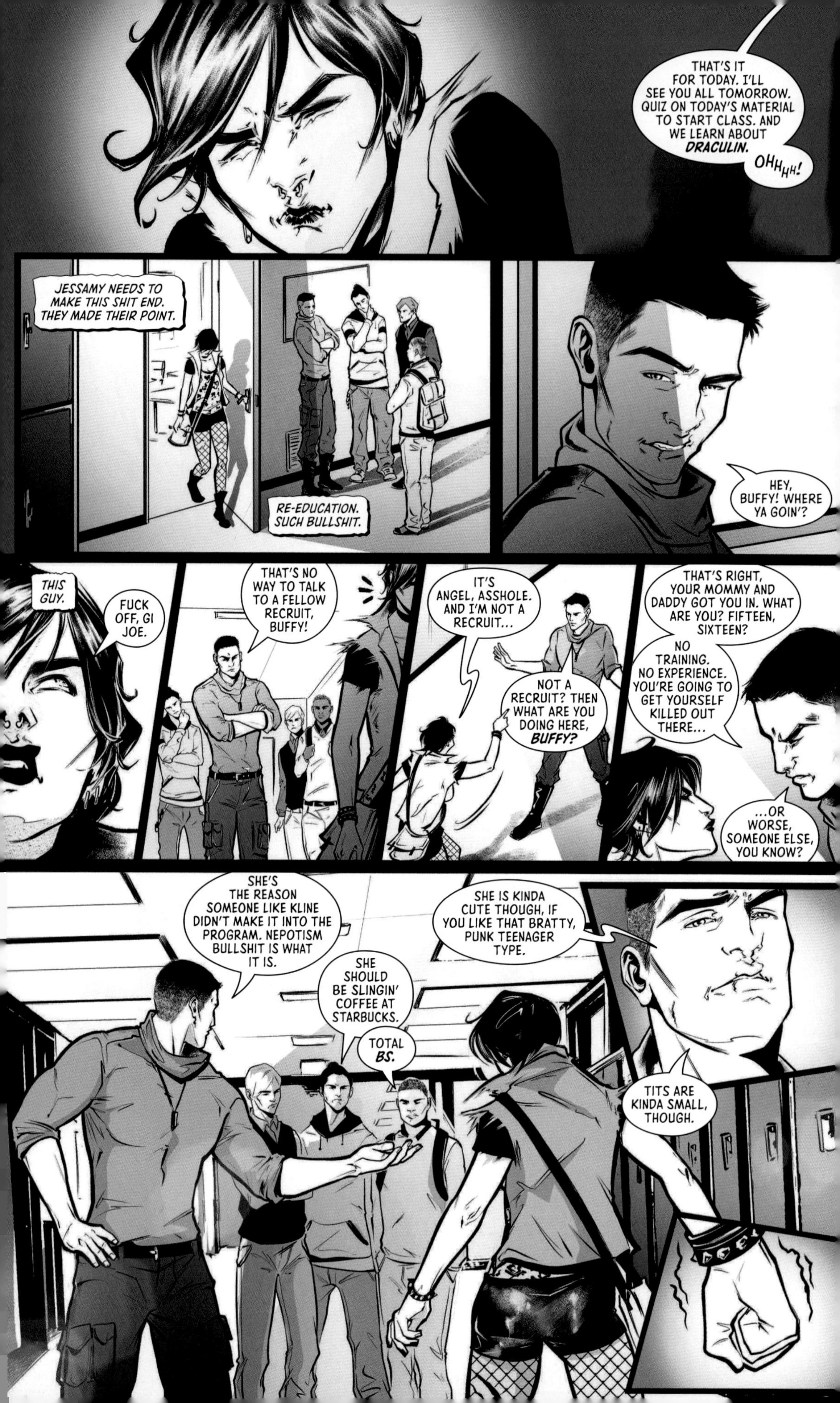
THAT'S IT FOR TODAY. I'LL SEE YOU ALL TOMORROW. QUIZ ON TODAY'S MATERIAL TO START CLASS. AND WE LEARN ABOUT DRACULIN.
OHHHH!
JESSAMY NEEDS TO MAKE THIS SHIT END. THEY MADE THEIR POINT.
RE-EDUCATION. SUCH BULLSHIT.
HEY, BUFFY! WHERE YA GOIN'?
THIS GUY.
FUCK OFF, GI JOE.
THAT'S NO WAY TO TALK TO A FELLOW RECRUIT, BUFFY!
IT'S ANGEL, ASSHOLE. AND I'M NOT A RECRUIT...
NOT A RECRUIT? THEN WHAT ARE YOU DOING HERE, BUFFY?
THAT'S RIGHT, YOUR MOMMY AND DADDY GOT YOU IN. WHAT ARE YOU? FIFTEEN, SIXTEEN?
NO TRAINING. NO EXPERIENCE. YOU'RE GOING TO GET YOURSELF KILLED OUT THERE...
...OR WORSE, SOMEONE ELSE, YOU KNOW?
SHE'S THE REASON SOMEONE LIKE KLINE DIDN'T MAKE IT INTO THE PROGRAM. NEPOTISM BULLSHIT IS WHAT IT IS.
SHE SHOULD BE SLINGIN' COFFEE AT STARBUCKS.
TOTAL BS.
SHE IS KINDA CUTE THOUGH, IF YOU LIKE THAT BRATTY, PUNK TEENAGER TYPE.
TITS ARE KINDA SMALL, THOUGH.

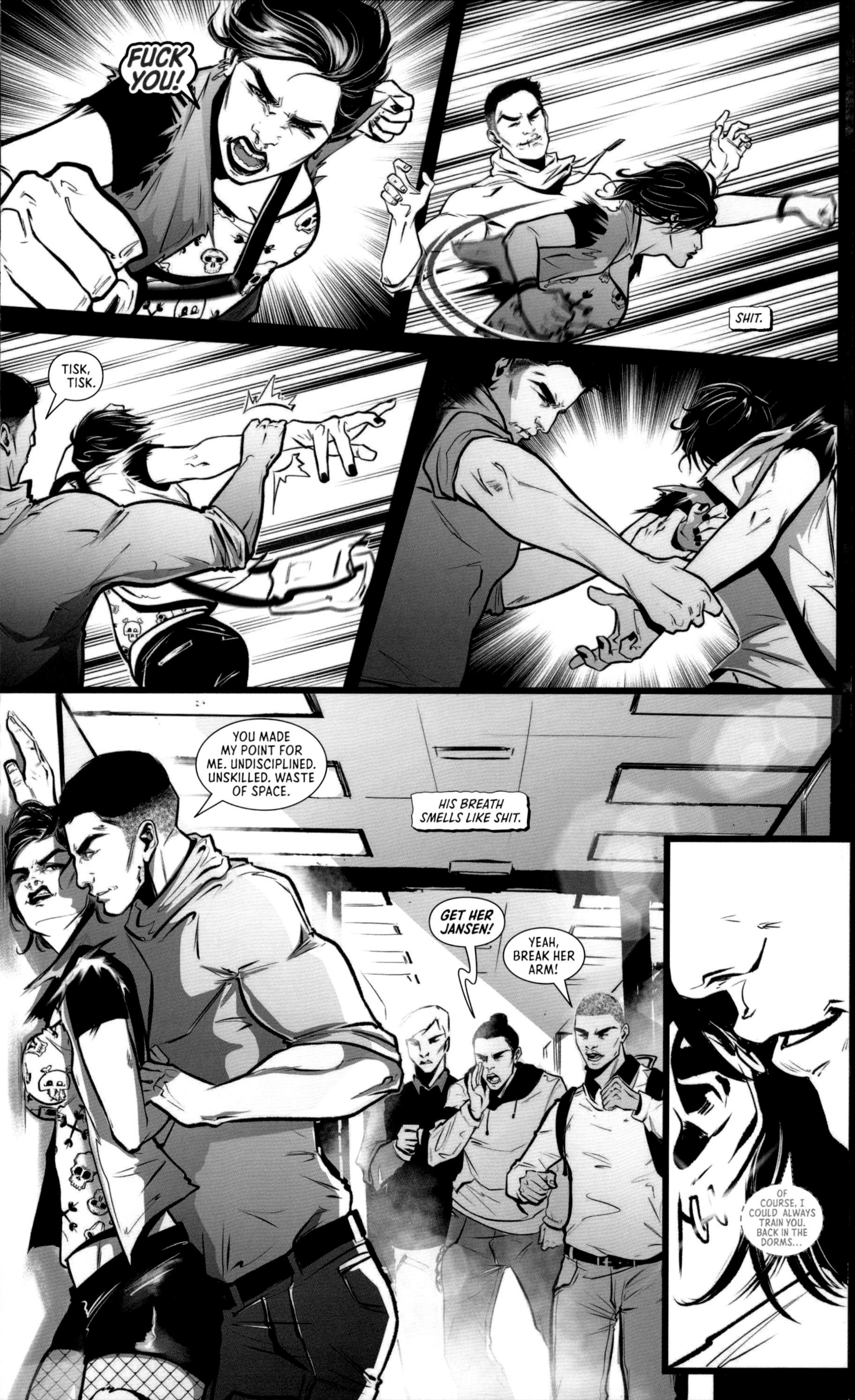
FUCK YOU!
SHIT.
TISK, TISK.
YOU MADE MY POINT FOR ME. UNDISCIPLINED. UNSKILLED. WASTE OF SPACE.
HIS BREATH SMELLS LIKE SHIT.
GET HER JANSEN!
YEAH, BREAK HER ARM!
OF COURSE, I COULD ALWAYS TRAIN YOU. BACK IN THE DORMS...

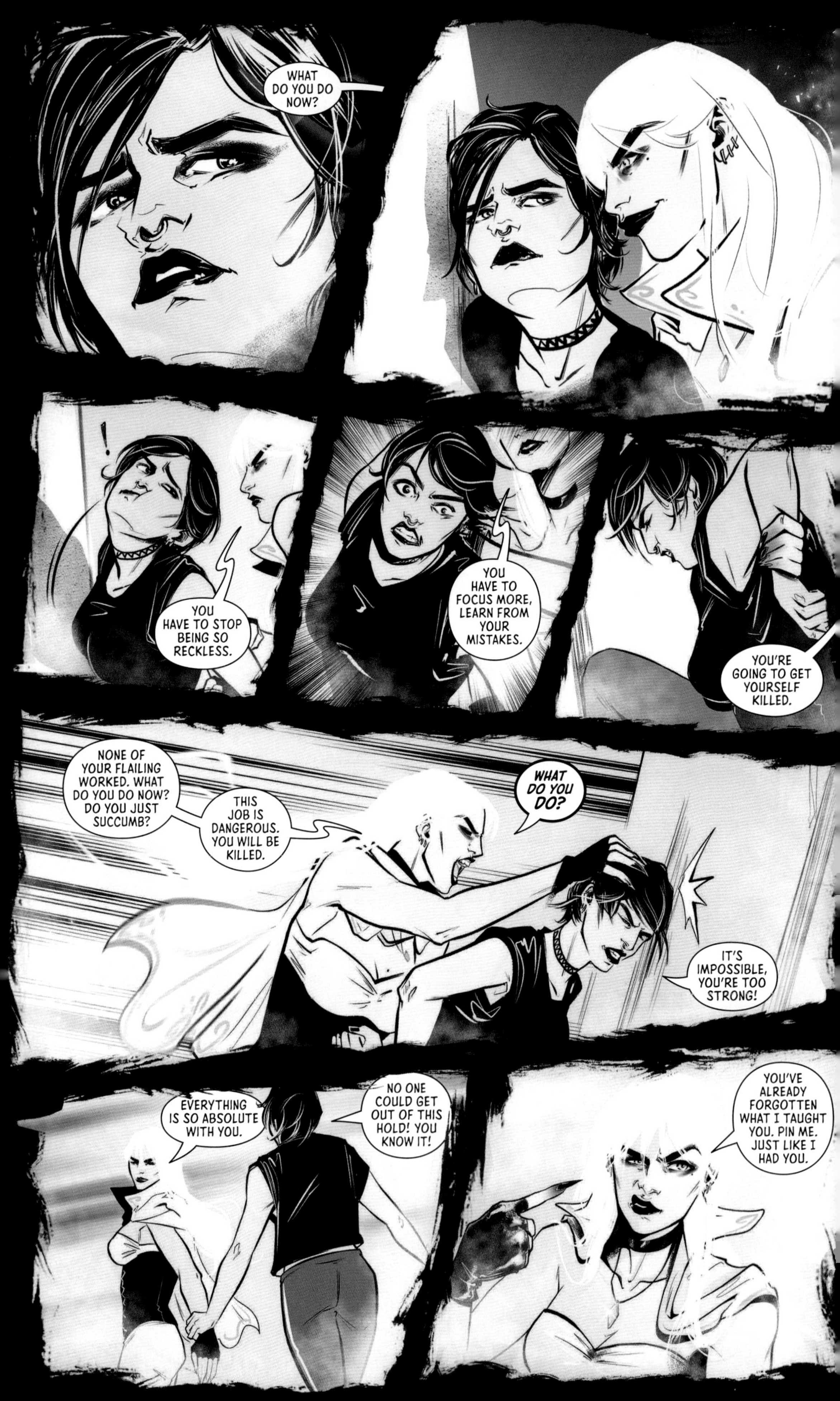
WHAT DO YOU DO NOW?
YOU HAVE TO STOP BEING SO RECKLESS.
YOU HAVE TO FOCUS MORE, LEARN FROM YOUR MISTAKES.
YOU'RE GOING TO GET YOURSELF KILLED.
NONE OF YOUR FLAILING WORKED. WHAT DO YOU DO NOW? DO YOU JUST SUCCUMB?
THIS JOB IS DANGEROUS. YOU WILL BE KILLED.
WHAT DO YOU DO?
IT'S IMPOSSIBLE, YOU'RE TOO STRONG!
EVERYTHING IS SO ABSOLUTE WITH YOU.
NO ONE COULD GET OUT OF THIS HOLD! YOU KNOW IT!
YOU'VE ALREADY FORGOTTEN WHAT I TAUGHT YOU. PIN ME. JUST LIKE I HAD YOU.

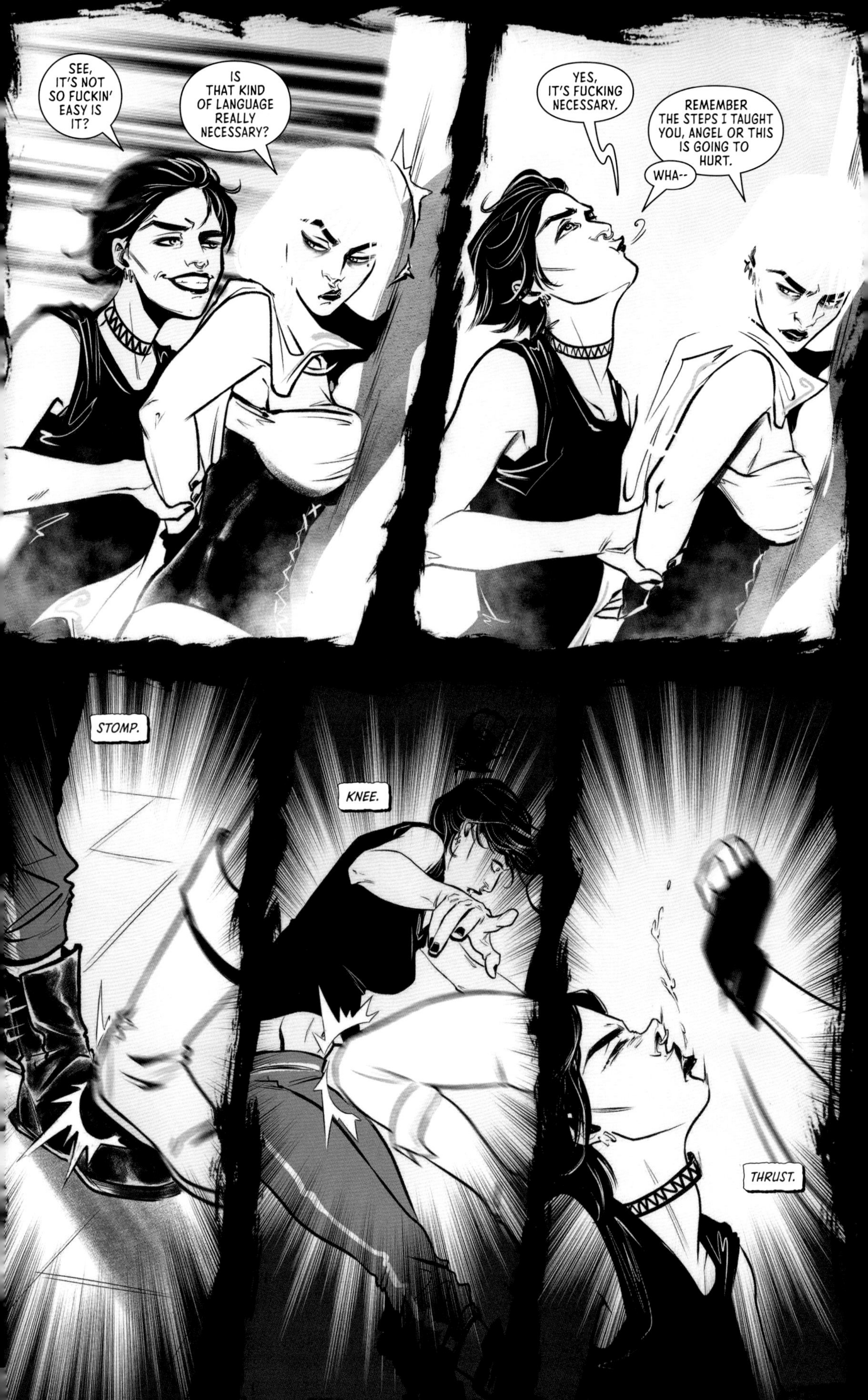
SEE, IT'S NOT SO FUCKIN' EASY IS IT?
IS THAT KIND OF LANGUAGE REALLY NECESSARY?
YES, IT'S FUCKING NECESSARY.
REMEMBER THE STEPS I TAUGHT YOU, ANGEL OR THIS IS GOING TO HURT.
WHA--
STOMP.
KNEE.
THRUST.

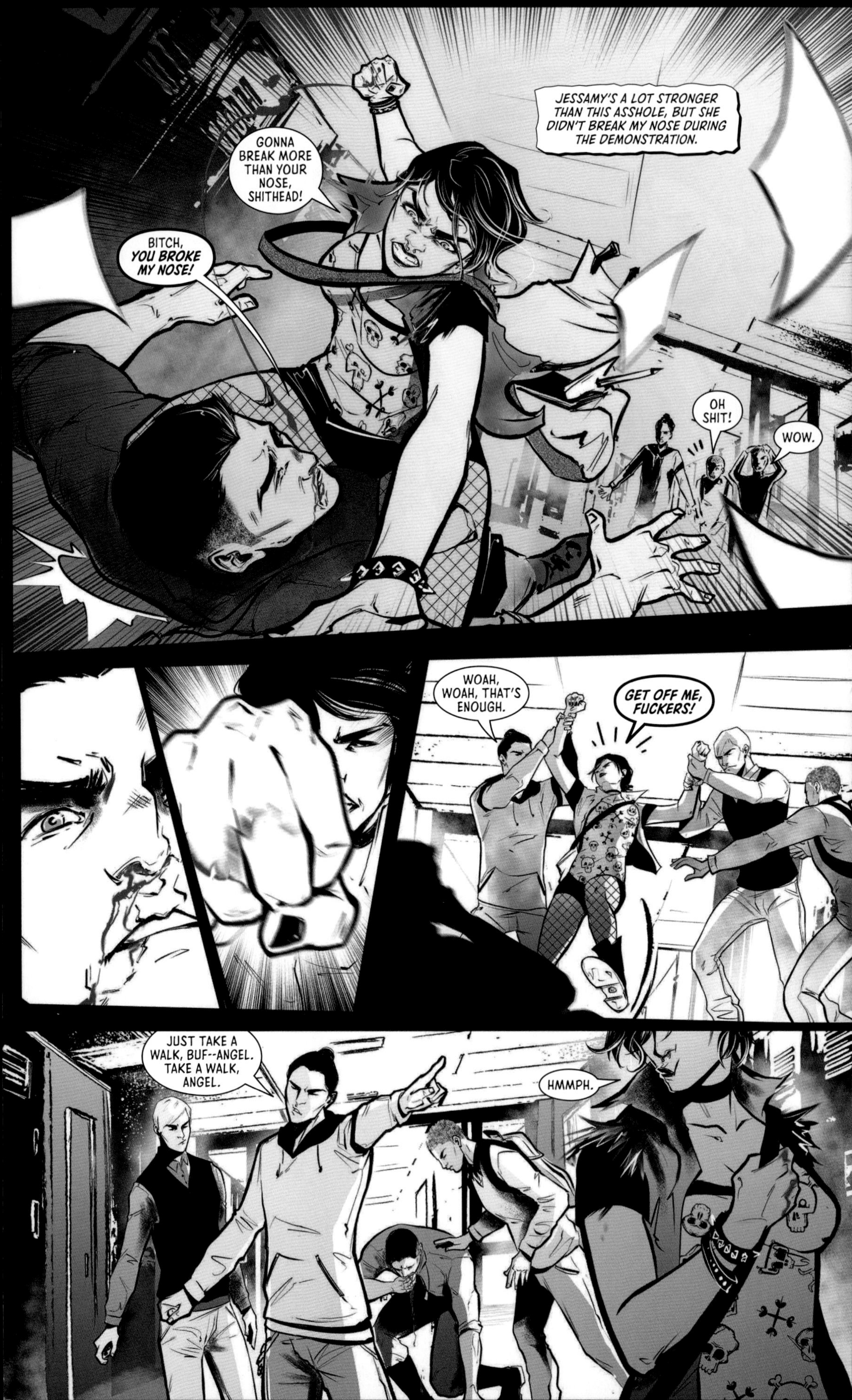
JESSAMY'S A LOT STRONGER THAN THIS ASSHOLE, BUT SHE DIDN'T BREAK MY NOSE DURING THE DEMONSTRATION.
GONNA BREAK MORE THAN YOUR NOSE, SHITHEAD!
BITCH, YOU BROKE MY NOSE!
OH SHIT!
WOW.
WOAH, WOAH, THAT'S ENOUGH.
GET OFF ME, FUCKERS!
JUST TAKE A WALK, BUF--ANGEL. TAKE A WALK, ANGEL.
HMMPH.

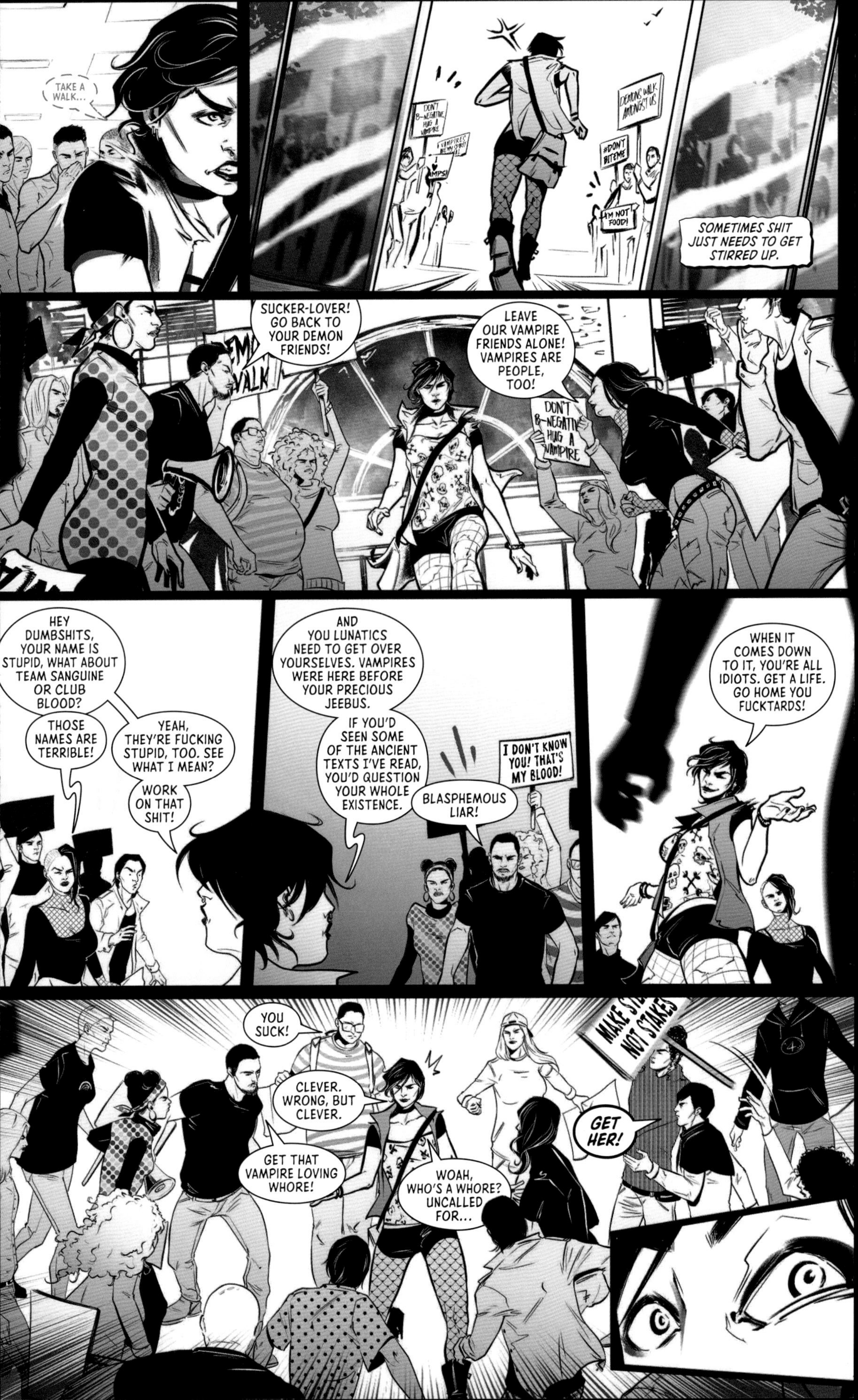
TAKE A WALK...
DON'T B-NEGATIVE HUG A VAMPIRE
DEMONS WALK AMONGST US
#DON'T BITEME
I'M NOT FOOD!
SOMETIMES SHIT JUST NEEDS TO GET STIRRED UP.
SUCKER-LOVER! GO BACK TO YOUR DEMON FRIENDS!
LEAVE OUR VAMPIRE FRIENDS ALONE! VAMPIRES ARE PEOPLE, TOO!
DON'T B-NEGATIVE HUG A VAMPIRE
HEY DUMBSHITS, YOUR NAME IS STUPID, WHAT ABOUT TEAM SANGUINE OR CLUB BLOOD?
THOSE NAMES ARE TERRIBLE!
YEAH, THEY'RE FUCKING STUPID, TOO. SEE WHAT I MEAN?
WORK ON THAT SHIT!
AND YOU LUNATICS NEED TO GET OVER YOURSELVES. VAMPIRES WERE HERE BEFORE YOUR PRECIOUS JEEBUS.
IF YOU'D SEEN SOME OF THE ANCIENT TEXTS I'VE READ, YOU'D QUESTION YOUR WHOLE EXISTENCE.
I DON'T KNOW YOU! THAT'S MY BLOOD!
BLASPHEMOUS LIAR!
WHEN IT COMES DOWN TO IT, YOU'RE ALL IDIOTS. GET A LIFE. GO HOME YOU FUCKTARDS!
YOU SUCK!
CLEVER. WRONG, BUT CLEVER.
GET THAT VAMPIRE LOVING WHORE!
WOAH, WHO'S A WHORE? UNCALLED FOR...
GET HER!

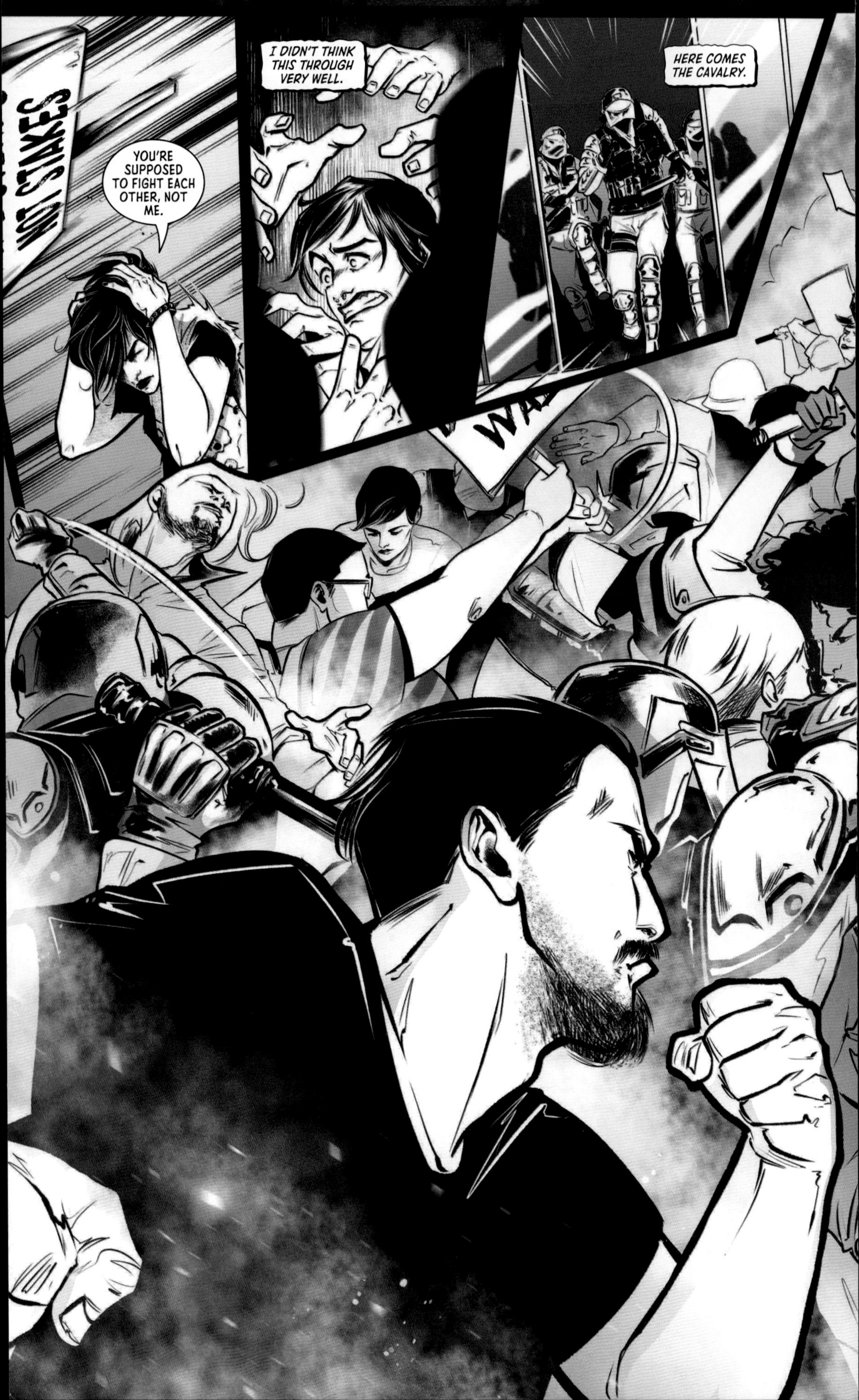
NOT STAKES
YOU'RE SUPPOSED TO FIGHT EACH OTHER, NOT ME.
I DIDN'T THINK THIS THROUGH VERY WELL.
HERE COMES THE CAVALRY.

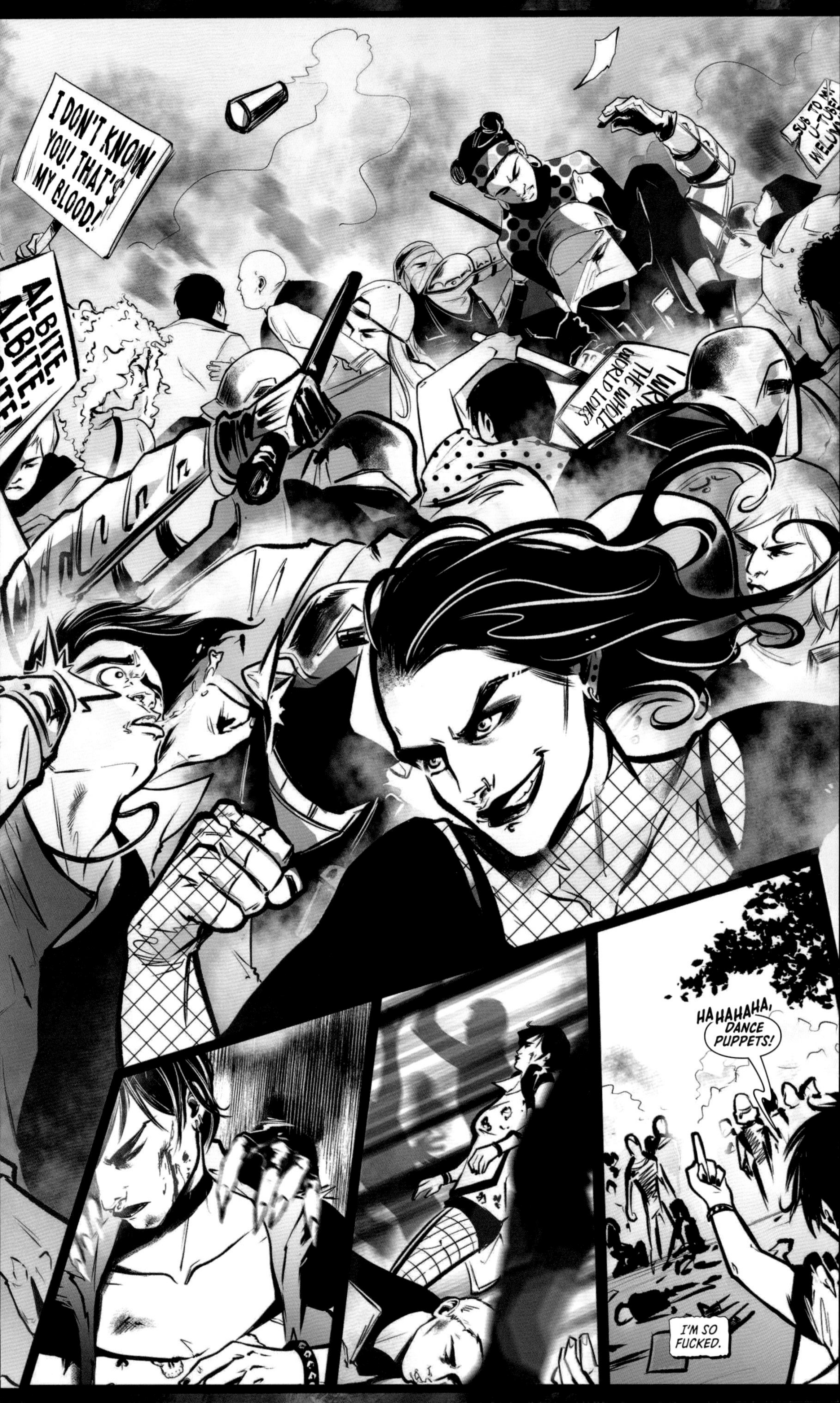

I DON'T KNOW YOU! THAT'S MY BLOOD!
HAHAHAHA, DANCE PUPPETS!
I'M SO FUCKED.

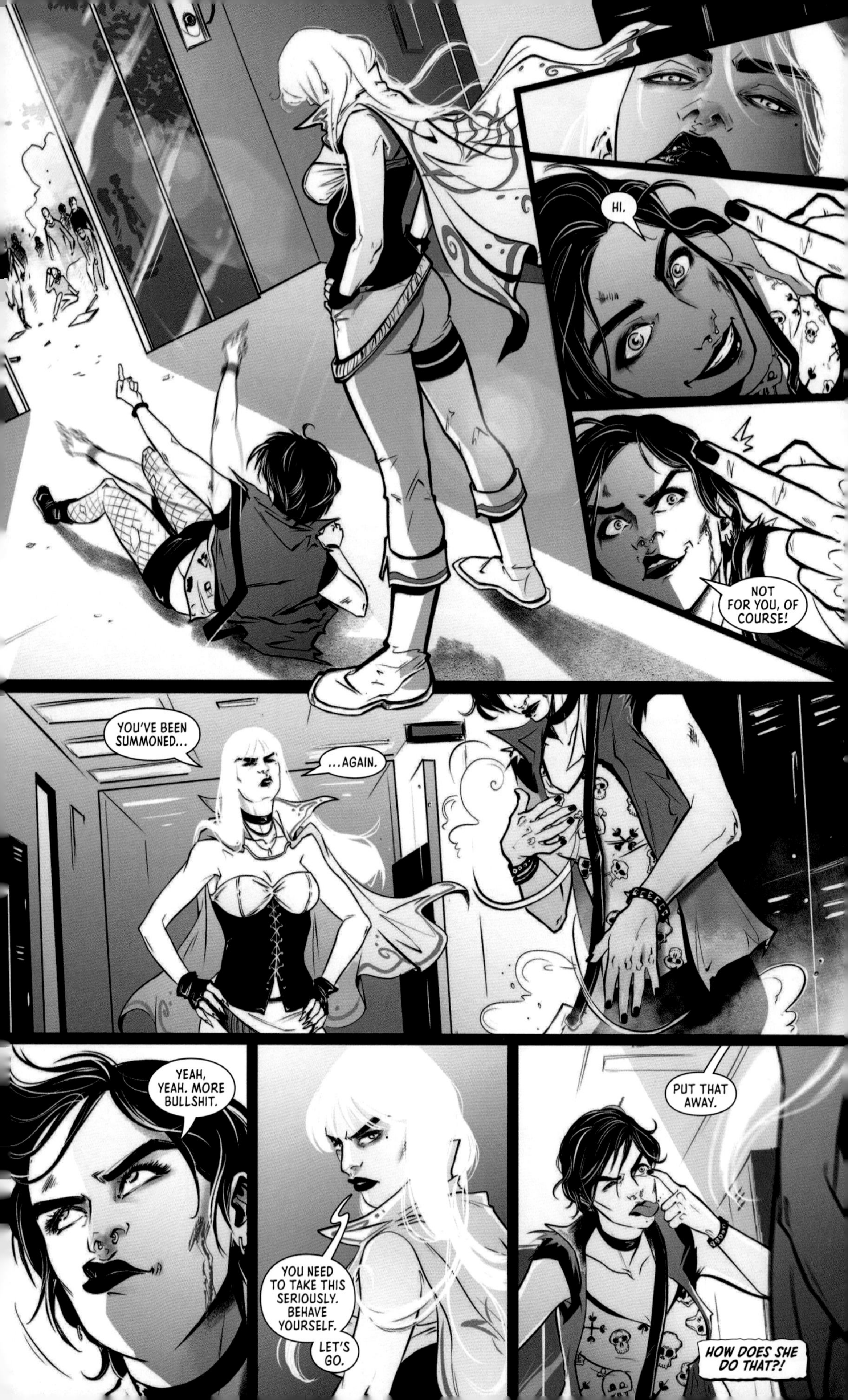
HI.
NOT FOR YOU, OF COURSE!
YOU'VE BEEN SUMMONED...
...AGAIN.
YEAH, YEAH. MORE BULLSHIT.
YOU NEED TO TAKE THIS SERIOUSLY. BEHAVE YOURSELF.
LET'S GO.
PUT THAT AWAY.
HOW DOES SHE DO THAT?!

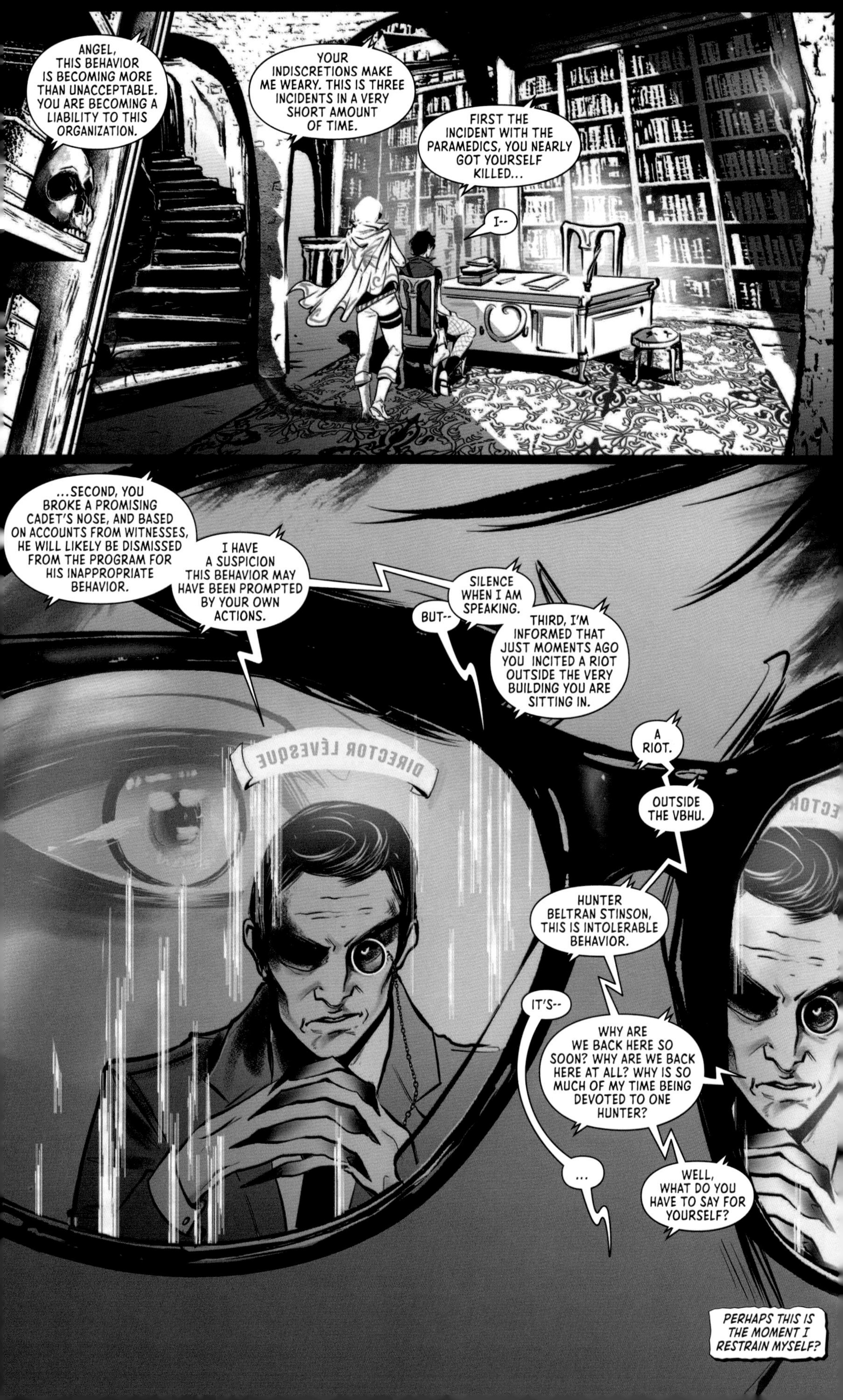

ANGEL, THIS BEHAVIOR IS BECOMING MORE THAN UNACCEPTABLE. YOU ARE BECOMING A LIABILITY TO THIS ORGANIZATION.
YOUR INDISCRETIONS MAKE ME WEARY. THIS IS THREE INCIDENTS IN A VERY SHORT AMOUNT OF TIME.
FIRST THE INCIDENT WITH THE PARAMEDICS, YOU NEARLY GOT YOURSELF KILLED...
I--
...SECOND, YOU BROKE A PROMISING CADET'S NOSE, AND BASED ON ACCOUNTS FROM WITNESSES, HE WILL LIKELY BE DISMISSED FROM THE PROGRAM FOR HIS INAPPROPRIATE BEHAVIOR.
I HAVE A SUSPICION THIS BEHAVIOR MAY HAVE BEEN PROMPTED BY YOUR OWN ACTIONS.
BUT--
SILENCE WHEN I AM SPEAKING.
THIRD, I'M INFORMED THAT JUST MOMENTS AGO YOU INCITED A RIOT OUTSIDE THE VERY BUILDING YOU ARE SITTING IN.
A RIOT.
OUTSIDE THE VBHU.
HUNTER BELTRAN STINSON, THIS IS INTOLERABLE BEHAVIOR.
IT'S--
WHY ARE WE BACK HERE SO SOON? WHY ARE WE BACK HERE AT ALL? WHY IS SO MUCH OF MY TIME BEING DEVOTED TO ONE HUNTER?
...
WELL, WHAT DO YOU HAVE TO SAY FOR YOURSELF?
PERHAPS THIS IS THE MOMENT I RESTRAIN MYSELF?

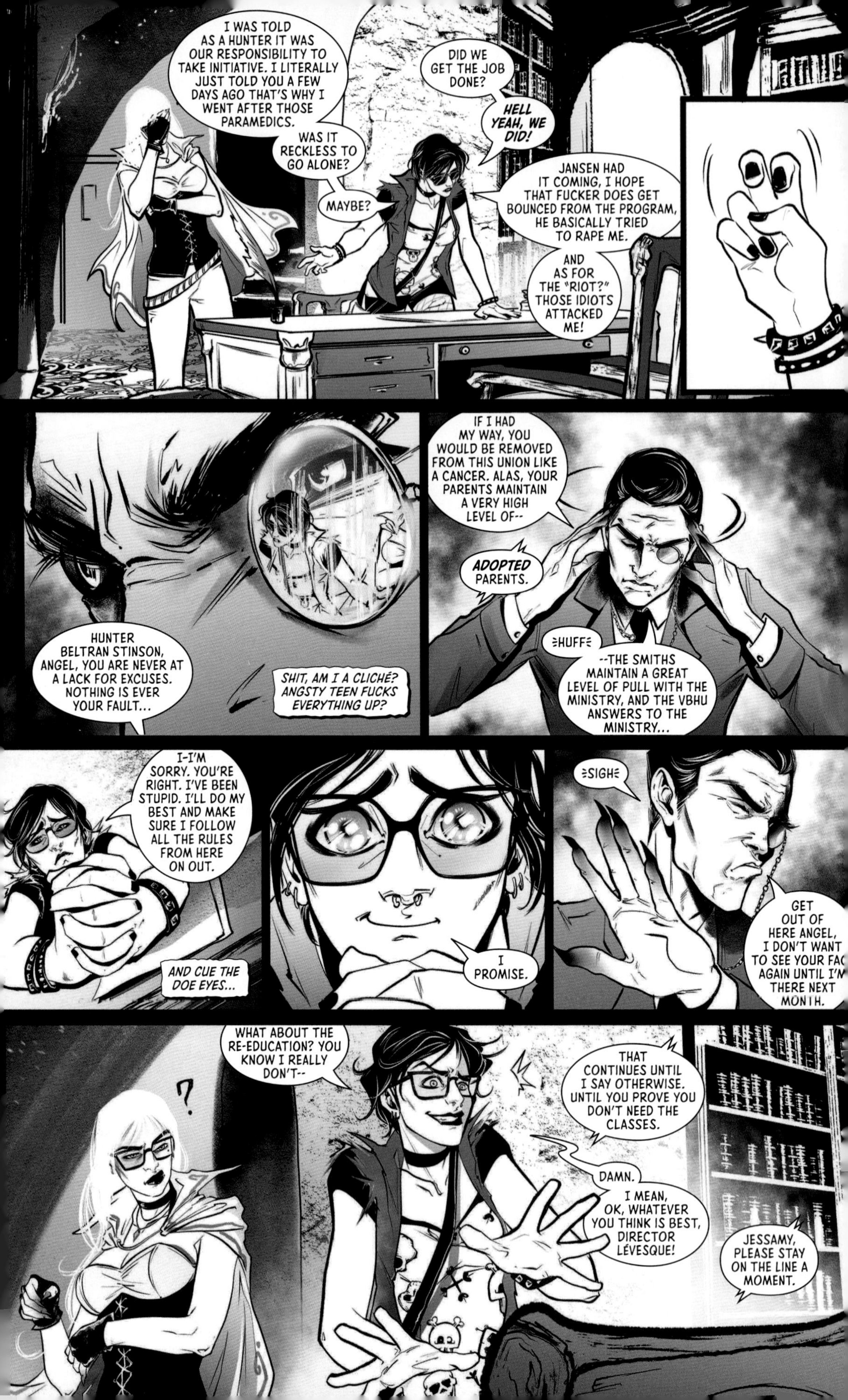
I WAS TOLD AS A HUNTER IT WAS OUR RESPONSIBILITY TO TAKE INITIATIVE. I LITERALLY JUST TOLD YOU A FEW DAYS AGO THAT'S WHY I WENT AFTER THOSE PARAMEDICS.
WAS IT RECKLESS TO GO ALONE?
MAYBE?
DID WE GET THE JOB DONE?
HELL YEAH, WE DID!
JANSEN HAD IT COMING, I HOPE THAT FUCKER DOES GET BOUNCED FROM THE PROGRAM, HE BASICALLY TRIED TO RAPE ME.
AND AS FOR THE "RIOT?" THOSE IDIOTS ATTACKED ME!
HUNTER BELTRAN STINSON, ANGEL, YOU ARE NEVER AT A LACK FOR EXCUSES. NOTHING IS EVER YOUR FAULT...
SHIT, AM I A CLICHÉ? ANGSTY TEEN FUCKS EVERYTHING UP?
IF I HAD MY WAY, YOU WOULD BE REMOVED FROM THIS UNION LIKE A CANCER. ALAS, YOUR PARENTS MAINTAIN A VERY HIGH LEVEL OF--
ADOPTED PARENTS.
HUFF
--THE SMITHS MAINTAIN A GREAT LEVEL OF PULL WITH THE MINISTRY, AND THE VBHU ANSWERS TO THE MINISTRY...
I-I'M SORRY. YOU'RE RIGHT. I'VE BEEN STUPID. I'LL DO MY BEST AND MAKE SURE I FOLLOW ALL THE RULES FROM HERE ON OUT.
AND CUE THE DOE EYES...
I PROMISE.
SIGH
GET OUT OF HERE ANGEL, I DON'T WANT TO SEE YOUR FAC AGAIN UNTIL I'M THERE NEXT MONTH.
WHAT ABOUT THE RE-EDUCATION? YOU KNOW I REALLY DON'T--
?
THAT CONTINUES UNTIL I SAY OTHERWISE. UNTIL YOU PROVE YOU DON'T NEED THE CLASSES.
DAMN.
I MEAN, OK, WHATEVER YOU THINK IS BEST, DIRECTOR LÉVESQUE!
JESSAMY, PLEASE STAY ON THE LINE A MOMENT.

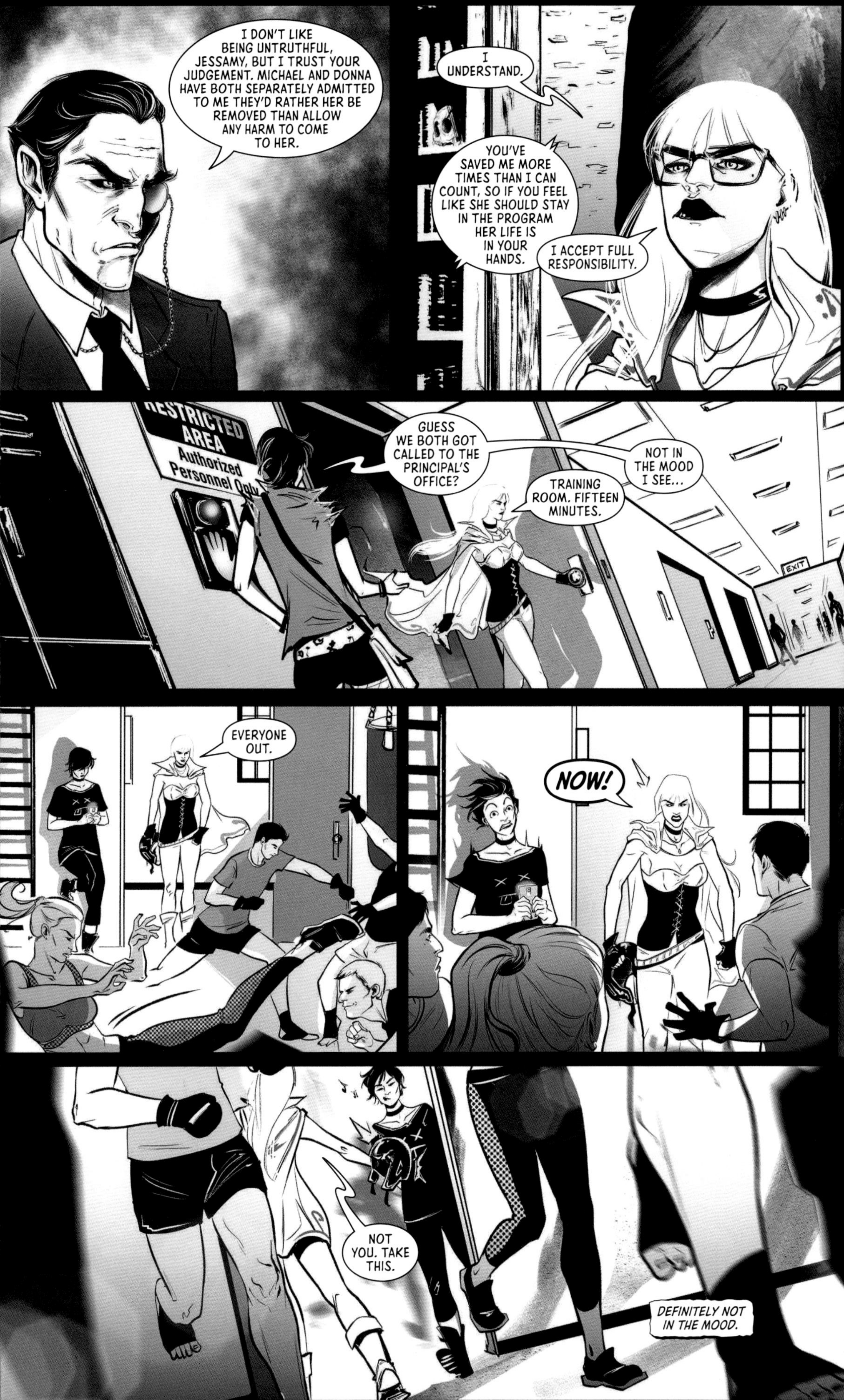

I DON'T LIKE BEING UNTRUTHFUL, JESSAMY, BUT I TRUST YOUR JUDGEMENT. MICHAEL AND DONNA HAVE BOTH SEPARATELY ADMITTED TO ME THEY'D RATHER HER BE REMOVED THAN ALLOW ANY HARM TO COME TO HER.
I UNDERSTAND.
YOU'VE SAVED ME MORE TIMES THAN I CAN COUNT, SO IF YOU FEEL LIKE SHE SHOULD STAY IN THE PROGRAM HER LIFE IS IN YOUR HANDS.
I ACCEPT FULL RESPONSIBILITY.
RESTRICTED AREA
Authorized Personnel Only
GUESS WE BOTH GOT CALLED TO THE PRINCIPAL'S OFFICE?
NOT IN THE MOOD I SEE...
TRAINING ROOM. FIFTEEN MINUTES.
EXIT
EVERYONE OUT.
NOW!
NOT YOU. TAKE THIS.
DEFINITELY NOT IN THE MOOD.

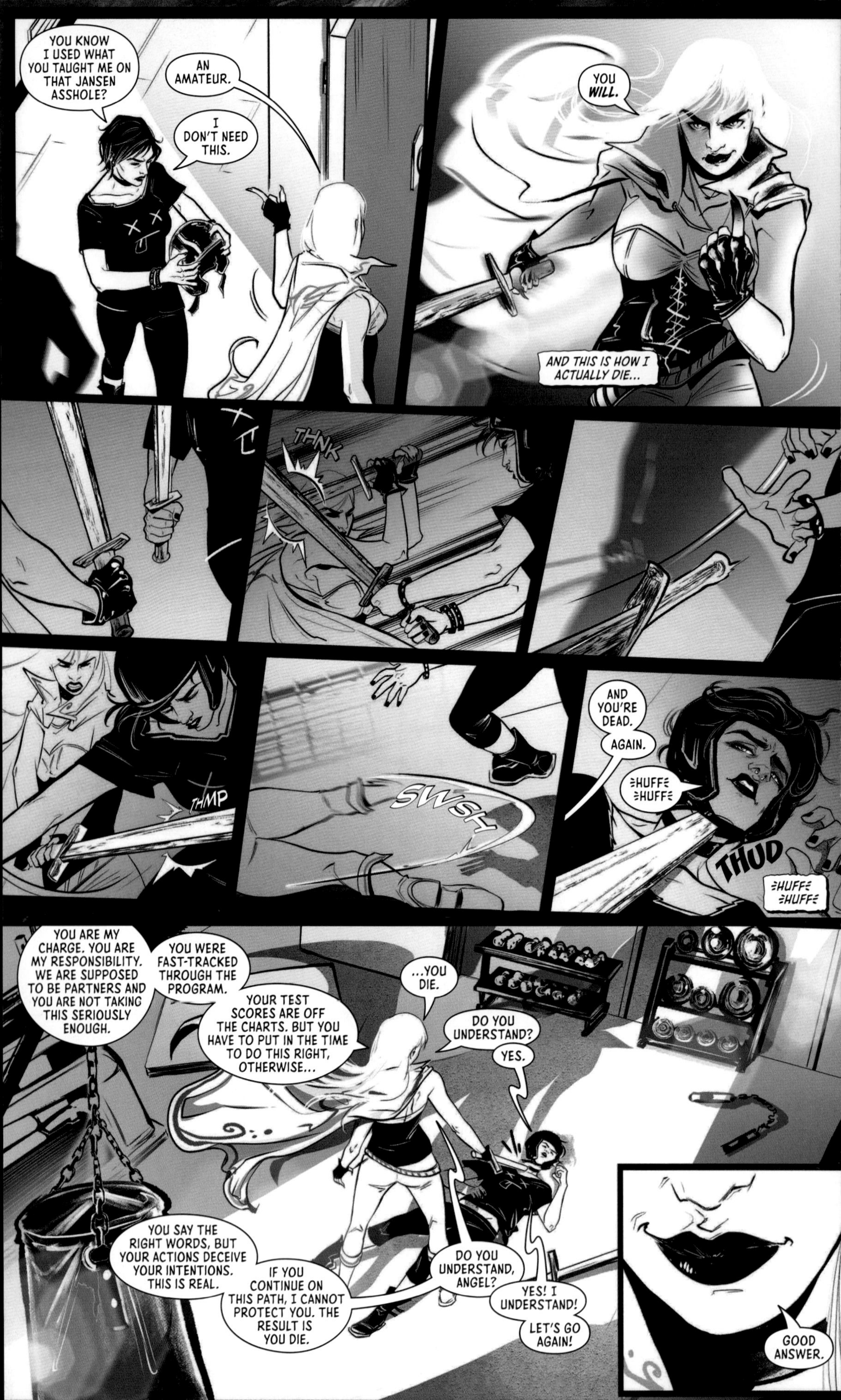

YOU KNOW I USED WHAT YOU TAUGHT ME ON THAT JANSEN ASSHOLE?
AN AMATEUR.
I DON'T NEED THIS.
YOU WILL.
AND THIS IS HOW I ACTUALLY DIE...
THNK
THMP
SWSH
AND YOU'RE DEAD.
AGAIN.
HUFF HUFF
THUD
HUFF HUFF
YOU ARE MY CHARGE. YOU ARE MY RESPONSIBILITY. WE ARE SUPPOSED TO BE PARTNERS AND YOU ARE NOT TAKING THIS SERIOUSLY ENOUGH.
YOU WERE FAST-TRACKED THROUGH THE PROGRAM.
YOUR TEST SCORES ARE OFF THE CHARTS. BUT YOU HAVE TO PUT IN THE TIME TO DO THIS RIGHT, OTHERWISE...
...YOU DIE.
DO YOU UNDERSTAND?
YES.
YOU SAY THE RIGHT WORDS, BUT YOUR ACTIONS DECEIVE YOUR INTENTIONS. THIS IS REAL.
IF YOU CONTINUE ON THIS PATH, I CANNOT PROTECT YOU. THE RESULT IS YOU DIE.
DO YOU UNDERSTAND, ANGEL?
YES! I UNDERSTAND!
LET'S GO AGAIN!
GOOD ANSWER.

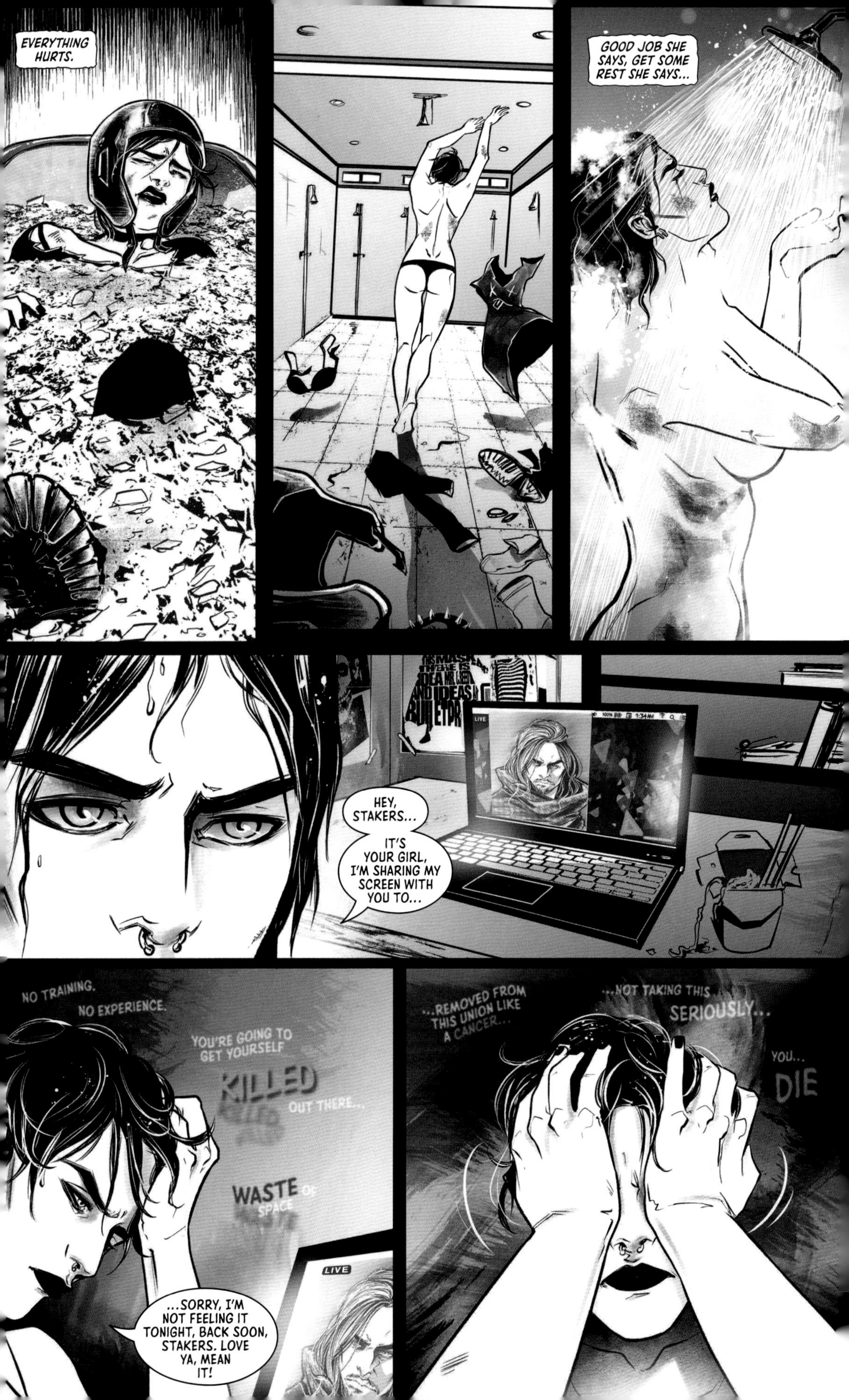
EVERYTHING HURTS.
GOOD JOB SHE SAYS, GET SOME REST SHE SAYS...
LIVE
HEY, STAKERS...
IT'S YOUR GIRL, I'M SHARING MY SCREEN WITH YOU TO...
NO TRAINING.
NO EXPERIENCE.
YOU'RE GOING TO GET YOURSELF
KILLED
OUT THERE...
WASTE OF
SPACE
LIVE
...SORRY, I'M NOT FEELING IT TONIGHT, BACK SOON, STAKERS. LOVE YA, MEAN IT!
...REMOVED FROM THIS UNION LIKE A CANCER...
...NOT TAKING THIS SERIOUSLY...
YOU...
DIE

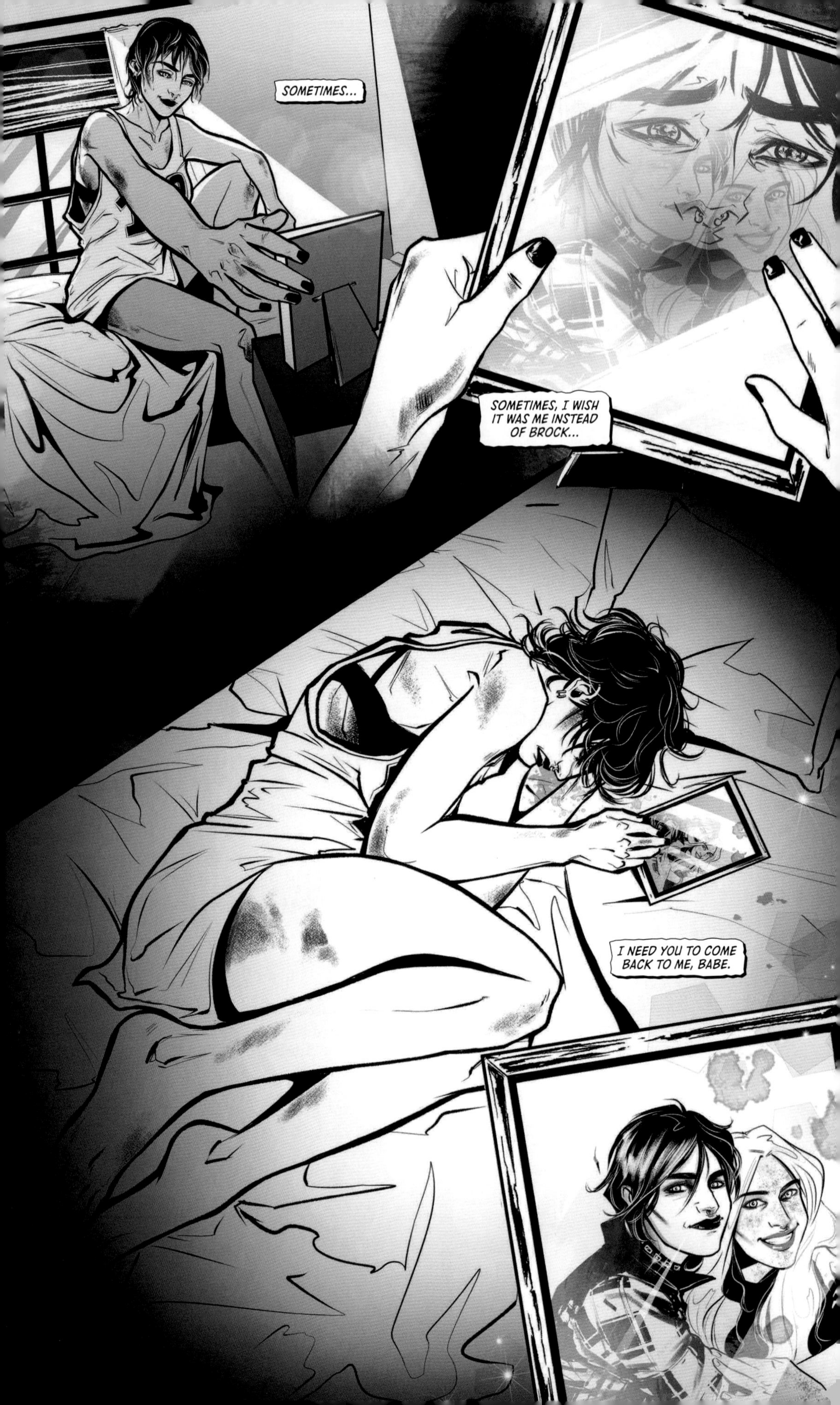
SOMETIMES...
SOMETIMES, I WISH IT WAS ME INSTEAD OF BROCK...
I NEED YOU TO COME BACK TO ME, BABE.

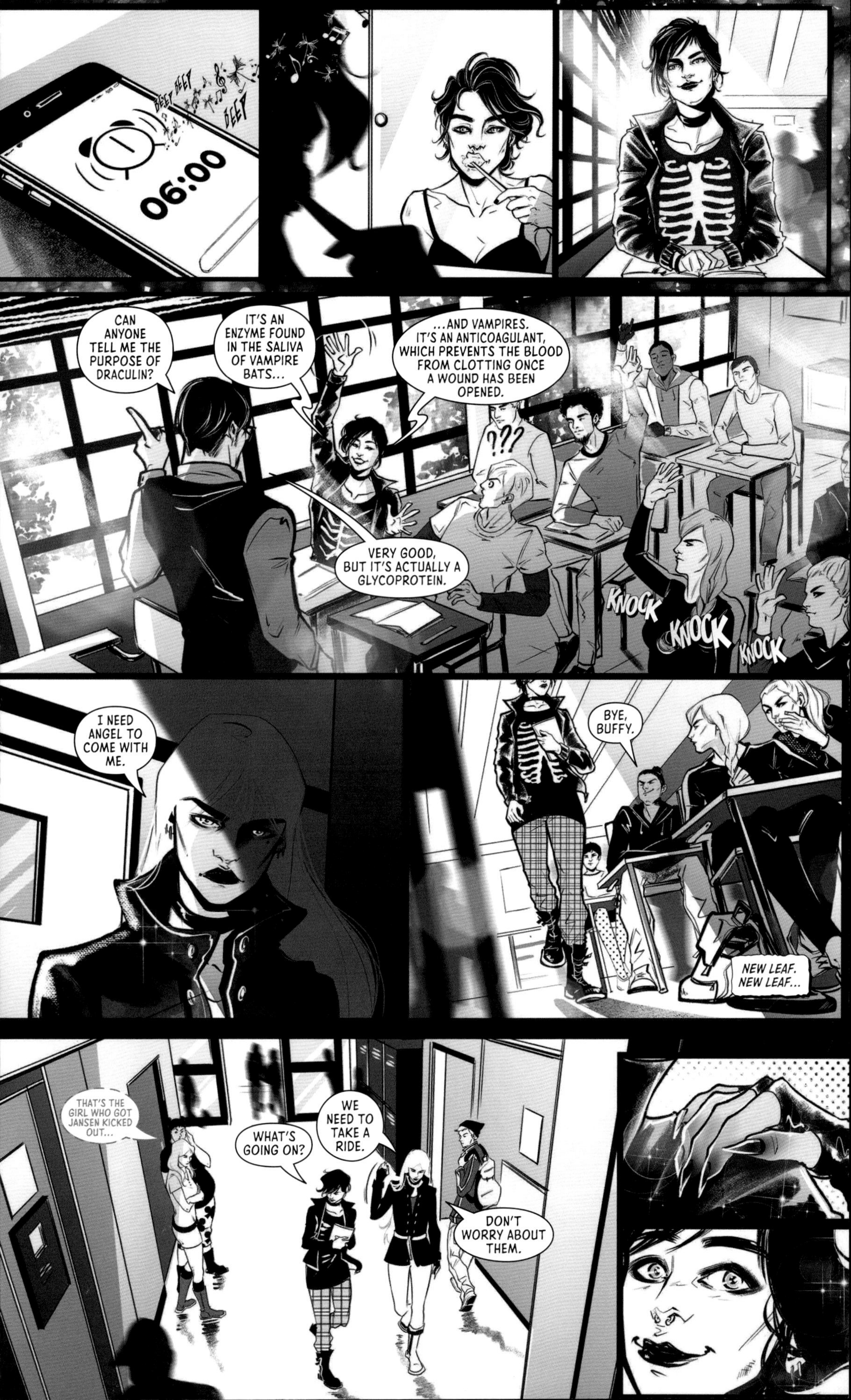
BEEP BEEP
BEEP
06:00
CAN ANYONE TELL ME THE PURPOSE OF DRACULIN?
IT'S AN ENZYME FOUND IN THE SALIVA OF VAMPIRE BATS...
...AND VAMPIRES. IT'S AN ANTICOAGULANT, WHICH PREVENTS THE BLOOD FROM CLOTTING ONCE A WOUND HAS BEEN OPENED.
???
VERY GOOD, BUT IT'S ACTUALLY A GLYCOPROTEIN.
KNOCK
KNOCK
KNOCK
I NEED ANGEL TO COME WITH ME.
BYE, BUFFY.
NEW LEAF. NEW LEAF...
THAT'S THE GIRL WHO GOT JANSEN KICKED OUT...
WHAT'S GOING ON?
WE NEED TO TAKE A RIDE.
DON'T WORRY ABOUT THEM.

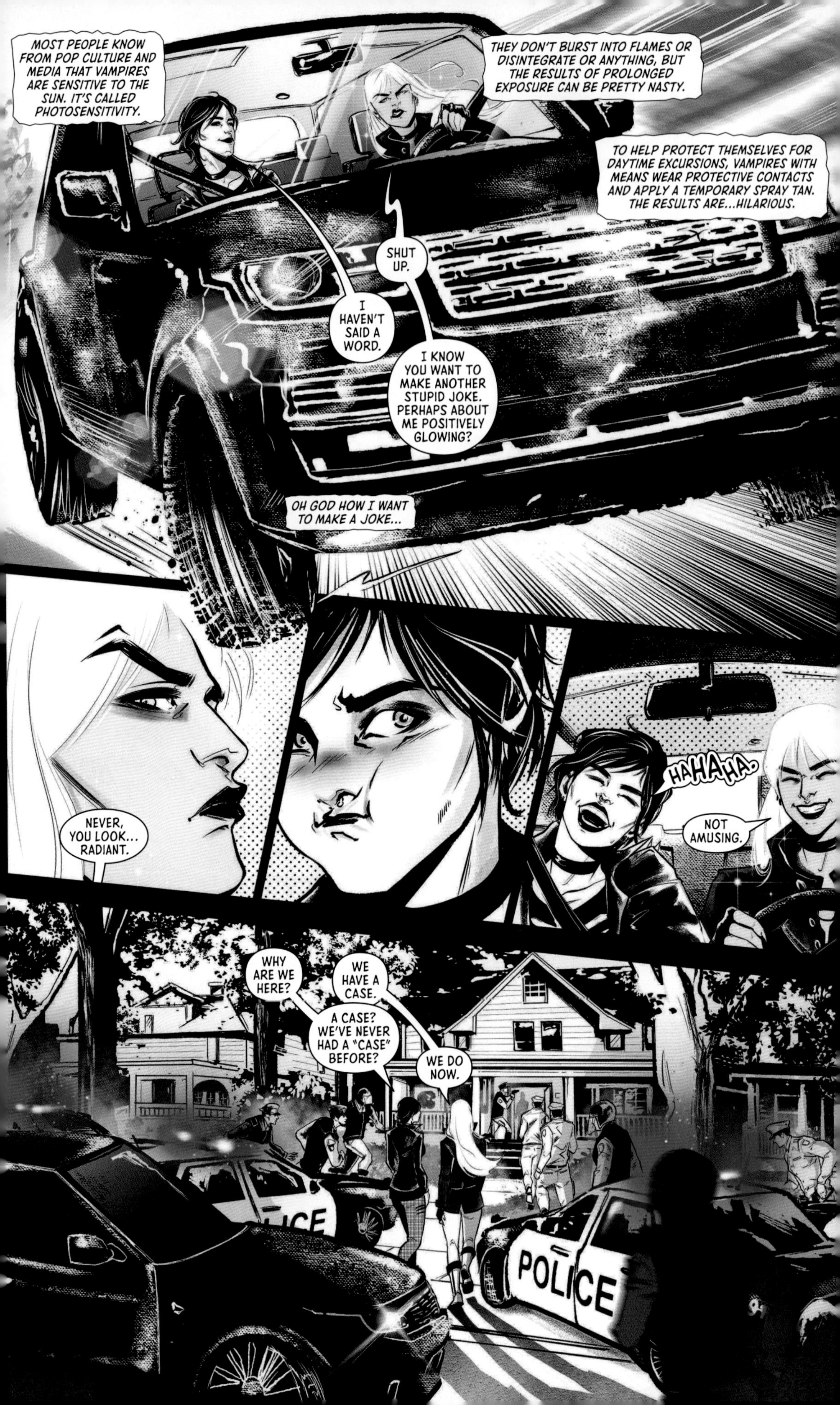

MOST PEOPLE KNOW FROM POP CULTURE AND MEDIA THAT VAMPIRES ARE SENSITIVE TO THE SUN. IT'S CALLED PHOTOSENSITIVITY.
THEY DON'T BURST INTO FLAMES OR DISINTEGRATE OR ANYTHING, BUT THE RESULTS OF PROLONGED EXPOSURE CAN BE PRETTY NASTY.
TO HELP PROTECT THEMSELVES FOR DAYTIME EXCURSIONS, VAMPIRES WITH MEANS WEAR PROTECTIVE CONTACTS AND APPLY A TEMPORARY SPRAY TAN. THE RESULTS ARE...HILARIOUS.
SHUT UP.
I HAVEN'T SAID A WORD.
I KNOW YOU WANT TO MAKE ANOTHER STUPID JOKE. PERHAPS ABOUT ME POSITIVELY GLOWING?
OH GOD HOW I WANT TO MAKE A JOKE...
NEVER, YOU LOOK... RADIANT.
HAHAHA
NOT AMUSING.
WHY ARE WE HERE?
WE HAVE A CASE.
A CASE? WE'VE NEVER HAD A "CASE" BEFORE?
WE DO NOW.
POLICE

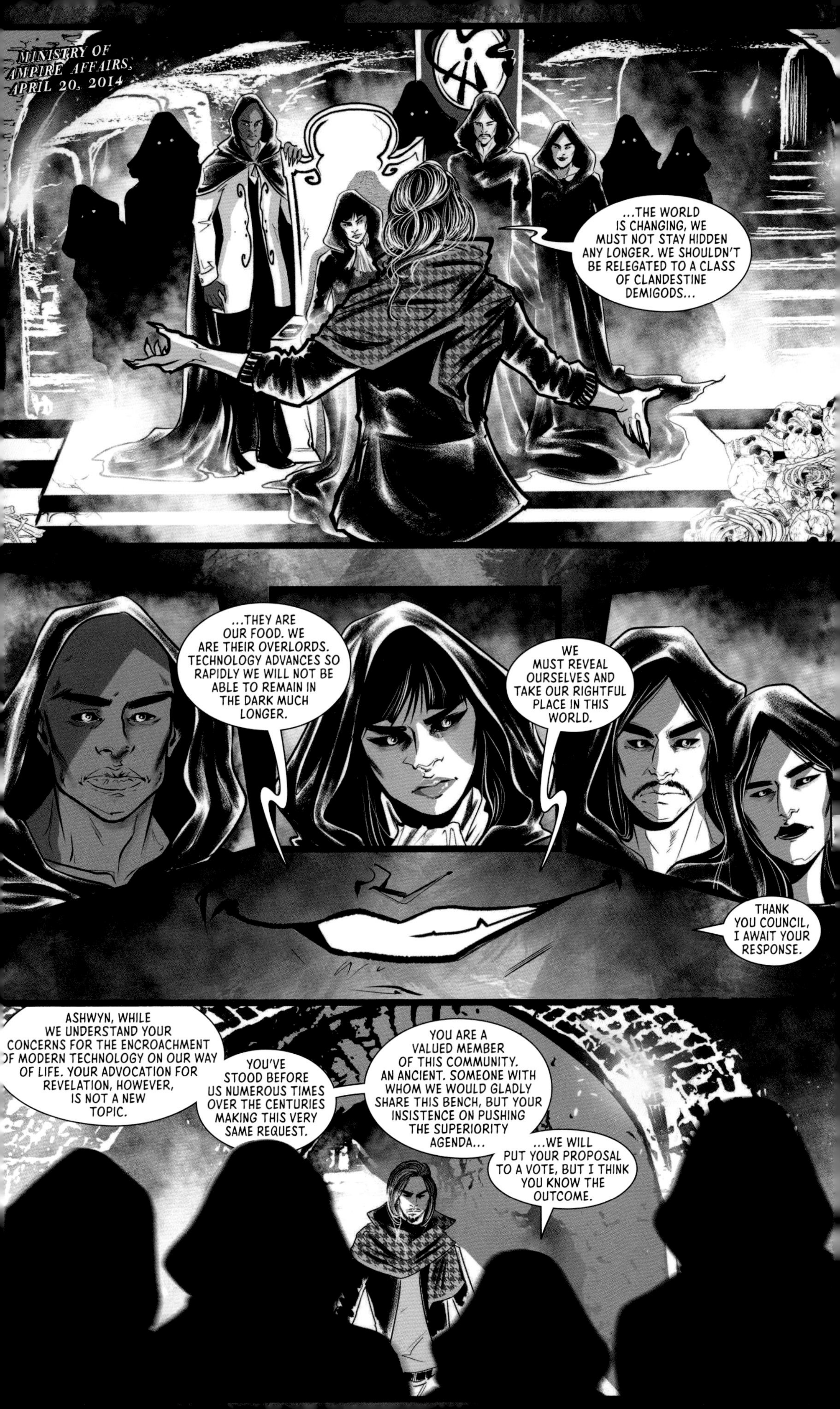
MINISTRY OF
AMPIRE AFFAIRS,
APRIL 20, 2014
...THE WORLD IS CHANGING, WE MUST NOT STAY HIDDEN ANY LONGER. WE SHOULDN'T BE RELEGATED TO A CLASS OF CLANDESTINE DEMIGODS...
...THEY ARE OUR FOOD. WE ARE THEIR OVERLORDS. TECHNOLOGY ADVANCES SO RAPIDLY WE WILL NOT BE ABLE TO REMAIN IN THE DARK MUCH LONGER.
WE MUST REVEAL OURSELVES AND TAKE OUR RIGHTFUL PLACE IN THIS WORLD.
THANK YOU COUNCIL, I AWAIT YOUR RESPONSE.
ASHWYN, WHILE WE UNDERSTAND YOUR CONCERNS FOR THE ENCROACHMENT OF MODERN TECHNOLOGY ON OUR WAY OF LIFE. YOUR ADVOCATION FOR REVELATION, HOWEVER, IS NOT A NEW TOPIC.
YOU'VE STOOD BEFORE US NUMEROUS TIMES OVER THE CENTURIES MAKING THIS VERY SAME REQUEST.
YOU ARE A VALUED MEMBER OF THIS COMMUNITY. AN ANCIENT. SOMEONE WITH WHOM WE WOULD GLADLY SHARE THIS BENCH, BUT YOUR INSISTENCE ON PUSHING THE SUPERIORITY AGENDA...
...WE WILL PUT YOUR PROPOSAL TO A VOTE, BUT I THINK YOU KNOW THE OUTCOME.

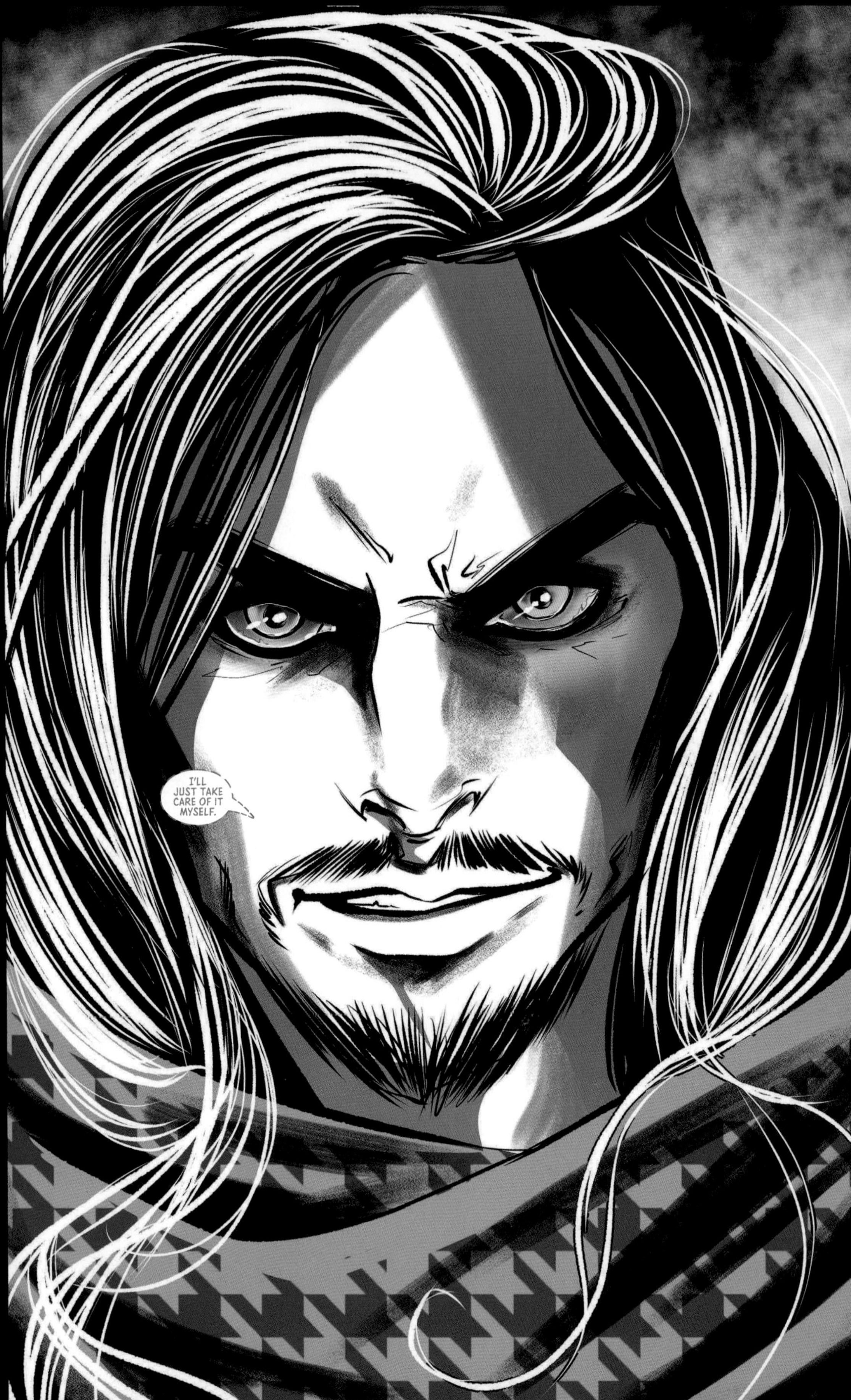
I'LL JUST TAKE CARE OF IT MYSELF.

End Chapter Two

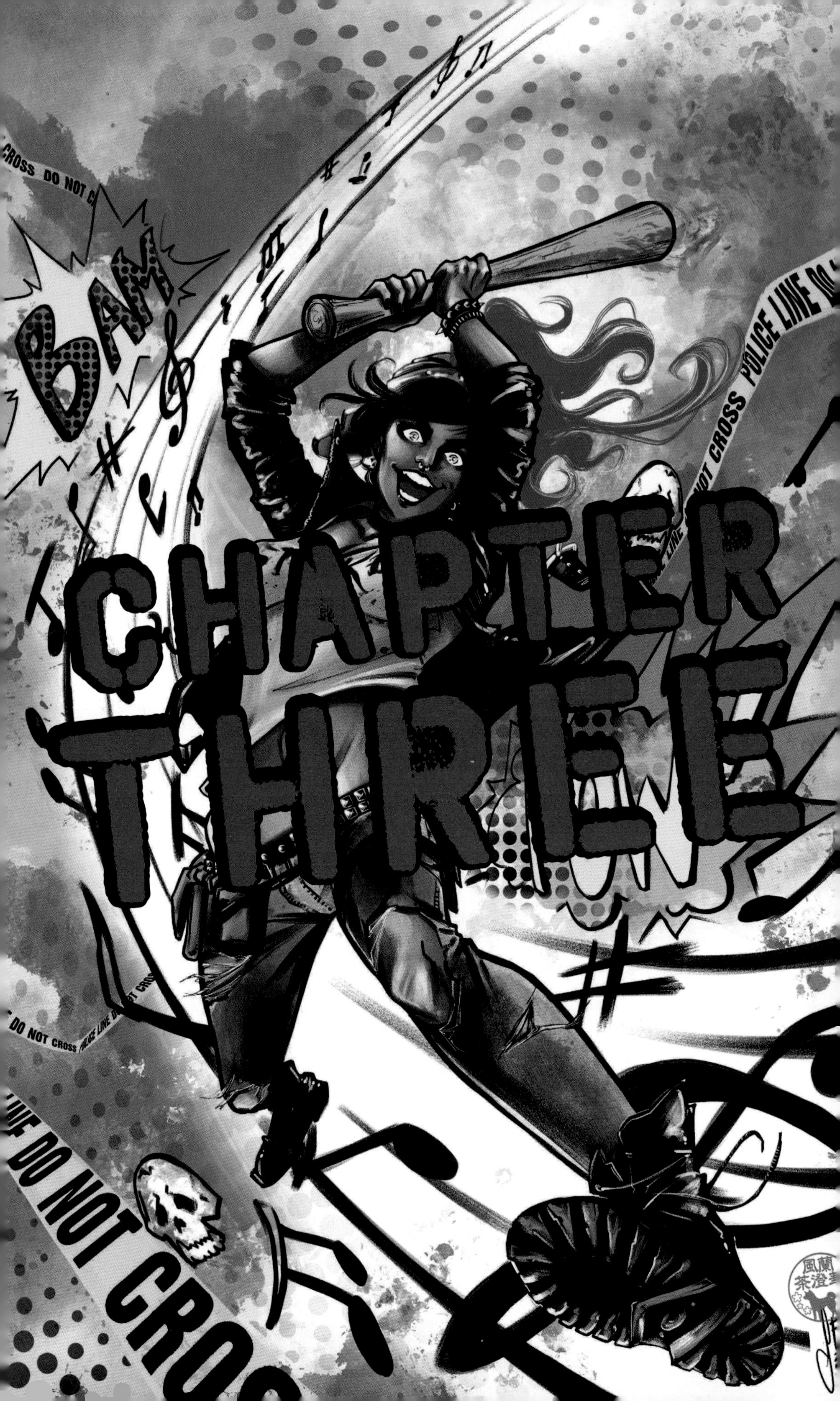
CHAPTER
THREE
BAM
POLICE LINE DO NOT CROSS
DO NOT CROSS

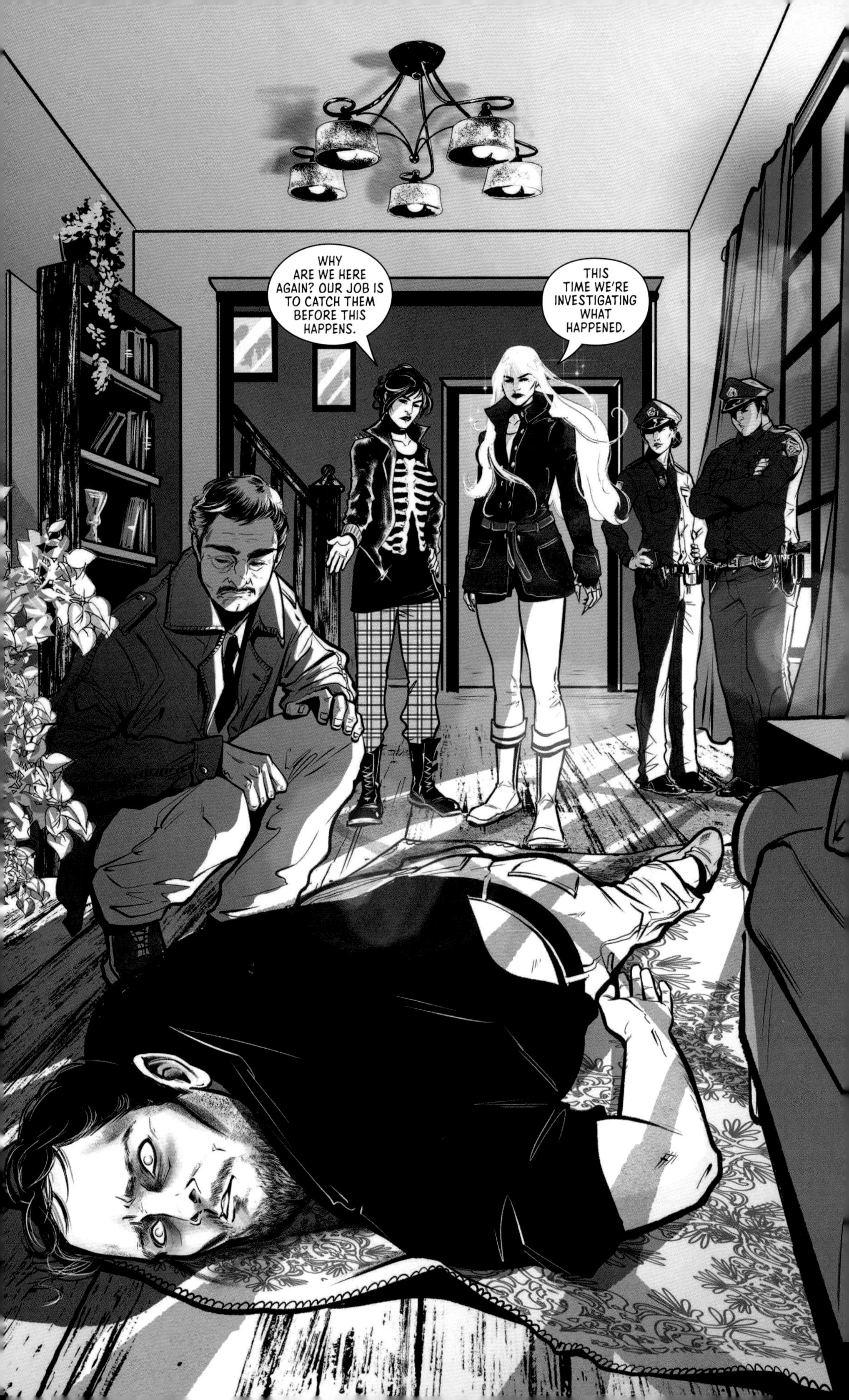
WHY ARE WE HERE AGAIN? OUR JOB IS TO CATCH THEM BEFORE THIS HAPPENS.
THIS TIME WE'RE INVESTIGATING WHAT HAPPENED.

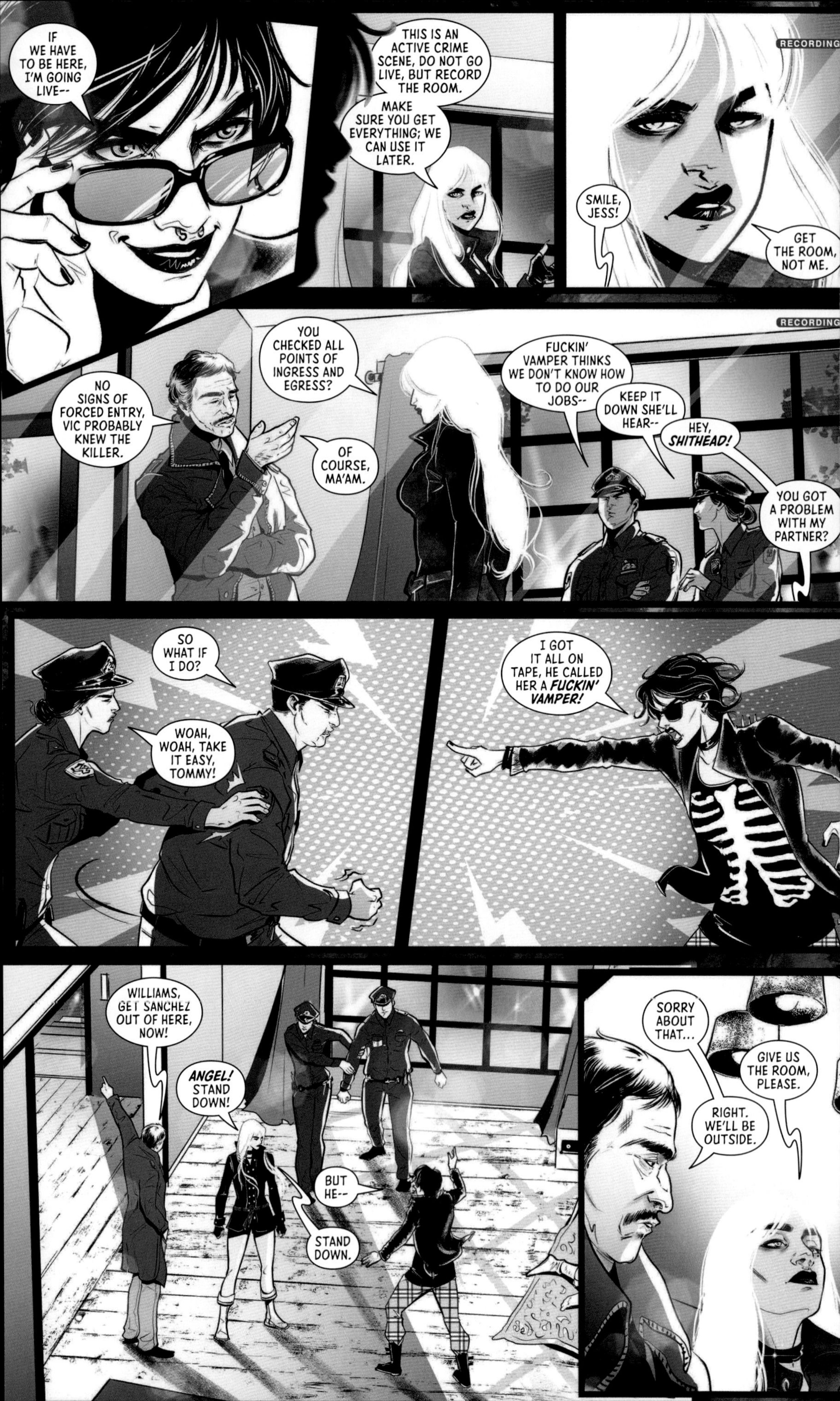
IF WE HAVE TO BE HERE, I'M GOING LIVE--
THIS IS AN ACTIVE CRIME SCENE, DO NOT GO LIVE, BUT RECORD THE ROOM.
MAKE SURE YOU GET EVERYTHING; WE CAN USE IT LATER.
RECORDING
SMILE, JESS!
GET THE ROOM, NOT ME.
RECORDING
YOU CHECKED ALL POINTS OF INGRESS AND EGRESS?
NO SIGNS OF FORCED ENTRY, VIC PROBABLY KNEW THE KILLER.
OF COURSE, MA'AM.
FUCKIN' VAMPER THINKS WE DON'T KNOW HOW TO DO OUR JOBS--
KEEP IT DOWN SHE'LL HEAR--
HEY, ***SHITHEAD!***
YOU GOT A PROBLEM WITH MY PARTNER?
SO WHAT IF I DO?
WOAH, WOAH, TAKE IT EASY, TOMMY!
I GOT IT ALL ON TAPE, HE CALLED HER A ***FUCKIN' VAMPER!***
WILLIAMS, GET SANCHEZ OUT OF HERE, NOW!
ANGEL! STAND DOWN!
BUT HE--
STAND DOWN.
SORRY ABOUT THAT...
GIVE US THE ROOM, PLEASE.
RIGHT. WE'LL BE OUTSIDE.

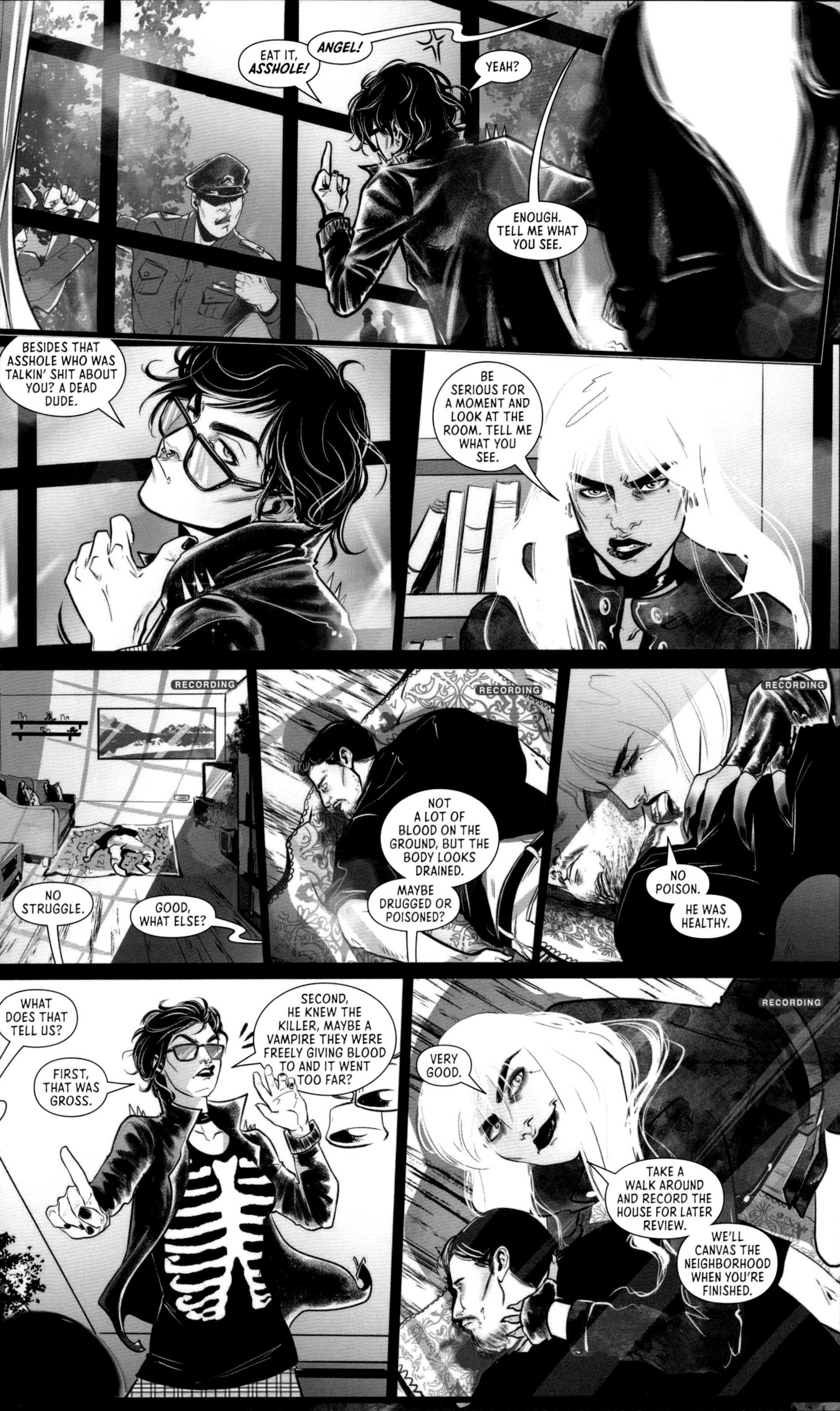
EAT IT, ASSHOLE!
ANGEL!
YEAH?
ENOUGH. TELL ME WHAT YOU SEE.
BESIDES THAT ASSHOLE WHO WAS TALKIN' SHIT ABOUT YOU? A DEAD DUDE.
BE SERIOUS FOR A MOMENT AND LOOK AT THE ROOM. TELL ME WHAT YOU SEE.
RECORDING
NO STRUGGLE.
GOOD, WHAT ELSE?
RECORDING
NOT A LOT OF BLOOD ON THE GROUND, BUT THE BODY LOOKS DRAINED.
MAYBE DRUGGED OR POISONED?
RECORDING
NO POISON.
HE WAS HEALTHY.
WHAT DOES THAT TELL US?
FIRST, THAT WAS GROSS.
SECOND, HE KNEW THE KILLER, MAYBE A VAMPIRE THEY WERE FREELY GIVING BLOOD TO AND IT WENT TOO FAR?
RECORDING
VERY GOOD.
TAKE A WALK AROUND AND RECORD THE HOUSE FOR LATER REVIEW.
WE'LL CANVAS THE NEIGHBORHOOD WHEN YOU'RE FINISHED.

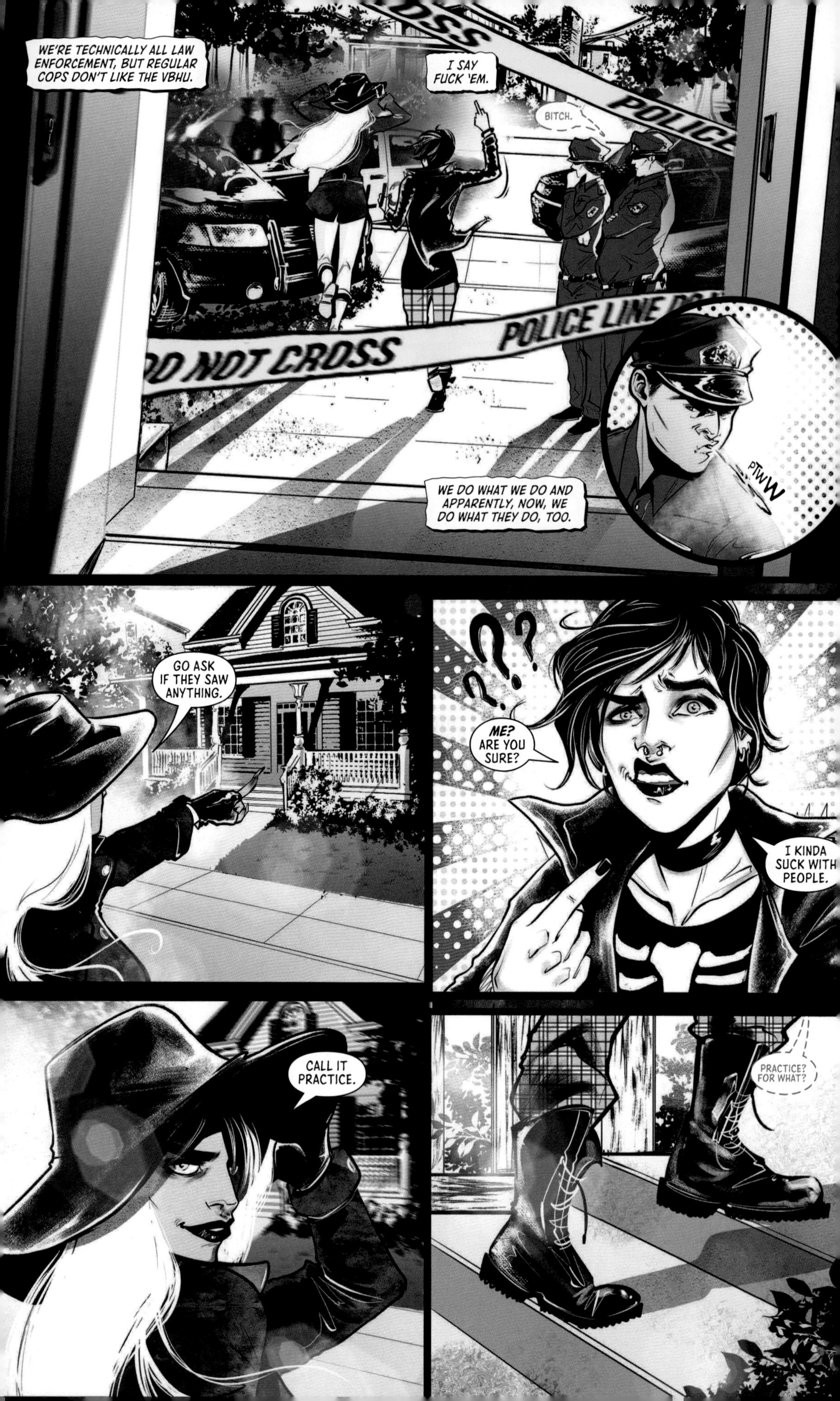
WE'RE TECHNICALLY ALL LAW ENFORCEMENT, BUT REGULAR COPS DON'T LIKE THE VBHU.
I SAY FUCK 'EM.
BITCH.
POLICE
POLICE LINE DO
DO NOT CROSS
WE DO WHAT WE DO AND APPARENTLY, NOW, WE DO WHAT THEY DO, TOO.
PTWW
GO ASK IF THEY SAW ANYTHING.
???
ME? ARE YOU SURE?
I KINDA SUCK WITH PEOPLE.
CALL IT PRACTICE.
PRACTICE? FOR WHAT?

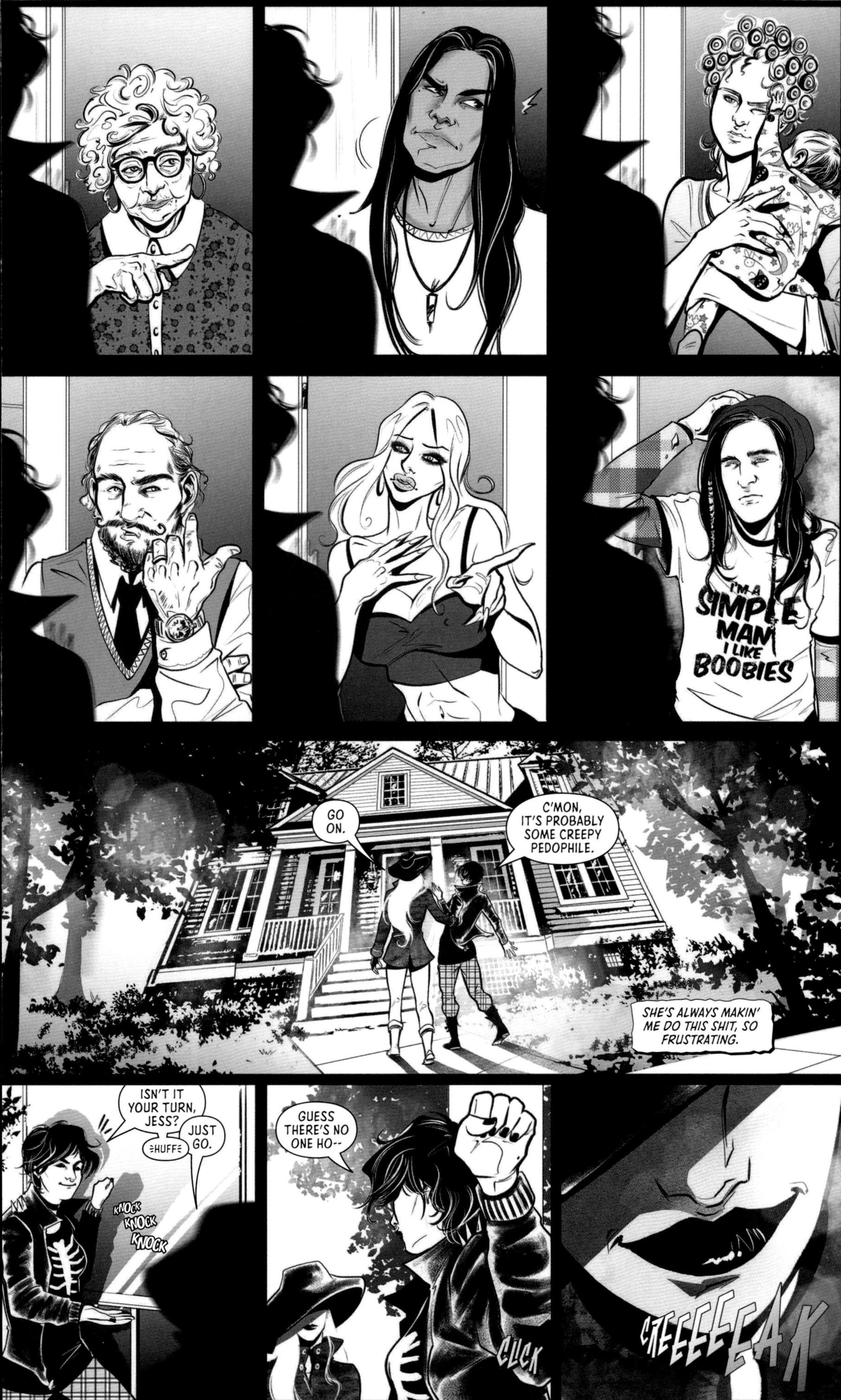
I'M A SIMPLE MAN I LIKE BOOBIES
GO ON.
C'MON, IT'S PROBABLY SOME CREEPY PEDOPHILE.
SHE'S ALWAYS MAKIN' ME DO THIS SHIT, SO FRUSTRATING.
ISN'T IT YOUR TURN, JESS?
HUFF
JUST GO.
KNOCK KNOCK KNOCK
GUESS THERE'S NO ONE HO--
CLICK
CREEEEEAK

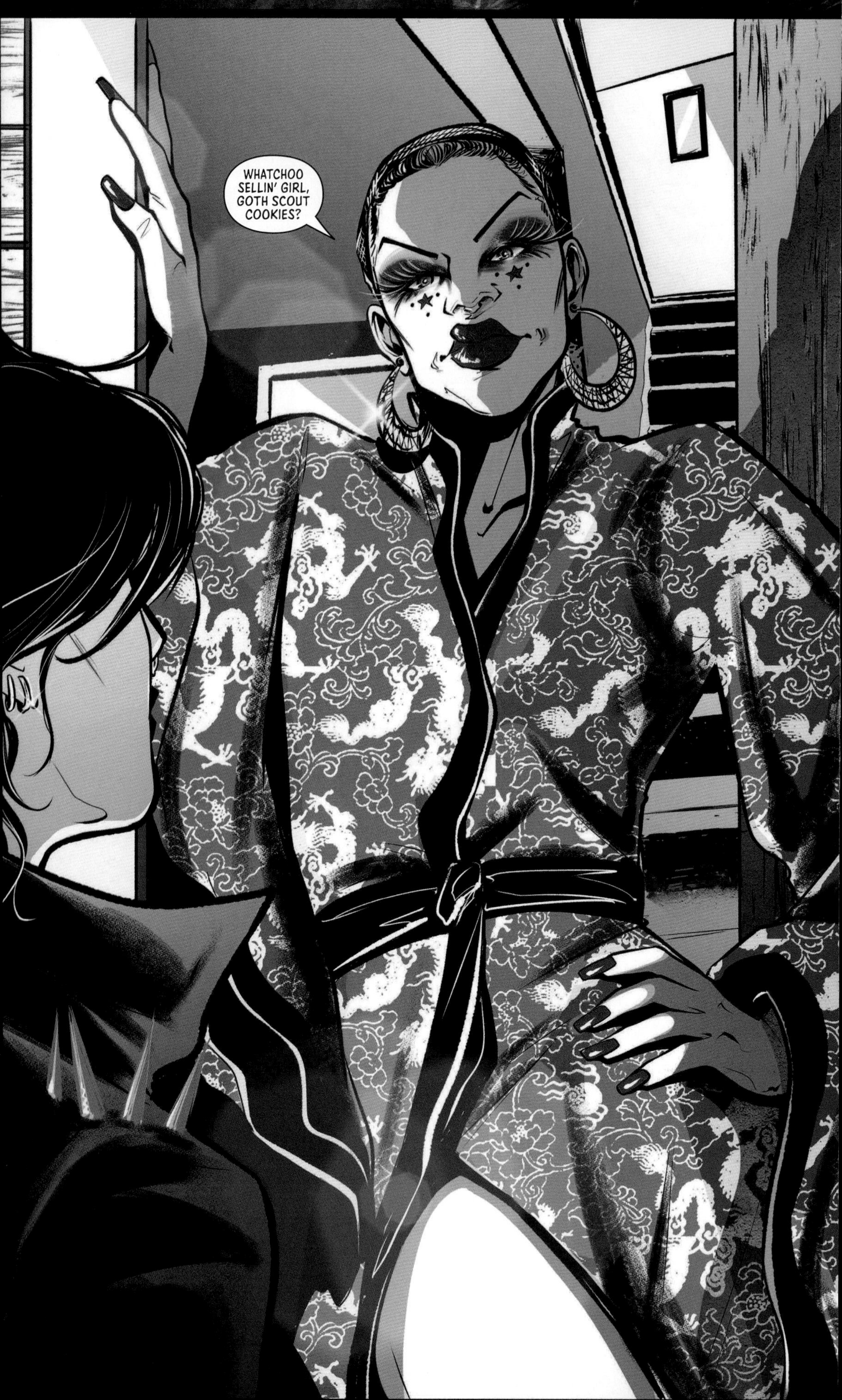
WHATCHOO SELLIN' GIRL, GOTH SCOUT COOKIES?

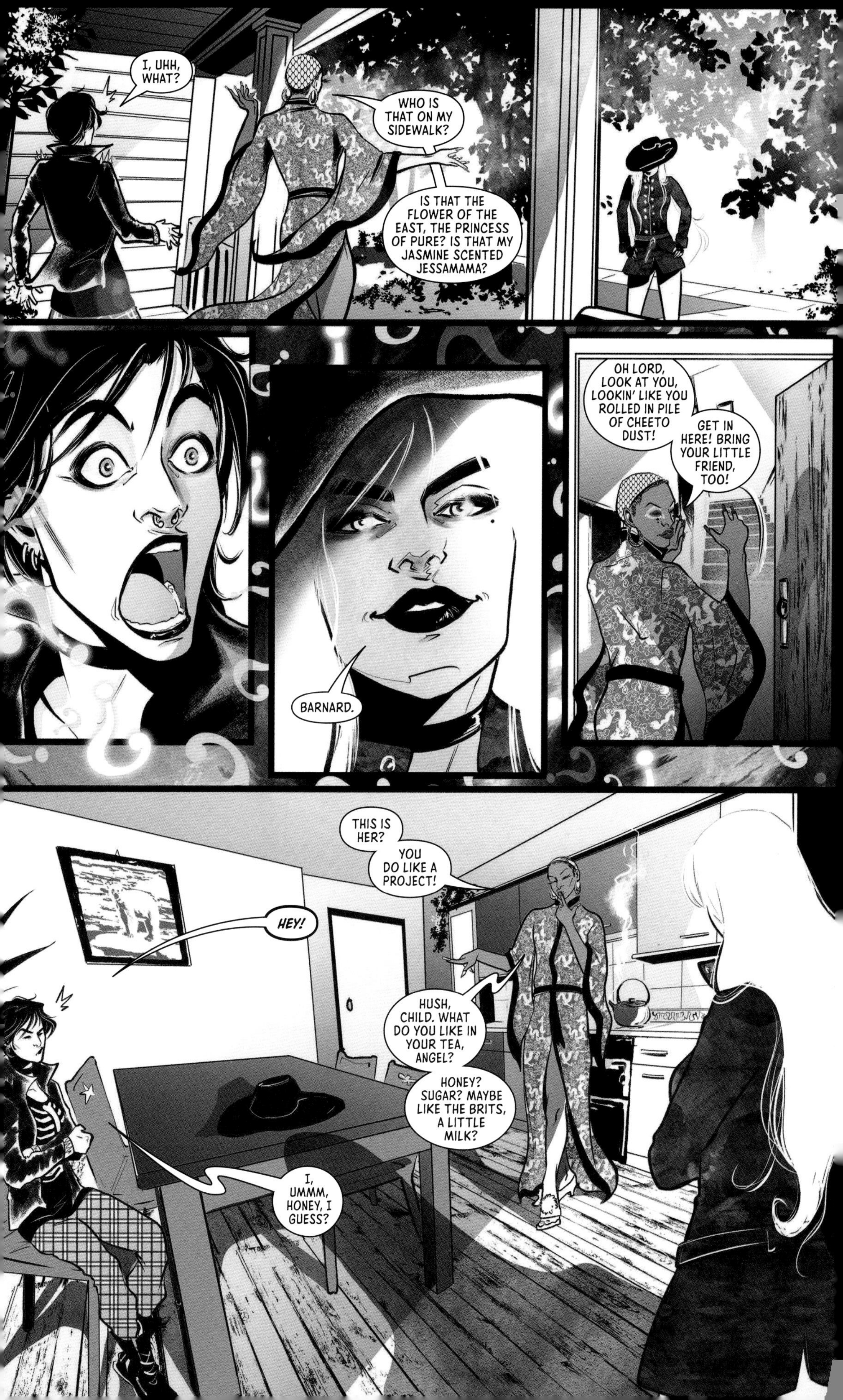

I, UHH, WHAT?
WHO IS THAT ON MY SIDEWALK?
IS THAT THE FLOWER OF THE EAST, THE PRINCESS OF PURE? IS THAT MY JASMINE SCENTED JESSAMAMA?
BARNARD.
OH LORD, LOOK AT YOU, LOOKIN' LIKE YOU ROLLED IN PILE OF CHEETO DUST!
GET IN HERE! BRING YOUR LITTLE FRIEND, TOO!
THIS IS HER?
YOU DO LIKE A PROJECT!
HEY!
HUSH, CHILD. WHAT DO YOU LIKE IN YOUR TEA, ANGEL?
HONEY? SUGAR? MAYBE LIKE THE BRITS, A LITTLE MILK?
I, UMMM, HONEY, I GUESS?

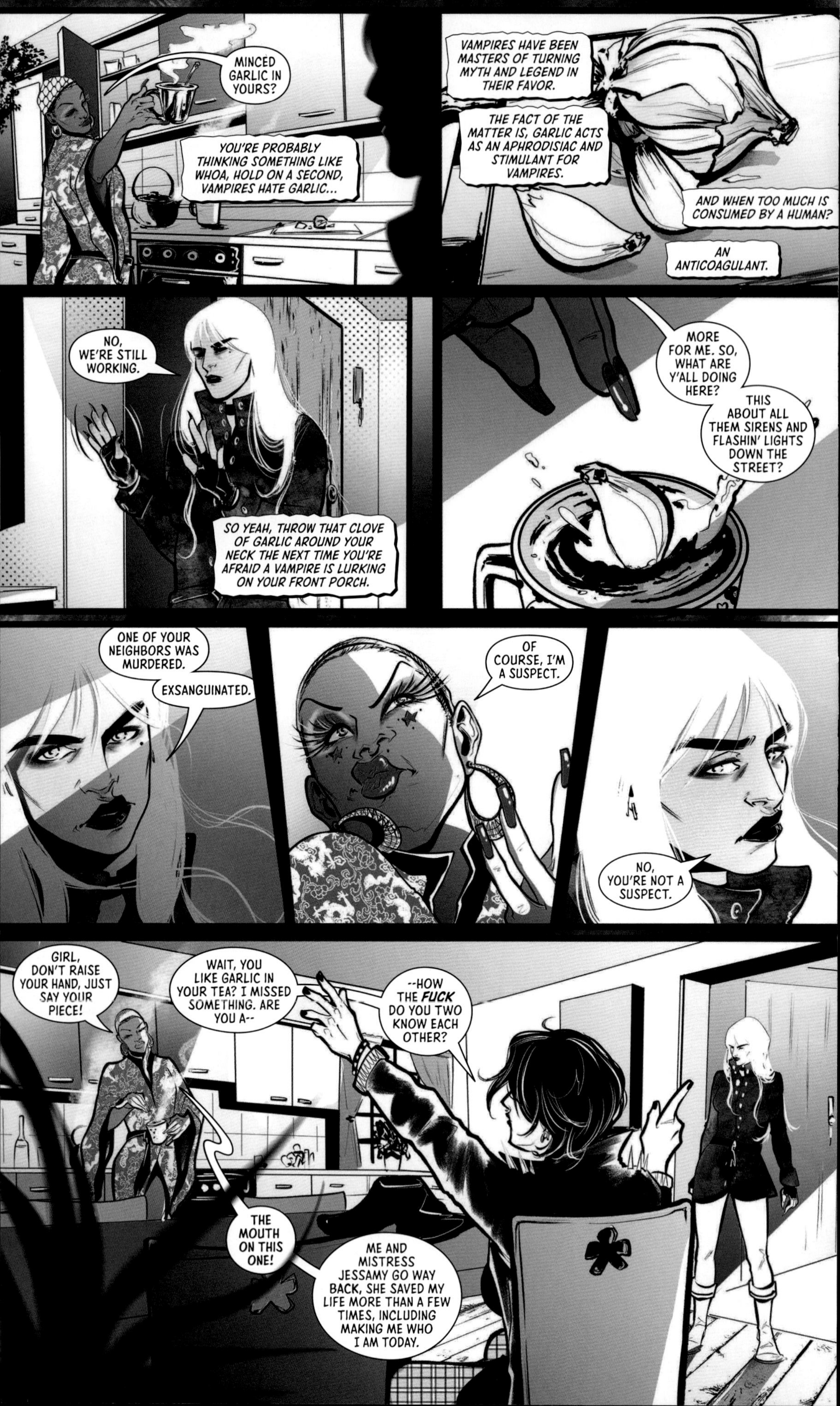

MINCED GARLIC IN YOURS?
YOU'RE PROBABLY THINKING SOMETHING LIKE WHOA, HOLD ON A SECOND, VAMPIRES HATE GARLIC...
VAMPIRES HAVE BEEN MASTERS OF TURNING MYTH AND LEGEND IN THEIR FAVOR.
THE FACT OF THE MATTER IS, GARLIC ACTS AS AN APHRODISIAC AND STIMULANT FOR VAMPIRES.
AND WHEN TOO MUCH IS CONSUMED BY A HUMAN?
AN ANTICOAGULANT.
NO, WE'RE STILL WORKING.
SO YEAH, THROW THAT CLOVE OF GARLIC AROUND YOUR NECK THE NEXT TIME YOU'RE AFRAID A VAMPIRE IS LURKING ON YOUR FRONT PORCH.
MORE FOR ME. SO, WHAT ARE Y'ALL DOING HERE?
THIS ABOUT ALL THEM SIRENS AND FLASHIN' LIGHTS DOWN THE STREET?
ONE OF YOUR NEIGHBORS WAS MURDERED.
EXSANGUINATED.
OF COURSE, I'M A SUSPECT.
NO, YOU'RE NOT A SUSPECT.
GIRL, DON'T RAISE YOUR HAND, JUST SAY YOUR PIECE!
WAIT, YOU LIKE GARLIC IN YOUR TEA? I MISSED SOMETHING. ARE YOU A--
--HOW THE FUCK DO YOU TWO KNOW EACH OTHER?
THE MOUTH ON THIS ONE!
ME AND MISTRESS JESSAMY GO WAY BACK, SHE SAVED MY LIFE MORE THAN A FEW TIMES, INCLUDING MAKING ME WHO I AM TODAY.

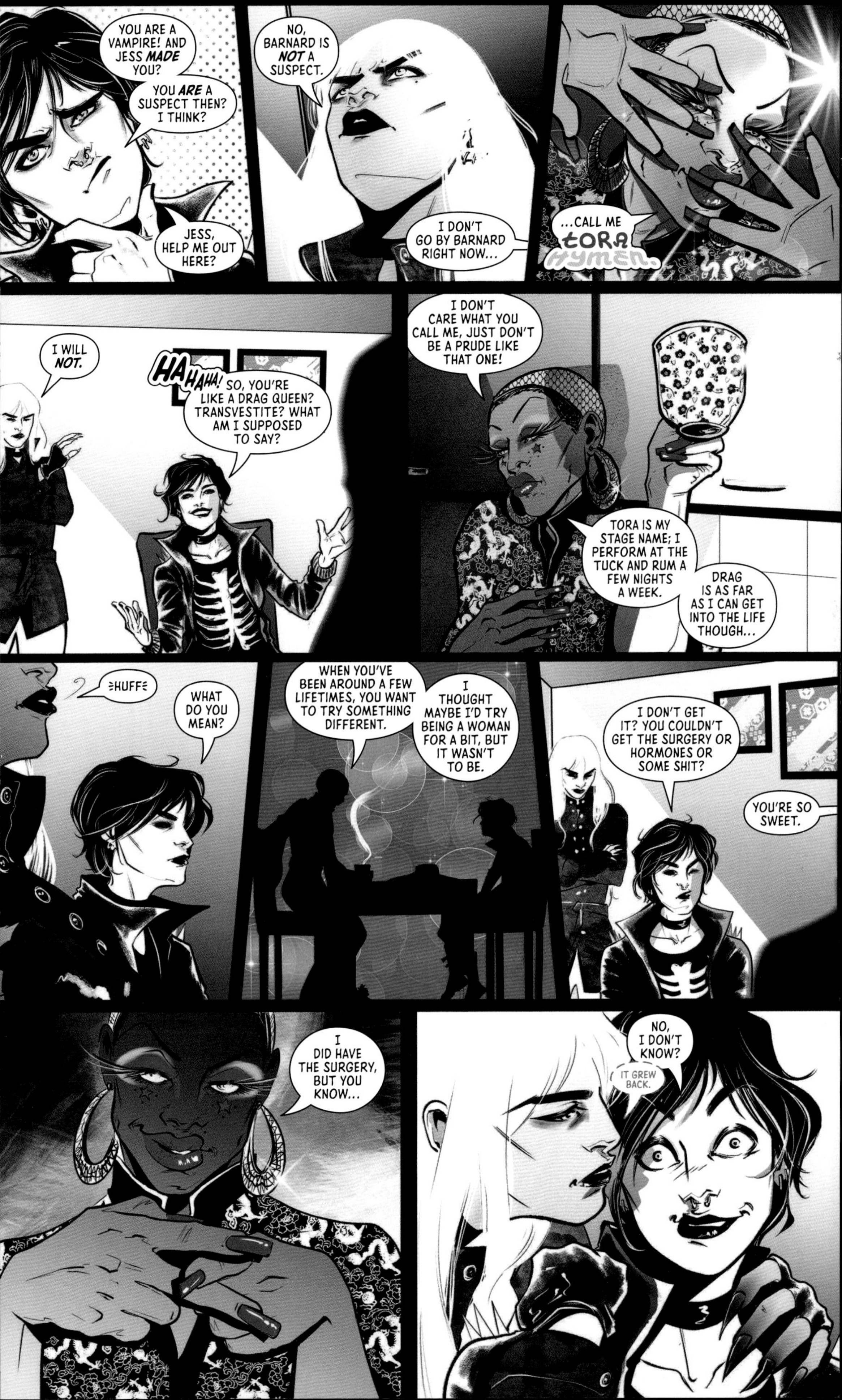
YOU ARE A VAMPIRE! AND JESS *MADE* YOU?
YOU *ARE* A SUSPECT THEN? I THINK?
JESS, HELP ME OUT HERE?
NO, BARNARD IS *NOT* A SUSPECT.
I DON'T GO BY BARNARD RIGHT NOW...
...CALL ME TORA HYMEN.
I WILL *NOT.*
HAHAHA! SO, YOU'RE LIKE A DRAG QUEEN? TRANSVESTITE? WHAT AM I SUPPOSED TO SAY?
I DON'T CARE WHAT YOU CALL ME, JUST DON'T BE A PRUDE LIKE THAT ONE!
TORA IS MY STAGE NAME; I PERFORM AT THE TUCK AND RUM A FEW NIGHTS A WEEK.
DRAG IS AS FAR AS I CAN GET INTO THE LIFE THOUGH...
HUFF
WHAT DO YOU MEAN?
WHEN YOU'VE BEEN AROUND A FEW LIFETIMES, YOU WANT TO TRY SOMETHING DIFFERENT.
I THOUGHT MAYBE I'D TRY BEING A WOMAN FOR A BIT, BUT IT WASN'T TO BE.
I DON'T GET IT? YOU COULDN'T GET THE SURGERY OR HORMONES OR SOME SHIT?
YOU'RE SO SWEET.
I DID HAVE THE SURGERY, BUT YOU KNOW...
NO, I DON'T KNOW?
IT GREW BACK.

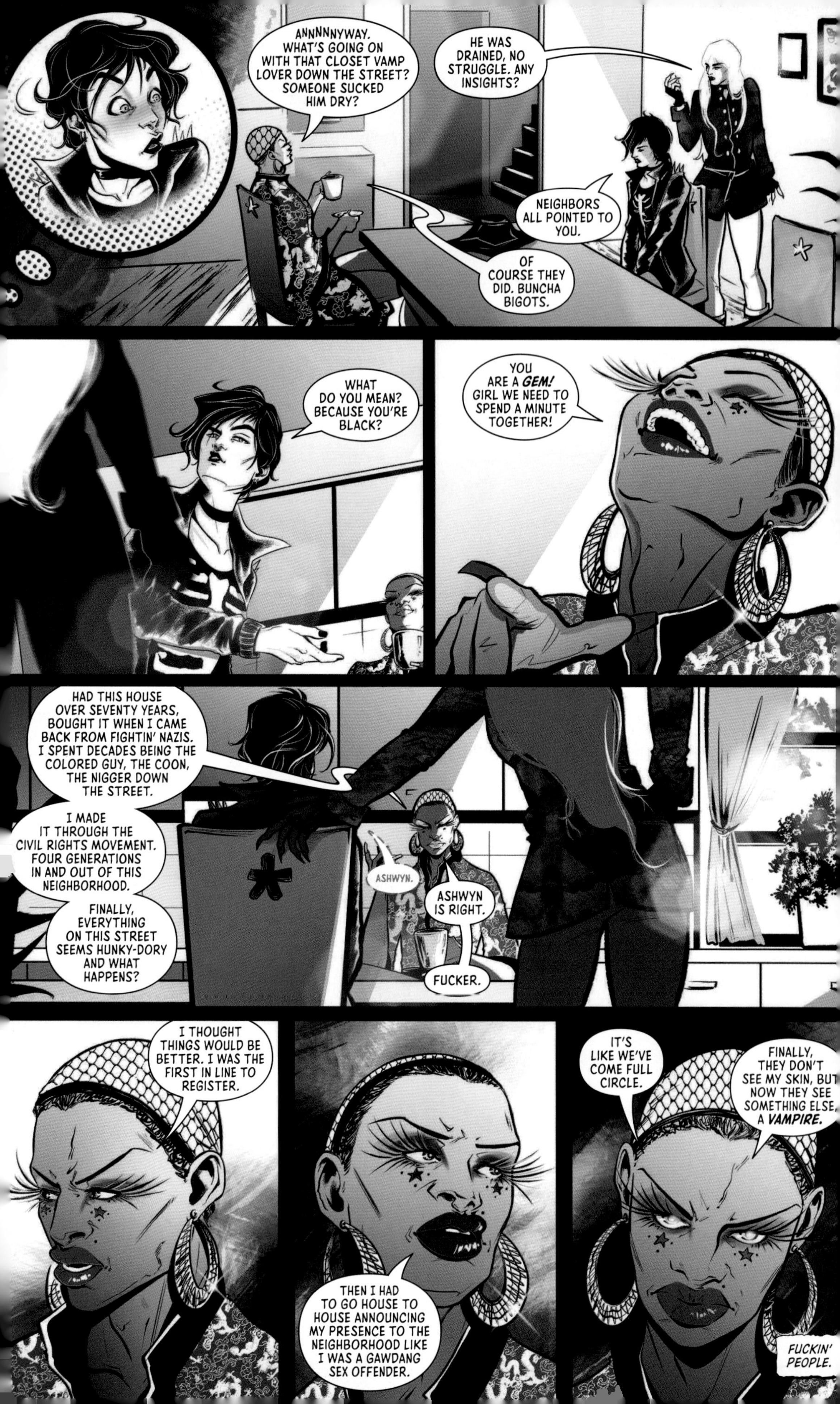

ANNNNNYWAY. WHAT'S GOING ON WITH THAT CLOSET VAMP LOVER DOWN THE STREET? SOMEONE SUCKED HIM DRY?
HE WAS DRAINED, NO STRUGGLE. ANY INSIGHTS?
NEIGHBORS ALL POINTED TO YOU.
OF COURSE THEY DID. BUNCHA BIGOTS.
WHAT DO YOU MEAN? BECAUSE YOU'RE BLACK?
YOU ARE A *GEM!* GIRL WE NEED TO SPEND A MINUTE TOGETHER!
HAD THIS HOUSE OVER SEVENTY YEARS, BOUGHT IT WHEN I CAME BACK FROM FIGHTIN' NAZIS. I SPENT DECADES BEING THE COLORED GUY, THE COON, THE NIGGER DOWN THE STREET.
I MADE IT THROUGH THE CIVIL RIGHTS MOVEMENT. FOUR GENERATIONS IN AND OUT OF THIS NEIGHBORHOOD.
FINALLY, EVERYTHING ON THIS STREET SEEMS HUNKY-DORY AND WHAT HAPPENS?
ASHWYN.
ASHWYN IS RIGHT.
FUCKER.
I THOUGHT THINGS WOULD BE BETTER. I WAS THE FIRST IN LINE TO REGISTER.
THEN I HAD TO GO HOUSE TO HOUSE ANNOUNCING MY PRESENCE TO THE NEIGHBORHOOD LIKE I WAS A GAWDANG SEX OFFENDER.
IT'S LIKE WE'VE COME FULL CIRCLE.
FINALLY, THEY DON'T SEE MY SKIN, BUT NOW THEY SEE SOMETHING ELSE, A *VAMPIRE.*
FUCKIN' PEOPLE.

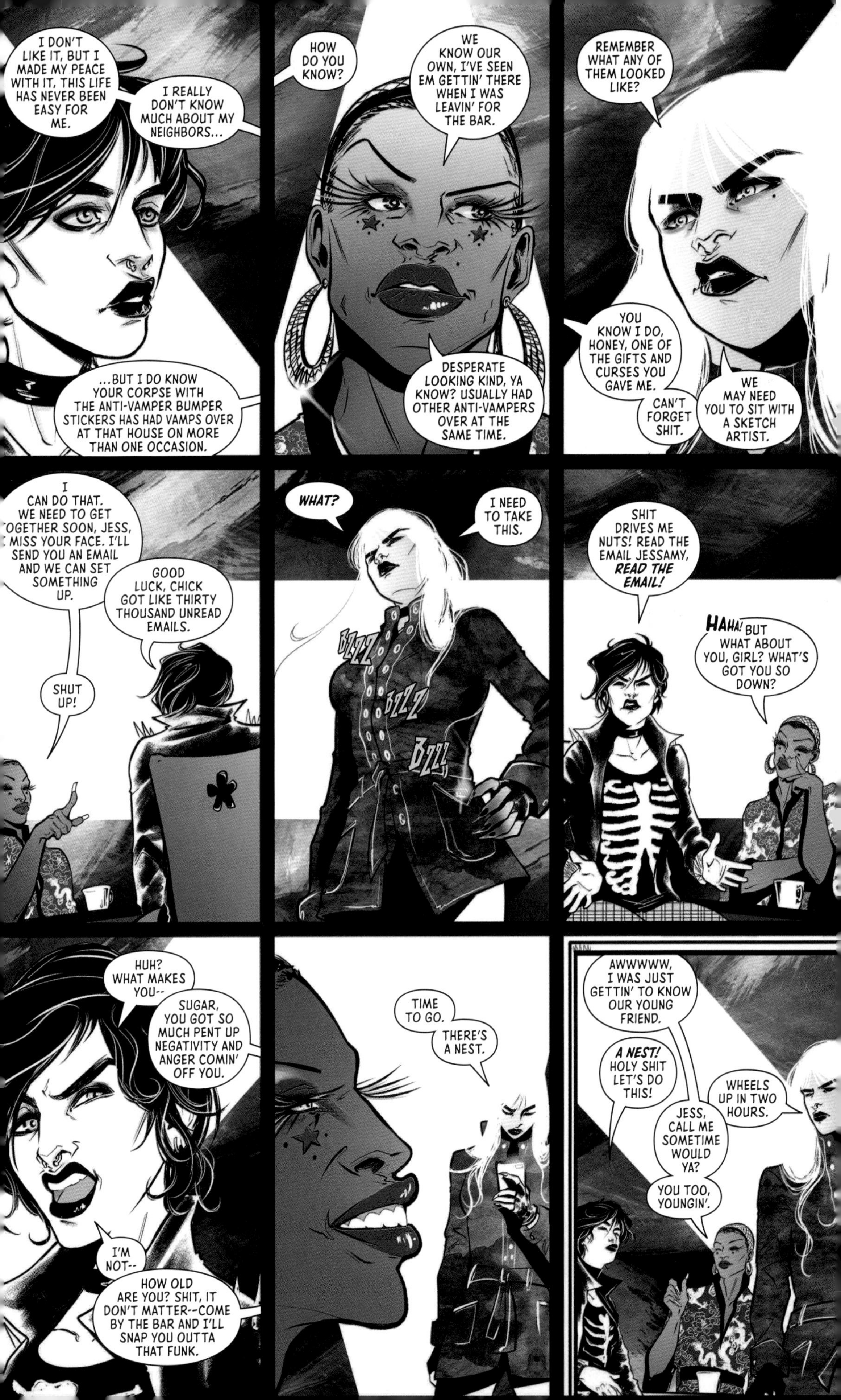
I DON'T LIKE IT, BUT I MADE MY PEACE WITH IT, THIS LIFE HAS NEVER BEEN EASY FOR ME.
I REALLY DON'T KNOW MUCH ABOUT MY NEIGHBORS...
...BUT I DO KNOW YOUR CORPSE WITH THE ANTI-VAMPER BUMPER STICKERS HAS HAD VAMPS OVER AT THAT HOUSE ON MORE THAN ONE OCCASION.
HOW DO YOU KNOW?
WE KNOW OUR OWN, I'VE SEEN EM GETTIN' THERE WHEN I WAS LEAVIN' FOR THE BAR.
DESPERATE LOOKING KIND, YA KNOW? USUALLY HAD OTHER ANTI-VAMPERS OVER AT THE SAME TIME.
REMEMBER WHAT ANY OF THEM LOOKED LIKE?
YOU KNOW I DO, HONEY, ONE OF THE GIFTS AND CURSES YOU GAVE ME.
CAN'T FORGET SHIT.
WE MAY NEED YOU TO SIT WITH A SKETCH ARTIST.
I CAN DO THAT. WE NEED TO GET TOGETHER SOON, JESS, I MISS YOUR FACE. I'LL SEND YOU AN EMAIL AND WE CAN SET SOMETHING UP.
GOOD LUCK, CHICK GOT LIKE THIRTY THOUSAND UNREAD EMAILS.
SHUT UP!
WHAT?
I NEED TO TAKE THIS.
BZZZ
BZZZ
BZZZ
SHIT DRIVES ME NUTS! READ THE EMAIL JESSAMY, READ THE EMAIL!
HAHA! BUT WHAT ABOUT YOU, GIRL? WHAT'S GOT YOU SO DOWN?
HUH? WHAT MAKES YOU--
SUGAR, YOU GOT SO MUCH PENT UP NEGATIVITY AND ANGER COMIN' OFF YOU.
I'M NOT--
HOW OLD ARE YOU? SHIT, IT DON'T MATTER--COME BY THE BAR AND I'LL SNAP YOU OUTTA THAT FUNK.
TIME TO GO.
THERE'S A NEST.
AWWWWW, I WAS JUST GETTIN' TO KNOW OUR YOUNG FRIEND.
A NEST! HOLY SHIT LET'S DO THIS!
WHEELS UP IN TWO HOURS.
JESS, CALL ME SOMETIME WOULD YA?
YOU TOO, YOUNGIN'.

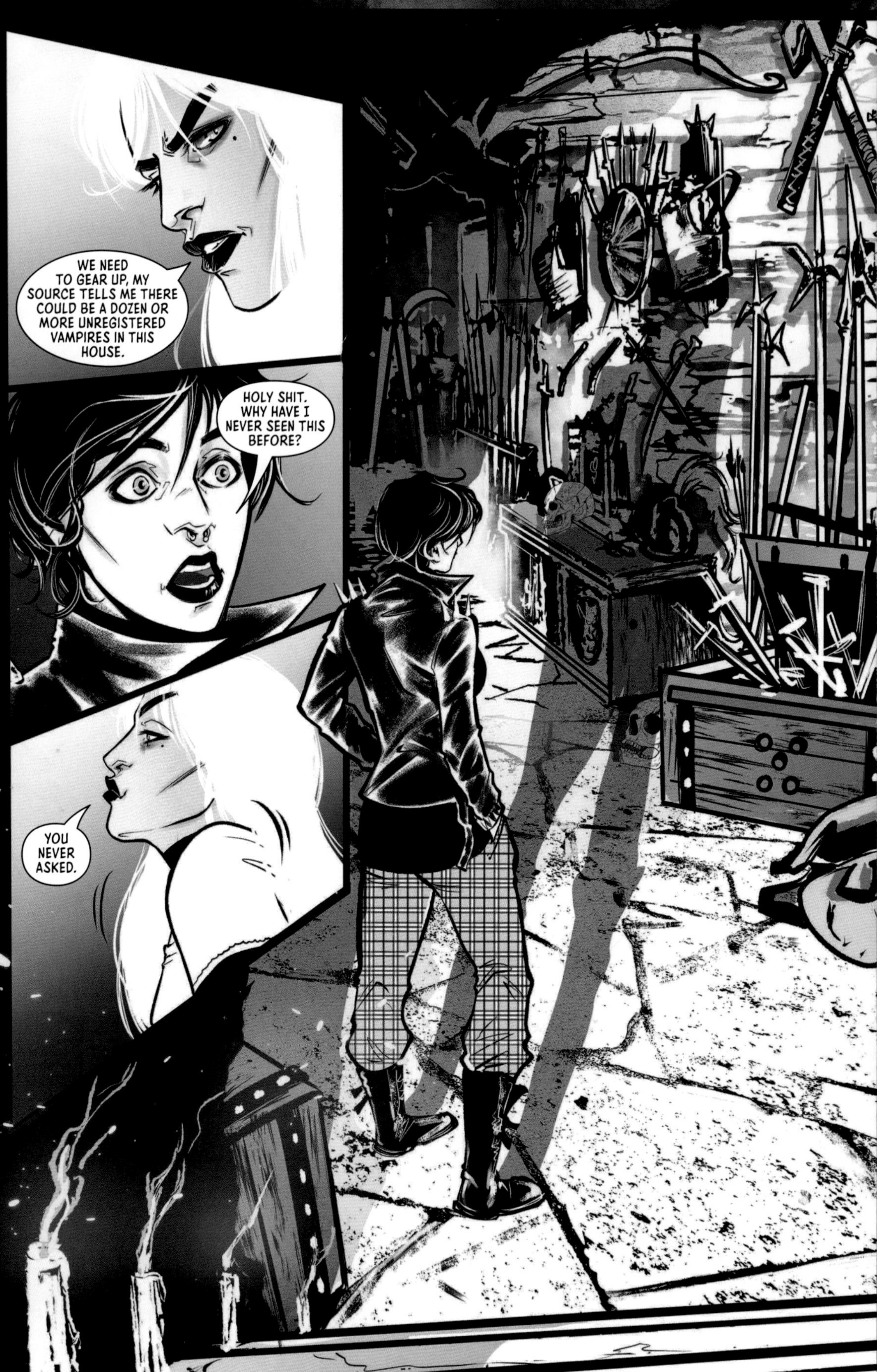
WE NEED TO GEAR UP, MY SOURCE TELLS ME THERE COULD BE A DOZEN OR MORE UNREGISTERED VAMPIRES IN THIS HOUSE.
HOLY SHIT. WHY HAVE I NEVER SEEN THIS BEFORE?
YOU NEVER ASKED.

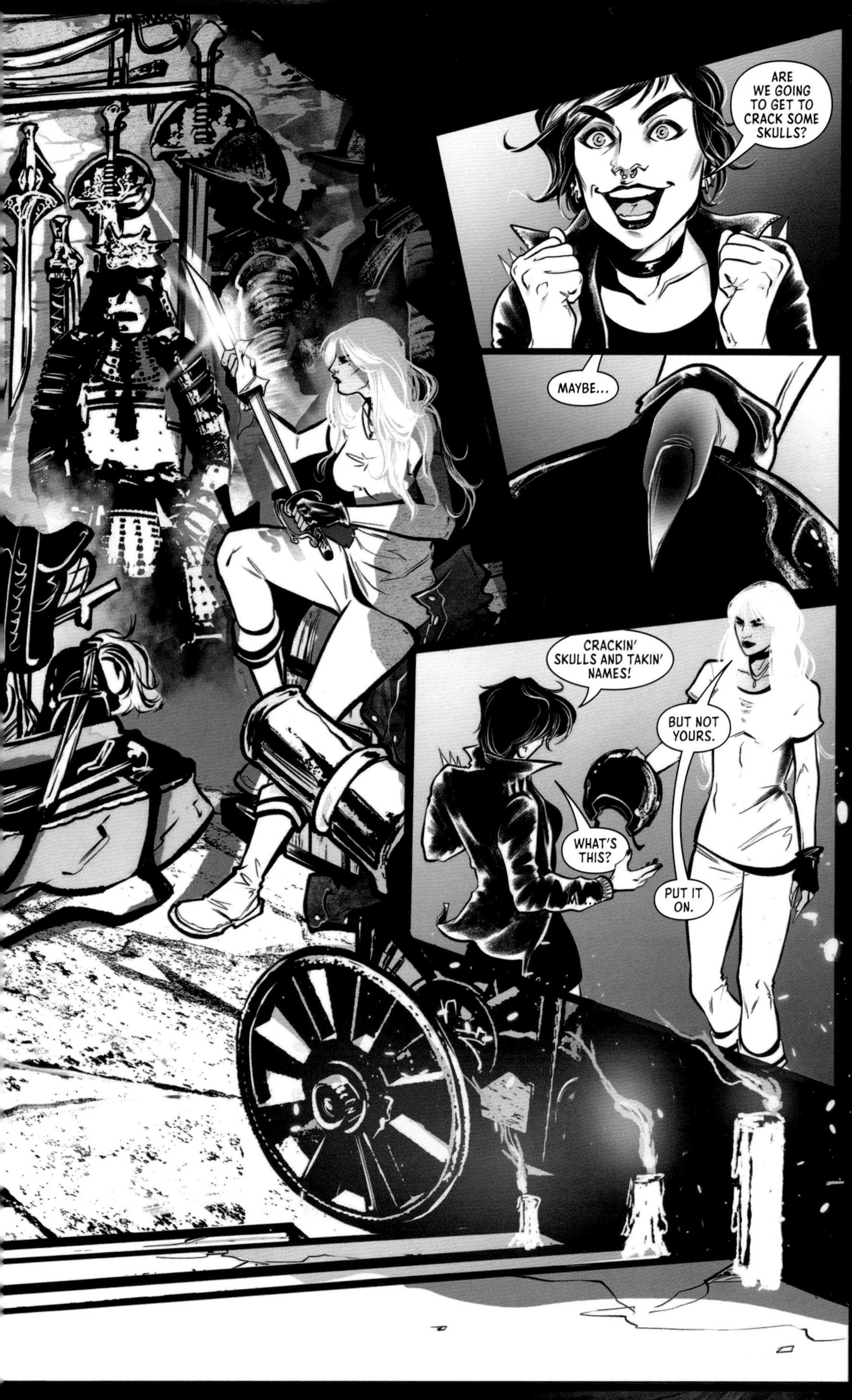
ARE WE GOING TO GET TO CRACK SOME SKULLS?
MAYBE...
CRACKIN' SKULLS AND TAKIN' NAMES!
BUT NOT YOURS.
WHAT'S THIS?
PUT IT ON.

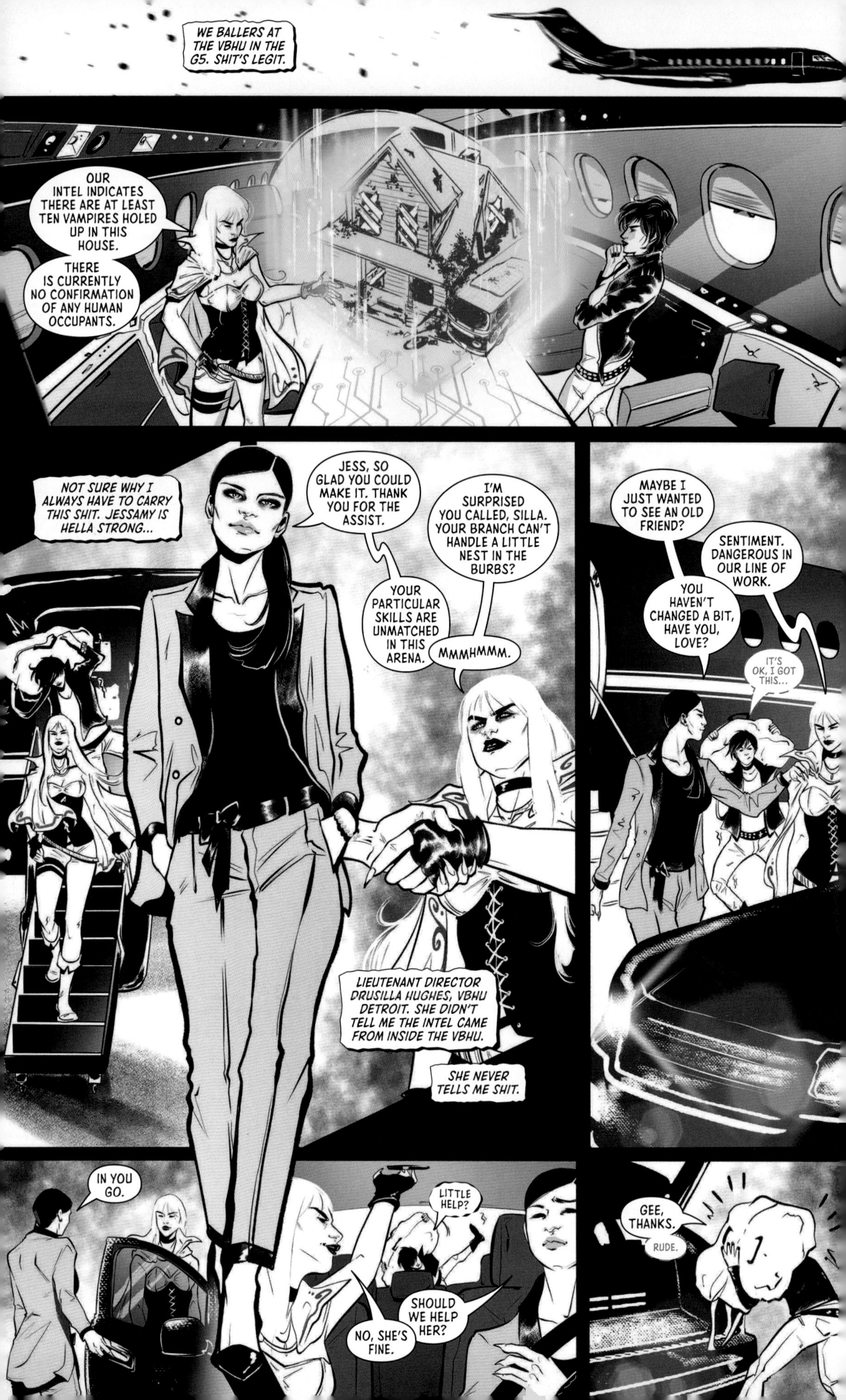
WE BALLERS AT THE VBHU IN THE G5. SHIT'S LEGIT.
OUR INTEL INDICATES THERE ARE AT LEAST TEN VAMPIRES HOLED UP IN THIS HOUSE.
THERE IS CURRENTLY NO CONFIRMATION OF ANY HUMAN OCCUPANTS.
NOT SURE WHY I ALWAYS HAVE TO CARRY THIS SHIT. JESSAMY IS HELLA STRONG...
JESS, SO GLAD YOU COULD MAKE IT. THANK YOU FOR THE ASSIST.
I'M SURPRISED YOU CALLED, SILLA. YOUR BRANCH CAN'T HANDLE A LITTLE NEST IN THE BURBS?
YOUR PARTICULAR SKILLS ARE UNMATCHED IN THIS ARENA.
MMMHMMM.
LIEUTENANT DIRECTOR DRUSILLA HUGHES, VBHU DETROIT. SHE DIDN'T TELL ME THE INTEL CAME FROM INSIDE THE VBHU.
SHE NEVER TELLS ME SHIT.
MAYBE I JUST WANTED TO SEE AN OLD FRIEND?
SENTIMENT. DANGEROUS IN OUR LINE OF WORK.
YOU HAVEN'T CHANGED A BIT, HAVE YOU, LOVE?
IT'S OK, I GOT THIS...
IN YOU GO.
LITTLE HELP?
SHOULD WE HELP HER?
NO, SHE'S FINE.
GEE, THANKS.
RUDE.

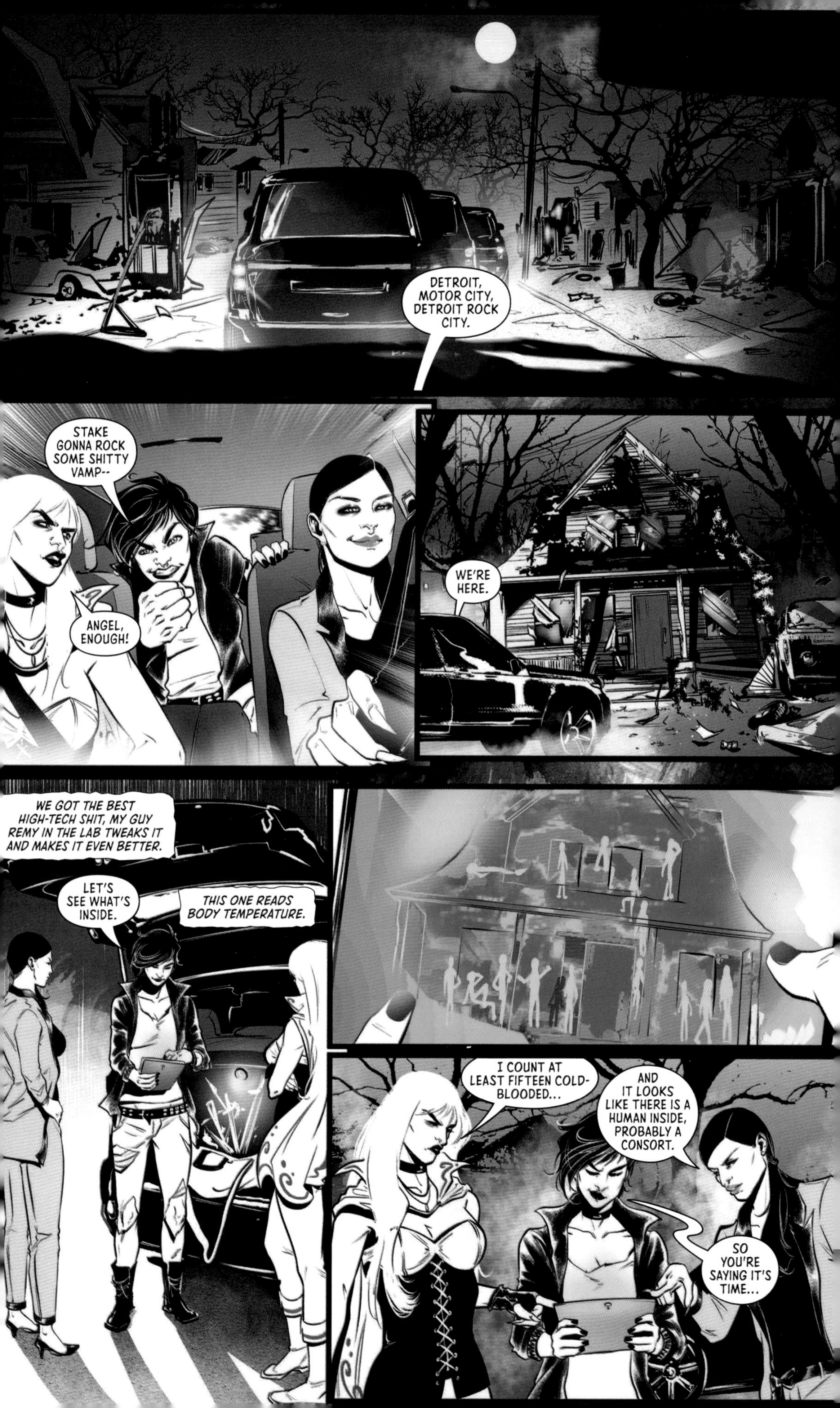
DETROIT, MOTOR CITY, DETROIT ROCK CITY.
STAKE GONNA ROCK SOME SHITTY VAMP--
ANGEL, ENOUGH!
WE'RE HERE.
WE GOT THE BEST HIGH-TECH SHIT, MY GUY REMY IN THE LAB TWEAKS IT AND MAKES IT EVEN BETTER.
LET'S SEE WHAT'S INSIDE.
THIS ONE READS BODY TEMPERATURE.
I COUNT AT LEAST FIFTEEN COLD-BLOODED...
AND IT LOOKS LIKE THERE IS A HUMAN INSIDE, PROBABLY A CONSORT.
SO YOU'RE SAYING IT'S TIME...

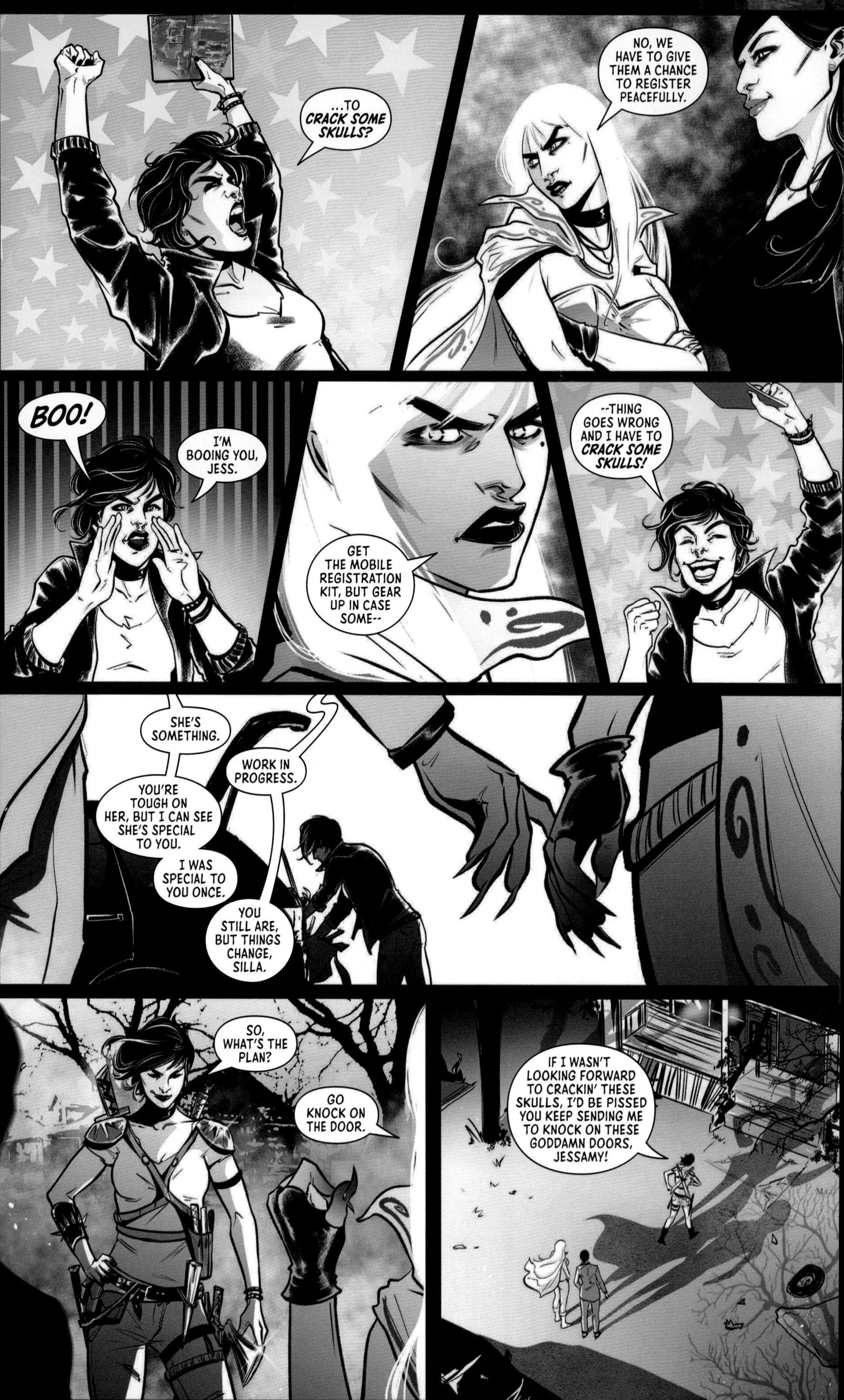
...TO CRACK SOME SKULLS?
NO, WE HAVE TO GIVE THEM A CHANCE TO REGISTER PEACEFULLY.
BOO!
I'M BOOING YOU, JESS.
GET THE MOBILE REGISTRATION KIT, BUT GEAR UP IN CASE SOME--
--THING GOES WRONG AND I HAVE TO CRACK SOME SKULLS!
SHE'S SOMETHING.
WORK IN PROGRESS.
YOU'RE TOUGH ON HER, BUT I CAN SEE SHE'S SPECIAL TO YOU.
I WAS SPECIAL TO YOU ONCE.
YOU STILL ARE, BUT THINGS CHANGE, SILLA.
SO, WHAT'S THE PLAN?
GO KNOCK ON THE DOOR.
IF I WASN'T LOOKING FORWARD TO CRACKIN' THESE SKULLS, I'D BE PISSED YOU KEEP SENDING ME TO KNOCK ON THESE GODDAMN DOORS, JESSAMY!

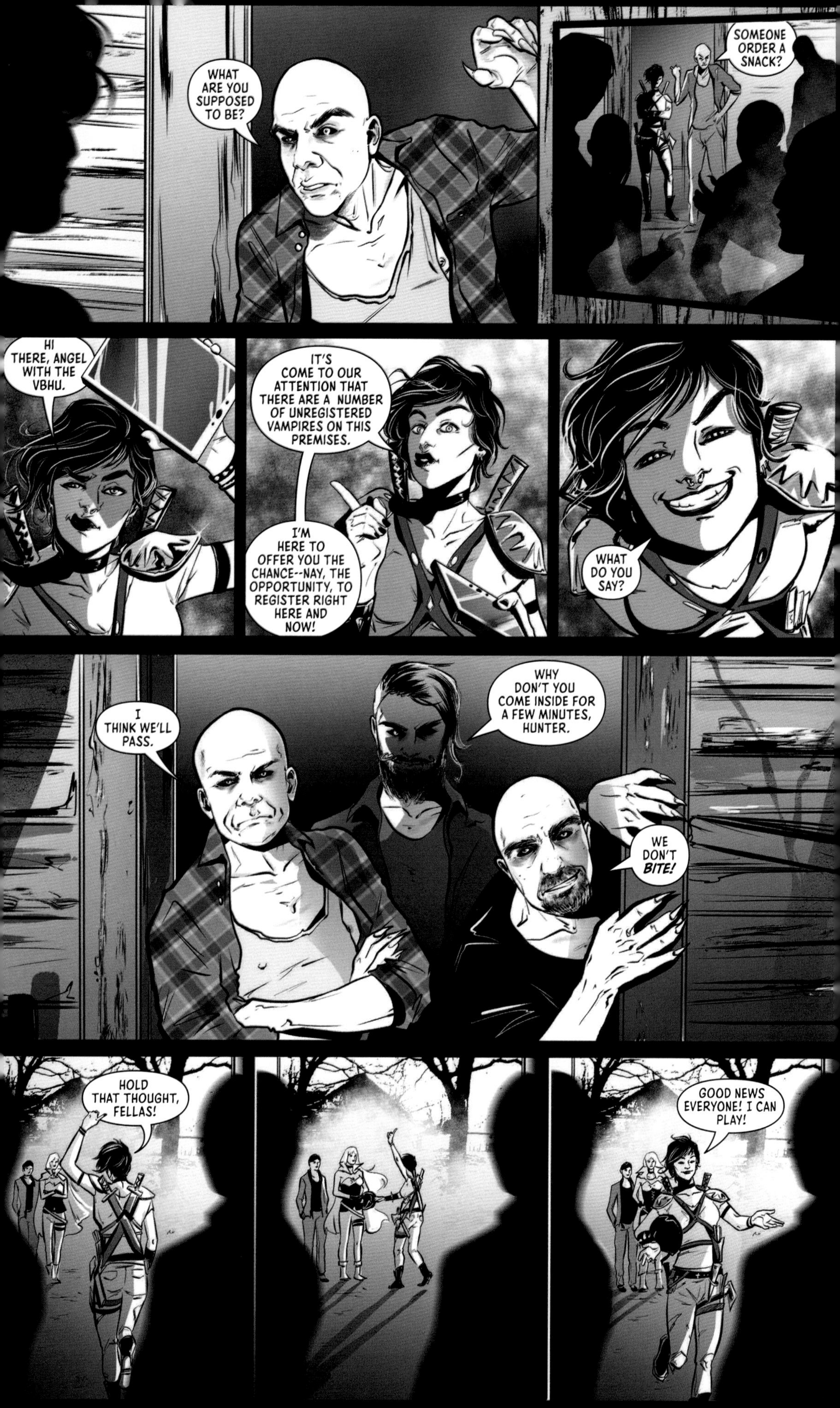

WHAT ARE YOU SUPPOSED TO BE?
SOMEONE ORDER A SNACK?
HI THERE, ANGEL WITH THE VBHU.
IT'S COME TO OUR ATTENTION THAT THERE ARE A NUMBER OF UNREGISTERED VAMPIRES ON THIS PREMISES.
I'M HERE TO OFFER YOU THE CHANCE--NAY, THE OPPORTUNITY, TO REGISTER RIGHT HERE AND NOW!
WHAT DO YOU SAY?
I THINK WE'LL PASS.
WHY DON'T YOU COME INSIDE FOR A FEW MINUTES, HUNTER.
WE DON'T *BITE!*
HOLD THAT THOUGHT, FELLAS!
GOOD NEWS EVERYONE! I CAN PLAY!

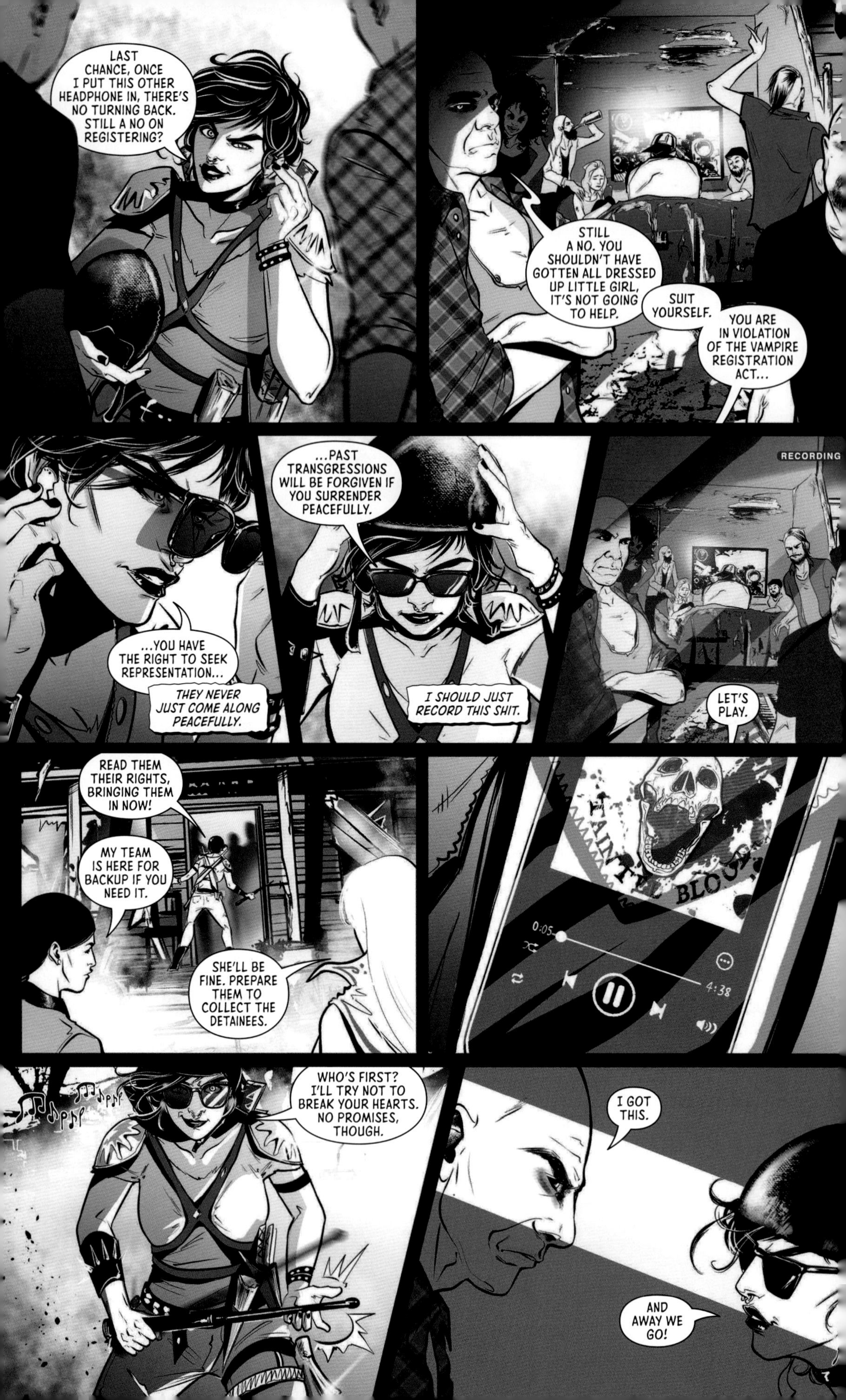

LAST CHANCE, ONCE I PUT THIS OTHER HEADPHONE IN, THERE'S NO TURNING BACK. STILL A NO ON REGISTERING?
STILL A NO. YOU SHOULDN'T HAVE GOTTEN ALL DRESSED UP LITTLE GIRL, IT'S NOT GOING TO HELP.
SUIT YOURSELF.
YOU ARE IN VIOLATION OF THE VAMPIRE REGISTRATION ACT...
...YOU HAVE THE RIGHT TO SEEK REPRESENTATION...
THEY NEVER JUST COME ALONG PEACEFULLY.
...PAST TRANSGRESSIONS WILL BE FORGIVEN IF YOU SURRENDER PEACEFULLY.
I SHOULD JUST RECORD THIS SHIT.
RECORDING
LET'S PLAY.
READ THEM THEIR RIGHTS, BRINGING THEM IN NOW!
MY TEAM IS HERE FOR BACKUP IF YOU NEED IT.
SHE'LL BE FINE. PREPARE THEM TO COLLECT THE DETAINEES.
0:05
4:38
WHO'S FIRST? I'LL TRY NOT TO BREAK YOUR HEARTS. NO PROMISES, THOUGH.
I GOT THIS.
AND AWAY WE GO!

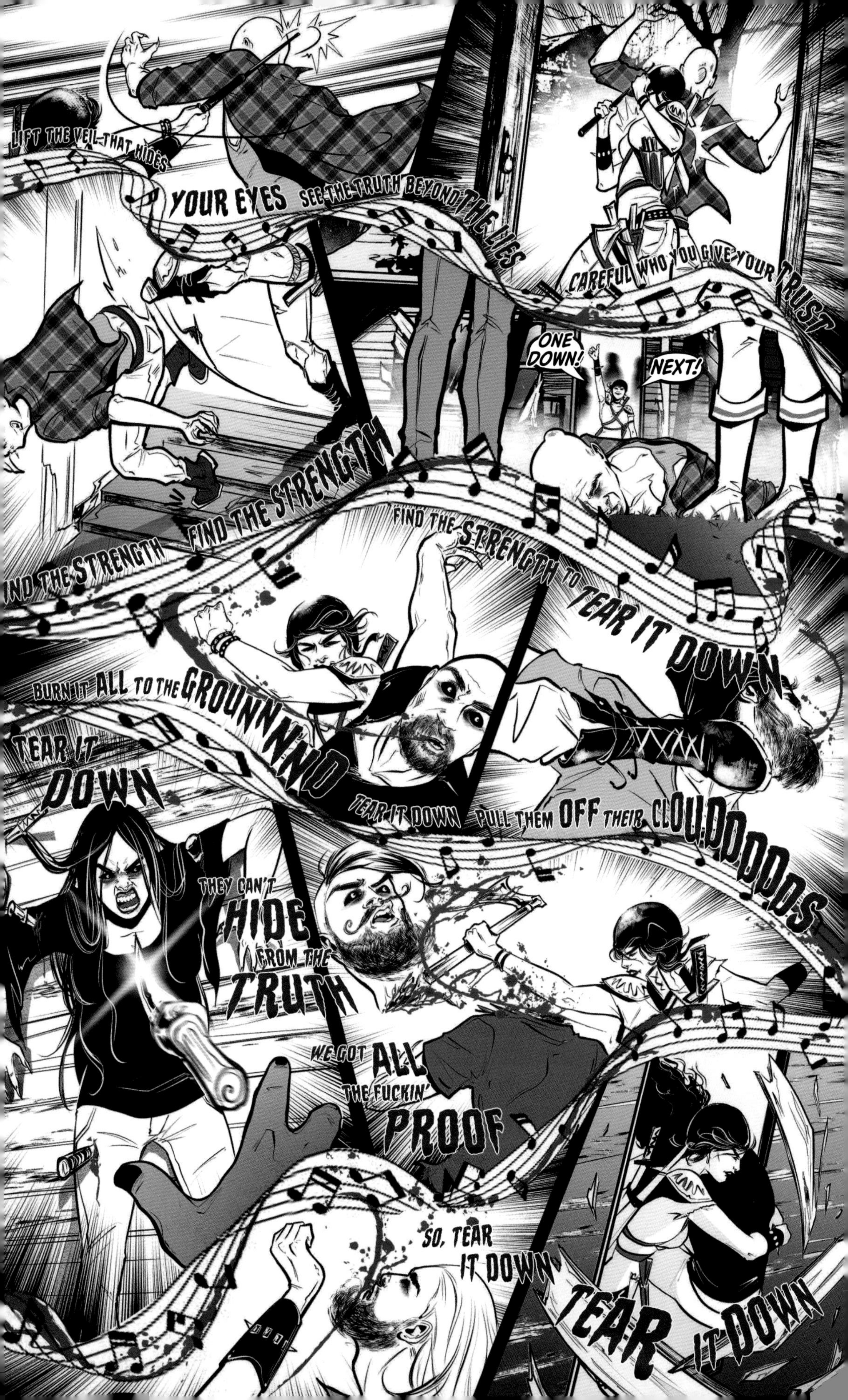

LIFT THE VEIL THAT HIDES
YOUR EYES
SEE THE TRUTH BEYOND THE LIES
CAREFUL WHO YOU GIVE YOUR TRUST
ONE DOWN!
NEXT!
FIND THE STRENGTH
FIND THE STRENGTH
FIND THE STRENGTH TO TEAR IT DOWN
BURN IT ALL TO THE GROUNNNND
TEAR IT DOWN
TEAR IT DOWN
PULL THEM OFF THEIR CLOUDDDDDS
THEY CAN'T HIDE FROM THE TRUTH
WE GOT ALL THE FUCKIN' PROOF
SO, TEAR IT DOWN
TEAR IT DOWN

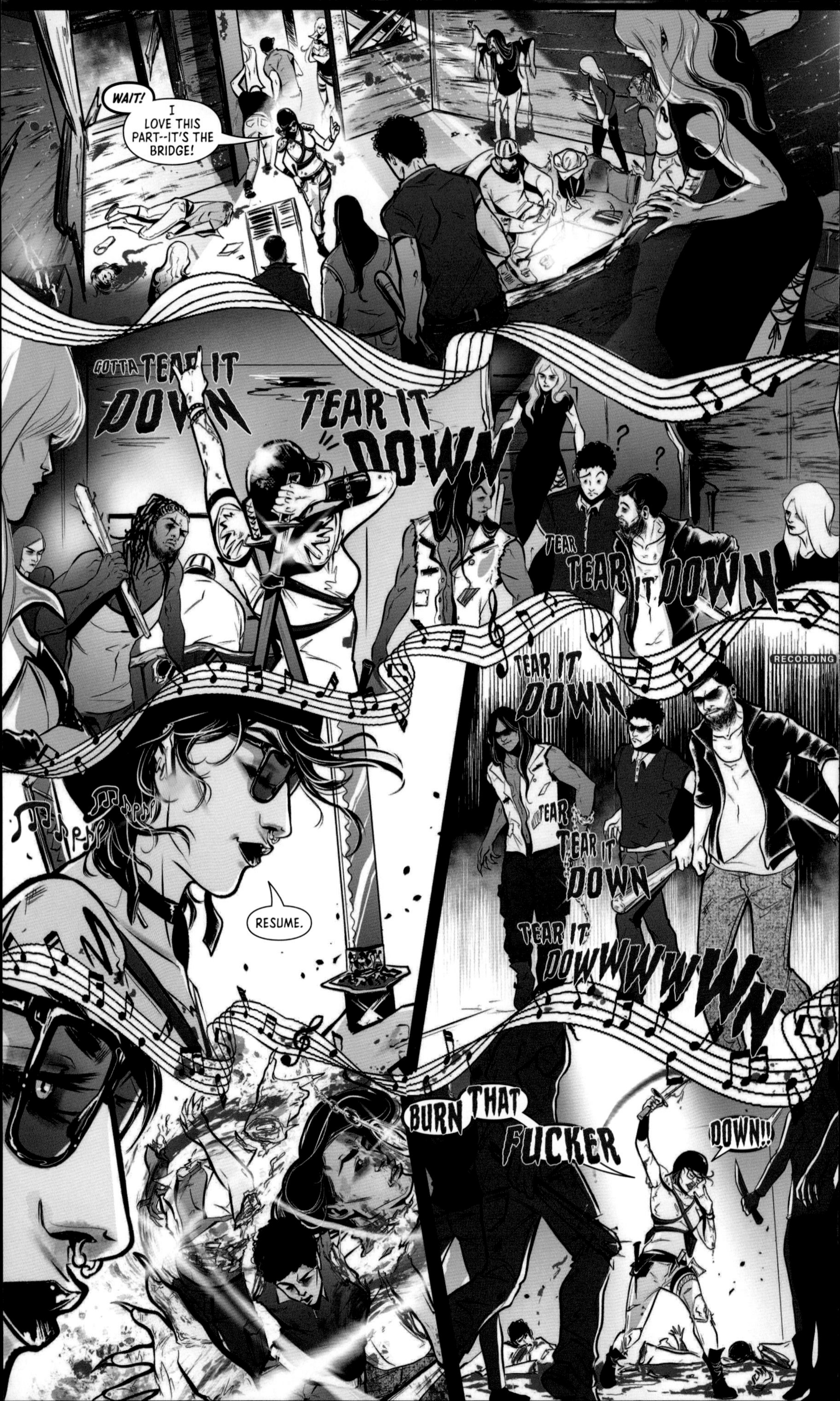

WAIT!
I LOVE THIS PART--IT'S THE BRIDGE!
GOTTA TEAR IT DOWN
TEAR IT DOWN
TEAR TEAR IT DOWN
RECORDING
TEAR IT DOWN
RESUME.
TEAR TEAR IT DOWN
TEAR IT DOWWWWWN
BURN THAT FUCKER
DOWN!!

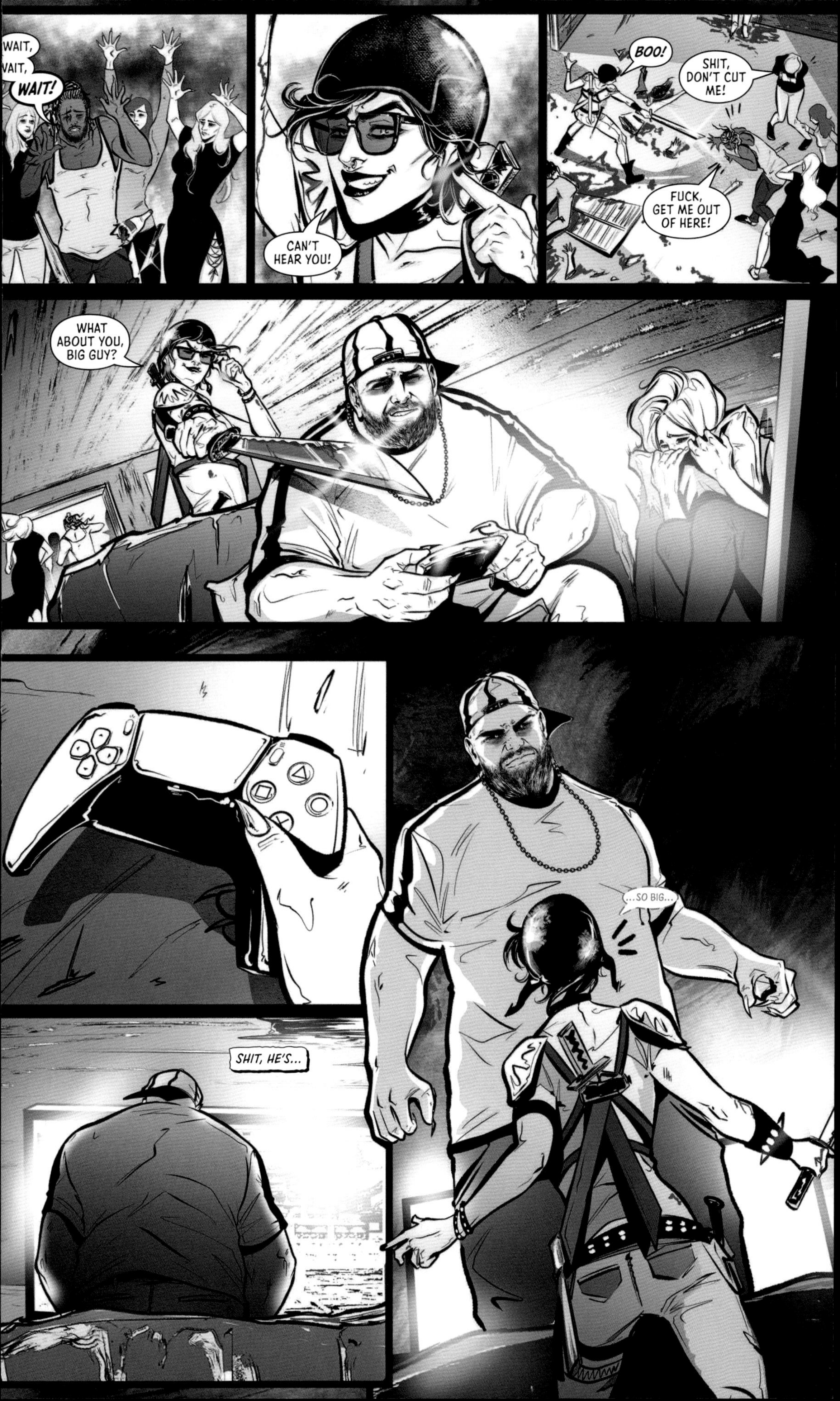
WAIT, WAIT, WAIT!
CAN'T HEAR YOU!
BOO!
SHIT, DON'T CUT ME!
FUCK, GET ME OUT OF HERE!
WHAT ABOUT YOU, BIG GUY?
SHIT, HE'S...
...SO BIG...

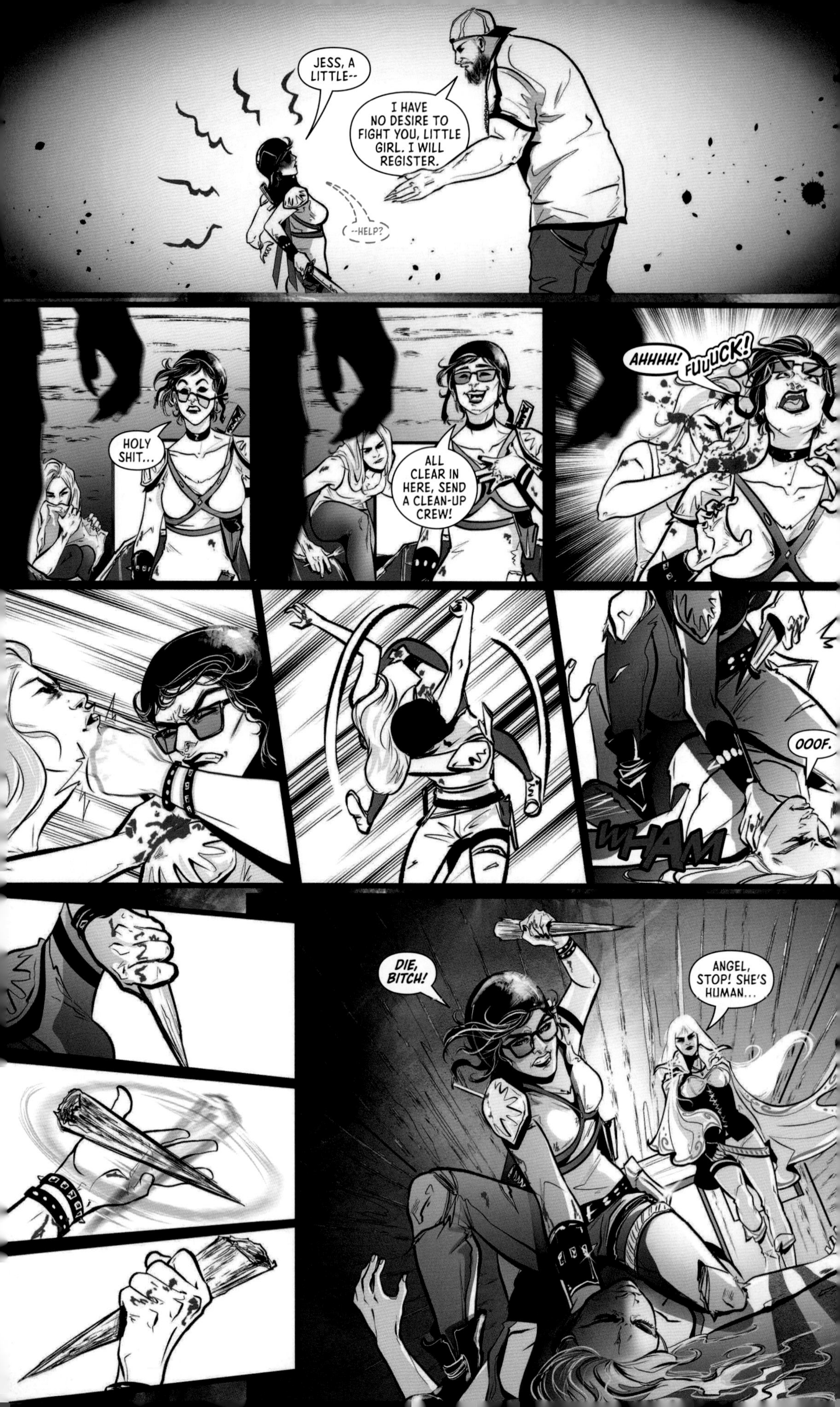
JESS, A LITTLE--
I HAVE NO DESIRE TO FIGHT YOU, LITTLE GIRL. I WILL REGISTER.
--HELP?
HOLY SHIT...
ALL CLEAR IN HERE, SEND A CLEAN-UP CREW!
AHHHH!
FUUUCK!
OOOF.
WHAM
DIE, BITCH!
ANGEL, STOP! SHE'S HUMAN...

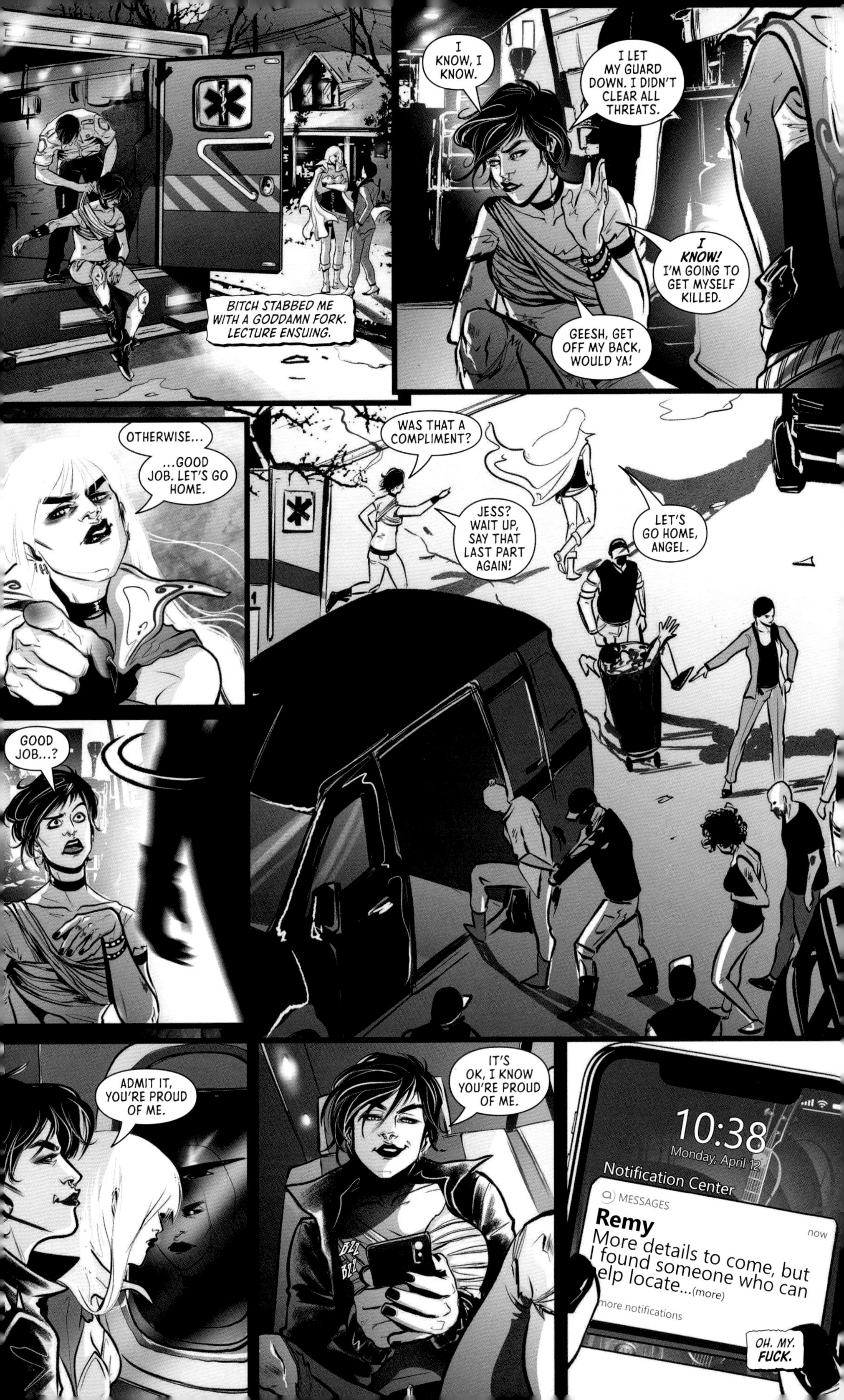
BITCH STABBED ME WITH A GODDAMN FORK. LECTURE ENSUING.
I KNOW, I KNOW.
I LET MY GUARD DOWN. I DIDN'T CLEAR ALL THREATS.
I KNOW! I'M GOING TO GET MYSELF KILLED.
GEESH, GET OFF MY BACK, WOULD YA!
OTHERWISE...
...GOOD JOB. LET'S GO HOME.
GOOD JOB...?
WAS THAT A COMPLIMENT?
JESS? WAIT UP, SAY THAT LAST PART AGAIN!
LET'S GO HOME, ANGEL.
ADMIT IT, YOU'RE PROUD OF ME.
IT'S OK, I KNOW YOU'RE PROUD OF ME.
BZZ BZZ
10:38
Monday, April 12
Notification Center
MESSAGES
Remy
now
More details to come, but I found someone who can help locate...(more)
more notifications
OH. MY. FUCK.

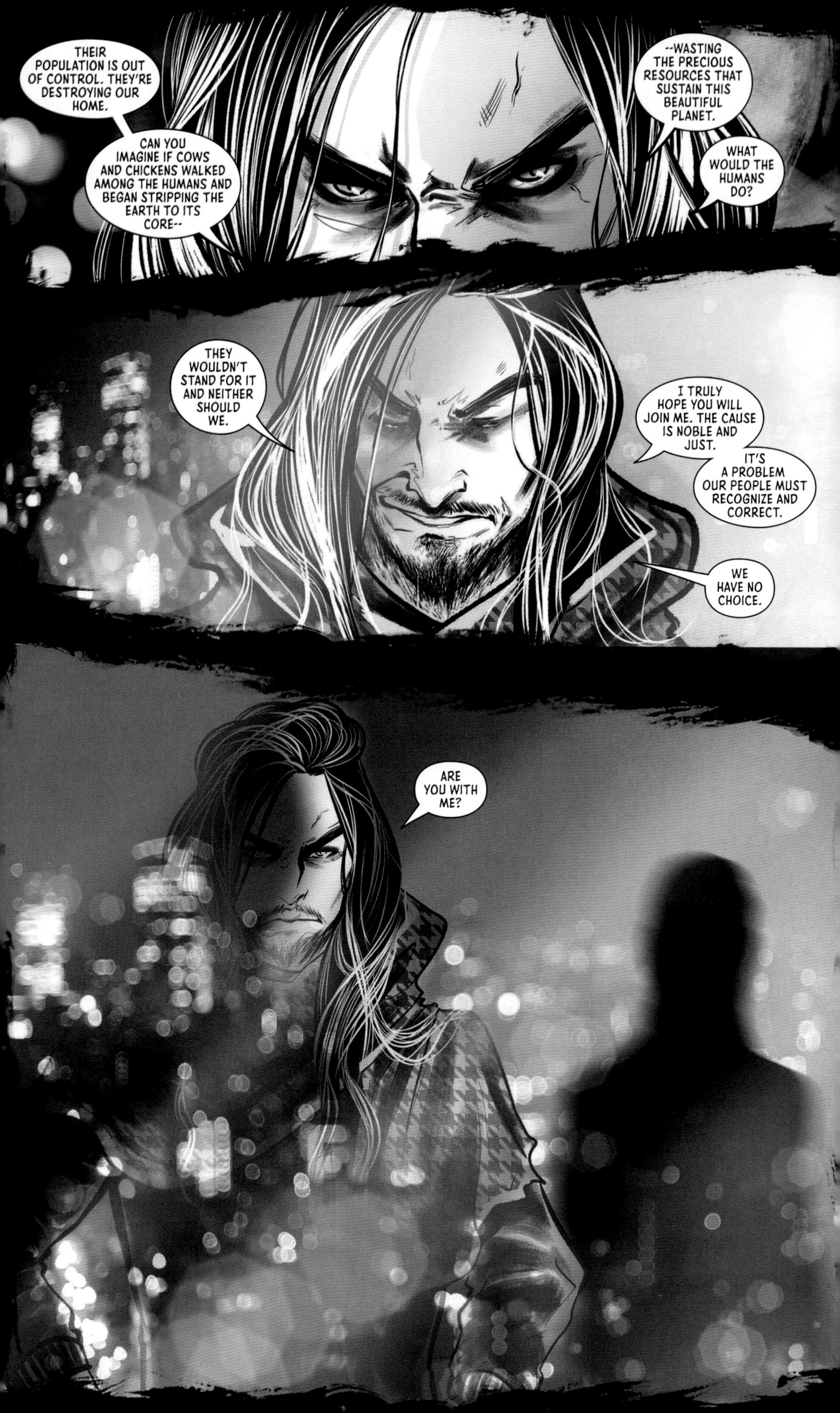

THEIR POPULATION IS OUT OF CONTROL. THEY'RE DESTROYING OUR HOME.
CAN YOU IMAGINE IF COWS AND CHICKENS WALKED AMONG THE HUMANS AND BEGAN STRIPPING THE EARTH TO ITS CORE--
--WASTING THE PRECIOUS RESOURCES THAT SUSTAIN THIS BEAUTIFUL PLANET.
WHAT WOULD THE HUMANS DO?
THEY WOULDN'T STAND FOR IT AND NEITHER SHOULD WE.
I TRULY HOPE YOU WILL JOIN ME. THE CAUSE IS NOBLE AND JUST.
IT'S A PROBLEM OUR PEOPLE MUST RECOGNIZE AND CORRECT.
WE HAVE NO CHOICE.
ARE YOU WITH ME?

End Chapter Three

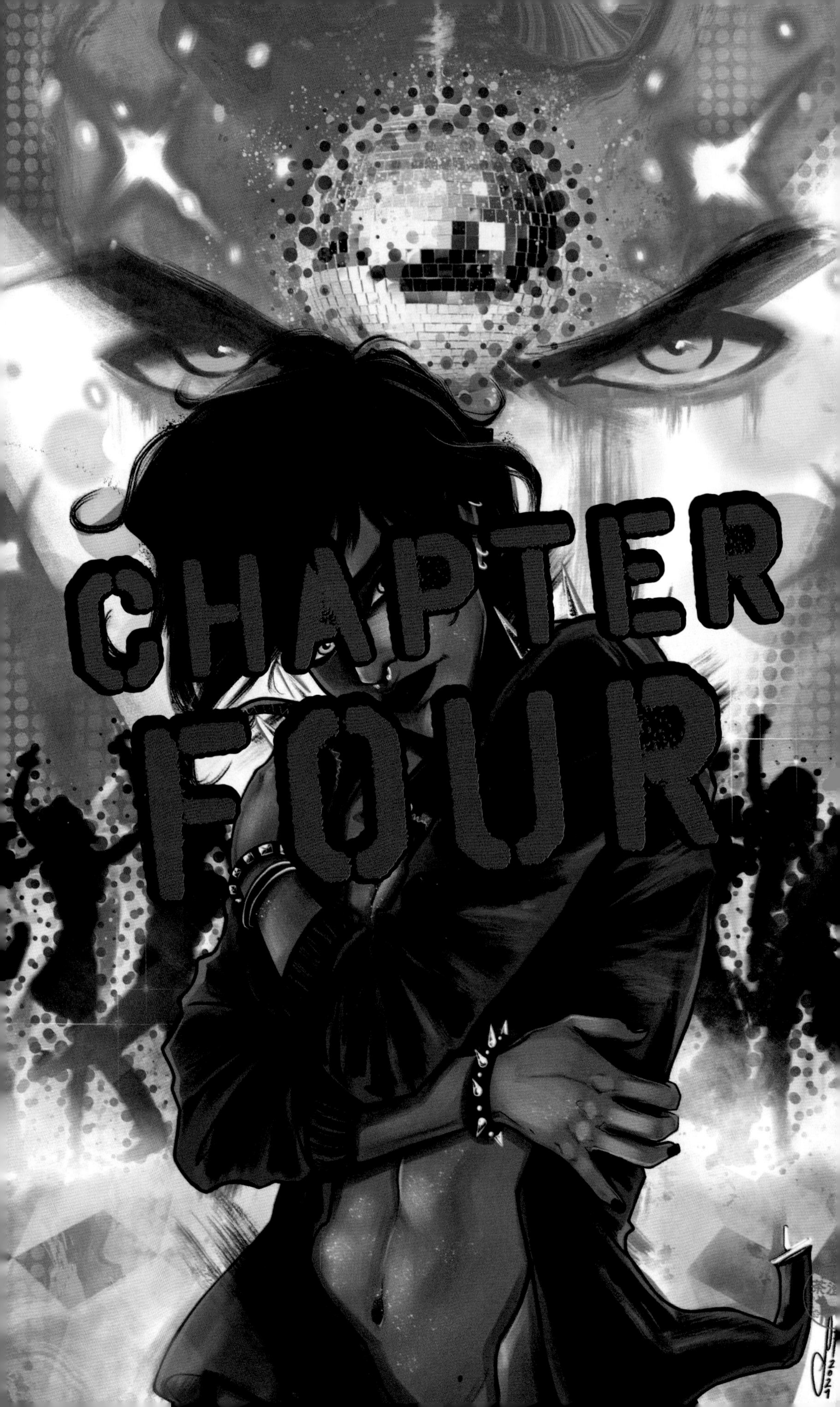

CHAPTER
FOUR

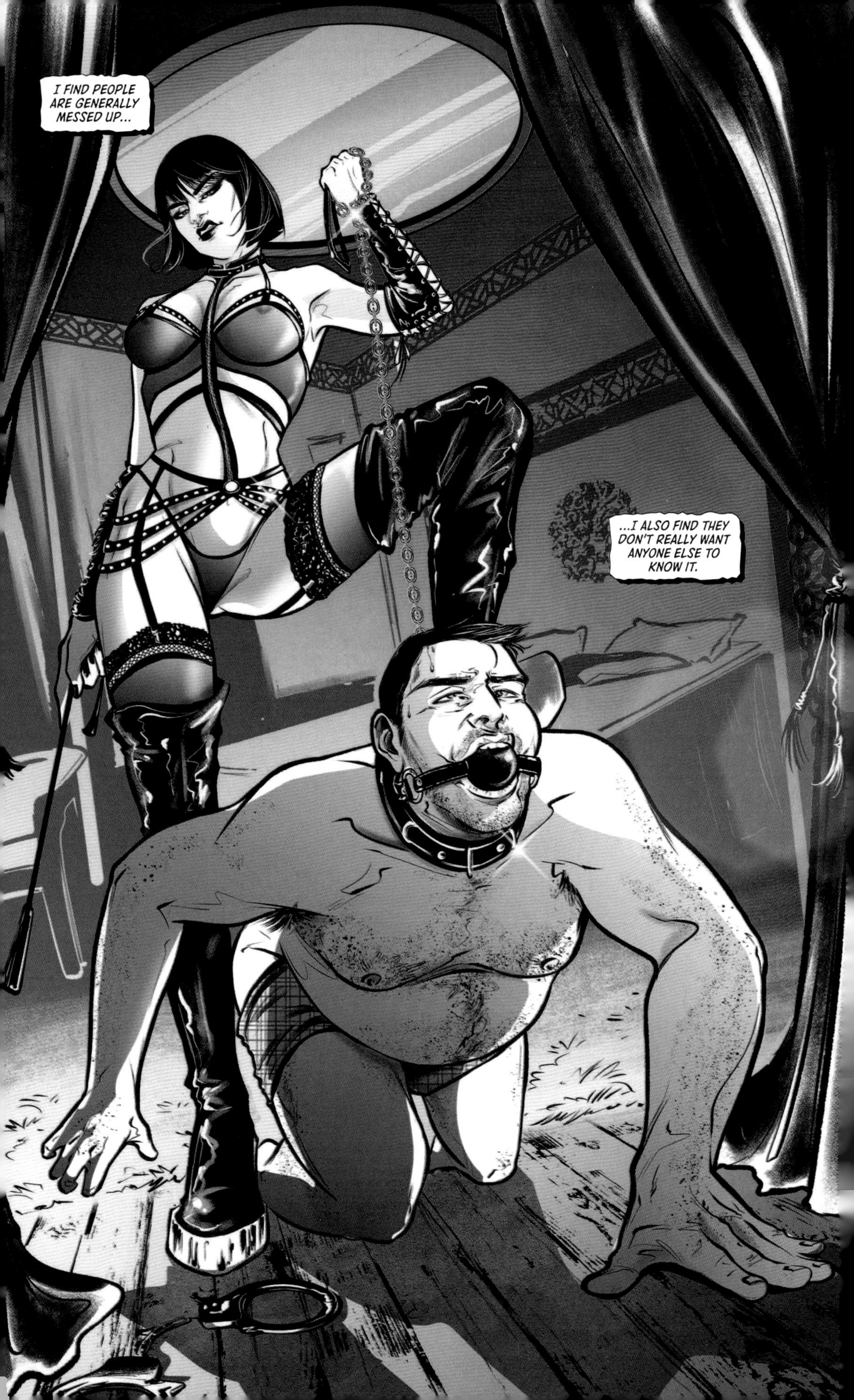
I FIND PEOPLE ARE GENERALLY MESSED UP...
...I ALSO FIND THEY DON'T REALLY WANT ANYONE ELSE TO KNOW IT.

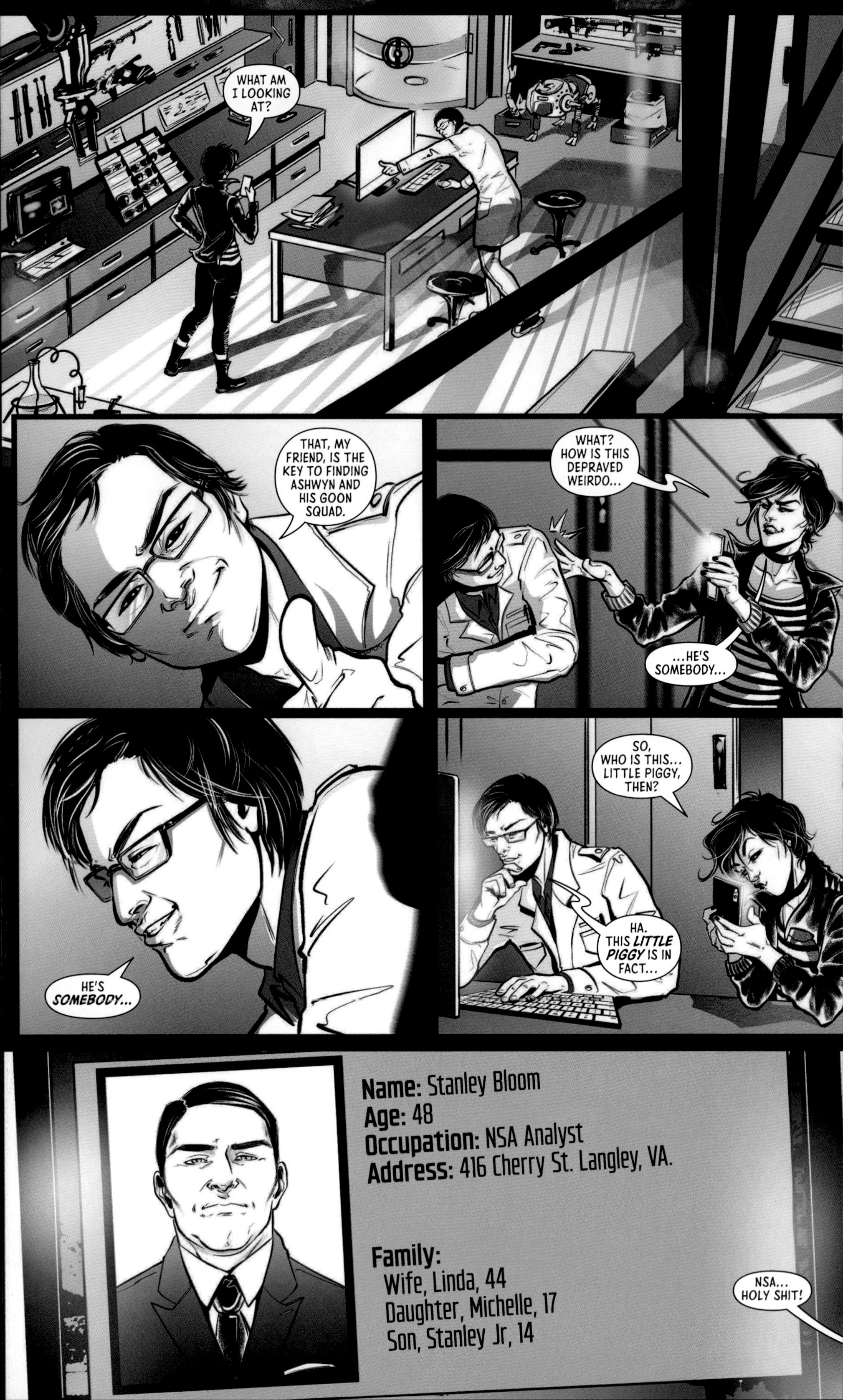
WHAT AM I LOOKING AT?
THAT, MY FRIEND, IS THE KEY TO FINDING ASHWYN AND HIS GOON SQUAD.
WHAT? HOW IS THIS DEPRAVED WEIRDO...
...HE'S SOMEBODY...
HE'S *SOMEBODY*...
SO, WHO IS THIS... LITTLE PIGGY, THEN?
HA. THIS *LITTLE PIGGY* IS IN FACT...
Name: Stanley Bloom
Age: 48
Occupation: NSA Analyst
Address: 416 Cherry St. Langley, VA.
Family:
Wife, Linda, 44
Daughter, Michelle, 17
Son, Stanley Jr, 14
NSA... HOLY SHIT!

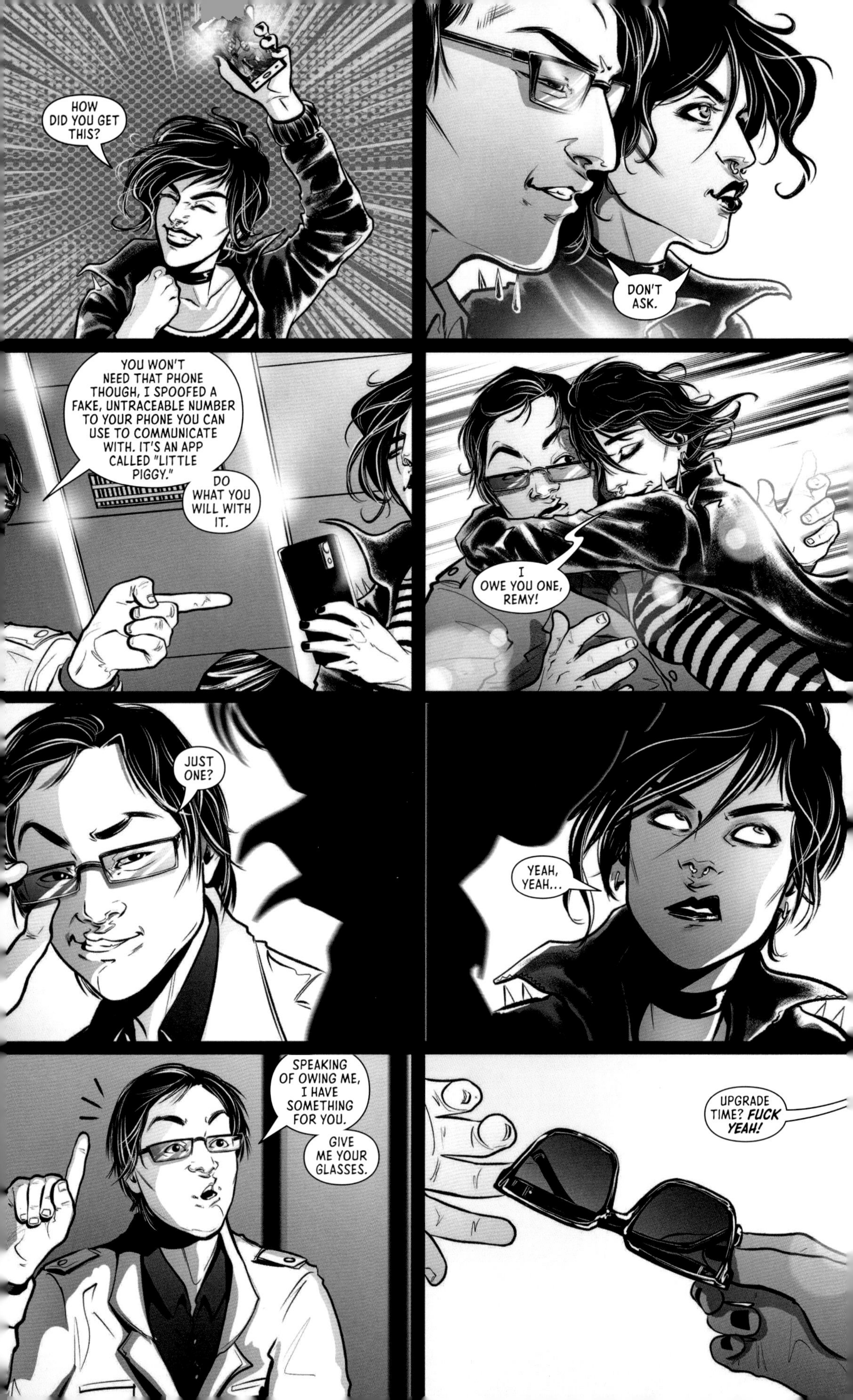
HOW DID YOU GET THIS?
DON'T ASK.
YOU WON'T NEED THAT PHONE THOUGH, I SPOOFED A FAKE, UNTRACEABLE NUMBER TO YOUR PHONE YOU CAN USE TO COMMUNICATE WITH. IT'S AN APP CALLED "LITTLE PIGGY."
DO WHAT YOU WILL WITH IT.
I OWE YOU ONE, REMY!
JUST ONE?
YEAH, YEAH...
SPEAKING OF OWING ME, I HAVE SOMETHING FOR YOU.
GIVE ME YOUR GLASSES.
UPGRADE TIME? ***FUCK YEAH!***

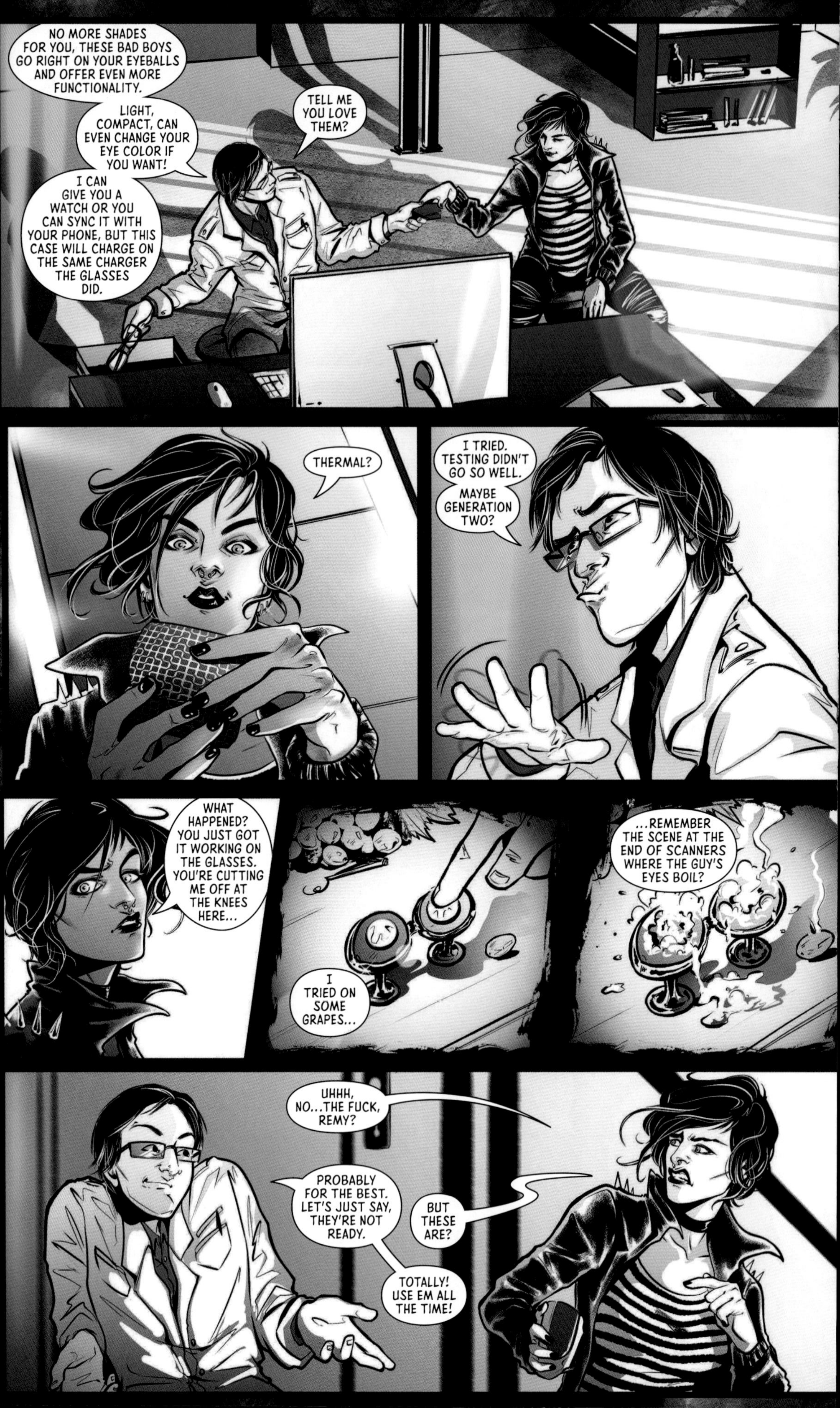

NO MORE SHADES FOR YOU, THESE BAD BOYS GO RIGHT ON YOUR EYEBALLS AND OFFER EVEN MORE FUNCTIONALITY.
LIGHT, COMPACT, CAN EVEN CHANGE YOUR EYE COLOR IF YOU WANT!
I CAN GIVE YOU A WATCH OR YOU CAN SYNC IT WITH YOUR PHONE, BUT THIS CASE WILL CHARGE ON THE SAME CHARGER THE GLASSES DID.
TELL ME YOU LOVE THEM?
THERMAL?
I TRIED. TESTING DIDN'T GO SO WELL.
MAYBE GENERATION TWO?
WHAT HAPPENED? YOU JUST GOT IT WORKING ON THE GLASSES. YOU'RE CUTTING ME OFF AT THE KNEES HERE...
I TRIED ON SOME GRAPES...
...REMEMBER THE SCENE AT THE END OF SCANNERS WHERE THE GUY'S EYES BOIL?
UHHH, NO...THE FUCK, REMY?
PROBABLY FOR THE BEST. LET'S JUST SAY, THEY'RE NOT READY.
BUT THESE ARE?
TOTALLY! USE EM ALL THE TIME!

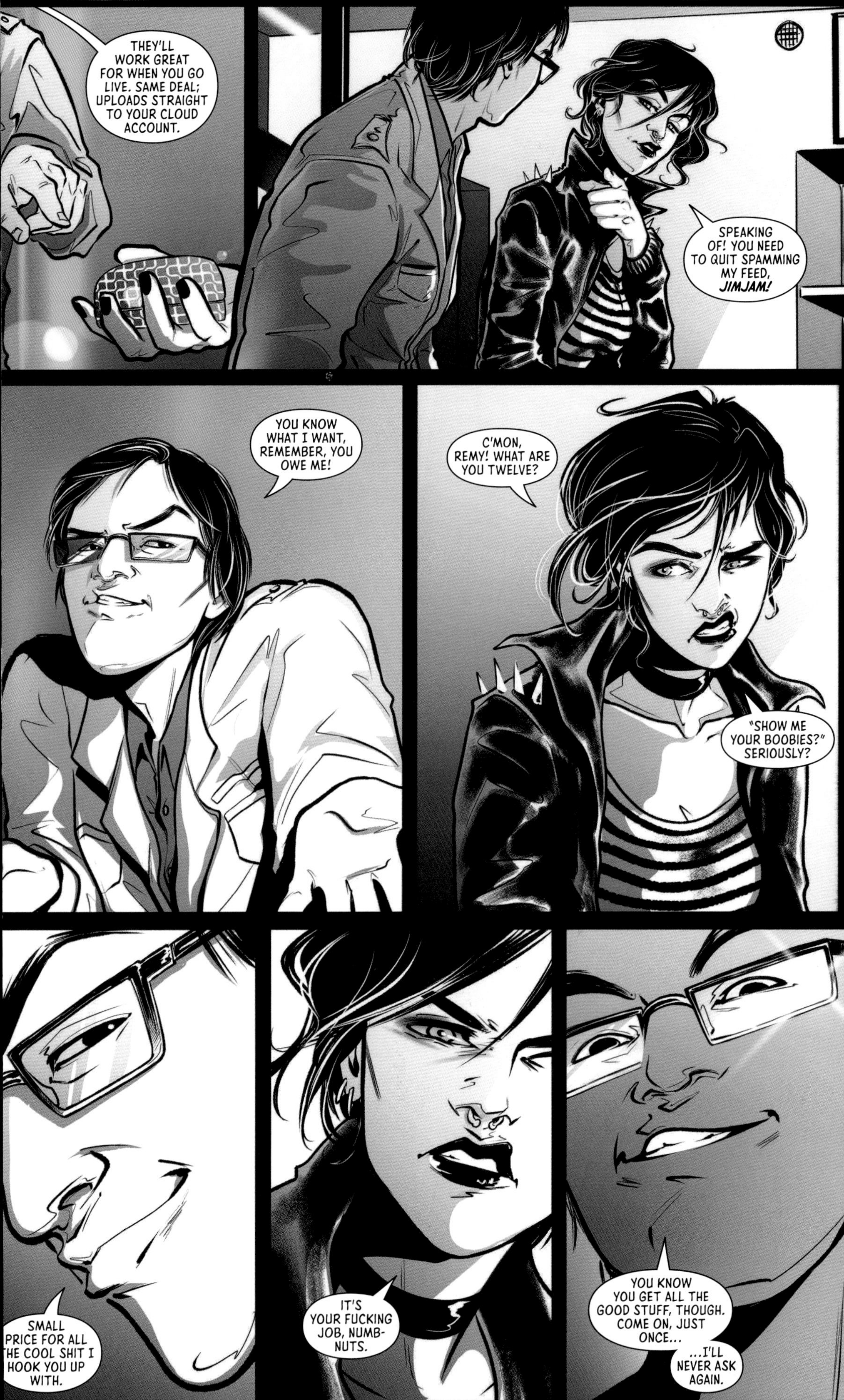
THEY'LL WORK GREAT FOR WHEN YOU GO LIVE. SAME DEAL; UPLOADS STRAIGHT TO YOUR CLOUD ACCOUNT.
SPEAKING OF! YOU NEED TO QUIT SPAMMING MY FEED, ***JIMJAM!***
YOU KNOW WHAT I WANT, REMEMBER, YOU OWE ME!
C'MON, REMY! WHAT ARE YOU TWELVE?
"SHOW ME YOUR BOOBIES?" SERIOUSLY?
SMALL PRICE FOR ALL THE COOL SHIT I HOOK YOU UP WITH.
IT'S YOUR FUCKING JOB, NUMB-NUTS.
YOU KNOW YOU GET ALL THE GOOD STUFF, THOUGH. COME ON, JUST ONCE...
...I'LL NEVER ASK AGAIN.

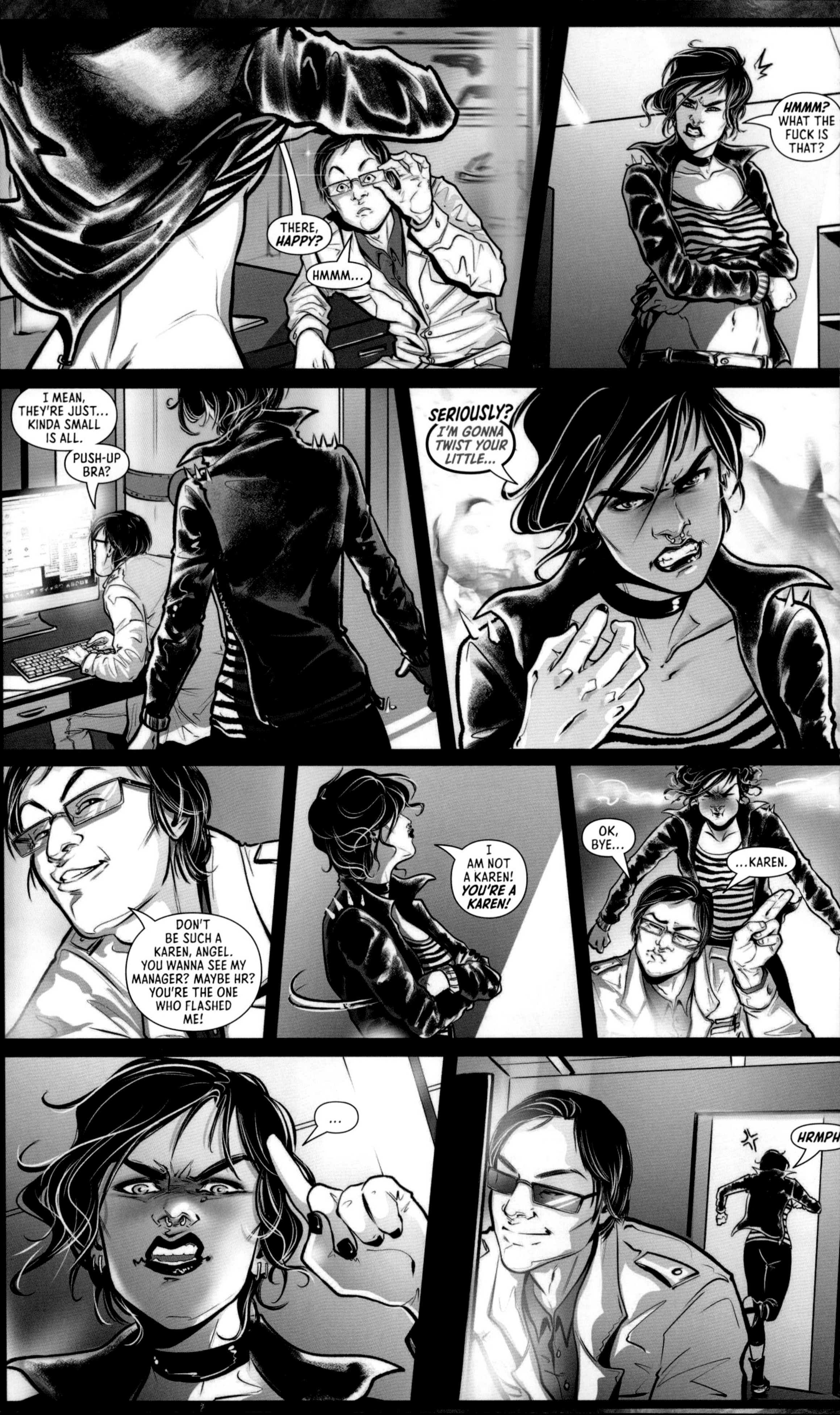
THERE, HAPPY?
HMMM...
HMMM? WHAT THE FUCK IS THAT?
I MEAN, THEY'RE JUST... KINDA SMALL IS ALL.
PUSH-UP BRA?
SERIOUSLY? I'M GONNA TWIST YOUR LITTLE...
DON'T BE SUCH A KAREN, ANGEL. YOU WANNA SEE MY MANAGER? MAYBE HR? YOU'RE THE ONE WHO FLASHED ME!
I AM NOT A KAREN! YOU'RE A KAREN!
OK, BYE...
...KAREN.
...
HRMPH

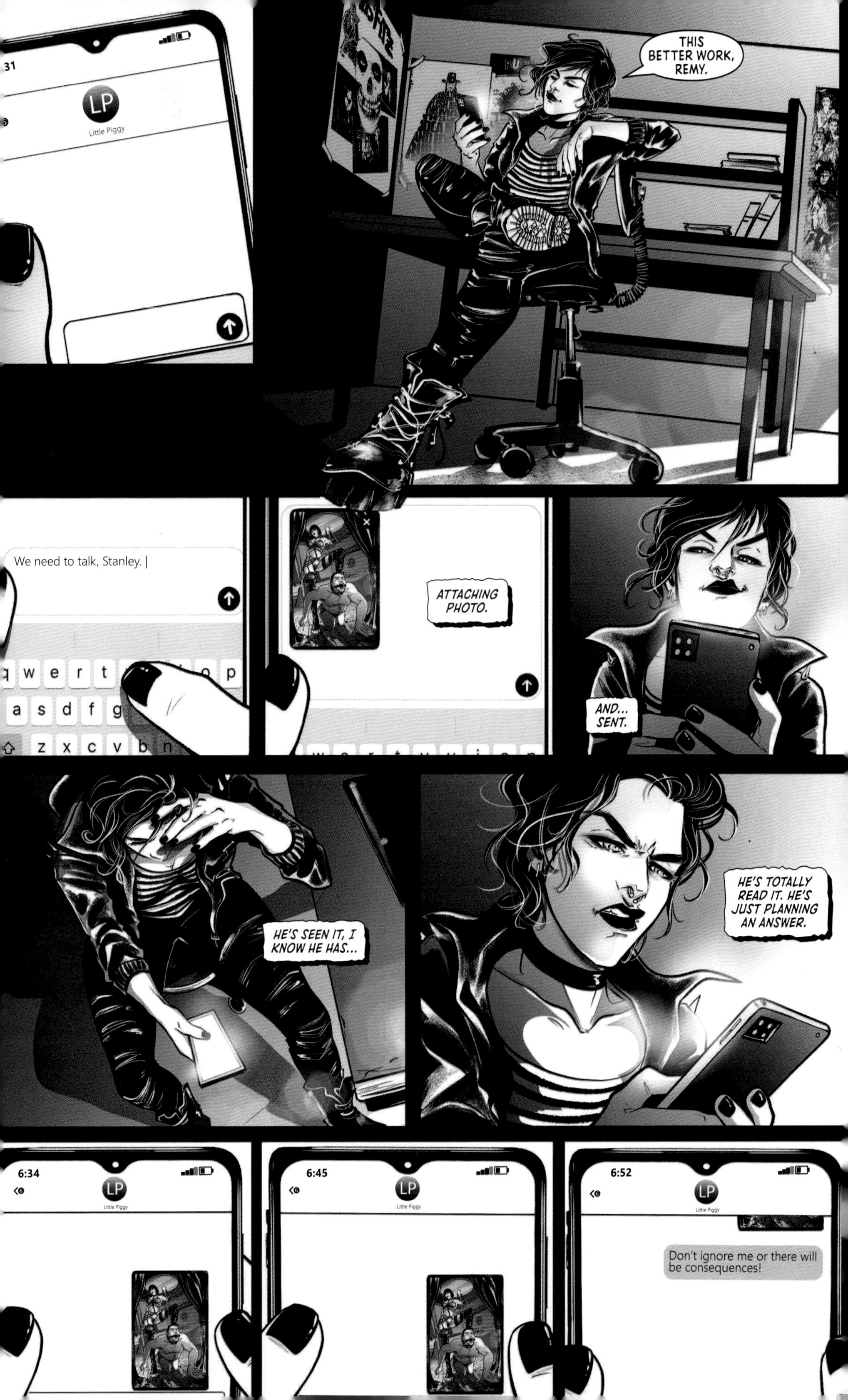

31
LP
Little Piggy
THIS BETTER WORK, REMY.
We need to talk, Stanley. |
ATTACHING PHOTO.
AND... SENT.
HE'S SEEN IT, I KNOW HE HAS...
HE'S TOTALLY READ IT. HE'S JUST PLANNING AN ANSWER.
6:34
LP
Little Piggy
6:45
LP
Little Piggy
6:52
LP
Little Piggy
Don't ignore me or there will be consequences!

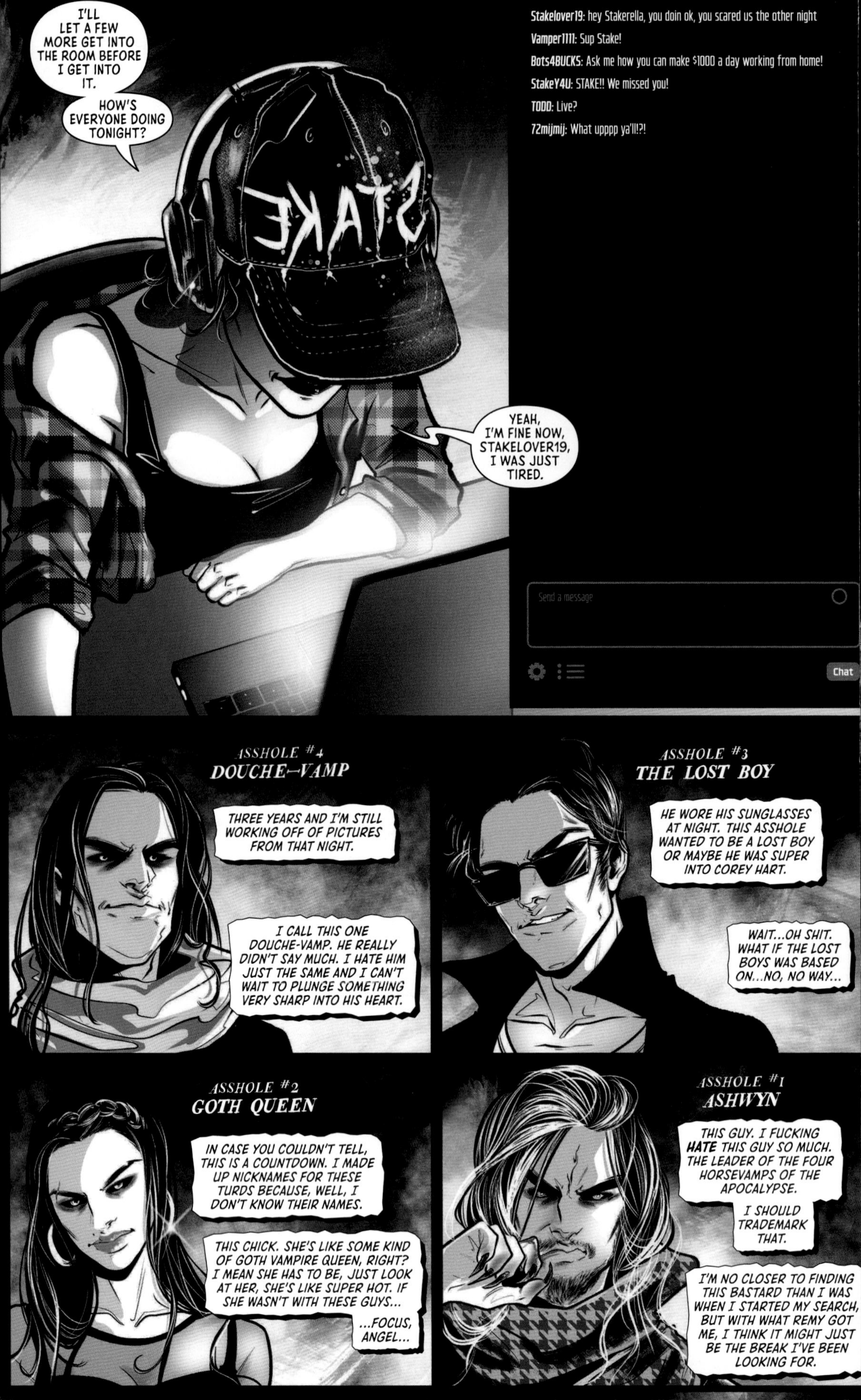
I'LL LET A FEW MORE GET INTO THE ROOM BEFORE I GET INTO IT.
HOW'S EVERYONE DOING TONIGHT?
Stakelover19: hey Stakerella, you doin ok, you scared us the other night
Vamper1111: Sup Stake!
Bots4BUCKS: Ask me how you can make $1000 a day working from home!
StakeY4U: STAKE!! We missed you!
TODD: Live?
72mijmij: What upppp ya'll!?!
STAKE
YEAH, I'M FINE NOW, STAKELOVER19, I WAS JUST TIRED.
Send a message
Chat
ASSHOLE #4 DOUCHE-VAMP
THREE YEARS AND I'M STILL WORKING OFF OF PICTURES FROM THAT NIGHT.
I CALL THIS ONE DOUCHE-VAMP. HE REALLY DIDN'T SAY MUCH. I HATE HIM JUST THE SAME AND I CAN'T WAIT TO PLUNGE SOMETHING VERY SHARP INTO HIS HEART.
ASSHOLE #3 THE LOST BOY
HE WORE HIS SUNGLASSES AT NIGHT. THIS ASSHOLE WANTED TO BE A LOST BOY OR MAYBE HE WAS SUPER INTO COREY HART.
WAIT...OH SHIT. WHAT IF THE LOST BOYS WAS BASED ON...NO, NO WAY...
ASSHOLE #2 GOTH QUEEN
IN CASE YOU COULDN'T TELL, THIS IS A COUNTDOWN. I MADE UP NICKNAMES FOR THESE TURDS BECAUSE, WELL, I DON'T KNOW THEIR NAMES.
THIS CHICK. SHE'S LIKE SOME KIND OF GOTH VAMPIRE QUEEN, RIGHT? I MEAN SHE HAS TO BE, JUST LOOK AT HER, SHE'S LIKE SUPER HOT. IF SHE WASN'T WITH THESE GUYS...
...FOCUS, ANGEL...
ASSHOLE #1 ASHWYN
THIS GUY. I FUCKING HATE THIS GUY SO MUCH. THE LEADER OF THE FOUR HORSEVAMPS OF THE APOCALYPSE.
I SHOULD TRADEMARK THAT.
I'M NO CLOSER TO FINDING THIS BASTARD THAN I WAS WHEN I STARTED MY SEARCH, BUT WITH WHAT REMY GOT ME, I THINK IT MIGHT JUST BE THE BREAK I'VE BEEN LOOKING FOR.

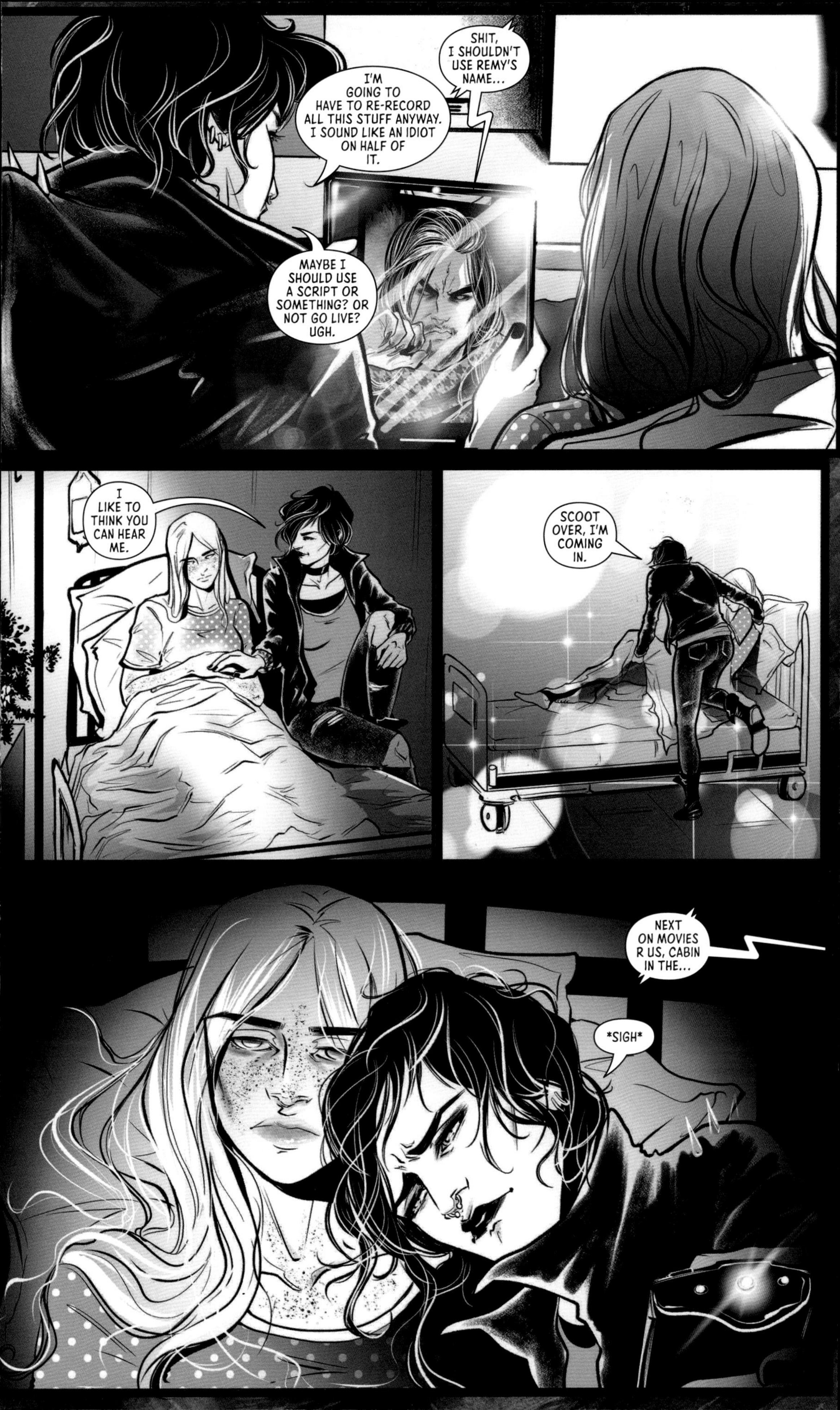
I'M GOING TO HAVE TO RE-RECORD ALL THIS STUFF ANYWAY. I SOUND LIKE AN IDIOT ON HALF OF IT.
SHIT, I SHOULDN'T USE REMY'S NAME...
MAYBE I SHOULD USE A SCRIPT OR SOMETHING? OR NOT GO LIVE? UGH.
I LIKE TO THINK YOU CAN HEAR ME.
SCOOT OVER, I'M COMING IN.
NEXT ON MOVIES R US, CABIN IN THE...
SIGH

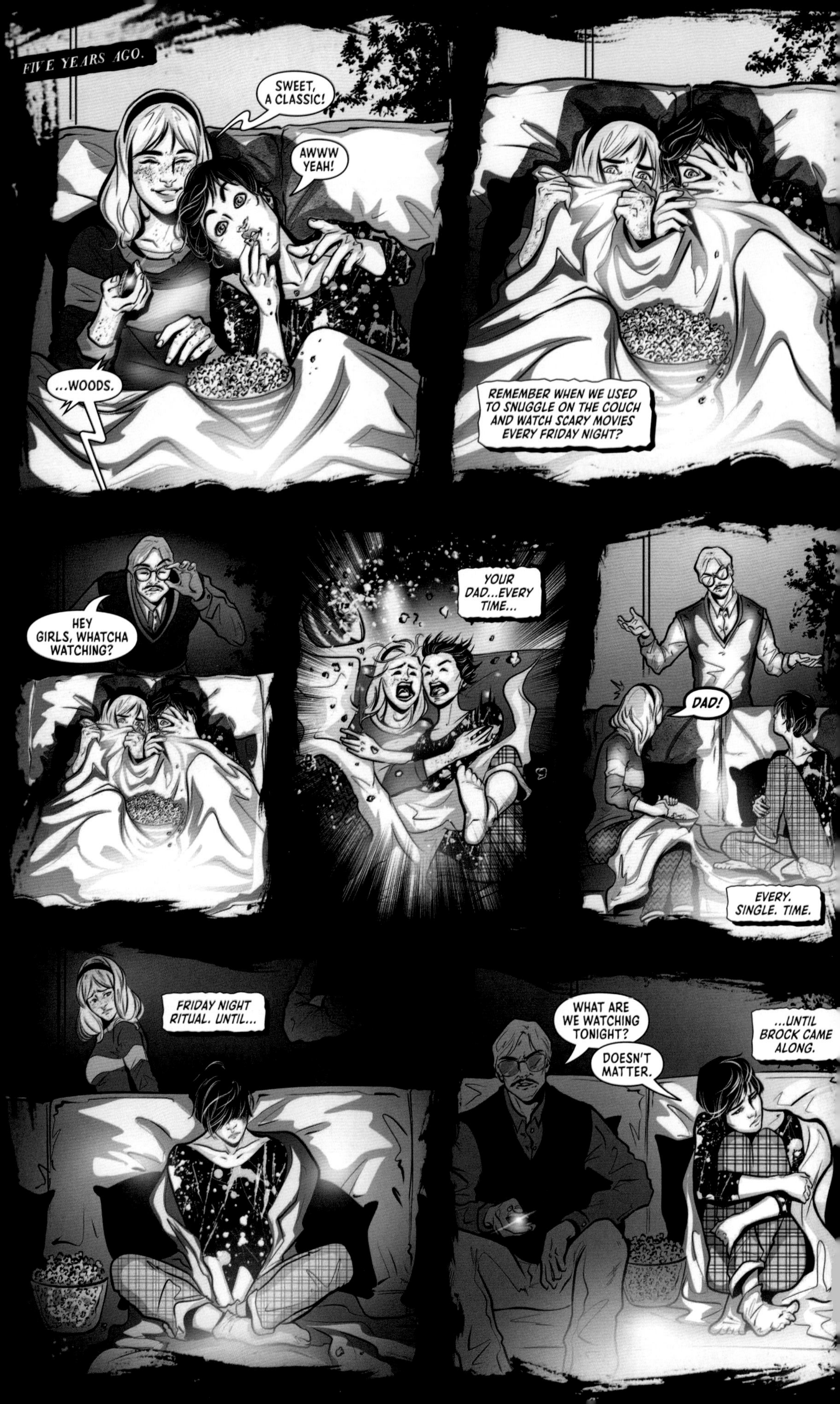

FIVE YEARS AGO.
SWEET, A CLASSIC!
AWWW YEAH!
...WOODS.
REMEMBER WHEN WE USED TO SNUGGLE ON THE COUCH AND WATCH SCARY MOVIES EVERY FRIDAY NIGHT?
HEY GIRLS, WHATCHA WATCHING?
YOUR DAD...EVERY TIME...
DAD!
EVERY. SINGLE. TIME.
FRIDAY NIGHT RITUAL. UNTIL...
WHAT ARE WE WATCHING TONIGHT?
DOESN'T MATTER.
...UNTIL BROCK CAME ALONG.

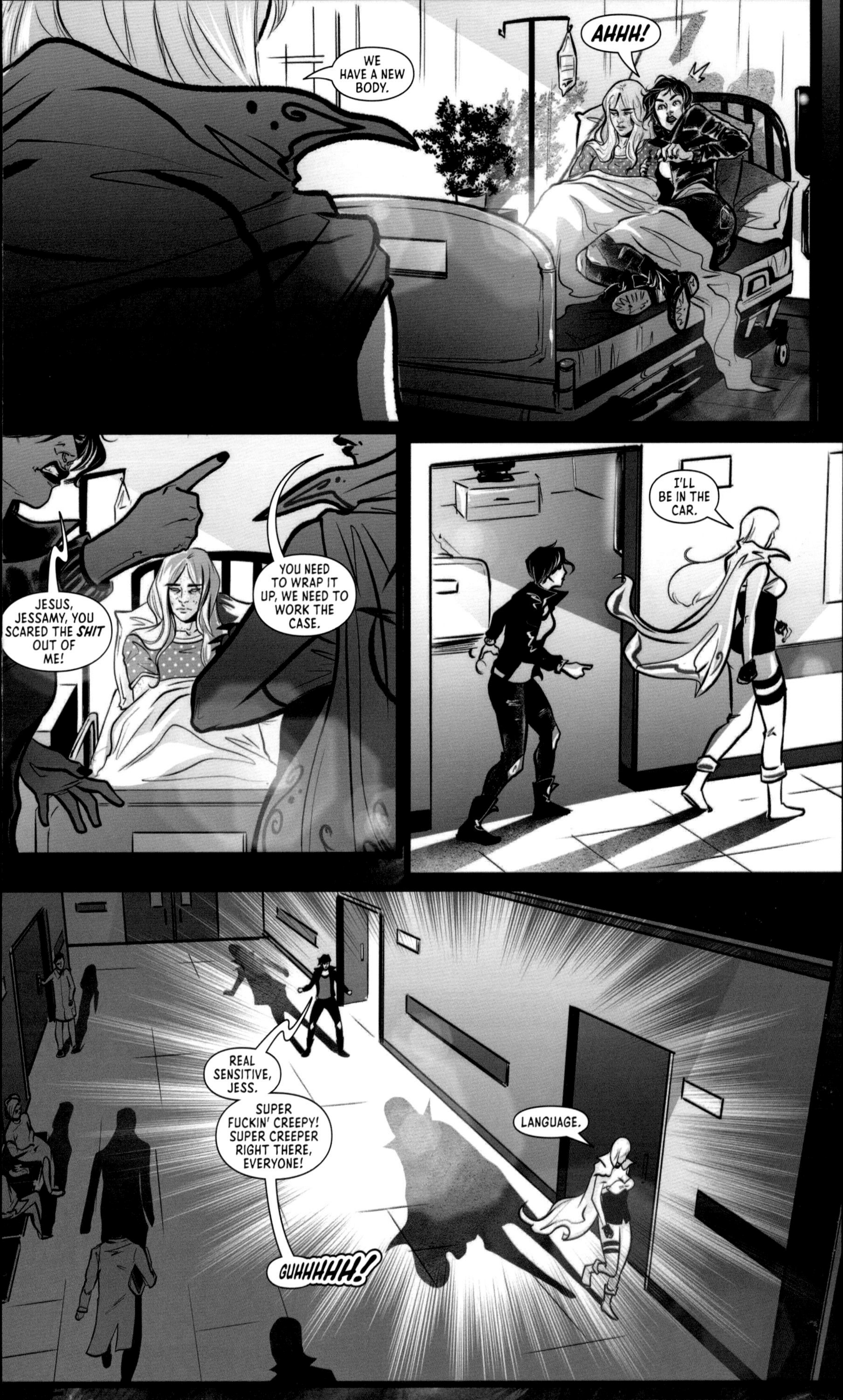
WE HAVE A NEW BODY.
AHHH!
JESUS, JESSAMY, YOU SCARED THE SHIT OUT OF ME!
YOU NEED TO WRAP IT UP, WE NEED TO WORK THE CASE.
I'LL BE IN THE CAR.
REAL SENSITIVE, JESS.
SUPER FUCKIN' CREEPY! SUPER CREEPER RIGHT THERE, EVERYONE!
GUHHHHH!
LANGUAGE.

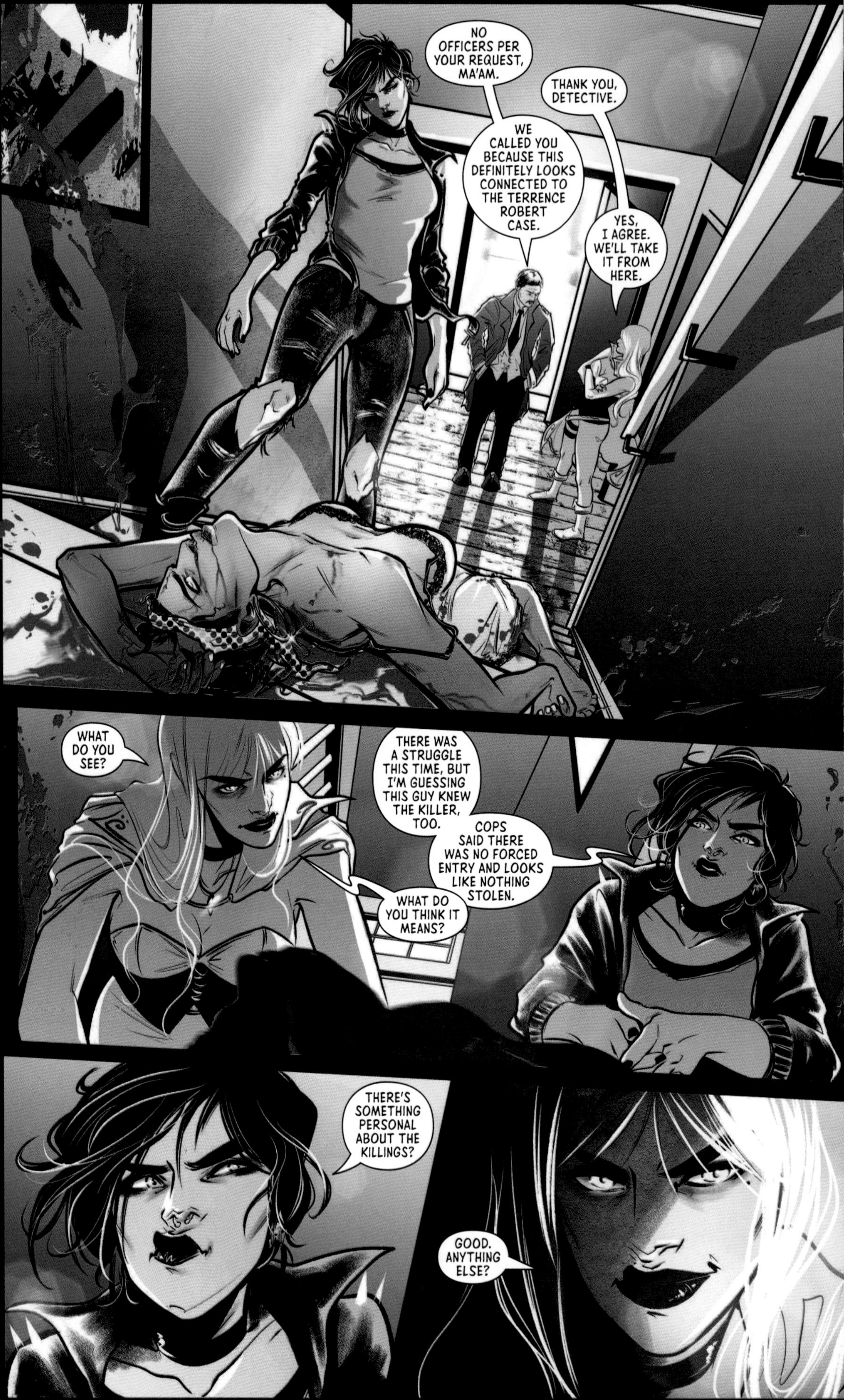
NO OFFICERS PER YOUR REQUEST, MA'AM.
WE CALLED YOU BECAUSE THIS DEFINITELY LOOKS CONNECTED TO THE TERRENCE ROBERT CASE.
THANK YOU, DETECTIVE.
YES, I AGREE. WE'LL TAKE IT FROM HERE.
WHAT DO YOU SEE?
THERE WAS A STRUGGLE THIS TIME, BUT I'M GUESSING THIS GUY KNEW THE KILLER, TOO.
COPS SAID THERE WAS NO FORCED ENTRY AND LOOKS LIKE NOTHING STOLEN.
WHAT DO YOU THINK IT MEANS?
THERE'S SOMETHING PERSONAL ABOUT THE KILLINGS?
GOOD. ANYTHING ELSE?

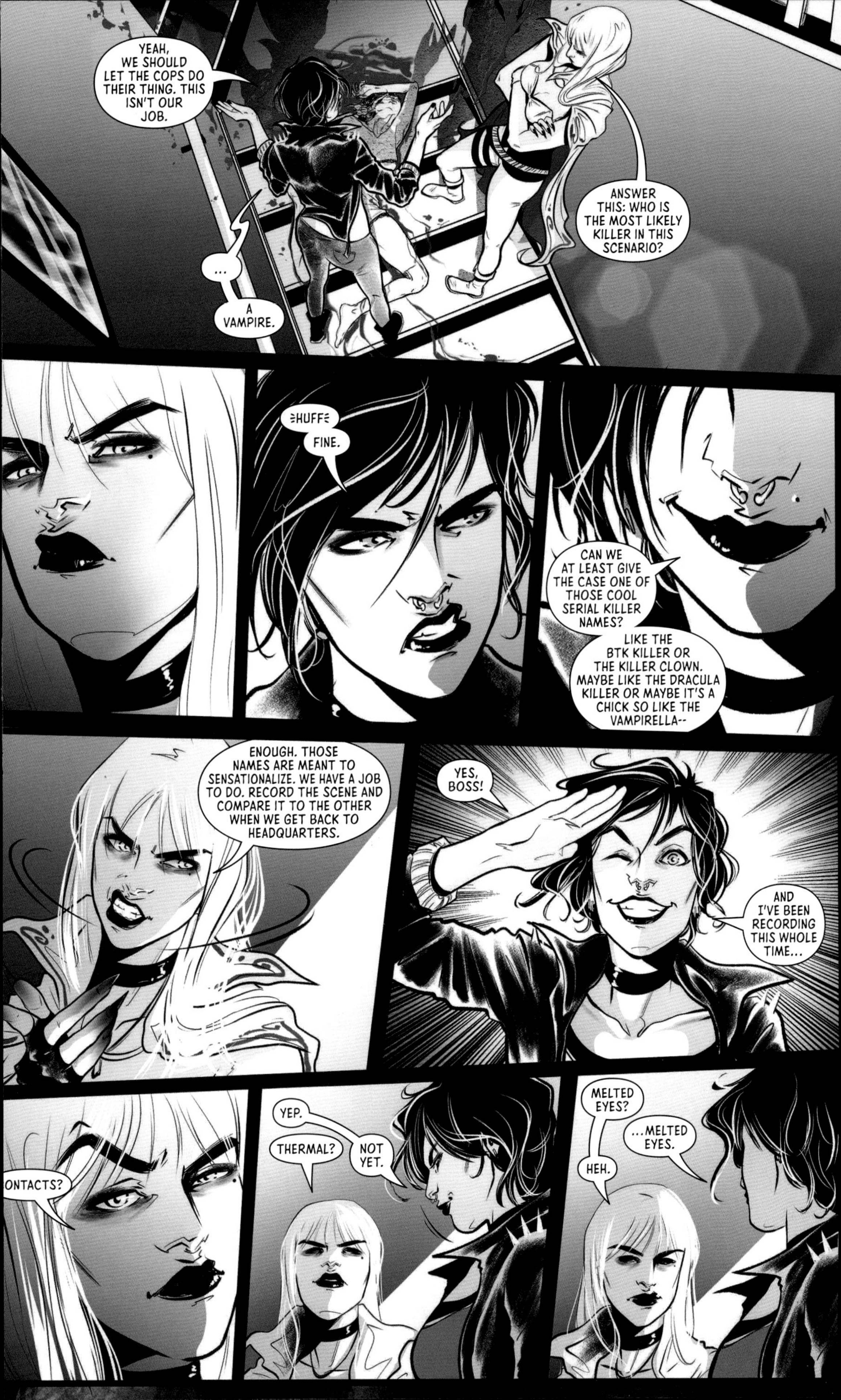
YEAH, WE SHOULD LET THE COPS DO THEIR THING. THIS ISN'T OUR JOB.
ANSWER THIS: WHO IS THE MOST LIKELY KILLER IN THIS SCENARIO?
...
A VAMPIRE.
HUFF
FINE.
CAN WE AT LEAST GIVE THE CASE ONE OF THOSE COOL SERIAL KILLER NAMES?
LIKE THE BTK KILLER OR THE KILLER CLOWN. MAYBE LIKE THE DRACULA KILLER OR MAYBE IT'S A CHICK SO LIKE THE VAMPIRELLA--
ENOUGH. THOSE NAMES ARE MEANT TO SENSATIONALIZE. WE HAVE A JOB TO DO. RECORD THE SCENE AND COMPARE IT TO THE OTHER WHEN WE GET BACK TO HEADQUARTERS.
YES, BOSS!
AND I'VE BEEN RECORDING THIS WHOLE TIME...
ONTACTS?
YEP.
THERMAL?
NOT YET.
MELTED EYES?
HEH.
...MELTED EYES.

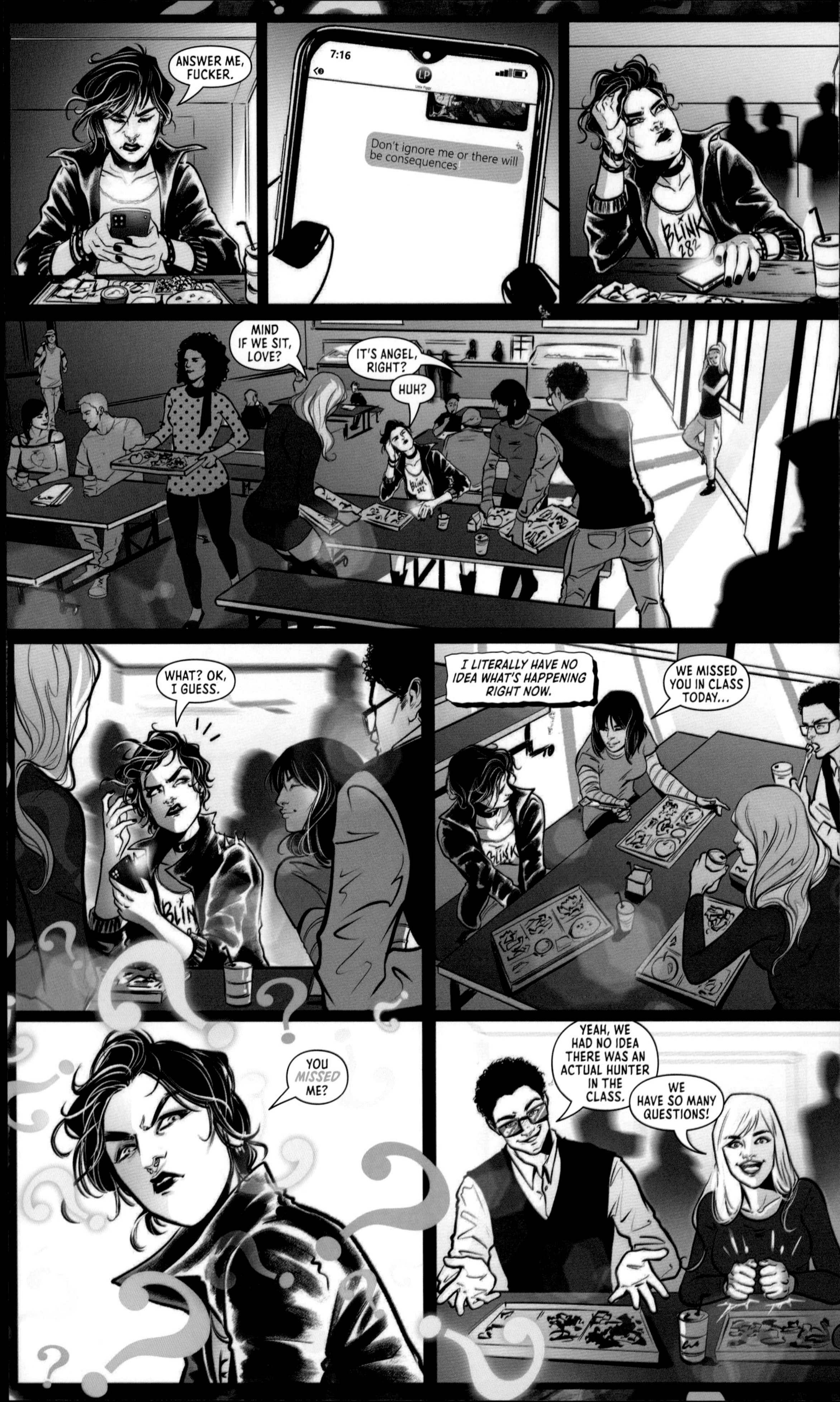
ANSWER ME, FUCKER.
7:16
LP
Don't ignore me or there will be consequences!
MIND IF WE SIT, LOVE?
IT'S ANGEL, RIGHT?
HUH?
WHAT? OK, I GUESS.
I LITERALLY HAVE NO IDEA WHAT'S HAPPENING RIGHT NOW.
WE MISSED YOU IN CLASS TODAY...
YOU *MISSED* ME?
YEAH, WE HAD NO IDEA THERE WAS AN ACTUAL HUNTER IN THE CLASS.
WE HAVE SO MANY QUESTIONS!

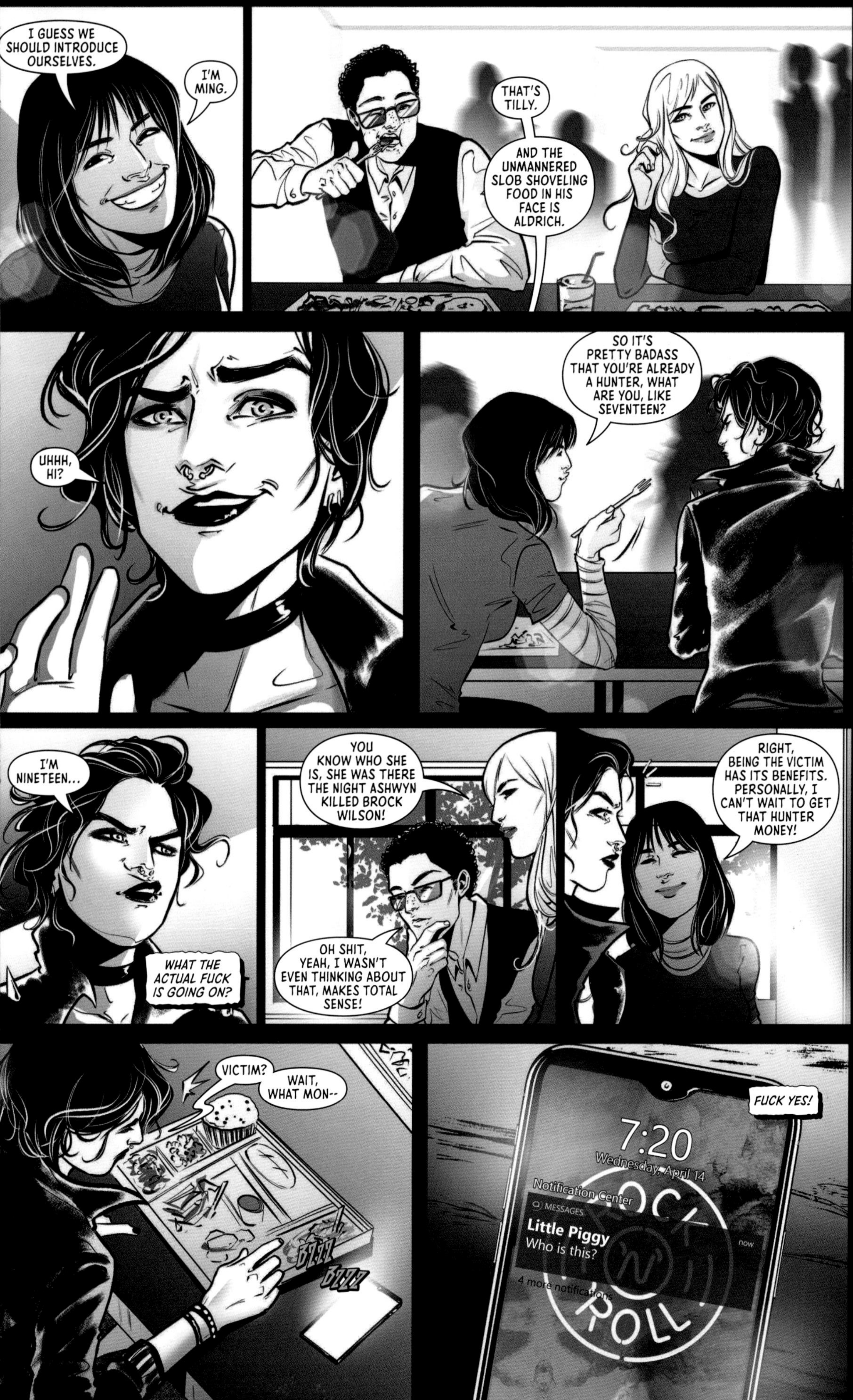
I GUESS WE SHOULD INTRODUCE OURSELVES.
I'M MING.
THAT'S TILLY.
AND THE UNMANNERED SLOB SHOVELING FOOD IN HIS FACE IS ALDRICH.
UHHH, HI?
SO IT'S PRETTY BADASS THAT YOU'RE ALREADY A HUNTER, WHAT ARE YOU, LIKE SEVENTEEN?
I'M NINETEEN...
WHAT THE ACTUAL FUCK IS GOING ON?
YOU KNOW WHO SHE IS, SHE WAS THERE THE NIGHT ASHWYN KILLED BROCK WILSON!
OH SHIT, YEAH, I WASN'T EVEN THINKING ABOUT THAT, MAKES TOTAL SENSE!
RIGHT, BEING THE VICTIM HAS ITS BENEFITS. PERSONALLY, I CAN'T WAIT TO GET THAT HUNTER MONEY!
VICTIM? WAIT, WHAT MON--
BZZZ
BZZZ
FUCK YES!
7:20
Wednesday, April 14
Notification Center
MESSAGES
Little Piggy
Who is this?
now
4 more notifications
ROCK N ROLL

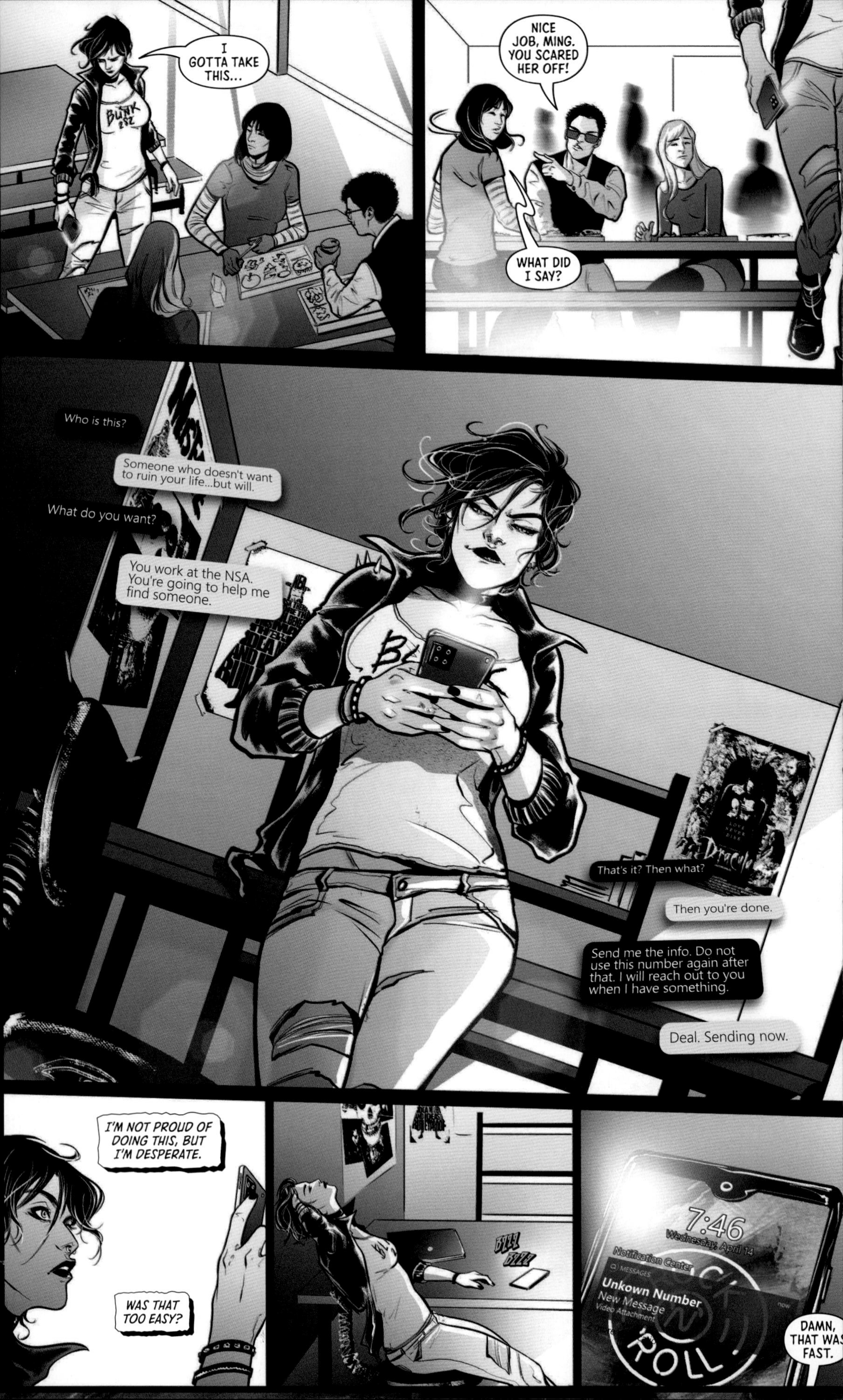
I GOTTA TAKE THIS...
BUNK 282
NICE JOB, MING. YOU SCARED HER OFF!
WHAT DID I SAY?
Who is this?
Someone who doesn't want to ruin your life...but will.
What do you want?
You work at the NSA. You're going to help me find someone.
That's it? Then what?
Then you're done.
Send me the info. Do not use this number again after that. I will reach out to you when I have something.
Deal. Sending now.
I'M NOT PROUD OF DOING THIS, BUT I'M DESPERATE.
WAS THAT TOO EASY?
7:46
Wednesday, April 14
Notification Center
Unkown Number
New Message
Video Attachment
ROLL
DAMN, THAT WAS FAST.

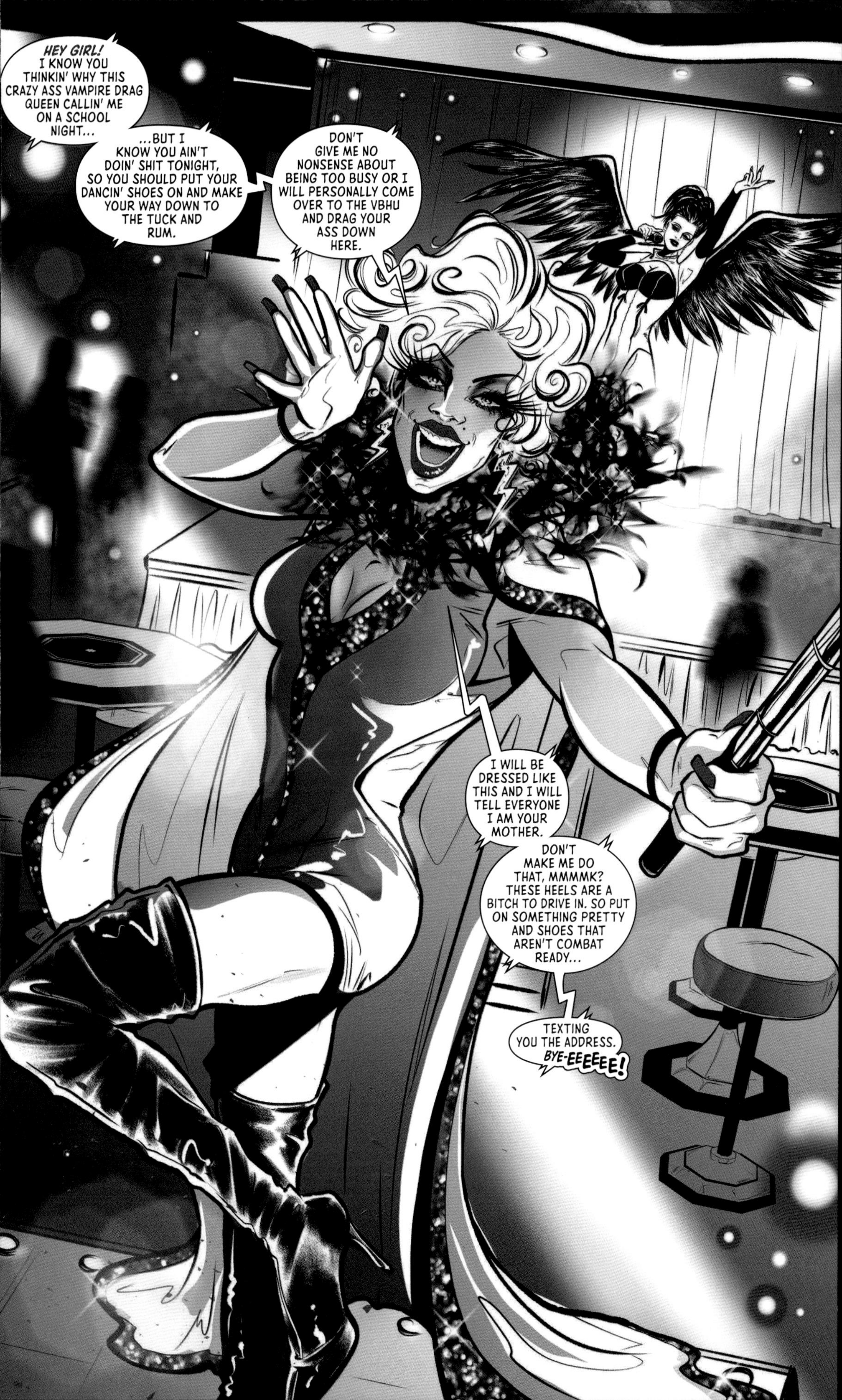
HEY GIRL! I KNOW YOU THINKIN' WHY THIS CRAZY ASS VAMPIRE DRAG QUEEN CALLIN' ME ON A SCHOOL NIGHT...
...BUT I KNOW YOU AIN'T DOIN' SHIT TONIGHT, SO YOU SHOULD PUT YOUR DANCIN' SHOES ON AND MAKE YOUR WAY DOWN TO THE TUCK AND RUM.
DON'T GIVE ME NO NONSENSE ABOUT BEING TOO BUSY OR I WILL PERSONALLY COME OVER TO THE VBHU AND DRAG YOUR ASS DOWN HERE.
I WILL BE DRESSED LIKE THIS AND I WILL TELL EVERYONE I AM YOUR MOTHER.
DON'T MAKE ME DO THAT, MMMMK? THESE HEELS ARE A BITCH TO DRIVE IN. SO PUT ON SOMETHING PRETTY AND SHOES THAT AREN'T COMBAT READY...
TEXTING YOU THE ADDRESS. BYE-EEEEEE!

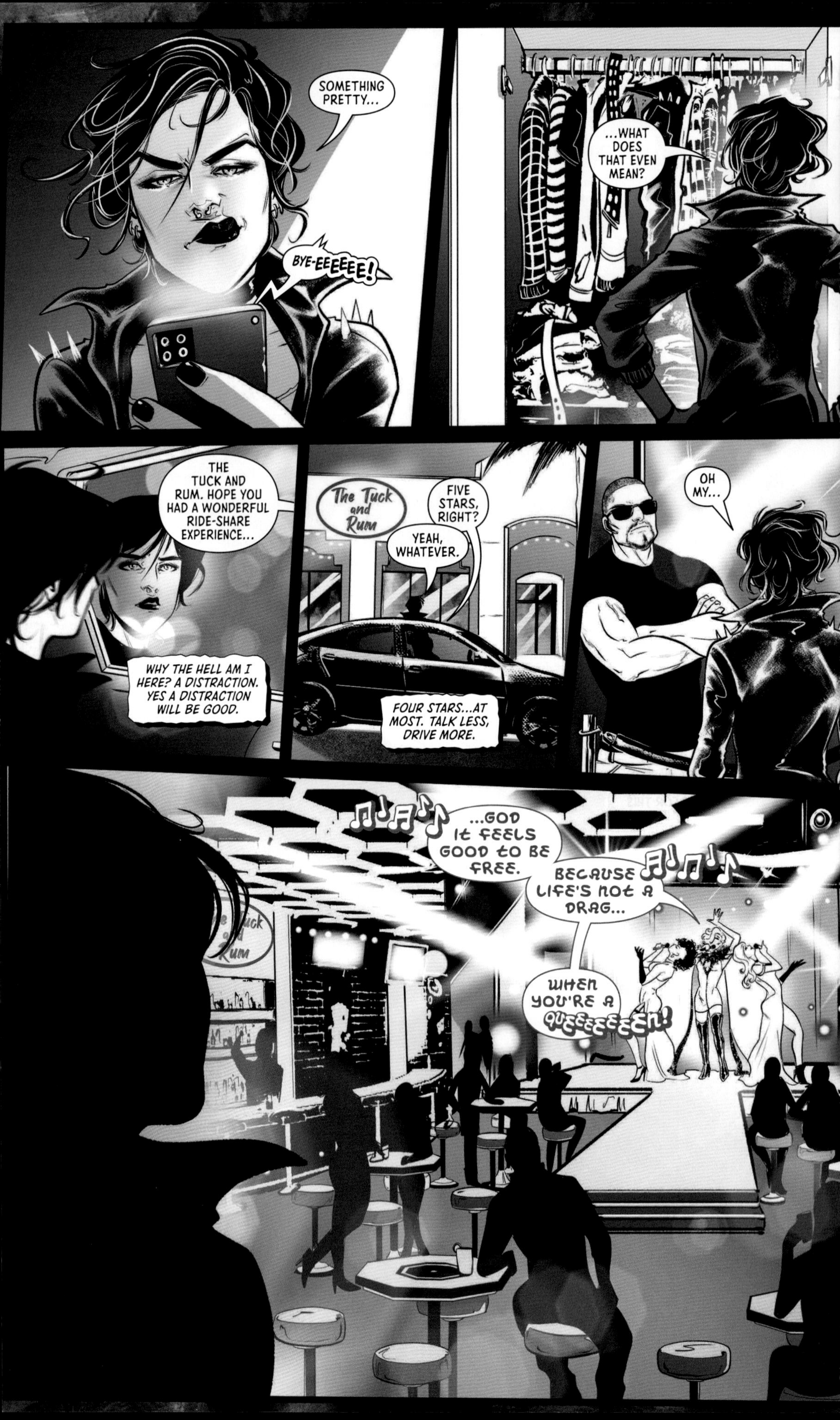
SOMETHING PRETTY...
BYE-EEEEEE!
...WHAT DOES THAT EVEN MEAN?
THE TUCK AND RUM. HOPE YOU HAD A WONDERFUL RIDE-SHARE EXPERIENCE...
WHY THE HELL AM I HERE? A DISTRACTION. YES A DISTRACTION WILL BE GOOD.
The Tuck and Rum
FIVE STARS, RIGHT?
YEAH, WHATEVER.
FOUR STARS...AT MOST. TALK LESS, DRIVE MORE.
OH MY...
...GOD IT FEELS GOOD TO BE FREE.
BECAUSE LIFE'S NOT A DRAG...
WHEN YOU'RE A QUEEEEEEEN!

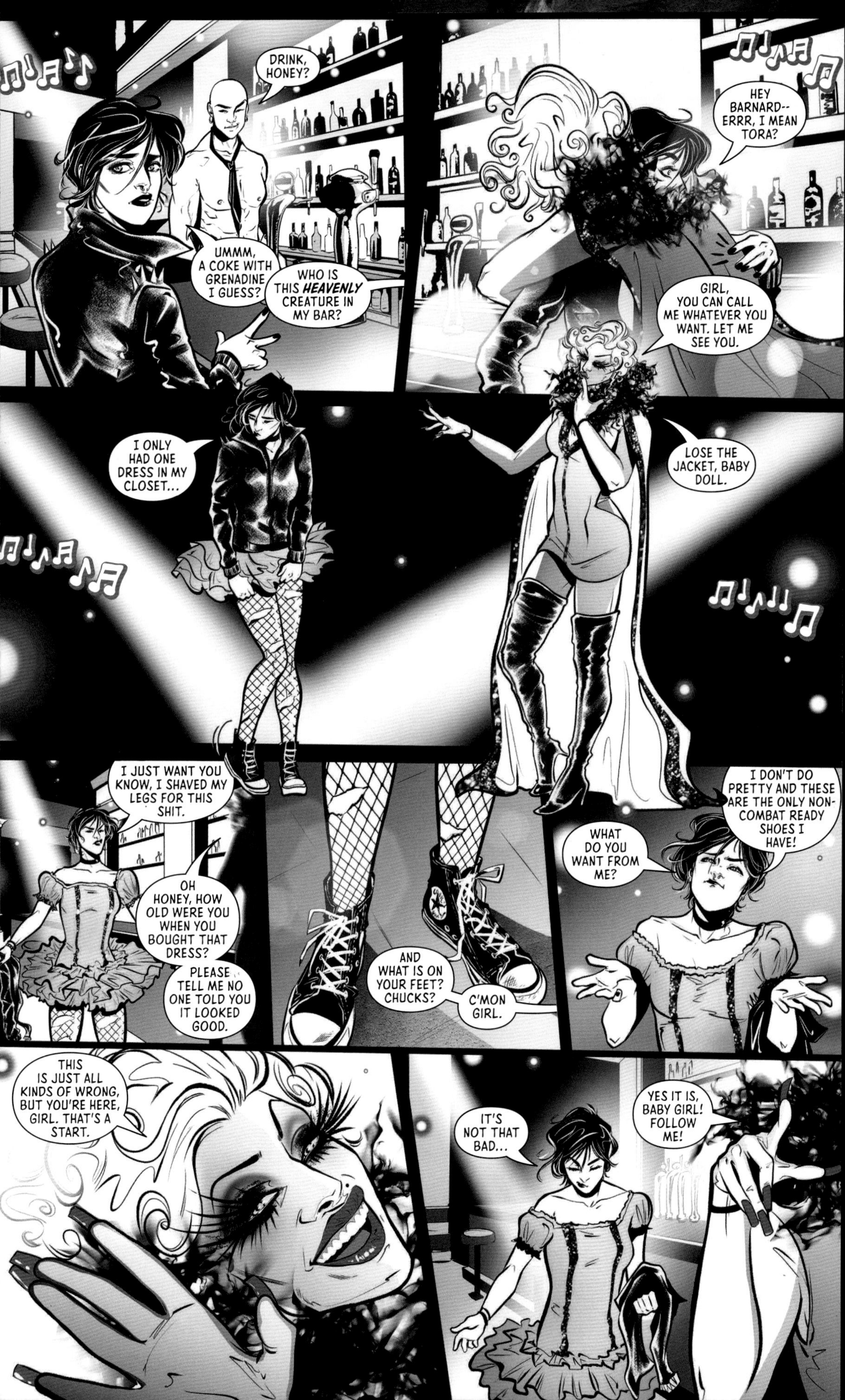
DRINK, HONEY?
UMMM, A COKE WITH GRENADINE I GUESS?
WHO IS THIS *HEAVENLY* CREATURE IN MY BAR?
HEY BARNARD-- ERRR, I MEAN TORA?
GIRL, YOU CAN CALL ME WHATEVER YOU WANT. LET ME SEE YOU.
I ONLY HAD ONE DRESS IN MY CLOSET...
LOSE THE JACKET, BABY DOLL.
I JUST WANT YOU KNOW, I SHAVED MY LEGS FOR THIS SHIT.
OH HONEY, HOW OLD WERE YOU WHEN YOU BOUGHT THAT DRESS?
PLEASE TELL ME NO ONE TOLD YOU IT LOOKED GOOD.
AND WHAT IS ON YOUR FEET? CHUCKS?
C'MON GIRL.
WHAT DO YOU WANT FROM ME?
I DON'T DO PRETTY AND THESE ARE THE ONLY NON-COMBAT READY SHOES I HAVE!
THIS IS JUST ALL KINDS OF WRONG, BUT YOU'RE HERE, GIRL. THAT'S A START.
IT'S NOT THAT BAD...
YES IT IS, BABY GIRL! FOLLOW ME!

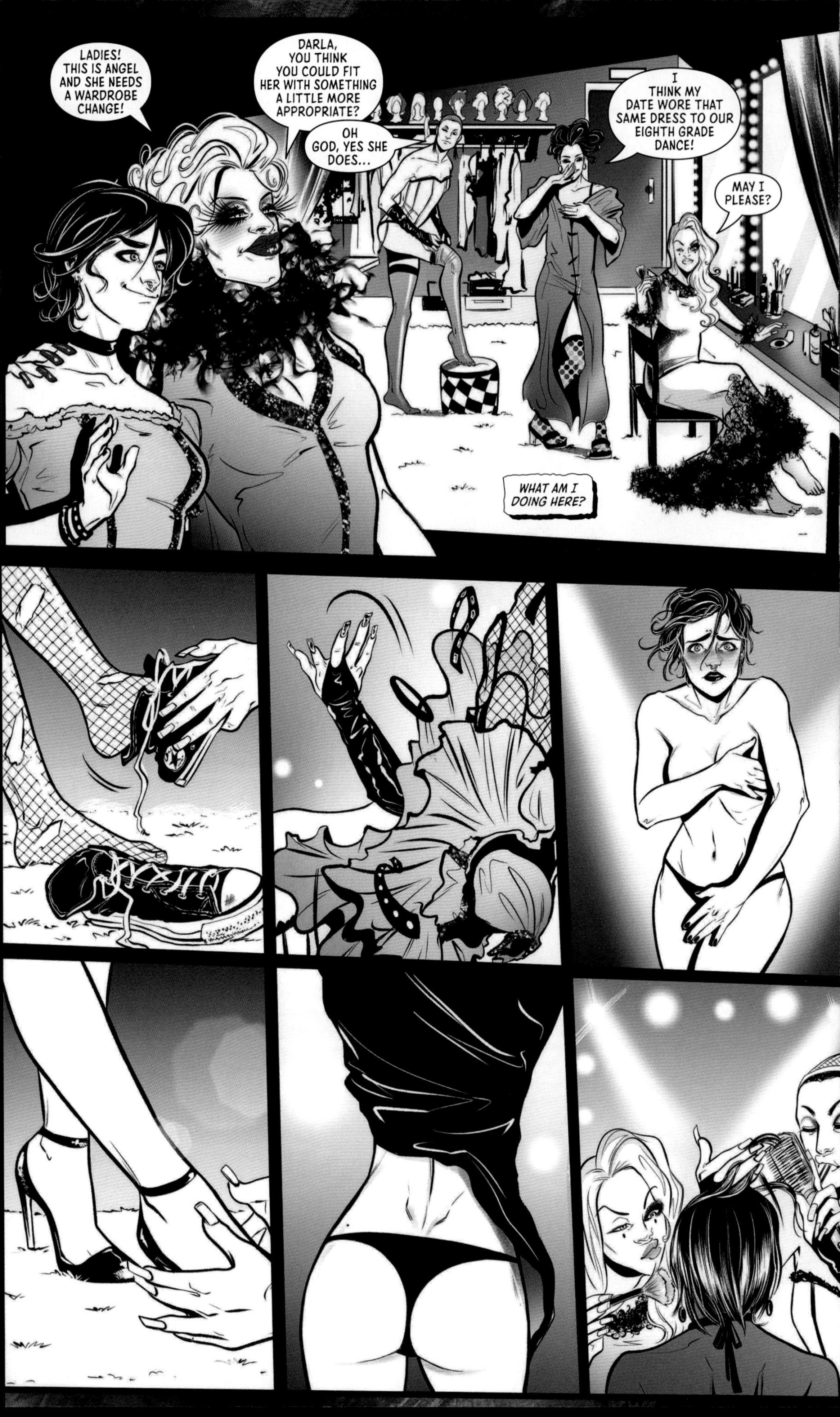
LADIES! THIS IS ANGEL AND SHE NEEDS A WARDROBE CHANGE!
DARLA, YOU THINK YOU COULD FIT HER WITH SOMETHING A LITTLE MORE APPROPRIATE?
OH GOD, YES SHE DOES...
I THINK MY DATE WORE THAT SAME DRESS TO OUR EIGHTH GRADE DANCE!
MAY I PLEASE?
WHAT AM I DOING HERE?

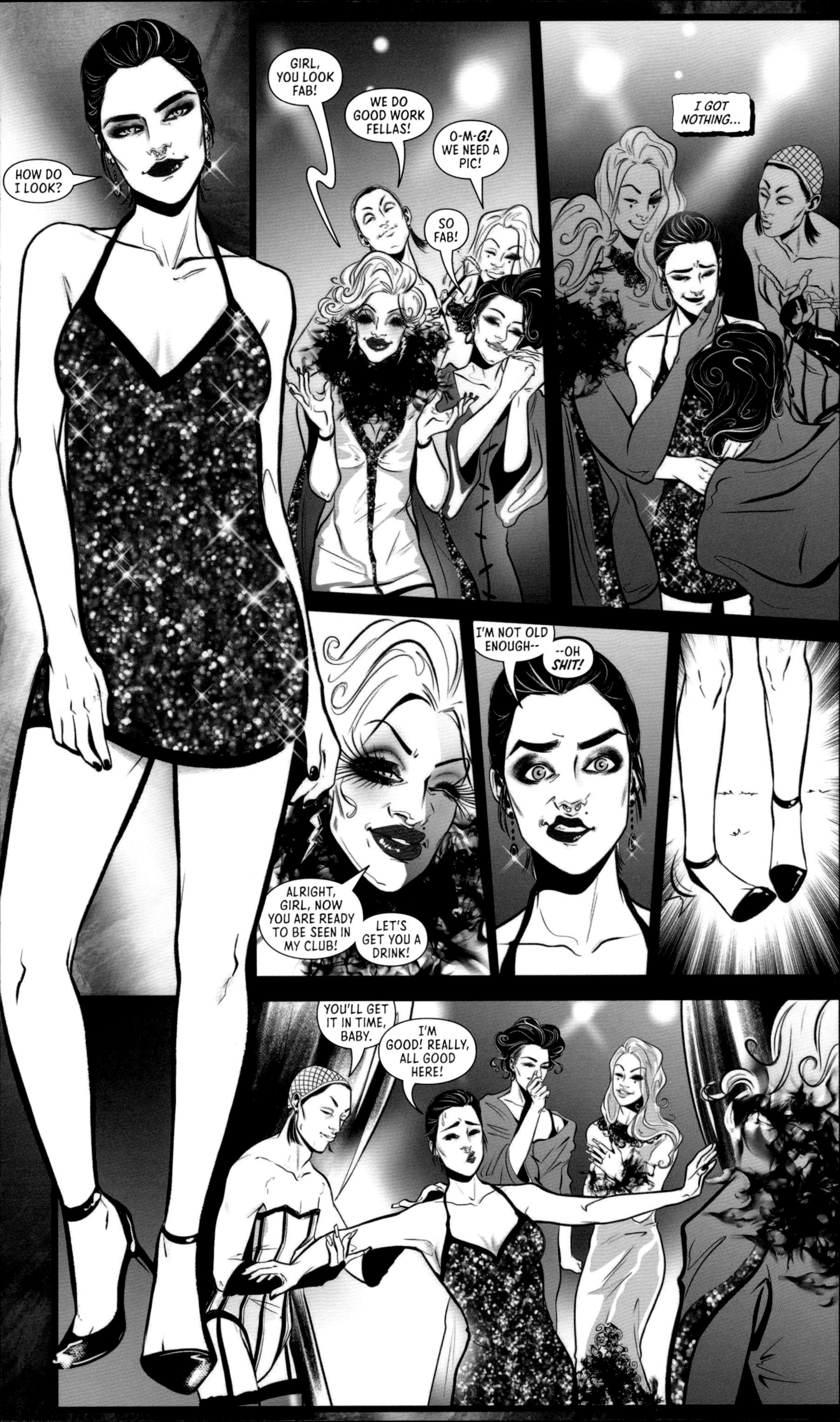
HOW DO I LOOK?
GIRL, YOU LOOK FAB!
WE DO GOOD WORK FELLAS!
O-M-G! WE NEED A PIC!
SO FAB!
I GOT NOTHING...
ALRIGHT, GIRL, NOW YOU ARE READY TO BE SEEN IN MY CLUB!
LET'S GET YOU A DRINK!
I'M NOT OLD ENOUGH--
--OH SHIT!
YOU'LL GET IT IN TIME, BABY.
I'M GOOD! REALLY, ALL GOOD HERE!

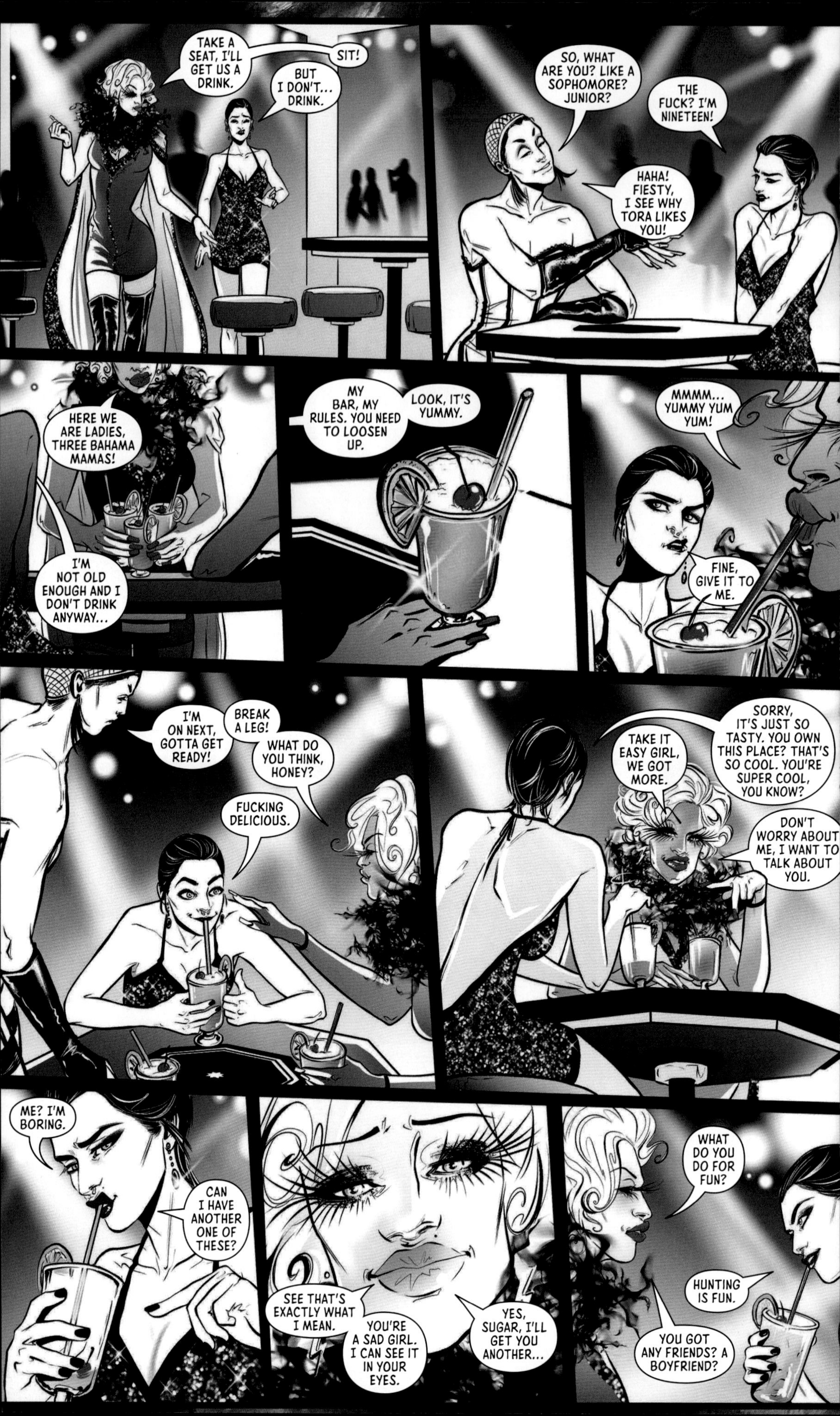
TAKE A SEAT, I'LL GET US A DRINK.
SIT!
BUT I DON'T... DRINK.
SO, WHAT ARE YOU? LIKE A SOPHOMORE? JUNIOR?
THE FUCK? I'M NINETEEN!
HAHA! FIESTY, I SEE WHY TORA LIKES YOU!
HERE WE ARE LADIES, THREE BAHAMA MAMAS!
I'M NOT OLD ENOUGH AND I DON'T DRINK ANYWAY...
MY BAR, MY RULES. YOU NEED TO LOOSEN UP.
LOOK, IT'S YUMMY.
MMMM... YUMMY YUM YUM!
FINE, GIVE IT TO ME.
I'M ON NEXT, GOTTA GET READY!
BREAK A LEG!
WHAT DO YOU THINK, HONEY?
FUCKING DELICIOUS.
TAKE IT EASY GIRL, WE GOT MORE.
SORRY, IT'S JUST SO TASTY. YOU OWN THIS PLACE? THAT'S SO COOL. YOU'RE SUPER COOL, YOU KNOW?
DON'T WORRY ABOUT ME, I WANT TO TALK ABOUT YOU.
ME? I'M BORING.
CAN I HAVE ANOTHER ONE OF THESE?
SEE THAT'S EXACTLY WHAT I MEAN.
YOU'RE A SAD GIRL. I CAN SEE IT IN YOUR EYES.
YES, SUGAR, I'LL GET YOU ANOTHER...
WHAT DO YOU DO FOR FUN?
HUNTING IS FUN.
YOU GOT ANY FRIENDS? A BOYFRIEND?

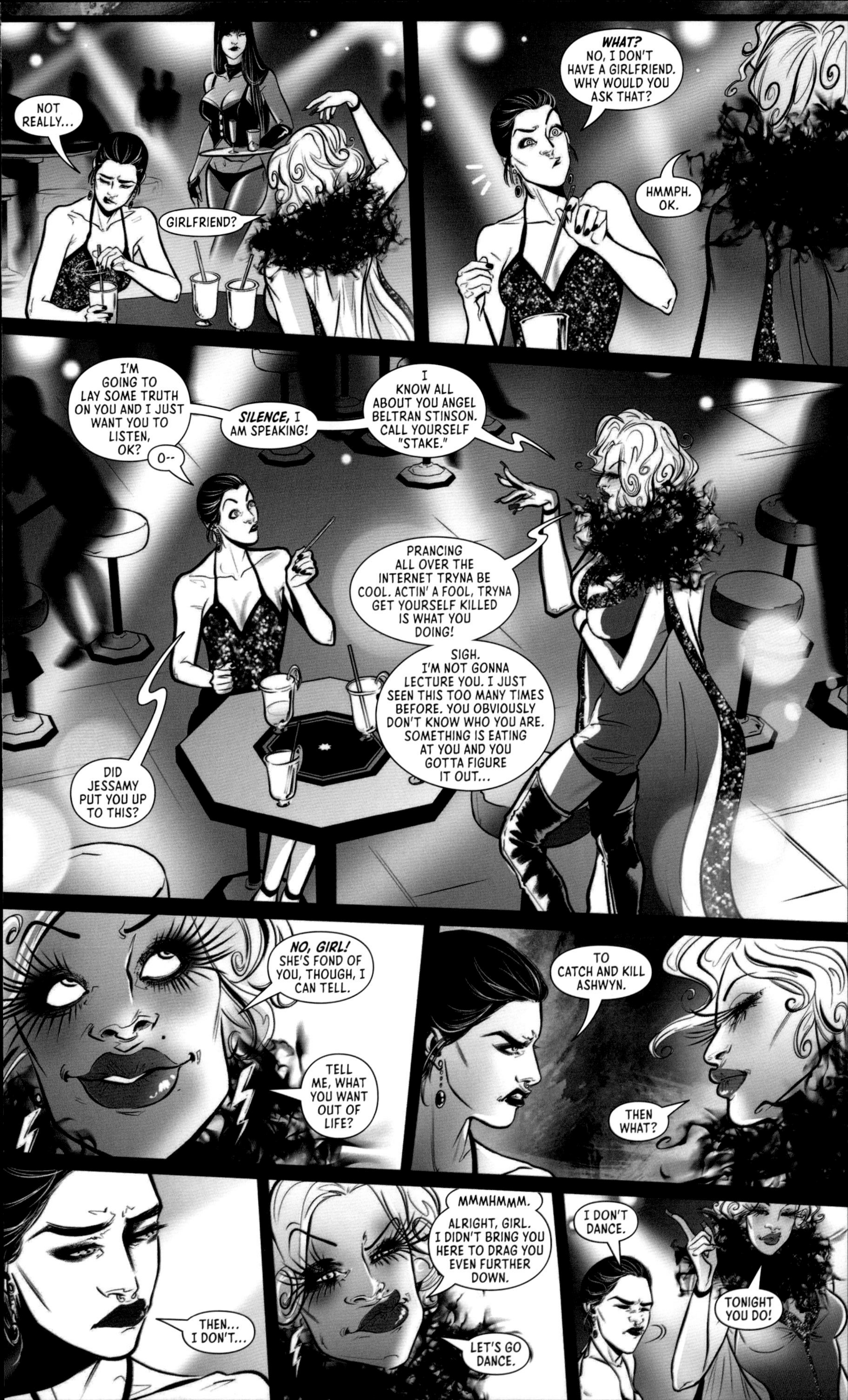
NOT REALLY...
GIRLFRIEND?
WHAT? NO, I DON'T HAVE A GIRLFRIEND. WHY WOULD YOU ASK THAT?
HMMPH. OK.
I'M GOING TO LAY SOME TRUTH ON YOU AND I JUST WANT YOU TO LISTEN, OK?
O--
SILENCE, I AM SPEAKING!
I KNOW ALL ABOUT YOU ANGEL BELTRAN STINSON. CALL YOURSELF "STAKE."
PRANCING ALL OVER THE INTERNET TRYNA BE COOL. ACTIN' A FOOL, TRYNA GET YOURSELF KILLED IS WHAT YOU DOING!
SIGH. I'M NOT GONNA LECTURE YOU. I JUST SEEN THIS TOO MANY TIMES BEFORE. YOU OBVIOUSLY DON'T KNOW WHO YOU ARE. SOMETHING IS EATING AT YOU AND YOU GOTTA FIGURE IT OUT...
DID JESSAMY PUT YOU UP TO THIS?
NO, GIRL! SHE'S FOND OF YOU, THOUGH, I CAN TELL.
TELL ME, WHAT YOU WANT OUT OF LIFE?
TO CATCH AND KILL ASHWYN.
THEN WHAT?
THEN... I DON'T...
MMMHMMM.
ALRIGHT, GIRL. I DIDN'T BRING YOU HERE TO DRAG YOU EVEN FURTHER DOWN.
LET'S GO DANCE.
I DON'T DANCE.
TONIGHT YOU DO!

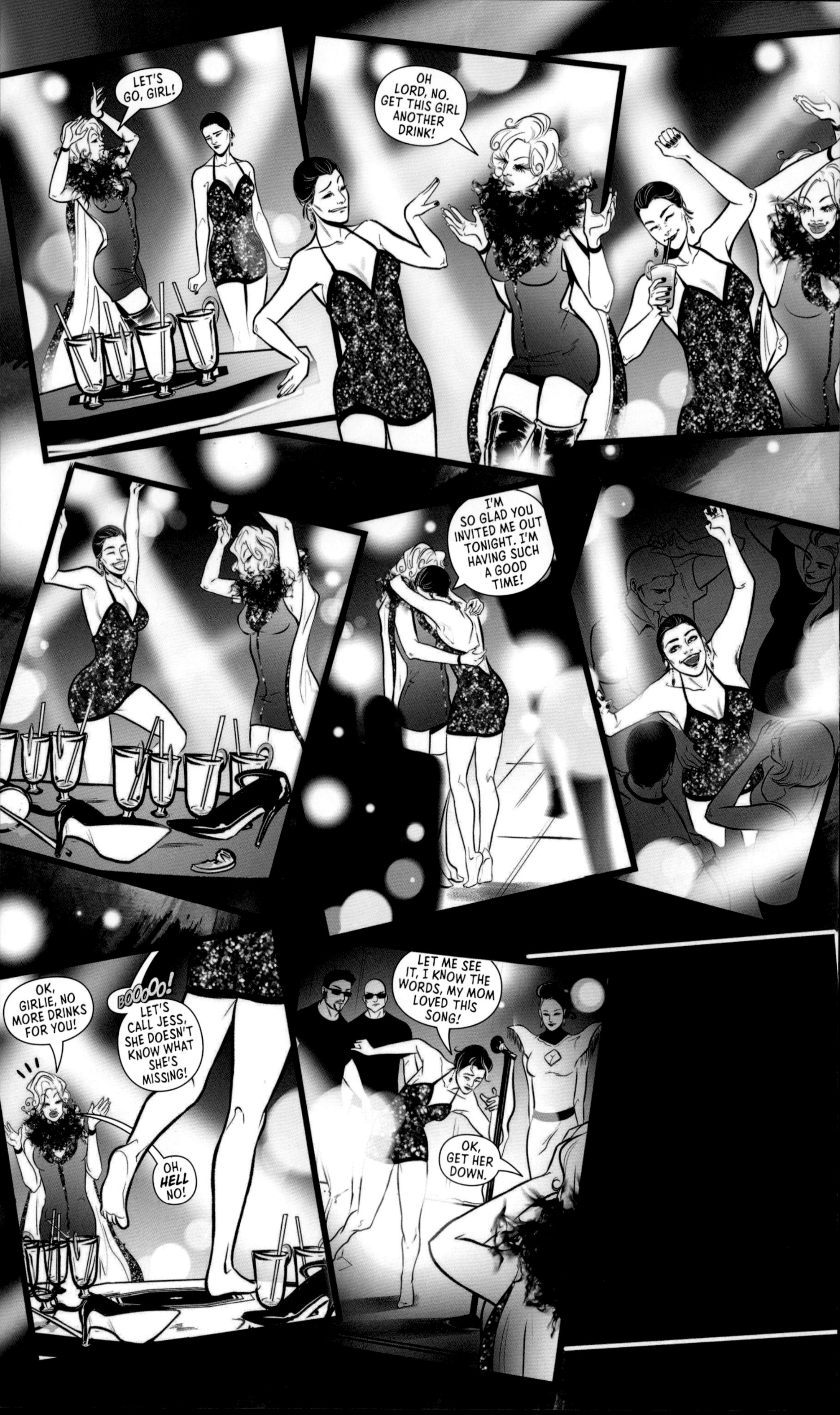
LET'S GO, GIRL!
OH LORD, NO. GET THIS GIRL ANOTHER DRINK!
I'M SO GLAD YOU INVITED ME OUT TONIGHT. I'M HAVING SUCH A GOOD TIME!
OK, GIRLIE, NO MORE DRINKS FOR YOU!
BOOOOO!
LET'S CALL JESS, SHE DOESN'T KNOW WHAT SHE'S MISSING!
OH, HELL NO!
LET ME SEE IT, I KNOW THE WORDS, MY MOM LOVED THIS SONG!
OK, GET HER DOWN.

End Chapter Four

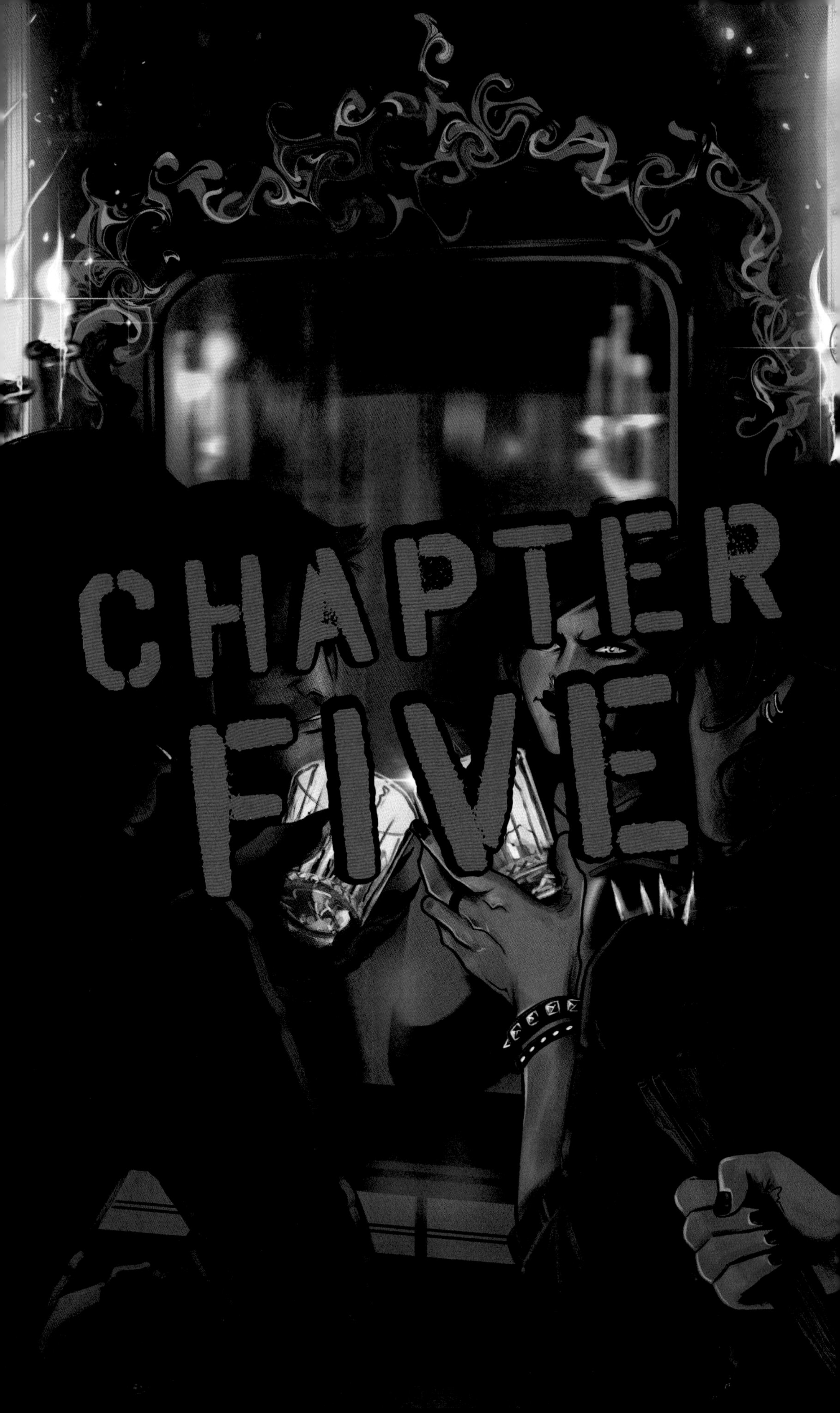
CHAPTER
FIVE

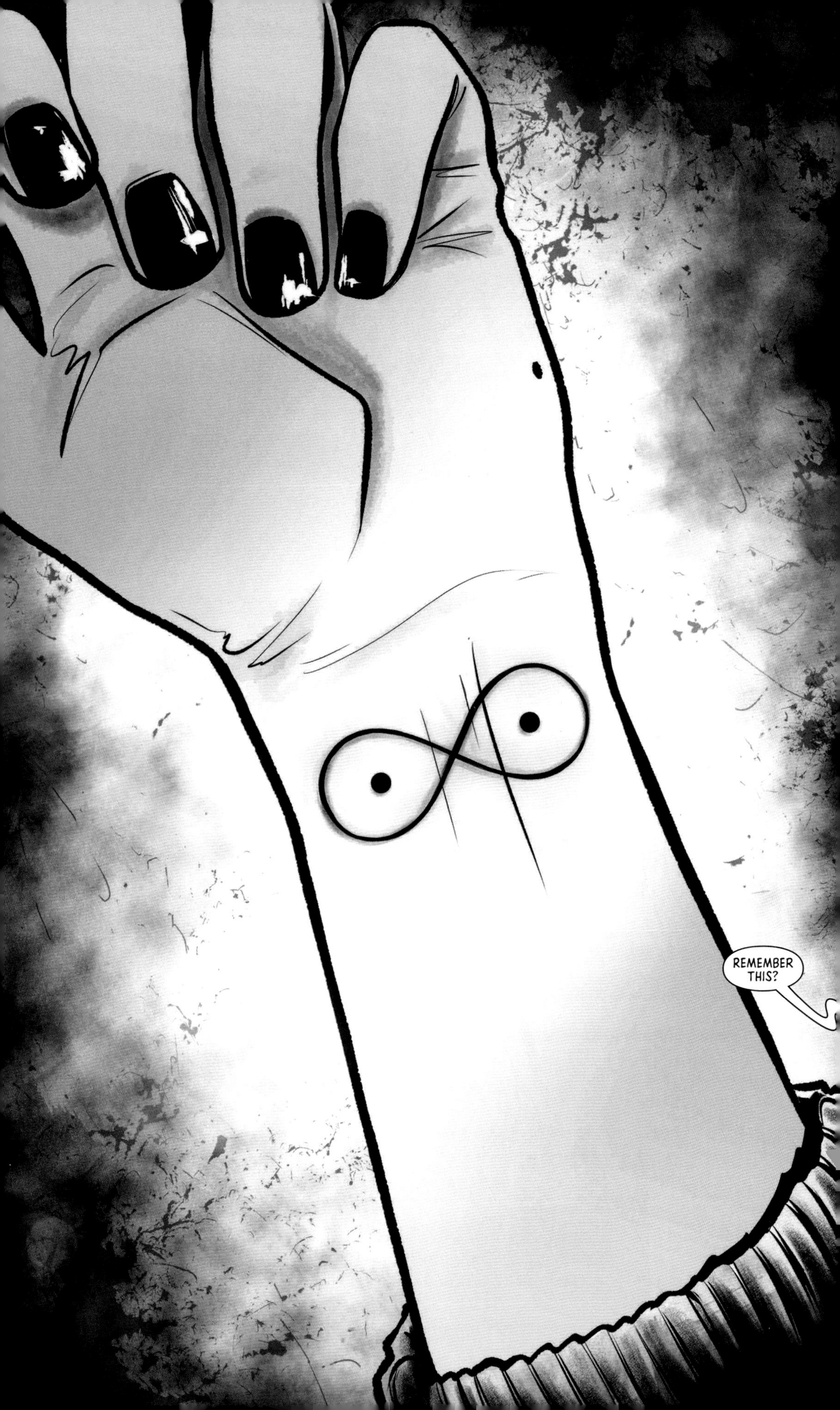
REMEMBER THIS?

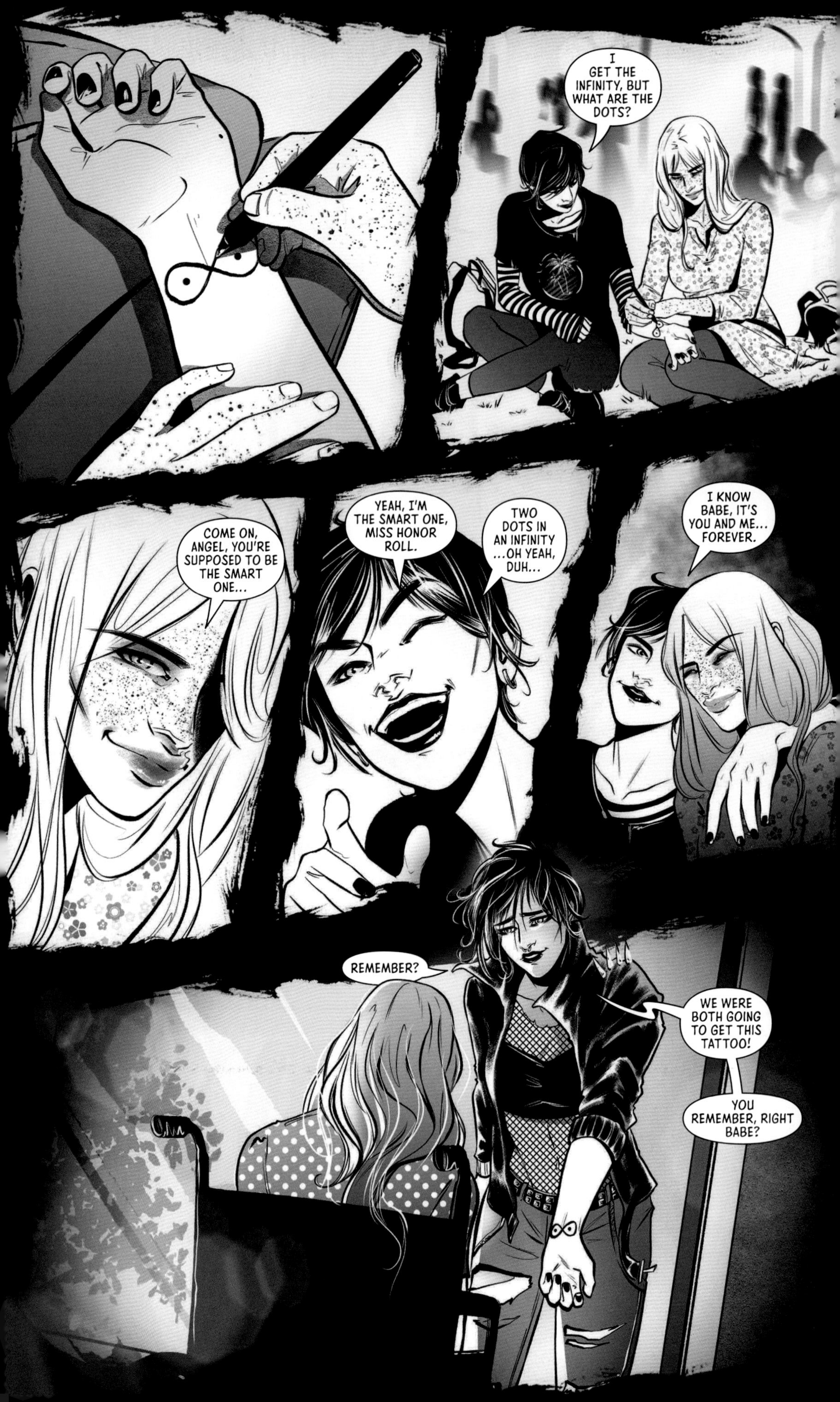
I GET THE INFINITY, BUT WHAT ARE THE DOTS?
COME ON, ANGEL, YOU'RE SUPPOSED TO BE THE SMART ONE...
YEAH, I'M THE SMART ONE, MISS HONOR ROLL.
TWO DOTS IN AN INFINITY ...OH YEAH, DUH...
I KNOW BABE, IT'S YOU AND ME... FOREVER.
REMEMBER?
WE WERE BOTH GOING TO GET THIS TATTOO!
YOU REMEMBER, RIGHT BABE?

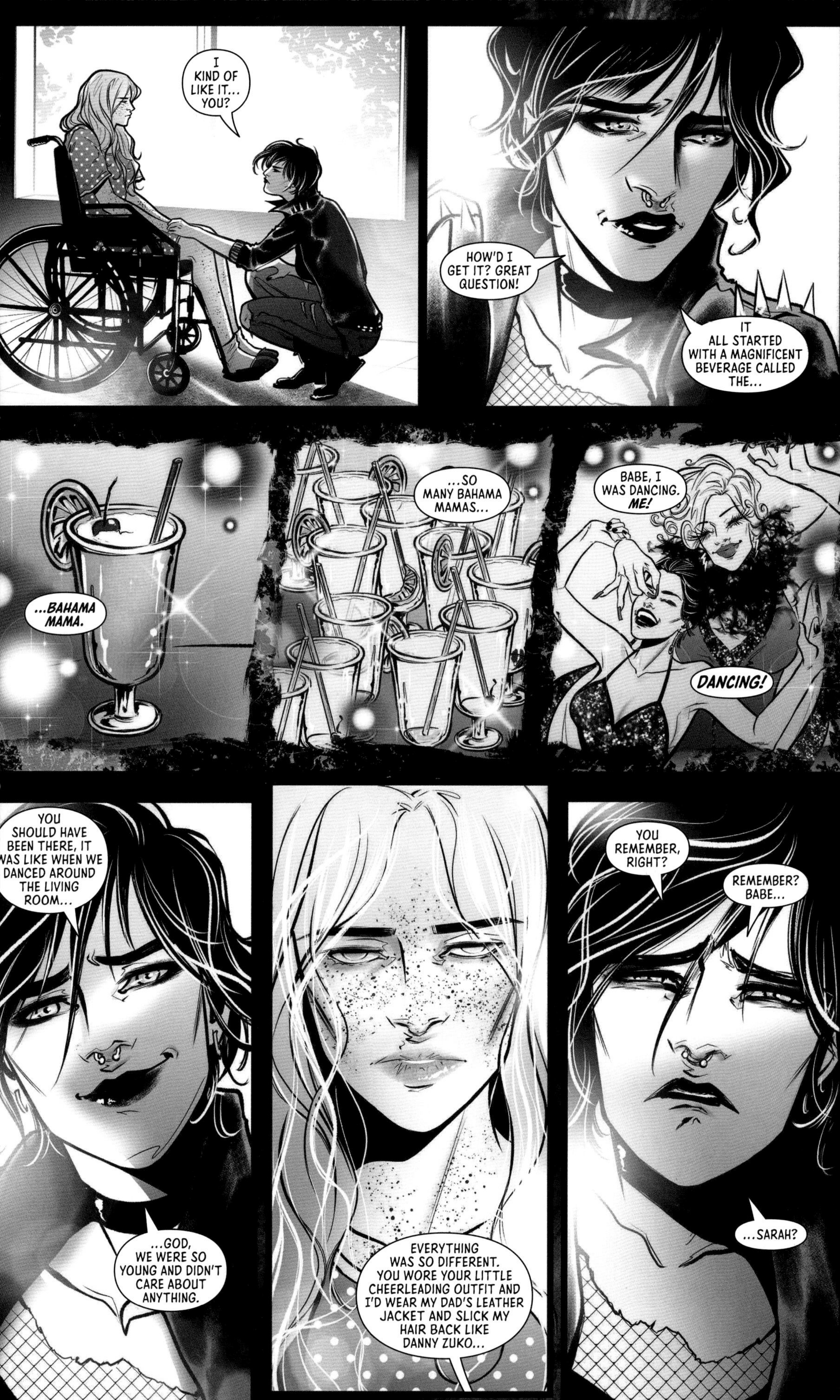

I KIND OF LIKE IT... YOU?
HOW'D I GET IT? GREAT QUESTION!
IT ALL STARTED WITH A MAGNIFICENT BEVERAGE CALLED THE...
...BAHAMA MAMA.
...SO MANY BAHAMA MAMAS...
BABE, I WAS DANCING. ME!
DANCING!
YOU SHOULD HAVE BEEN THERE, IT WAS LIKE WHEN WE DANCED AROUND THE LIVING ROOM...
...GOD, WE WERE SO YOUNG AND DIDN'T CARE ABOUT ANYTHING.
EVERYTHING WAS SO DIFFERENT. YOU WORE YOUR LITTLE CHEERLEADING OUTFIT AND I'D WEAR MY DAD'S LEATHER JACKET AND SLICK MY HAIR BACK LIKE DANNY ZUKO...
YOU REMEMBER, RIGHT?
REMEMBER? BABE...
...SARAH?

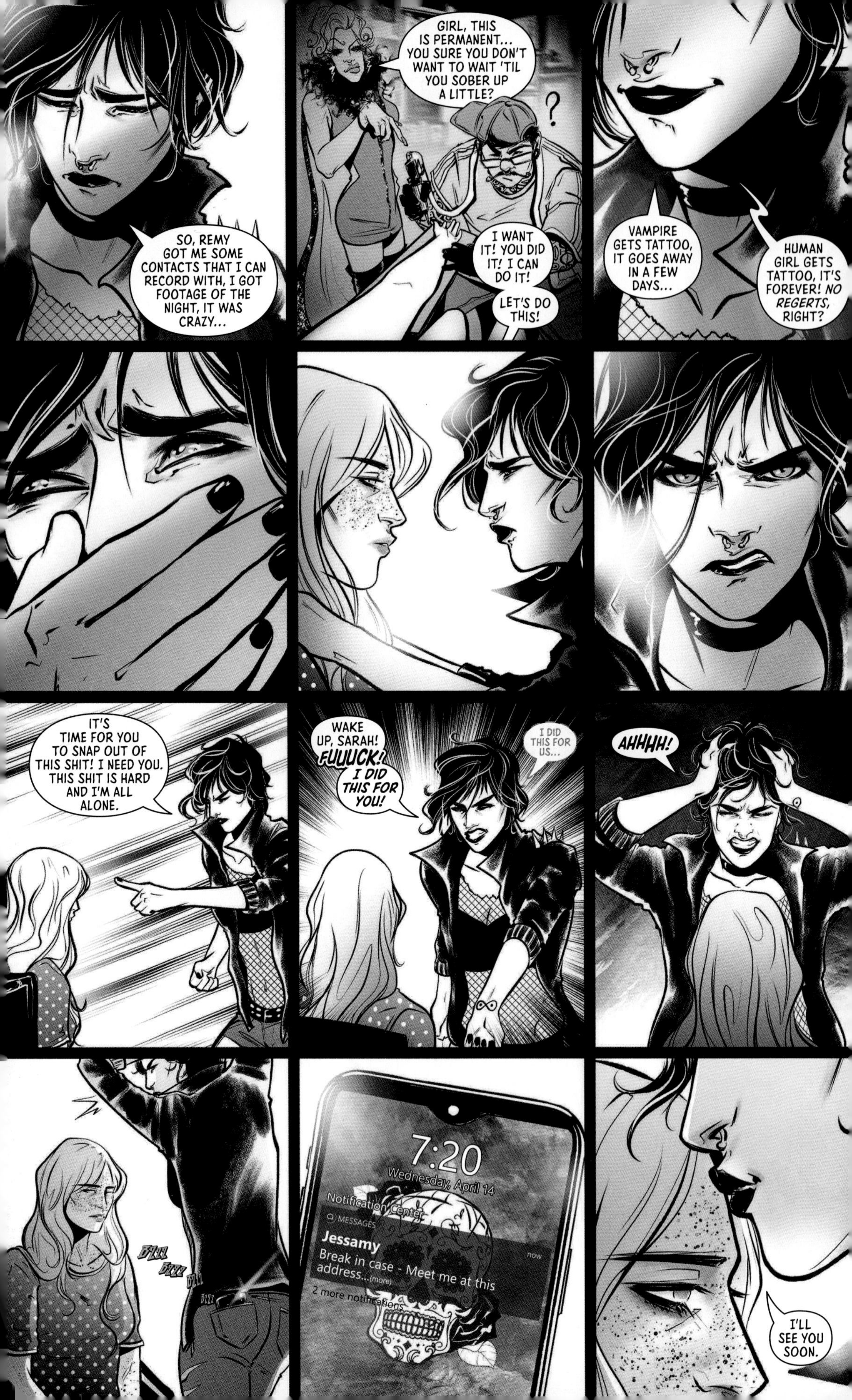

SO, REMY GOT ME SOME CONTACTS THAT I CAN RECORD WITH, I GOT FOOTAGE OF THE NIGHT, IT WAS CRAZY...
GIRL, THIS IS PERMANENT... YOU SURE YOU DON'T WANT TO WAIT 'TIL YOU SOBER UP A LITTLE?
?
I WANT IT! YOU DID IT! I CAN DO IT!
LET'S DO THIS!
VAMPIRE GETS TATTOO, IT GOES AWAY IN A FEW DAYS...
HUMAN GIRL GETS TATTOO, IT'S FOREVER! *NO REGERTS,* RIGHT?
IT'S TIME FOR YOU TO SNAP OUT OF THIS SHIT! I NEED YOU. THIS SHIT IS HARD AND I'M ALL ALONE.
WAKE UP, SARAH!
FUUUCK!
I DID THIS FOR YOU!
I DID THIS FOR US...
AHHHH!
BZZZ
BZZZ
BZZZ
BZZZ
7:20
Wednesday, April 14
Notification Center
MESSAGES
Jessamy
now
Break in case - Meet me at this address...(more)
2 more notifications
I'LL SEE YOU SOON.

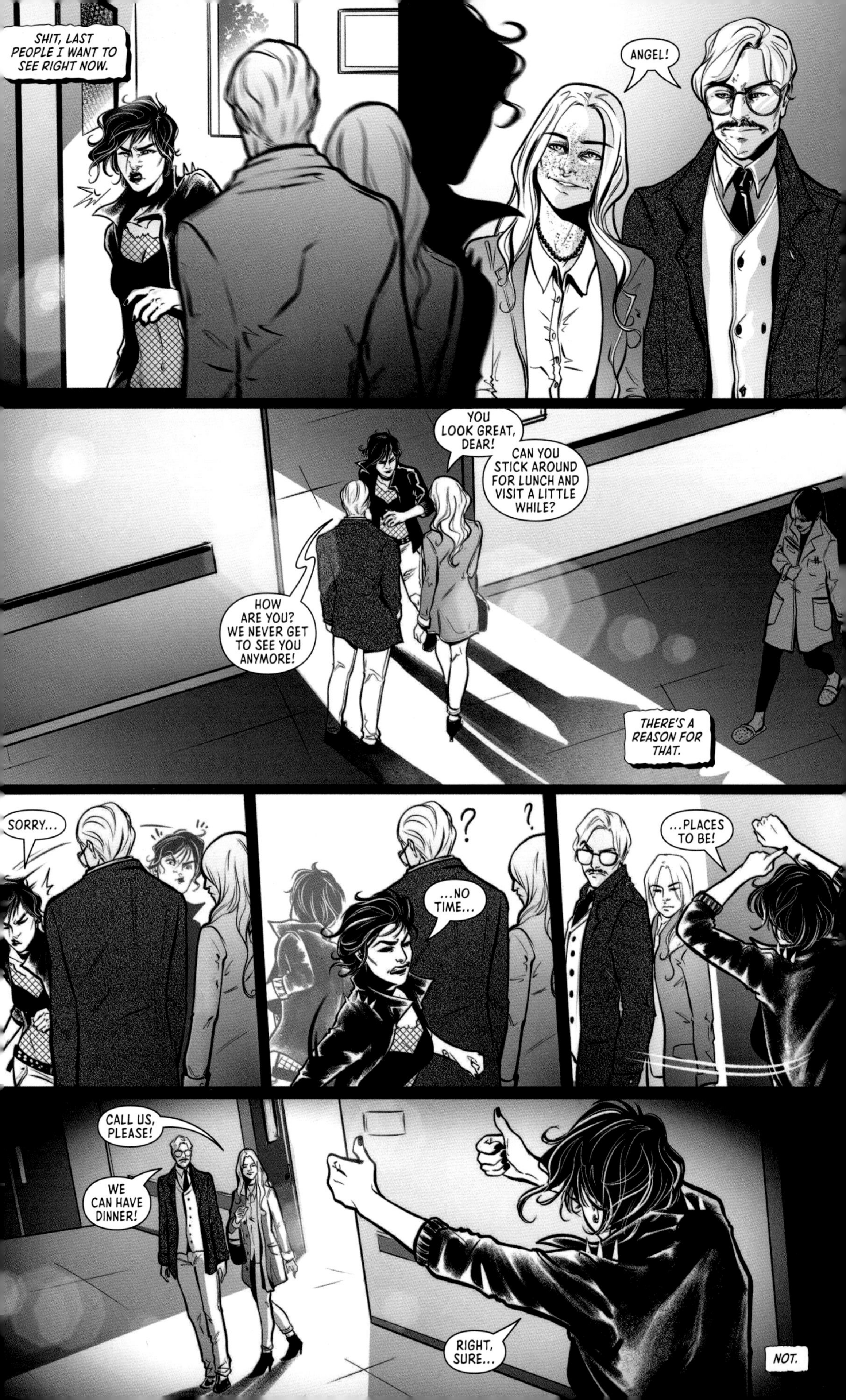

SHIT, LAST PEOPLE I WANT TO SEE RIGHT NOW.
ANGEL!
YOU LOOK GREAT, DEAR!
CAN YOU STICK AROUND FOR LUNCH AND VISIT A LITTLE WHILE?
HOW ARE YOU? WE NEVER GET TO SEE YOU ANYMORE!
THERE'S A REASON FOR THAT.
SORRY...
...NO TIME...
...PLACES TO BE!
CALL US, PLEASE!
WE CAN HAVE DINNER!
RIGHT, SURE...
NOT.

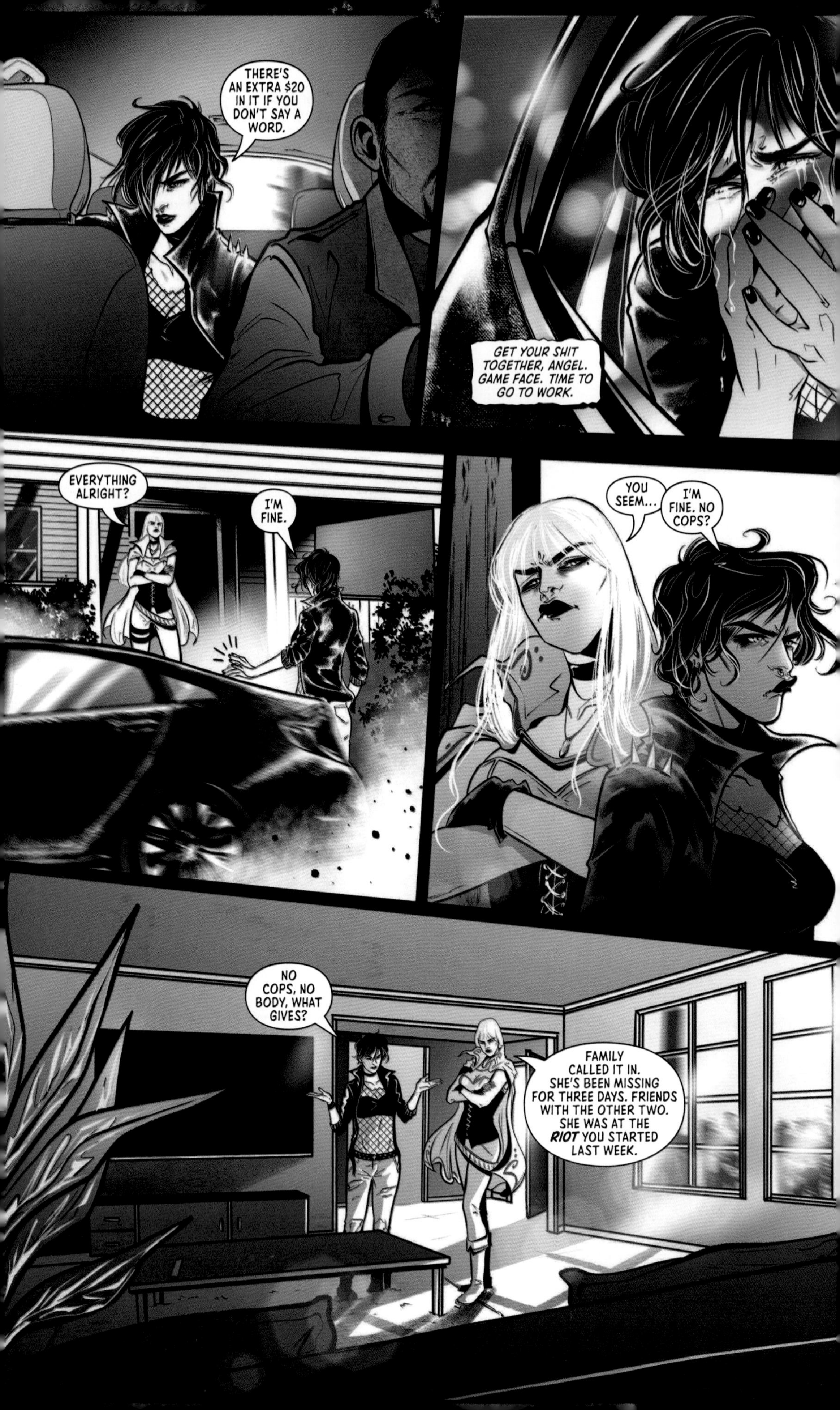
THERE'S AN EXTRA $20 IN IT IF YOU DON'T SAY A WORD.
GET YOUR SHIT TOGETHER, ANGEL. GAME FACE. TIME TO GO TO WORK.
EVERYTHING ALRIGHT?
I'M FINE.
YOU SEEM...
I'M FINE. NO COPS?
NO COPS, NO BODY, WHAT GIVES?
FAMILY CALLED IT IN. SHE'S BEEN MISSING FOR THREE DAYS. FRIENDS WITH THE OTHER TWO. SHE WAS AT THE RIOT YOU STARTED LAST WEEK.

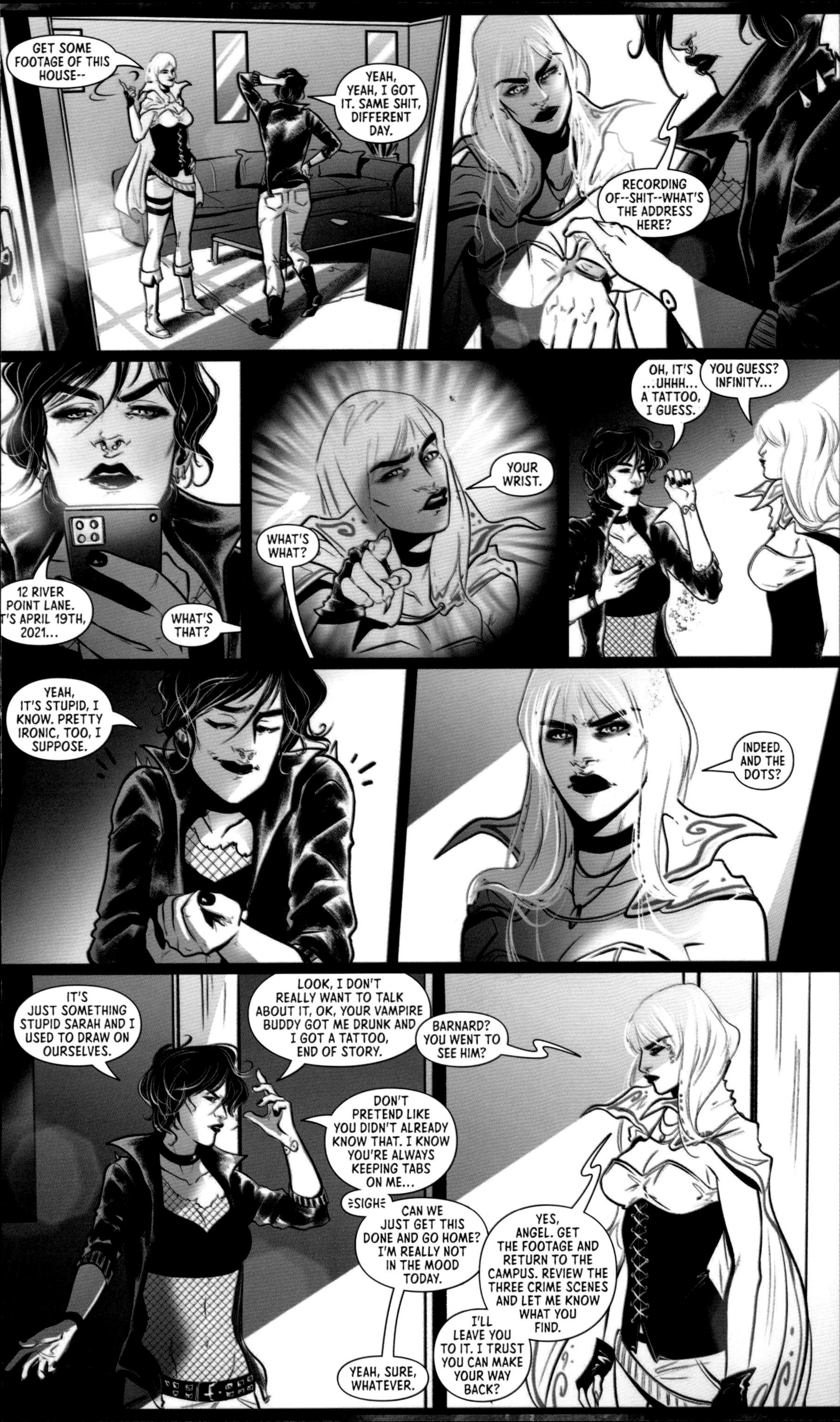

GET SOME FOOTAGE OF THIS HOUSE--
YEAH, YEAH, I GOT IT. SAME SHIT, DIFFERENT DAY.
RECORDING OF--SHIT--WHAT'S THE ADDRESS HERE?
12 RIVER POINT LANE. IT'S APRIL 19TH, 2021...
WHAT'S THAT?
WHAT'S WHAT?
YOUR WRIST.
OH, IT'S ...UHHH... A TATTOO, I GUESS.
YOU GUESS? INFINITY...
YEAH, IT'S STUPID, I KNOW. PRETTY IRONIC, TOO, I SUPPOSE.
INDEED. AND THE DOTS?
IT'S JUST SOMETHING STUPID SARAH AND I USED TO DRAW ON OURSELVES.
LOOK, I DON'T REALLY WANT TO TALK ABOUT IT, OK, YOUR VAMPIRE BUDDY GOT ME DRUNK AND I GOT A TATTOO, END OF STORY.
BARNARD? YOU WENT TO SEE HIM?
DON'T PRETEND LIKE YOU DIDN'T ALREADY KNOW THAT. I KNOW YOU'RE ALWAYS KEEPING TABS ON ME...
SIGH
CAN WE JUST GET THIS DONE AND GO HOME? I'M REALLY NOT IN THE MOOD TODAY.
YES, ANGEL. GET THE FOOTAGE AND RETURN TO THE CAMPUS. REVIEW THE THREE CRIME SCENES AND LET ME KNOW WHAT YOU FIND.
I'LL LEAVE YOU TO IT. I TRUST YOU CAN MAKE YOUR WAY BACK?
YEAH, SURE, WHATEVER.

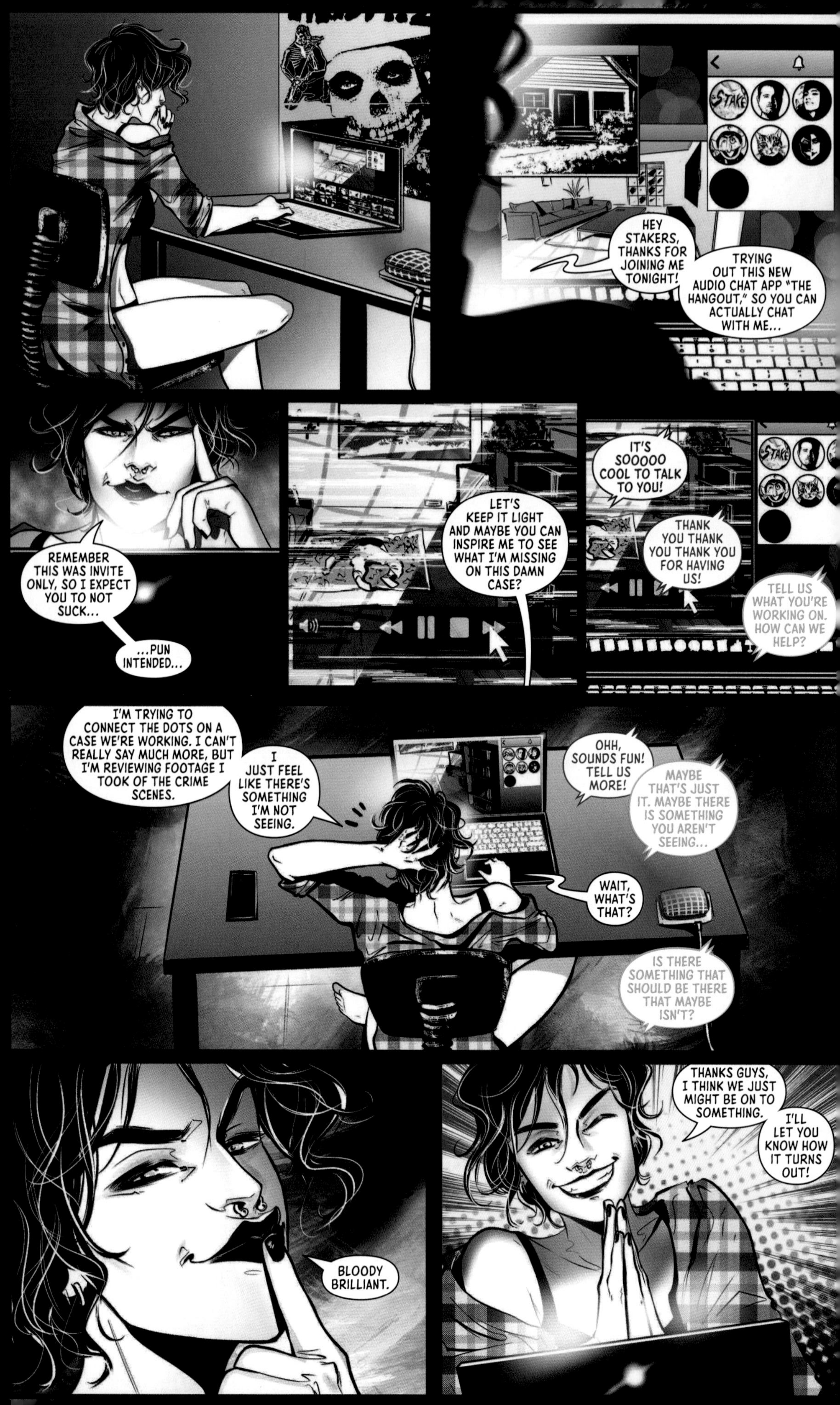

STAKE
HEY STAKERS, THANKS FOR JOINING ME TONIGHT!
TRYING OUT THIS NEW AUDIO CHAT APP "THE HANGOUT," SO YOU CAN ACTUALLY CHAT WITH ME...
REMEMBER THIS WAS INVITE ONLY, SO I EXPECT YOU TO NOT SUCK...
...PUN INTENDED...
LET'S KEEP IT LIGHT AND MAYBE YOU CAN INSPIRE ME TO SEE WHAT I'M MISSING ON THIS DAMN CASE?
IT'S SOOOOO COOL TO TALK TO YOU!
THANK YOU THANK YOU THANK YOU FOR HAVING US!
TELL US WHAT YOU'RE WORKING ON. HOW CAN WE HELP?
I'M TRYING TO CONNECT THE DOTS ON A CASE WE'RE WORKING. I CAN'T REALLY SAY MUCH MORE, BUT I'M REVIEWING FOOTAGE I TOOK OF THE CRIME SCENES.
I JUST FEEL LIKE THERE'S SOMETHING I'M NOT SEEING.
OHH, SOUNDS FUN! TELL US MORE!
MAYBE THAT'S JUST IT. MAYBE THERE IS SOMETHING YOU AREN'T SEEING...
WAIT, WHAT'S THAT?
IS THERE SOMETHING THAT SHOULD BE THERE THAT MAYBE ISN'T?
BLOODY BRILLIANT.
THANKS GUYS, I THINK WE JUST MIGHT BE ON TO SOMETHING.
I'LL LET YOU KNOW HOW IT TURNS OUT!

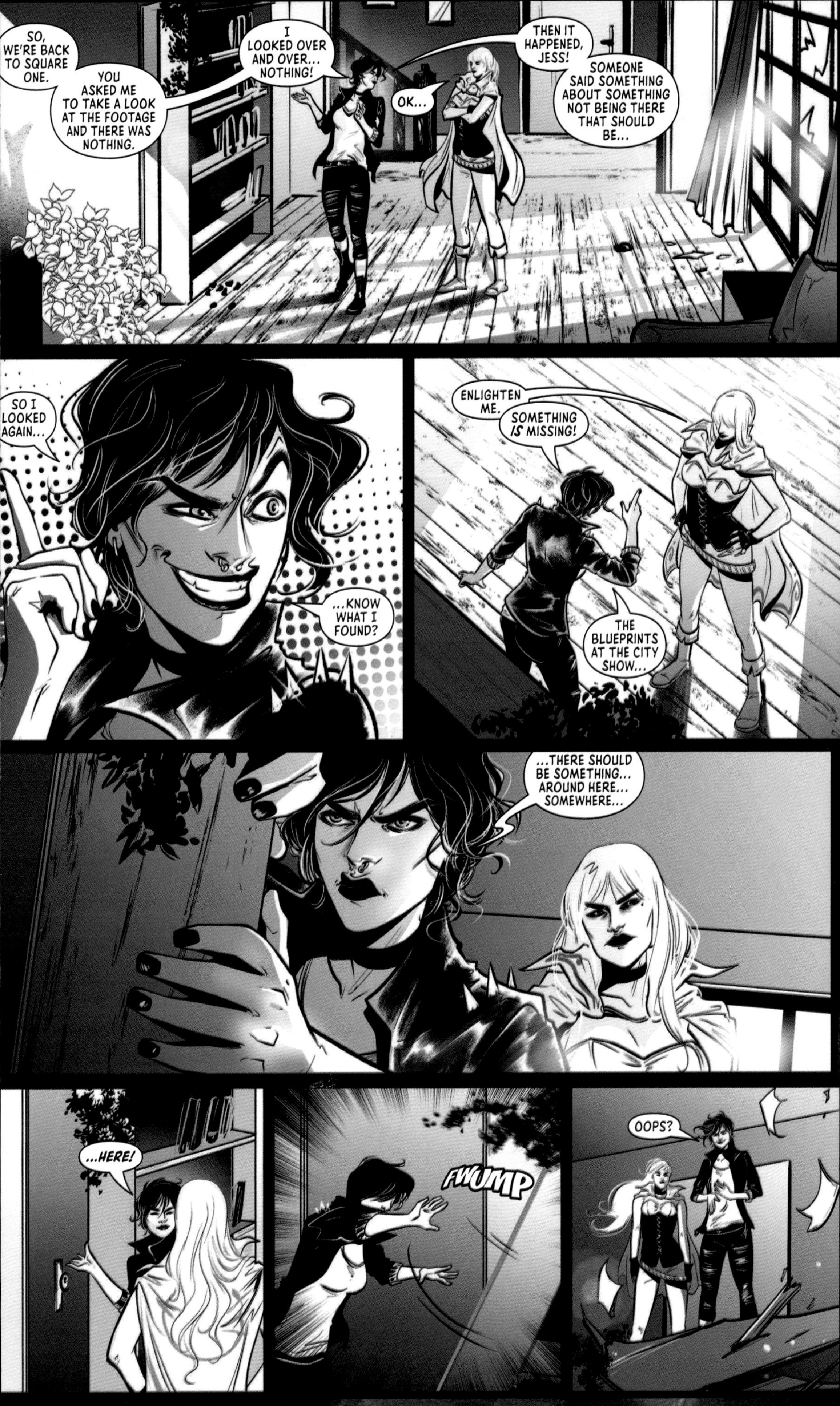
SO, WE'RE BACK TO SQUARE ONE.
YOU ASKED ME TO TAKE A LOOK AT THE FOOTAGE AND THERE WAS NOTHING.
I LOOKED OVER AND OVER... NOTHING!
OK...
THEN IT HAPPENED, JESS!
SOMEONE SAID SOMETHING ABOUT SOMETHING NOT BEING THERE THAT SHOULD BE...
SO I LOOKED AGAIN...
...KNOW WHAT I FOUND?
ENLIGHTEN ME.
SOMETHING *IS* MISSING!
THE BLUEPRINTS AT THE CITY SHOW...
...THERE SHOULD BE SOMETHING... AROUND HERE... SOMEWHERE...
...HERE!
FWUMP
OOPS?

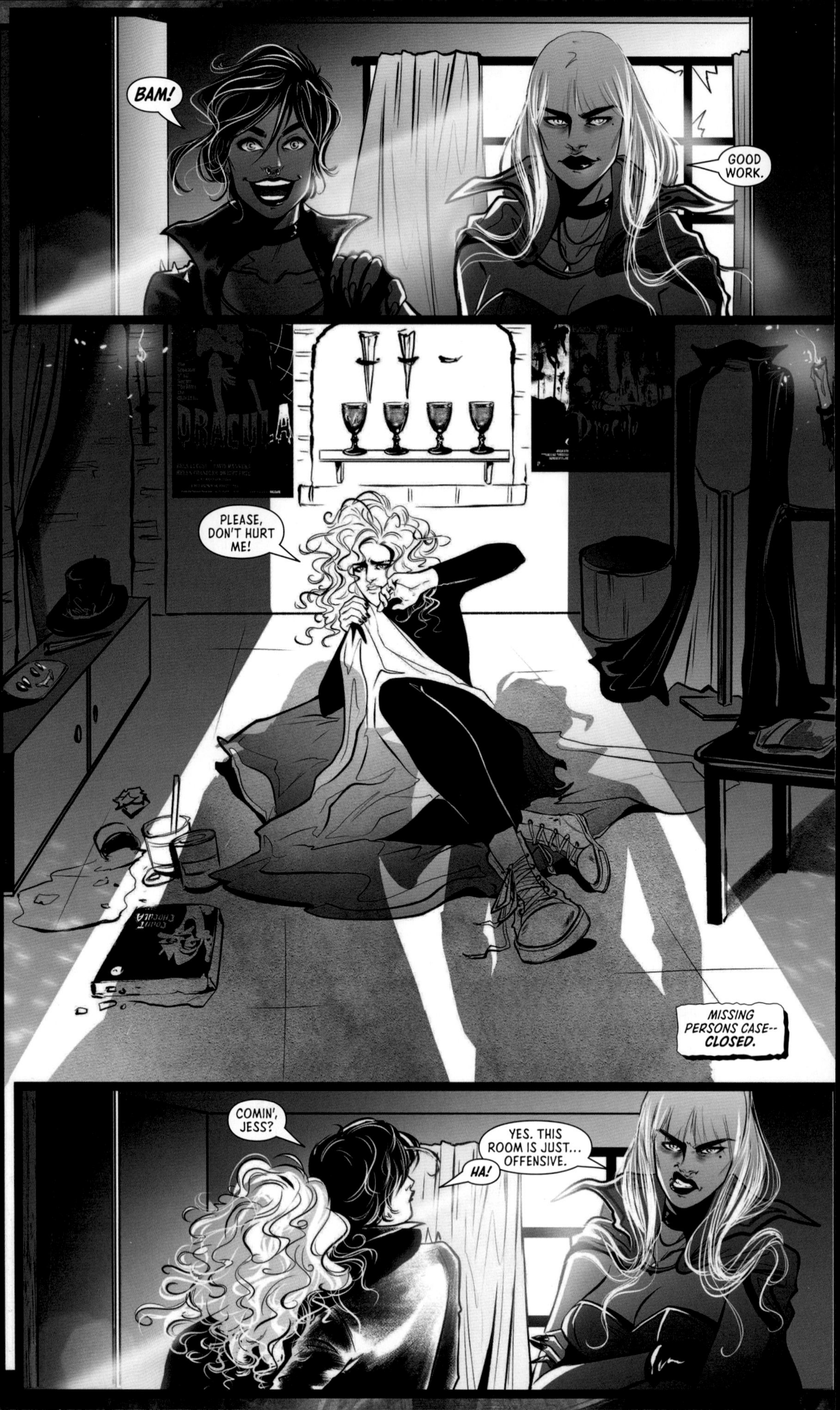
BAM!
GOOD WORK.
PLEASE, DON'T HURT ME!
MISSING PERSONS CASE-- CLOSED.
COMIN', JESS?
YES. THIS ROOM IS JUST... OFFENSIVE.
HA!

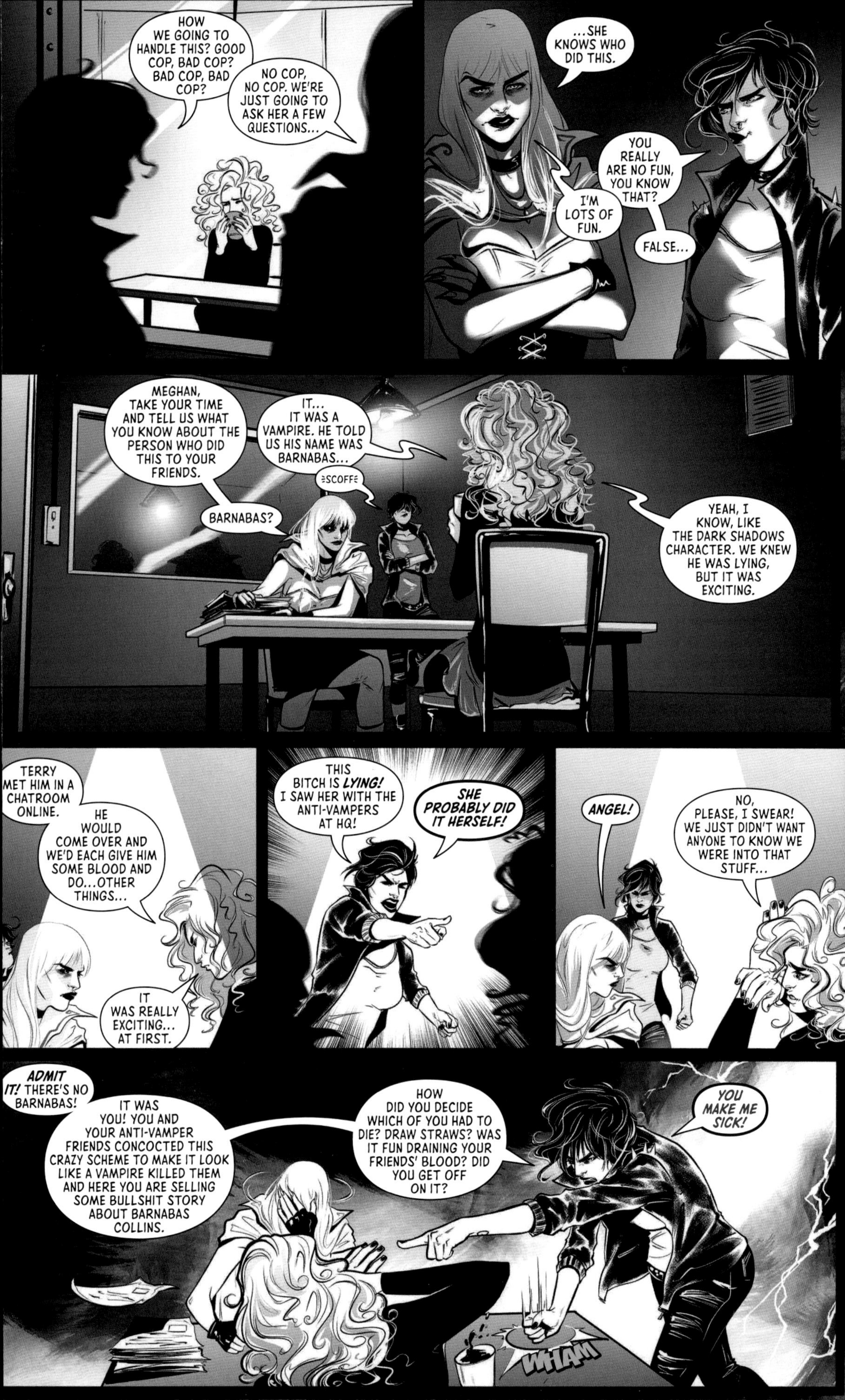
HOW WE GOING TO HANDLE THIS? GOOD COP, BAD COP? BAD COP, BAD COP?
NO COP, NO COP. WE'RE JUST GOING TO ASK HER A FEW QUESTIONS...
...SHE KNOWS WHO DID THIS.
YOU REALLY ARE NO FUN, YOU KNOW THAT?
I'M LOTS OF FUN.
FALSE...
MEGHAN, TAKE YOUR TIME AND TELL US WHAT YOU KNOW ABOUT THE PERSON WHO DID THIS TO YOUR FRIENDS.
IT... IT WAS A VAMPIRE. HE TOLD US HIS NAME WAS BARNABAS...
SCOFF
BARNABAS?
YEAH, I KNOW, LIKE THE DARK SHADOWS CHARACTER. WE KNEW HE WAS LYING, BUT IT WAS EXCITING.
TERRY MET HIM IN A CHATROOM ONLINE.
HE WOULD COME OVER AND WE'D EACH GIVE HIM SOME BLOOD AND DO...OTHER THINGS...
IT WAS REALLY EXCITING... AT FIRST.
THIS BITCH IS *LYING!* I SAW HER WITH THE ANTI-VAMPERS AT HQ!
SHE PROBABLY DID IT HERSELF!
ANGEL!
NO, PLEASE, I SWEAR! WE JUST DIDN'T WANT ANYONE TO KNOW WE WERE INTO THAT STUFF...
ADMIT IT! THERE'S NO BARNABAS!
IT WAS YOU! YOU AND YOUR ANTI-VAMPER FRIENDS CONCOCTED THIS CRAZY SCHEME TO MAKE IT LOOK LIKE A VAMPIRE KILLED THEM AND HERE YOU ARE SELLING SOME BULLSHIT STORY ABOUT BARNABAS COLLINS.
HOW DID YOU DECIDE WHICH OF YOU HAD TO DIE? DRAW STRAWS? WAS IT FUN DRAINING YOUR FRIENDS' BLOOD? DID YOU GET OFF ON IT?
YOU MAKE ME SICK!
WHAM

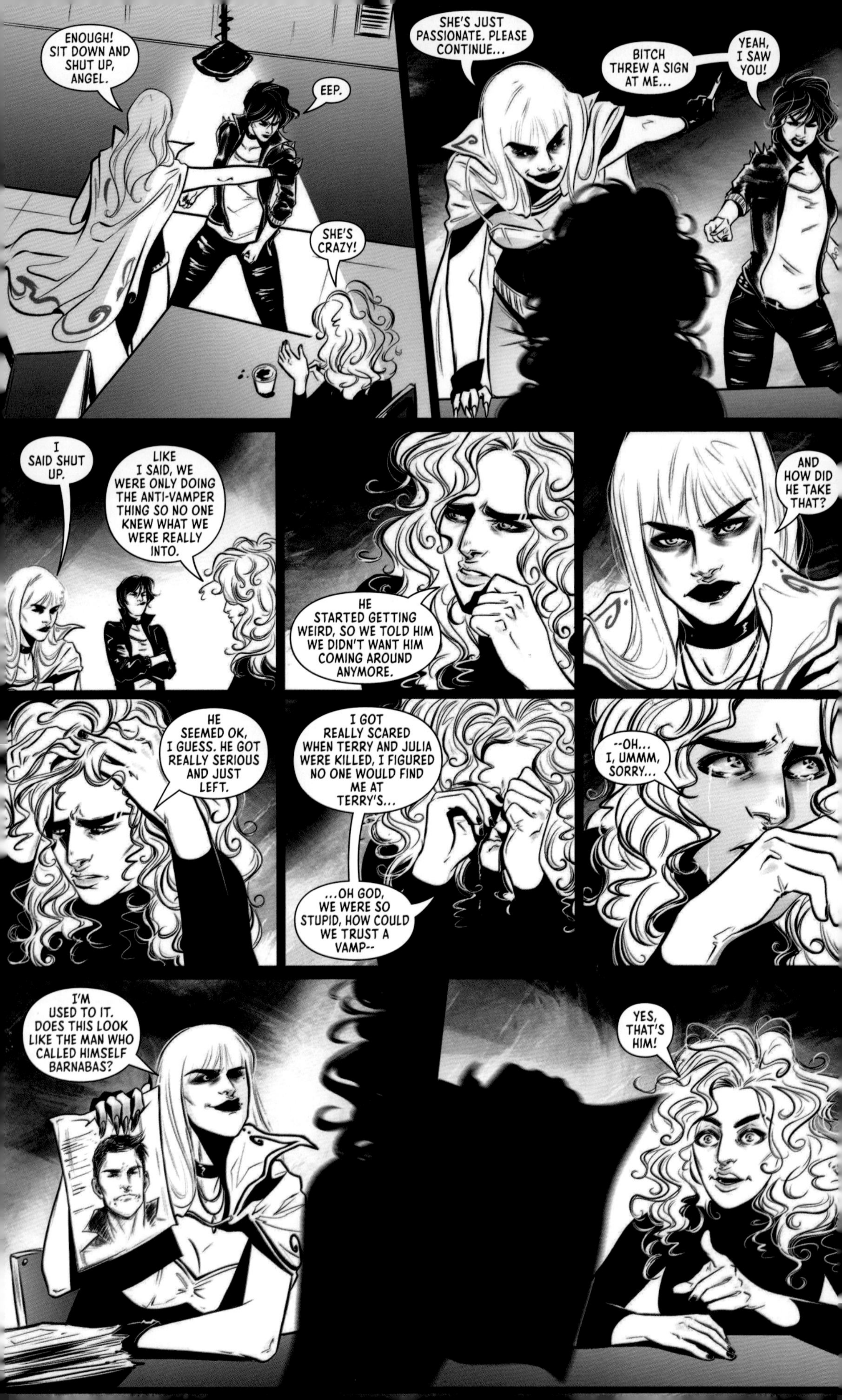
ENOUGH! SIT DOWN AND SHUT UP, ANGEL.
EEP.
SHE'S CRAZY!
SHE'S JUST PASSIONATE. PLEASE CONTINUE...
BITCH THREW A SIGN AT ME...
YEAH, I SAW YOU!
I SAID SHUT UP.
LIKE I SAID, WE WERE ONLY DOING THE ANTI-VAMPER THING SO NO ONE KNEW WHAT WE WERE REALLY INTO.
HE STARTED GETTING WEIRD, SO WE TOLD HIM WE DIDN'T WANT HIM COMING AROUND ANYMORE.
AND HOW DID HE TAKE THAT?
HE SEEMED OK, I GUESS. HE GOT REALLY SERIOUS AND JUST LEFT.
I GOT REALLY SCARED WHEN TERRY AND JULIA WERE KILLED, I FIGURED NO ONE WOULD FIND ME AT TERRY'S...
...OH GOD, WE WERE SO STUPID, HOW COULD WE TRUST A VAMP--
--OH... I, UMMM, SORRY...
I'M USED TO IT. DOES THIS LOOK LIKE THE MAN WHO CALLED HIMSELF BARNABAS?
YES, THAT'S HIM!

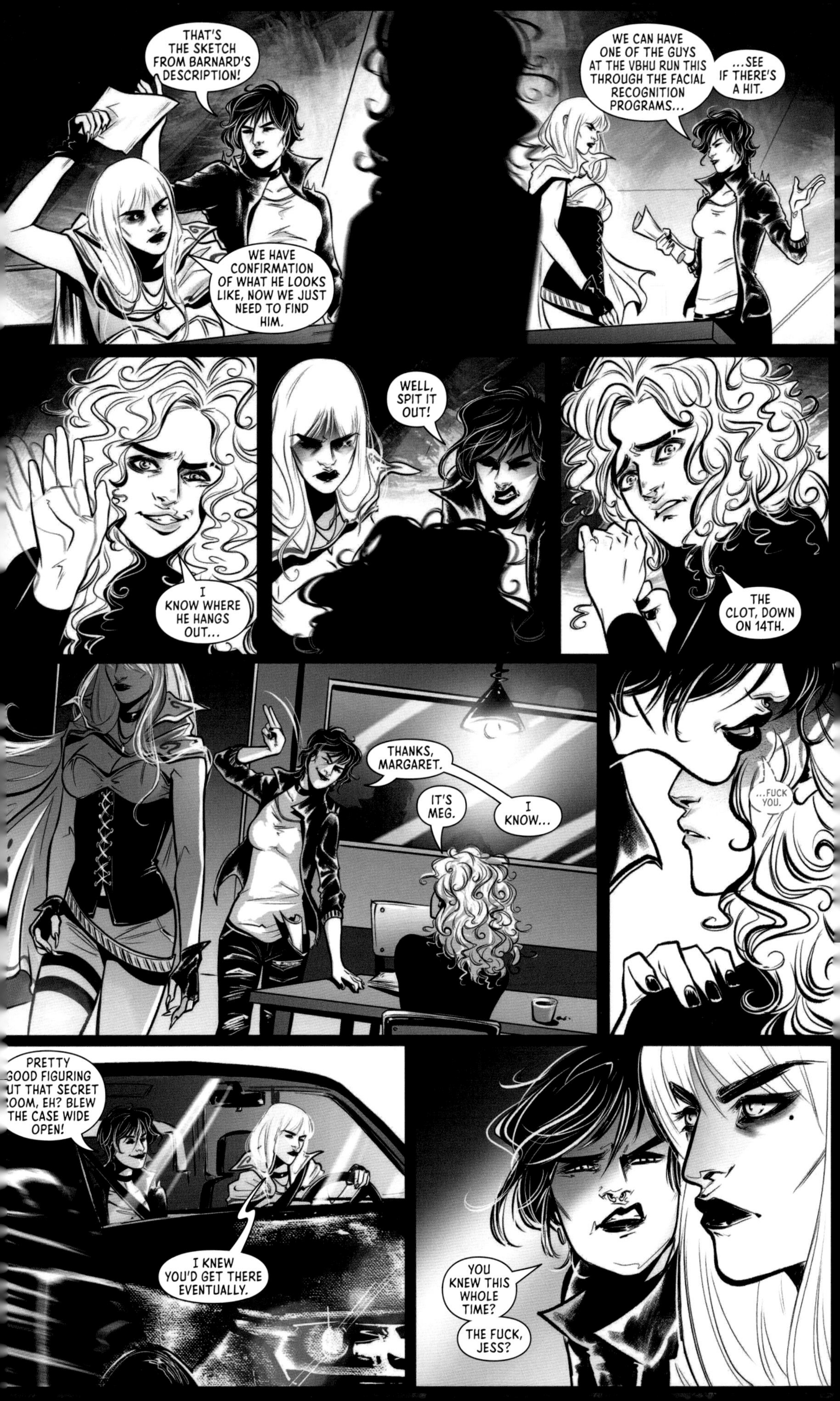
THAT'S THE SKETCH FROM BARNARD'S DESCRIPTION!
WE HAVE CONFIRMATION OF WHAT HE LOOKS LIKE, NOW WE JUST NEED TO FIND HIM.
WE CAN HAVE ONE OF THE GUYS AT THE VBHU RUN THIS THROUGH THE FACIAL RECOGNITION PROGRAMS...
...SEE IF THERE'S A HIT.
I KNOW WHERE HE HANGS OUT...
WELL, SPIT IT OUT!
THE CLOT, DOWN ON 14TH.
THANKS, MARGARET.
IT'S MEG.
I KNOW...
...FUCK YOU.
PRETTY GOOD FIGURING OUT THAT SECRET ROOM, EH? BLEW THE CASE WIDE OPEN!
I KNEW YOU'D GET THERE EVENTUALLY.
YOU KNEW THIS WHOLE TIME?
THE FUCK, JESS?

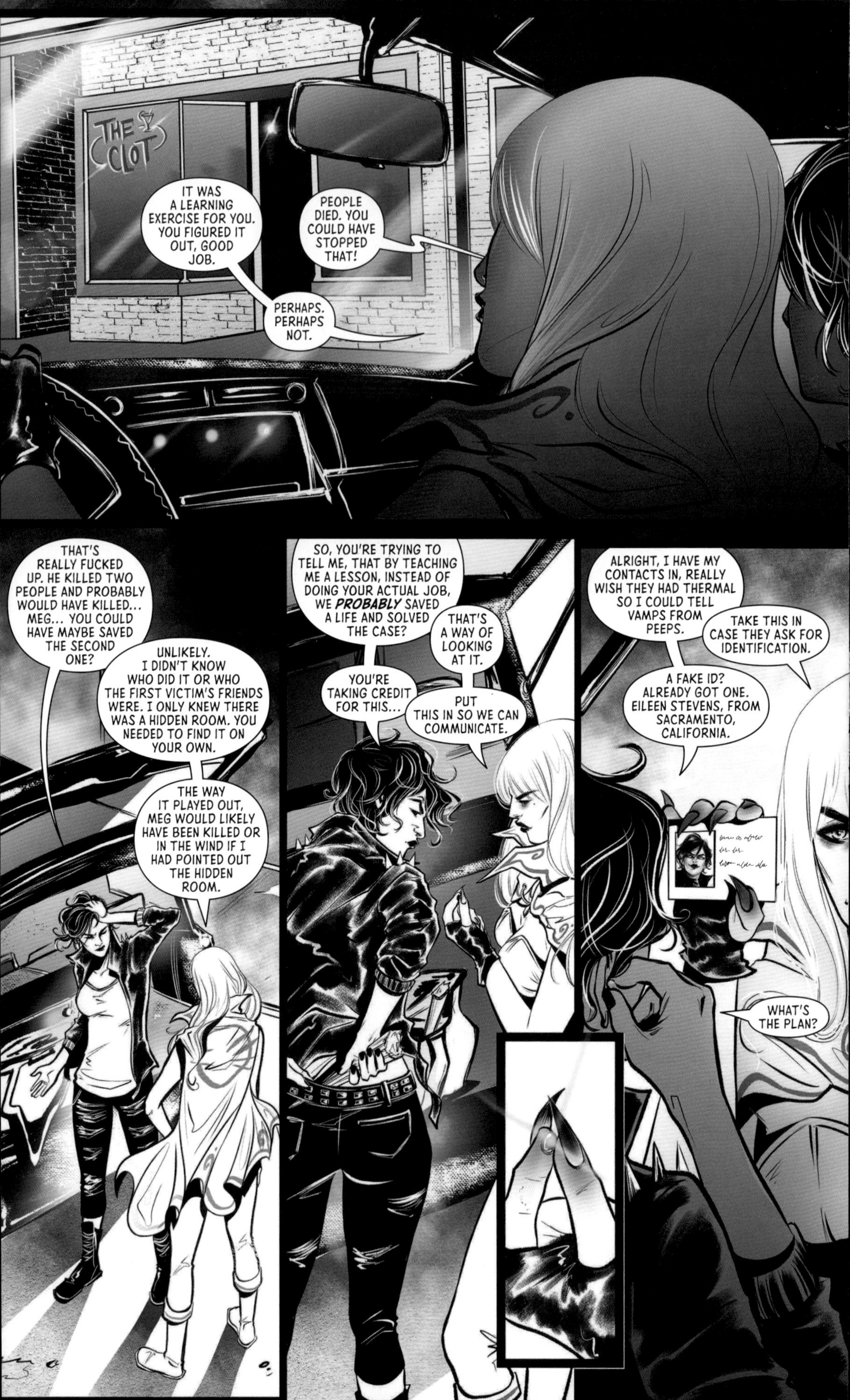
THE CLOT
IT WAS A LEARNING EXERCISE FOR YOU. YOU FIGURED IT OUT, GOOD JOB.
PEOPLE DIED. YOU COULD HAVE STOPPED THAT!
PERHAPS. PERHAPS NOT.
THAT'S REALLY FUCKED UP. HE KILLED TWO PEOPLE AND PROBABLY WOULD HAVE KILLED... MEG... YOU COULD HAVE MAYBE SAVED THE SECOND ONE?
UNLIKELY. I DIDN'T KNOW WHO DID IT OR WHO THE FIRST VICTIM'S FRIENDS WERE. I ONLY KNEW THERE WAS A HIDDEN ROOM. YOU NEEDED TO FIND IT ON YOUR OWN.
THE WAY IT PLAYED OUT, MEG WOULD LIKELY HAVE BEEN KILLED OR IN THE WIND IF I HAD POINTED OUT THE HIDDEN ROOM.
SO, YOU'RE TRYING TO TELL ME, THAT BY TEACHING ME A LESSON, INSTEAD OF DOING YOUR ACTUAL JOB, WE PROBABLY SAVED A LIFE AND SOLVED THE CASE?
THAT'S A WAY OF LOOKING AT IT.
YOU'RE TAKING CREDIT FOR THIS...
PUT THIS IN SO WE CAN COMMUNICATE.
ALRIGHT, I HAVE MY CONTACTS IN, REALLY WISH THEY HAD THERMAL SO I COULD TELL VAMPS FROM PEEPS.
TAKE THIS IN CASE THEY ASK FOR IDENTIFICATION.
A FAKE ID? ALREADY GOT ONE. EILEEN STEVENS, FROM SACRAMENTO, CALIFORNIA.
WHAT'S THE PLAN?

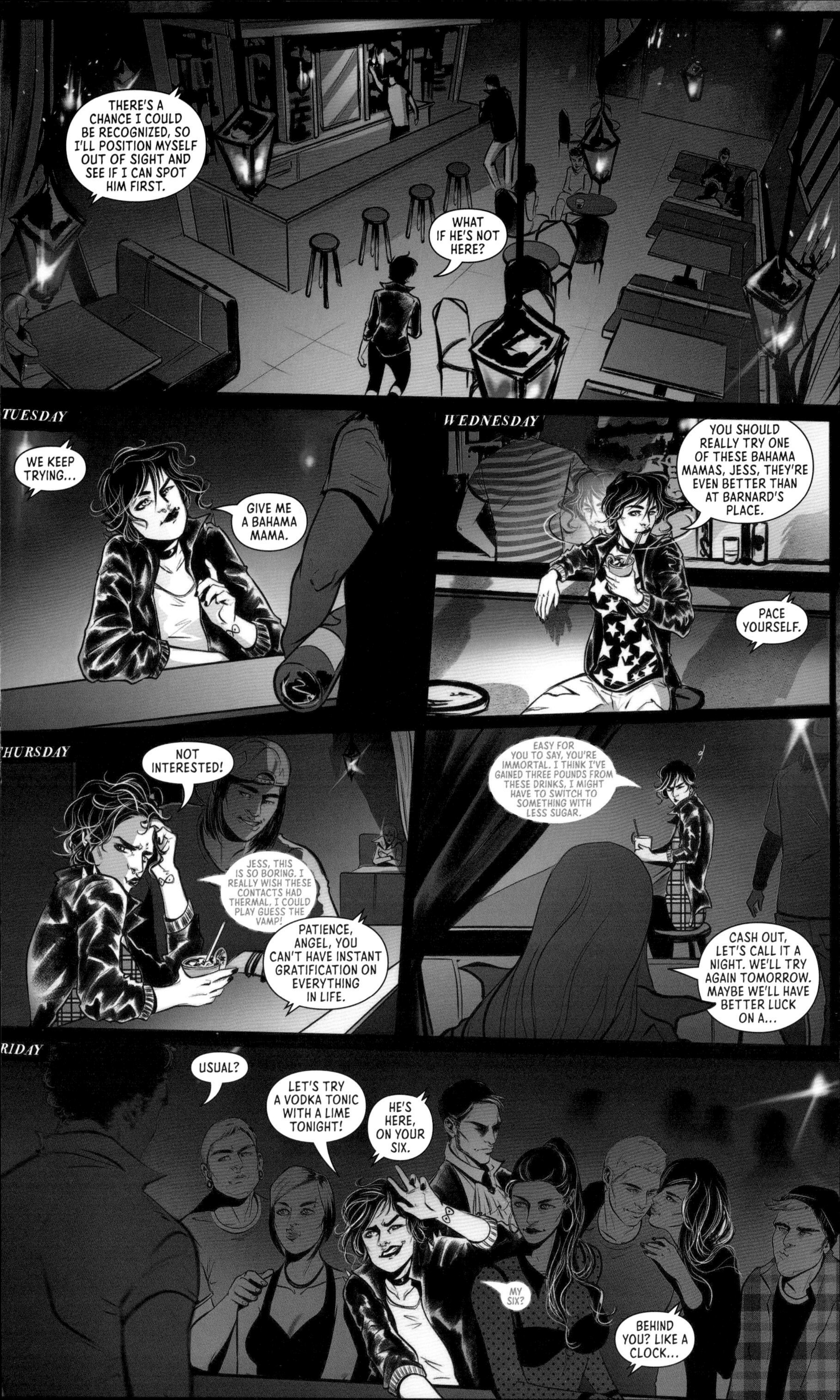

THERE'S A CHANCE I COULD BE RECOGNIZED, SO I'LL POSITION MYSELF OUT OF SIGHT AND SEE IF I CAN SPOT HIM FIRST.
WHAT IF HE'S NOT HERE?
TUESDAY
WE KEEP TRYING...
GIVE ME A BAHAMA MAMA.
WEDNESDAY
YOU SHOULD REALLY TRY ONE OF THESE BAHAMA MAMAS, JESS, THEY'RE EVEN BETTER THAN AT BARNARD'S PLACE.
PACE YOURSELF.
HURSDAY
NOT INTERESTED!
JESS, THIS IS SO BORING. I REALLY WISH THESE CONTACTS HAD THERMAL, I COULD PLAY GUESS THE VAMP!
PATIENCE, ANGEL, YOU CAN'T HAVE INSTANT GRATIFICATION ON EVERYTHING IN LIFE.
EASY FOR YOU TO SAY, YOU'RE IMMORTAL. I THINK I'VE GAINED THREE POUNDS FROM THESE DRINKS, I MIGHT HAVE TO SWITCH TO SOMETHING WITH LESS SUGAR.
CASH OUT, LET'S CALL IT A NIGHT. WE'LL TRY AGAIN TOMORROW. MAYBE WE'LL HAVE BETTER LUCK ON A...
RIDAY
USUAL?
LET'S TRY A VODKA TONIC WITH A LIME TONIGHT!
HE'S HERE, ON YOUR SIX.
MY SIX?
BEHIND YOU? LIKE A CLOCK...

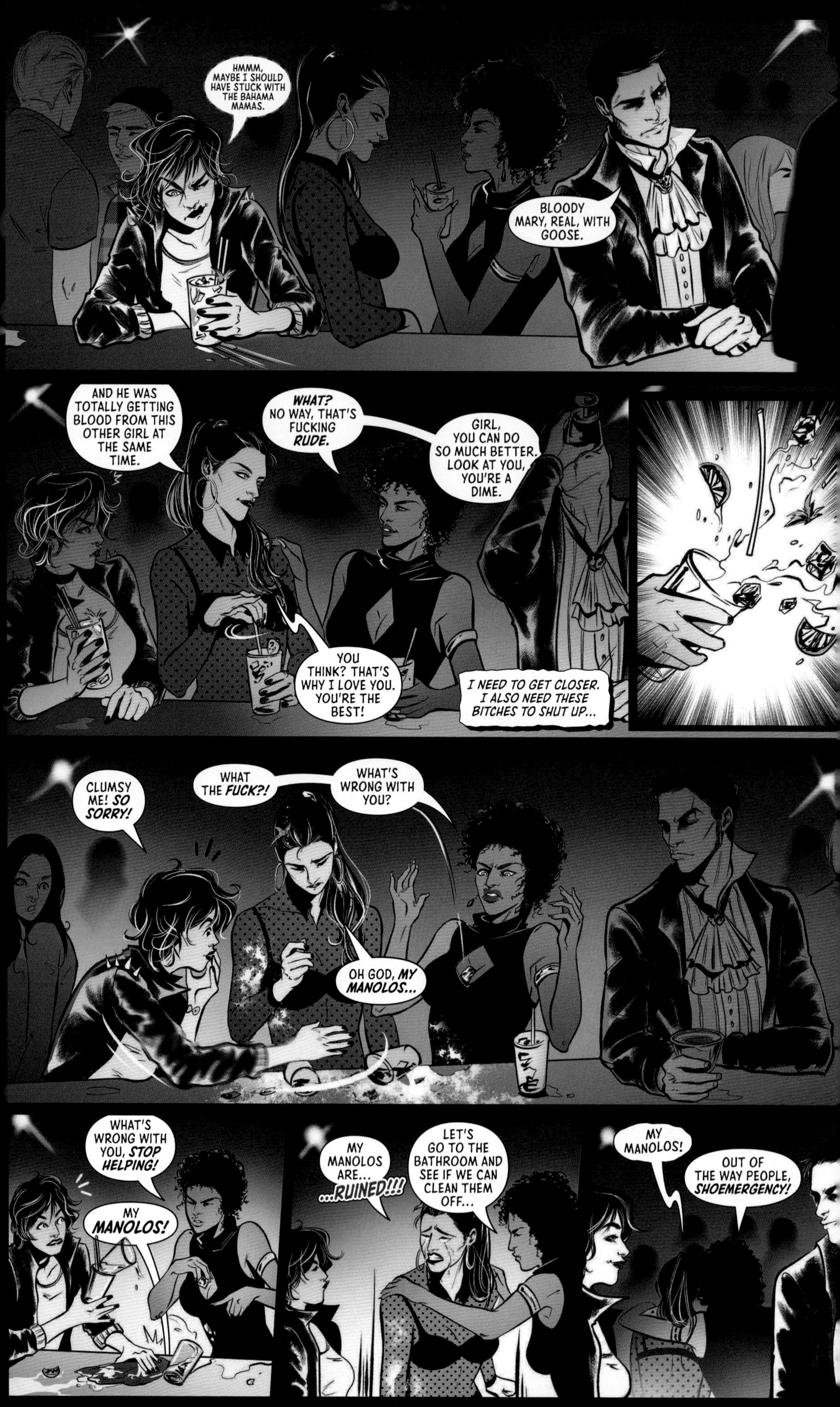
HMMM, MAYBE I SHOULD HAVE STUCK WITH THE BAHAMA MAMAS.
BLOODY MARY, REAL, WITH GOOSE.
AND HE WAS TOTALLY GETTING BLOOD FROM THIS OTHER GIRL AT THE SAME TIME.
WHAT? NO WAY, THAT'S FUCKING RUDE.
GIRL, YOU CAN DO SO MUCH BETTER. LOOK AT YOU, YOU'RE A DIME.
YOU THINK? THAT'S WHY I LOVE YOU. YOU'RE THE BEST!
I NEED TO GET CLOSER. I ALSO NEED THESE BITCHES TO SHUT UP...
CLUMSY ME! SO SORRY!
WHAT THE FUCK?!
WHAT'S WRONG WITH YOU?
OH GOD, MY MANOLOS...
WHAT'S WRONG WITH YOU, STOP HELPING!
MY MANOLOS!
MY MANOLOS ARE... ...RUINED!!!
LET'S GO TO THE BATHROOM AND SEE IF WE CAN CLEAN THEM OFF...
MY MANOLOS!
OUT OF THE WAY PEOPLE, SHOEMERGENCY!

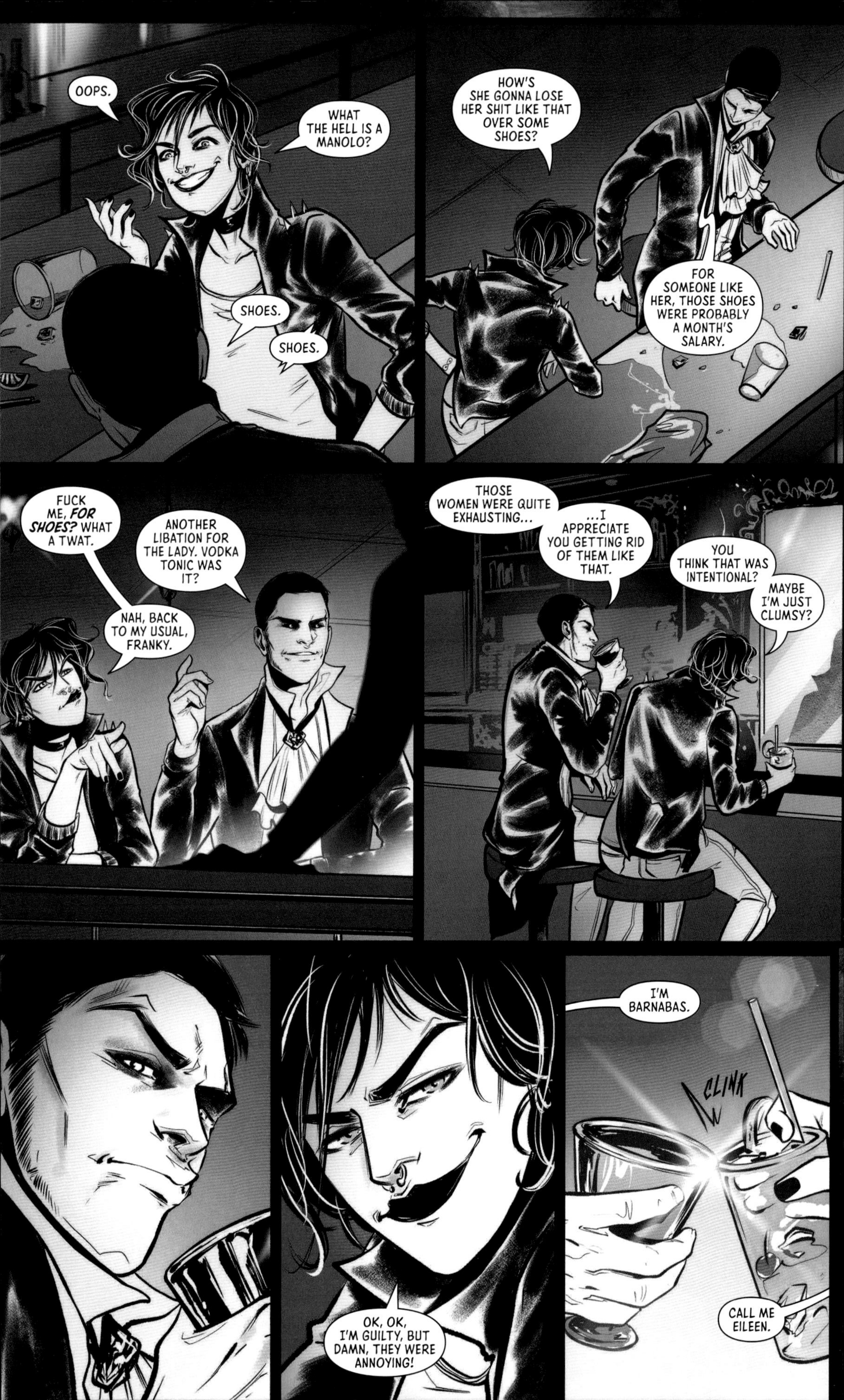
OOPS.
WHAT THE HELL IS A MANOLO?
SHOES.
SHOES.
HOW'S SHE GONNA LOSE HER SHIT LIKE THAT OVER SOME SHOES?
FOR SOMEONE LIKE HER, THOSE SHOES WERE PROBABLY A MONTH'S SALARY.
FUCK ME, **FOR SHOES?** WHAT A TWAT.
ANOTHER LIBATION FOR THE LADY. VODKA TONIC WAS IT?
NAH, BACK TO MY USUAL, FRANKY.
THOSE WOMEN WERE QUITE EXHAUSTING...
...I APPRECIATE YOU GETTING RID OF THEM LIKE THAT.
YOU THINK THAT WAS INTENTIONAL?
MAYBE I'M JUST CLUMSY?
OK, OK, I'M GUILTY, BUT DAMN, THEY WERE ANNOYING!
I'M BARNABAS.
CLINK
CALL ME EILEEN.

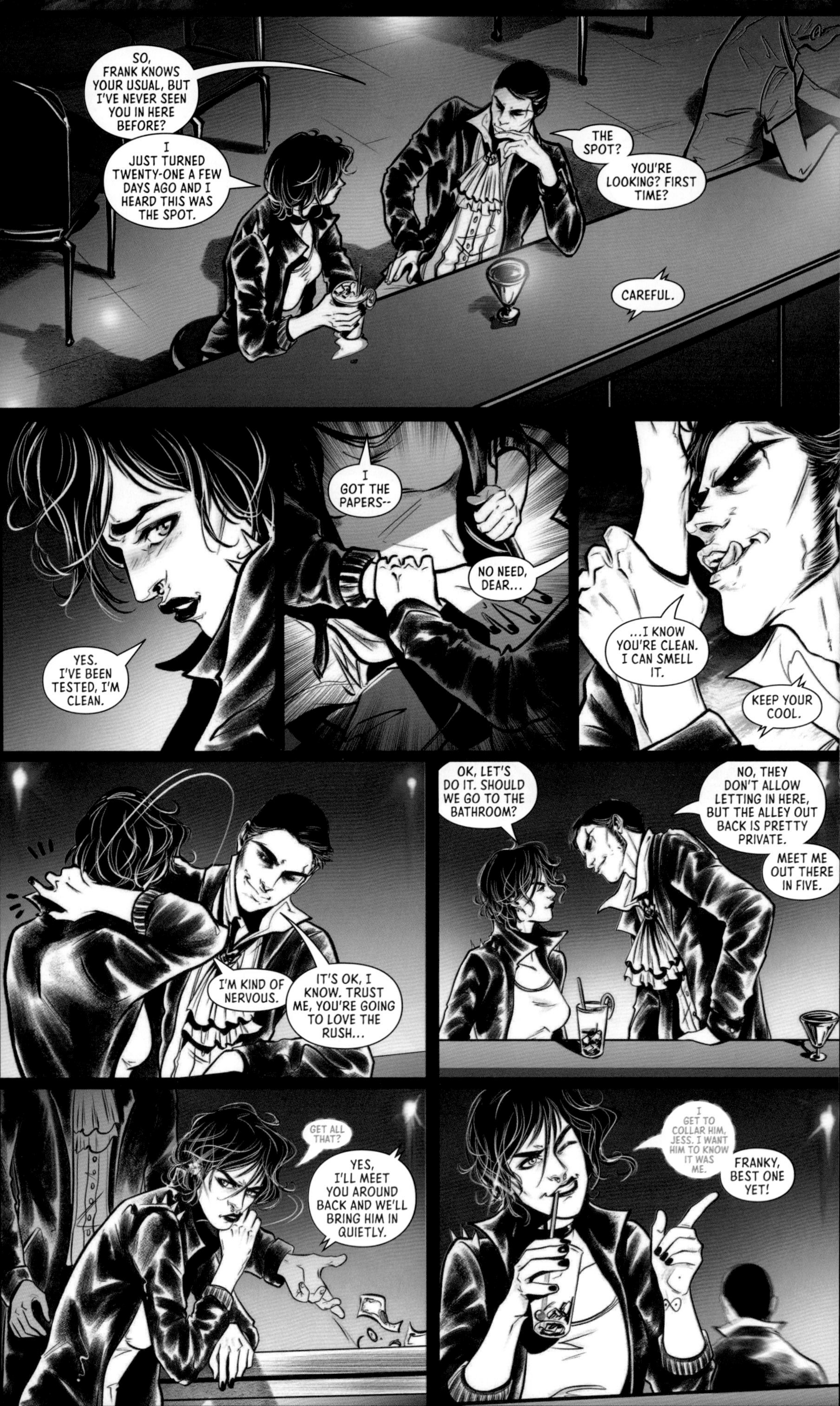
SO, FRANK KNOWS YOUR USUAL, BUT I'VE NEVER SEEN YOU IN HERE BEFORE?
I JUST TURNED TWENTY-ONE A FEW DAYS AGO AND I HEARD THIS WAS THE SPOT.
THE SPOT?
YOU'RE LOOKING? FIRST TIME?
CAREFUL.
YES. I'VE BEEN TESTED, I'M CLEAN.
I GOT THE PAPERS--
NO NEED, DEAR...
...I KNOW YOU'RE CLEAN. I CAN SMELL IT.
KEEP YOUR COOL.
I'M KIND OF NERVOUS.
IT'S OK, I KNOW. TRUST ME, YOU'RE GOING TO LOVE THE RUSH...
OK, LET'S DO IT. SHOULD WE GO TO THE BATHROOM?
NO, THEY DON'T ALLOW LETTING IN HERE, BUT THE ALLEY OUT BACK IS PRETTY PRIVATE.
MEET ME OUT THERE IN FIVE.
GET ALL THAT?
YES, I'LL MEET YOU AROUND BACK AND WE'LL BRING HIM IN QUIETLY.
I GET TO COLLAR HIM, JESS. I WANT HIM TO KNOW IT WAS ME.
FRANKY, BEST ONE YET!

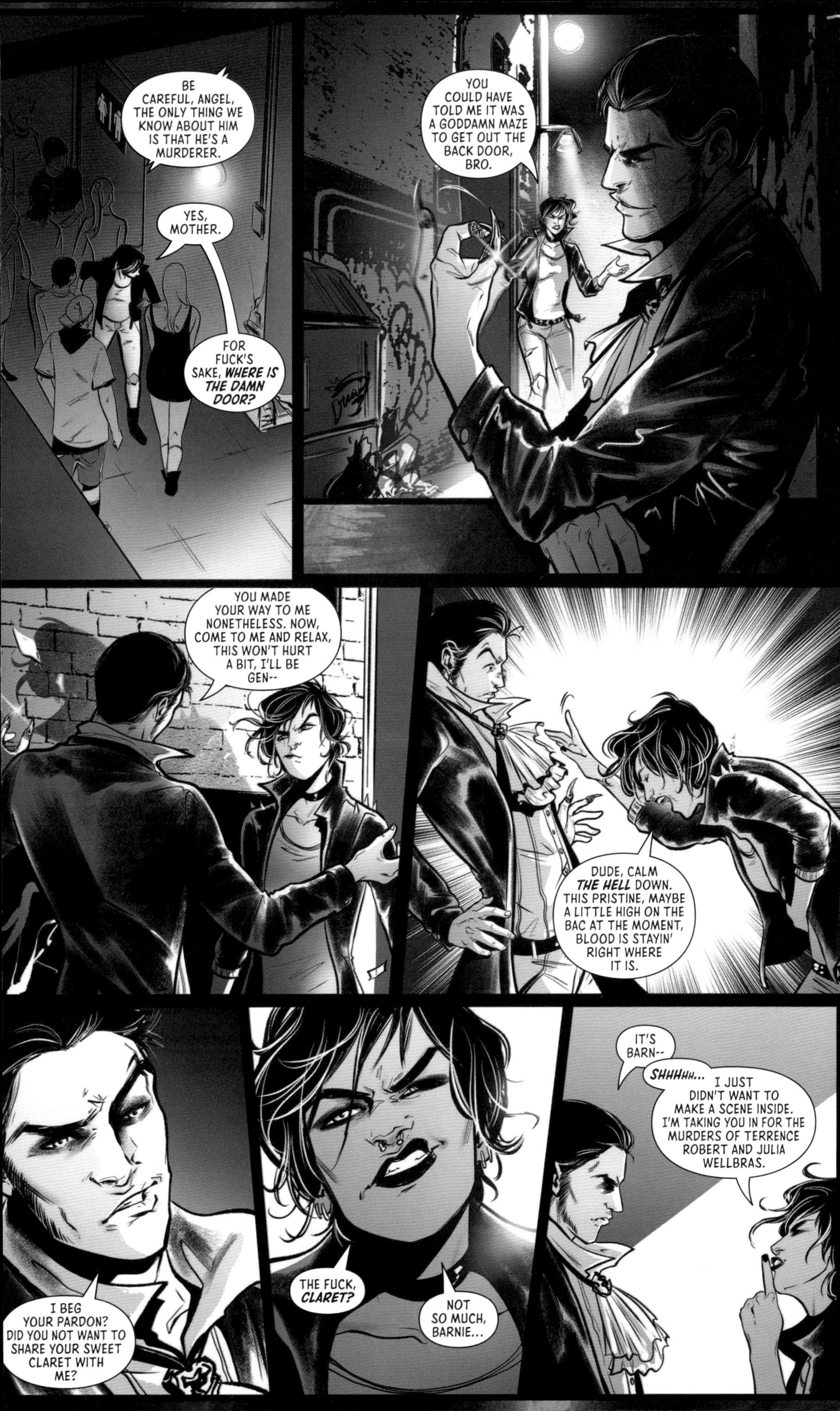
BE CAREFUL, ANGEL, THE ONLY THING WE KNOW ABOUT HIM IS THAT HE'S A MURDERER.
YES, MOTHER.
FOR FUCK'S SAKE, WHERE IS THE DAMN DOOR?
YOU COULD HAVE TOLD ME IT WAS A GODDAMN MAZE TO GET OUT THE BACK DOOR, BRO.
YOU MADE YOUR WAY TO ME NONETHELESS. NOW, COME TO ME AND RELAX, THIS WON'T HURT A BIT, I'LL BE GEN--
DUDE, CALM THE HELL DOWN. THIS PRISTINE, MAYBE A LITTLE HIGH ON THE BAC AT THE MOMENT, BLOOD IS STAYIN' RIGHT WHERE IT IS.
I BEG YOUR PARDON? DID YOU NOT WANT TO SHARE YOUR SWEET CLARET WITH ME?
THE FUCK, CLARET?
NOT SO MUCH, BARNIE...
IT'S BARN--
SHHHHH... I JUST DIDN'T WANT TO MAKE A SCENE INSIDE. I'M TAKING YOU IN FOR THE MURDERS OF TERRENCE ROBERT AND JULIA WELLBRAS.

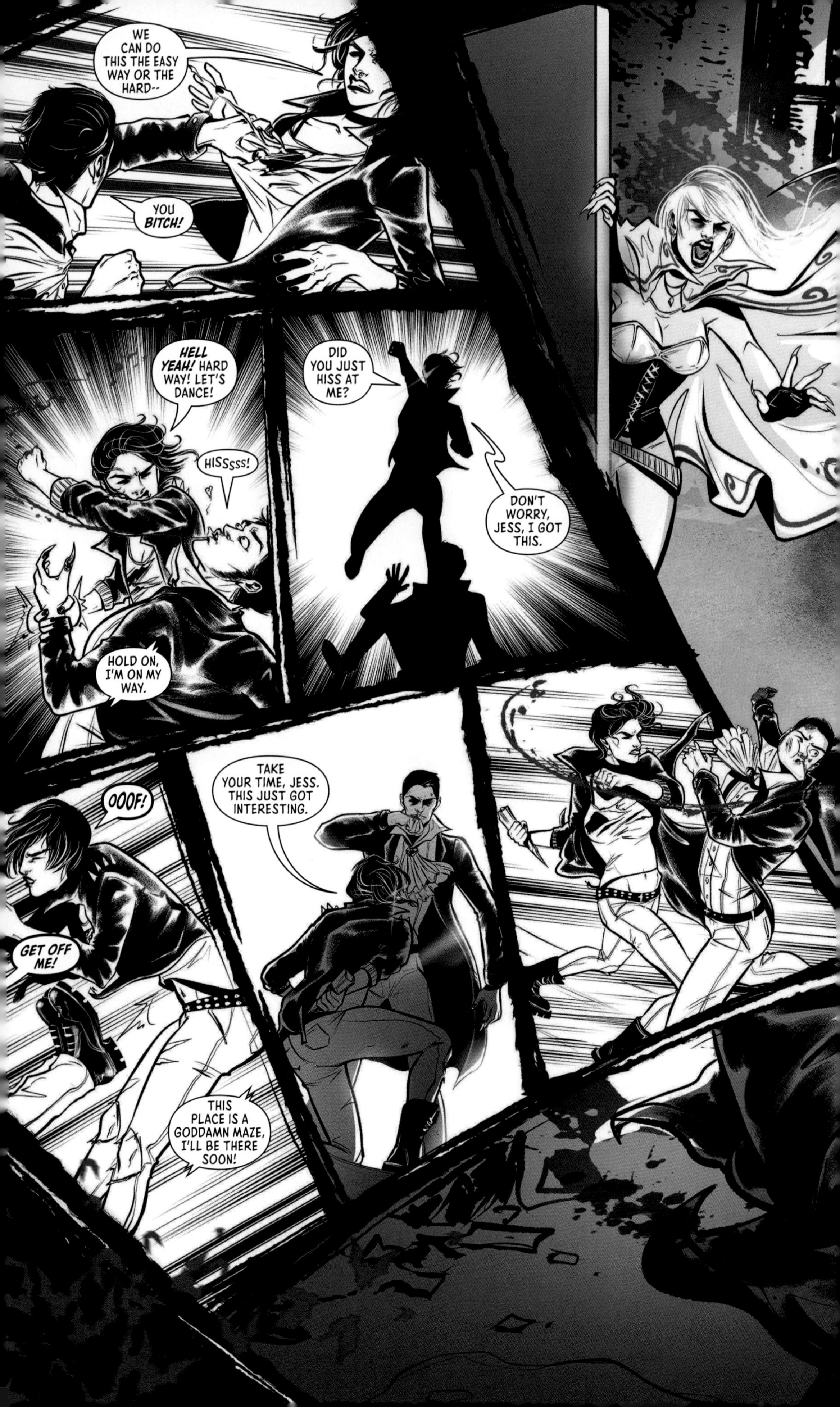
WE CAN DO THIS THE EASY WAY OR THE HARD--
YOU BITCH!
HELL YEAH! HARD WAY! LET'S DANCE!
HISSSSS!
HOLD ON, I'M ON MY WAY.
DID YOU JUST HISS AT ME?
DON'T WORRY, JESS, I GOT THIS.
OOOF!
GET OFF ME!
TAKE YOUR TIME, JESS. THIS JUST GOT INTERESTING.
THIS PLACE IS A GODDAMN MAZE, I'LL BE THERE SOON!

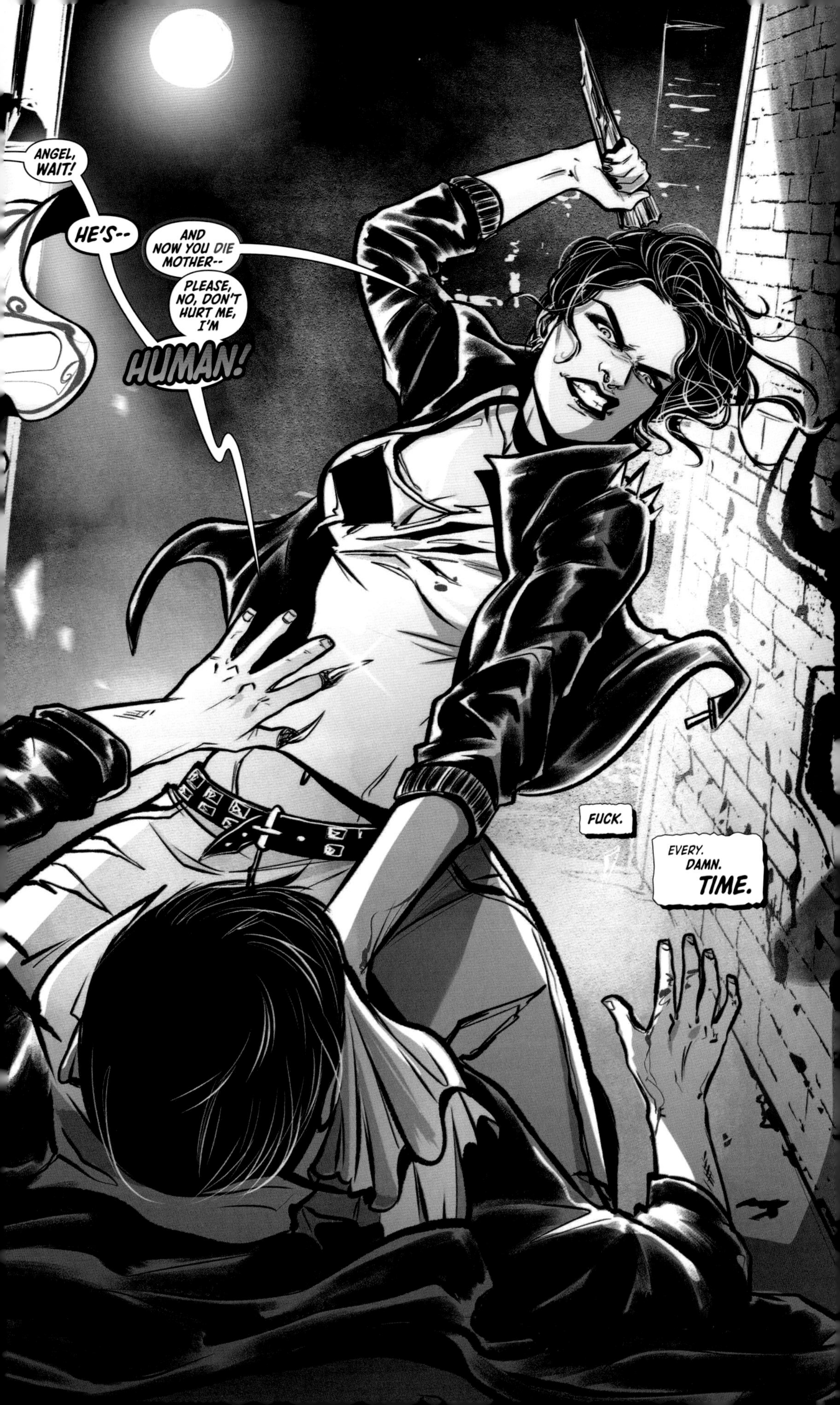

ANGEL, WAIT!
HE'S--
AND NOW YOU DIE MOTHER--
PLEASE, NO, DON'T HURT ME, I'M
HUMAN!
FUCK.
EVERY. DAMN. TIME.

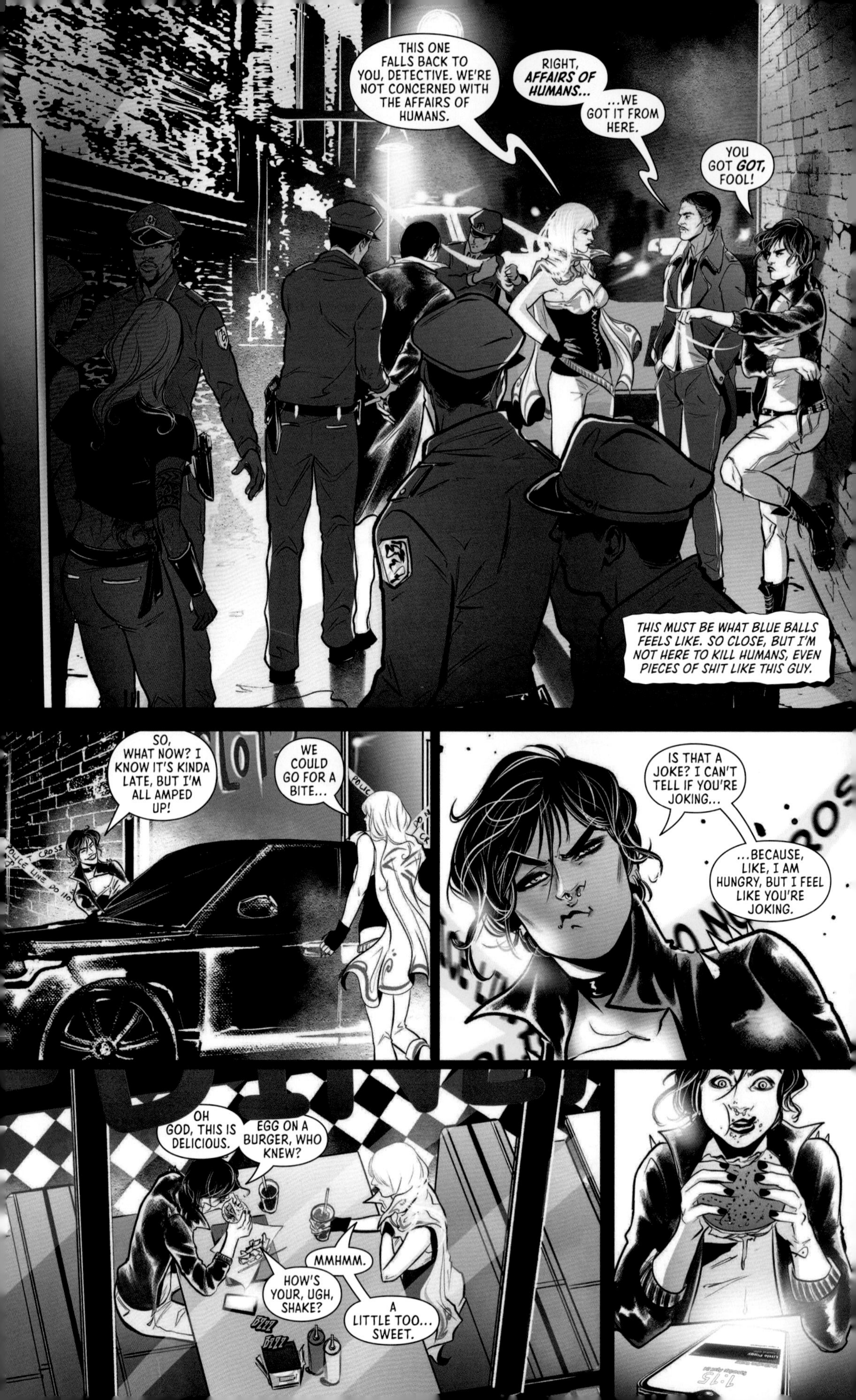
THIS ONE FALLS BACK TO YOU, DETECTIVE. WE'RE NOT CONCERNED WITH THE AFFAIRS OF HUMANS.
RIGHT, AFFAIRS OF HUMANS...
...WE GOT IT FROM HERE.
YOU GOT GOT, FOOL!
THIS MUST BE WHAT BLUE BALLS FEELS LIKE. SO CLOSE, BUT I'M NOT HERE TO KILL HUMANS, EVEN PIECES OF SHIT LIKE THIS GUY.
SO, WHAT NOW? I KNOW IT'S KINDA LATE, BUT I'M ALL AMPED UP!
WE COULD GO FOR A BITE...
IS THAT A JOKE? I CAN'T TELL IF YOU'RE JOKING...
...BECAUSE, LIKE, I AM HUNGRY, BUT I FEEL LIKE YOU'RE JOKING.
OH GOD, THIS IS DELICIOUS.
EGG ON A BURGER, WHO KNEW?
MMHMM.
HOW'S YOUR, UGH, SHAKE?
A LITTLE TOO... SWEET.

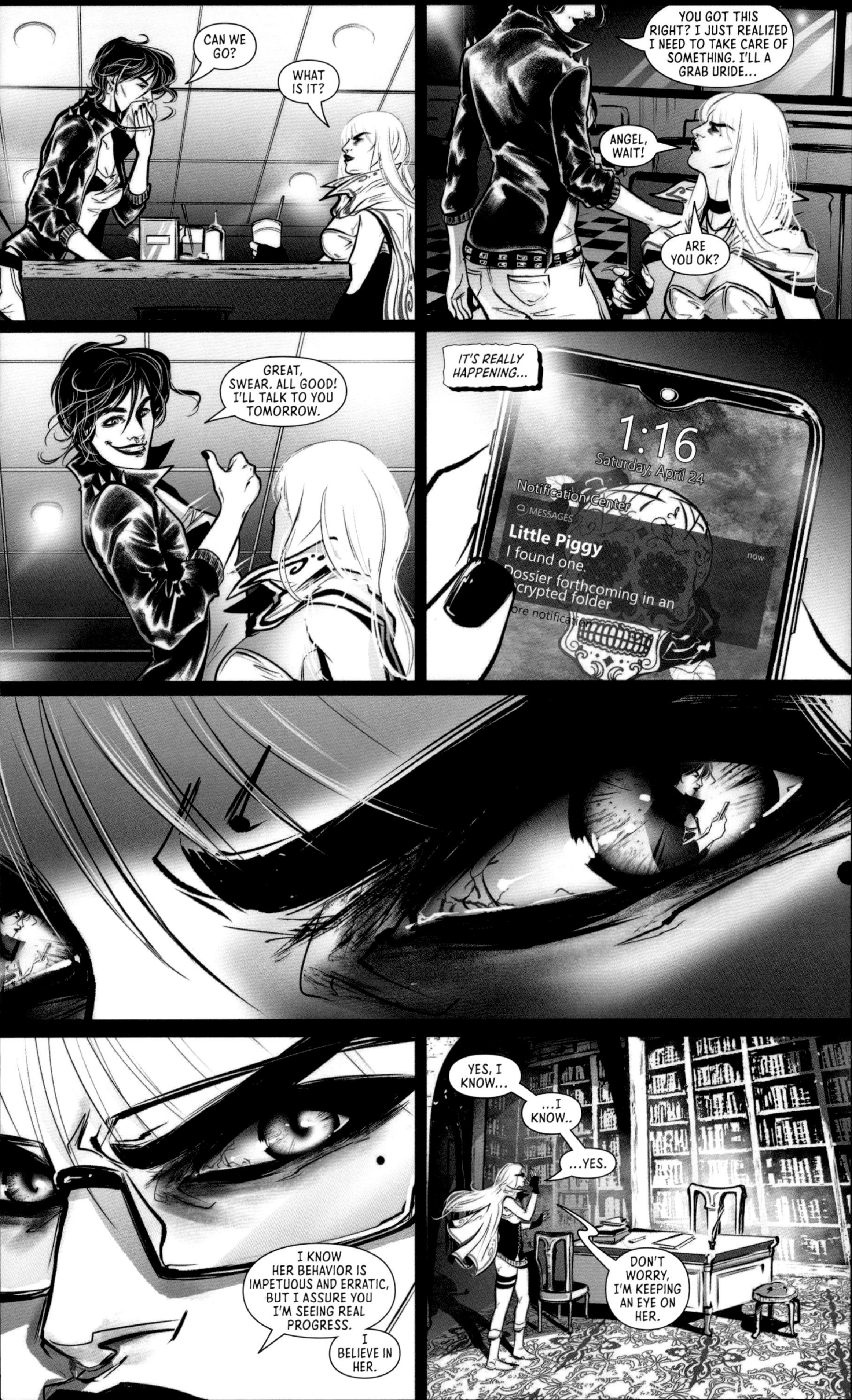
CAN WE GO?
WHAT IS IT?
YOU GOT THIS RIGHT? I JUST REALIZED I NEED TO TAKE CARE OF SOMETHING. I'LL A GRAB URIDE...
ANGEL, WAIT!
ARE YOU OK?
GREAT, SWEAR. ALL GOOD! I'LL TALK TO YOU TOMORROW.
IT'S REALLY HAPPENING...
1:16
Saturday, April 24
Notification Center
MESSAGES
Little Piggy
now
I found one.
Dossier forthcoming in an
crypted folder
YES, I KNOW...
...I KNOW..
...YES.
I KNOW HER BEHAVIOR IS IMPETUOUS AND ERRATIC, BUT I ASSURE YOU I'M SEEING REAL PROGRESS.
I BELIEVE IN HER.
DON'T WORRY, I'M KEEPING AN EYE ON HER.

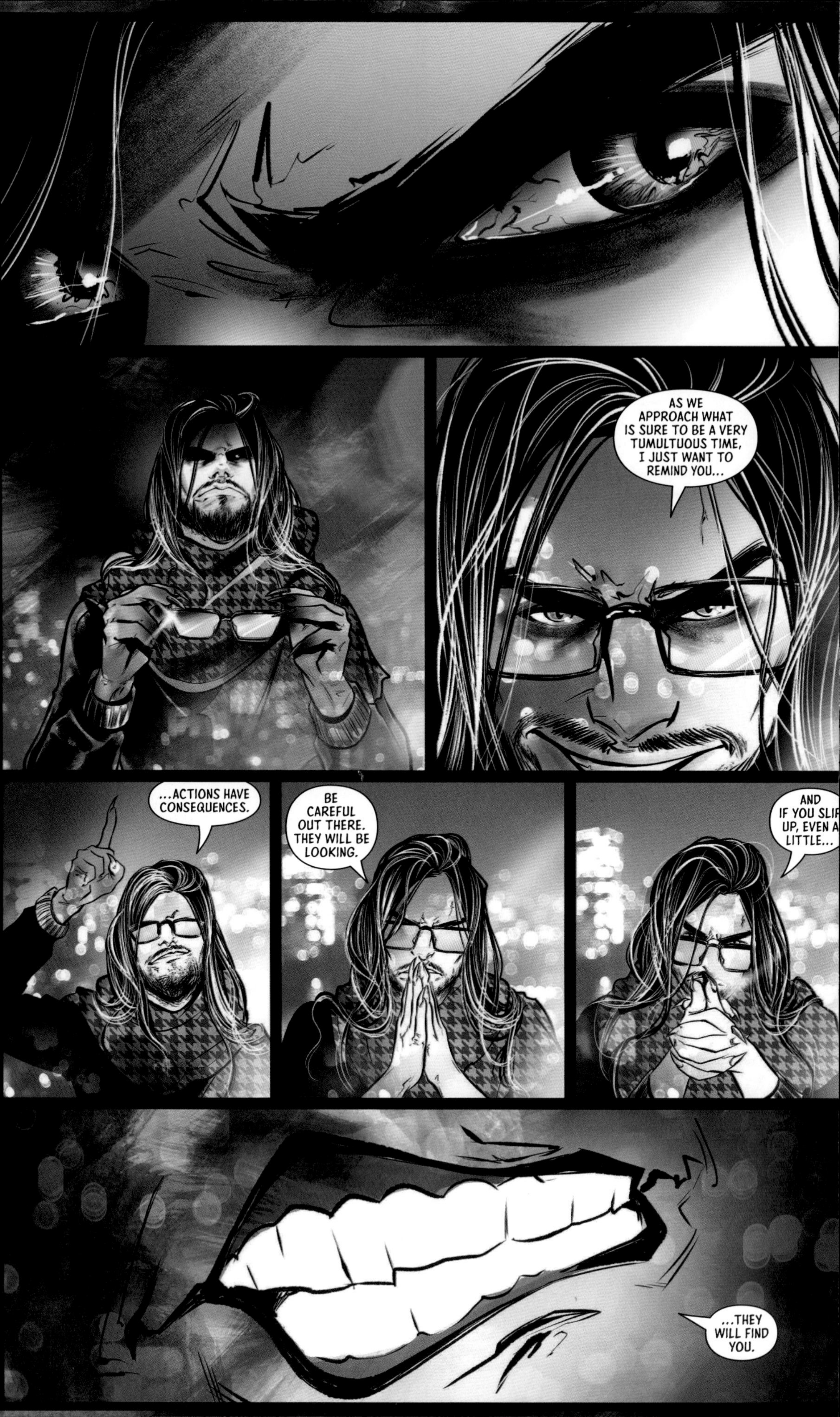
AS WE APPROACH WHAT IS SURE TO BE A VERY TUMULTUOUS TIME, I JUST WANT TO REMIND YOU...
...ACTIONS HAVE CONSEQUENCES.
BE CAREFUL OUT THERE. THEY WILL BE LOOKING.
AND IF YOU SLIP UP, EVEN A LITTLE...
...THEY WILL FIND YOU.

End Chapter Five

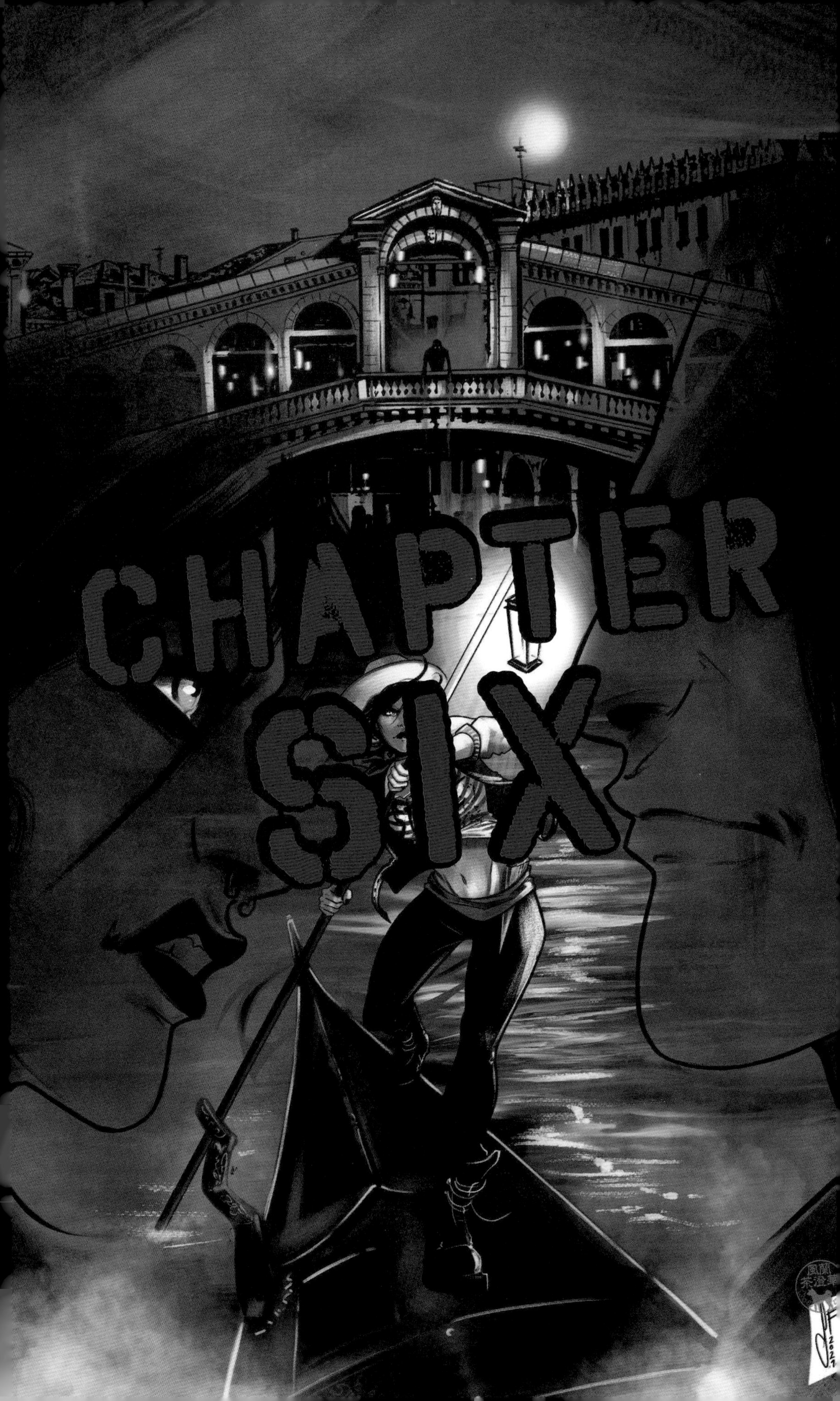
CHAPTER
SIX

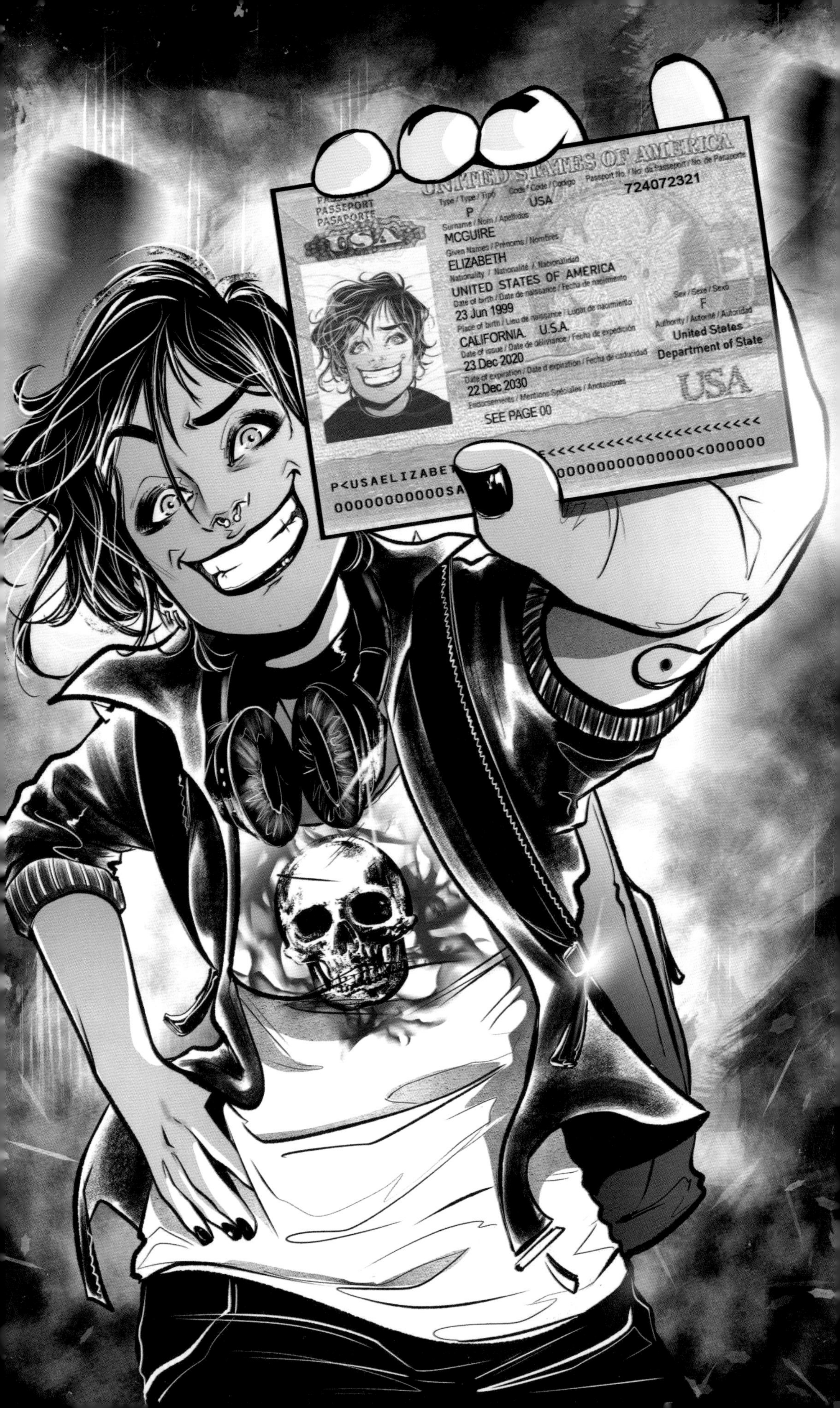
UNITED STATES OF AMERICA
PASSPORT
PASAPORTE
Type / Type / Tipo
P
Code / Code / Código
USA
Passport No. / No du Passeport / No. de Pasaporte
724072321
Surname / Nom / Apellidos
MCGUIRE
Given Names / Prénoms / Nombres
ELIZABETH
Nationality / Nationalité / Nacionalidad
UNITED STATES OF AMERICA
Date of birth / Date de naissance / Fecha de nacimiento
23 Jun 1999
Sex / Sexe / Sexo
F
Place of birth / Lieu de naissance / Lugar de nacimiento
CALIFORNIA. U.S.A.
Authority / Autorité / Autoridad
United States
Department of State
Date of issue / Date de délivrance / Fecha de expedición
23 Dec 2020
Date of expiration / Date d'expiration / Fecha de caducidad
22 Dec 2030
USA
Endorsements / Mentions Spéciales / Anotaciones
SEE PAGE 00
P<USAELIZABET
00000000000SA

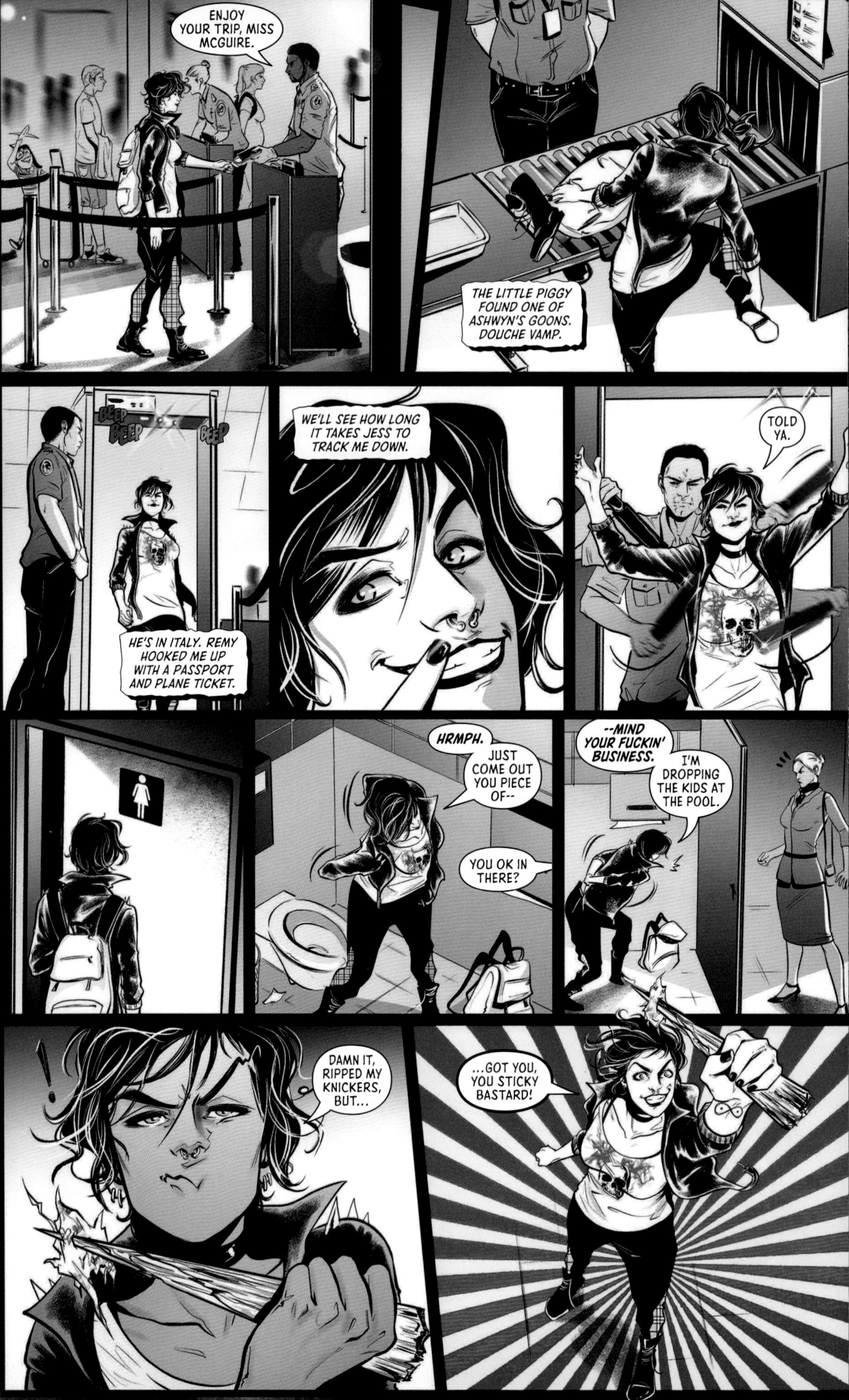
ENJOY YOUR TRIP, MISS MCGUIRE.
THE LITTLE PIGGY FOUND ONE OF ASHWYN'S GOONS. DOUCHE VAMP.
BEEP
BEEP
BEEP
HE'S IN ITALY. REMY HOOKED ME UP WITH A PASSPORT AND PLANE TICKET.
WE'LL SEE HOW LONG IT TAKES JESS TO TRACK ME DOWN.
TOLD YA.
HRMPH.
JUST COME OUT YOU PIECE OF--
YOU OK IN THERE?
--MIND YOUR FUCKIN' BUSINESS.
I'M DROPPING THE KIDS AT THE POOL.
!
DAMN IT, RIPPED MY KNICKERS, BUT...
...GOT YOU, YOU STICKY BASTARD!

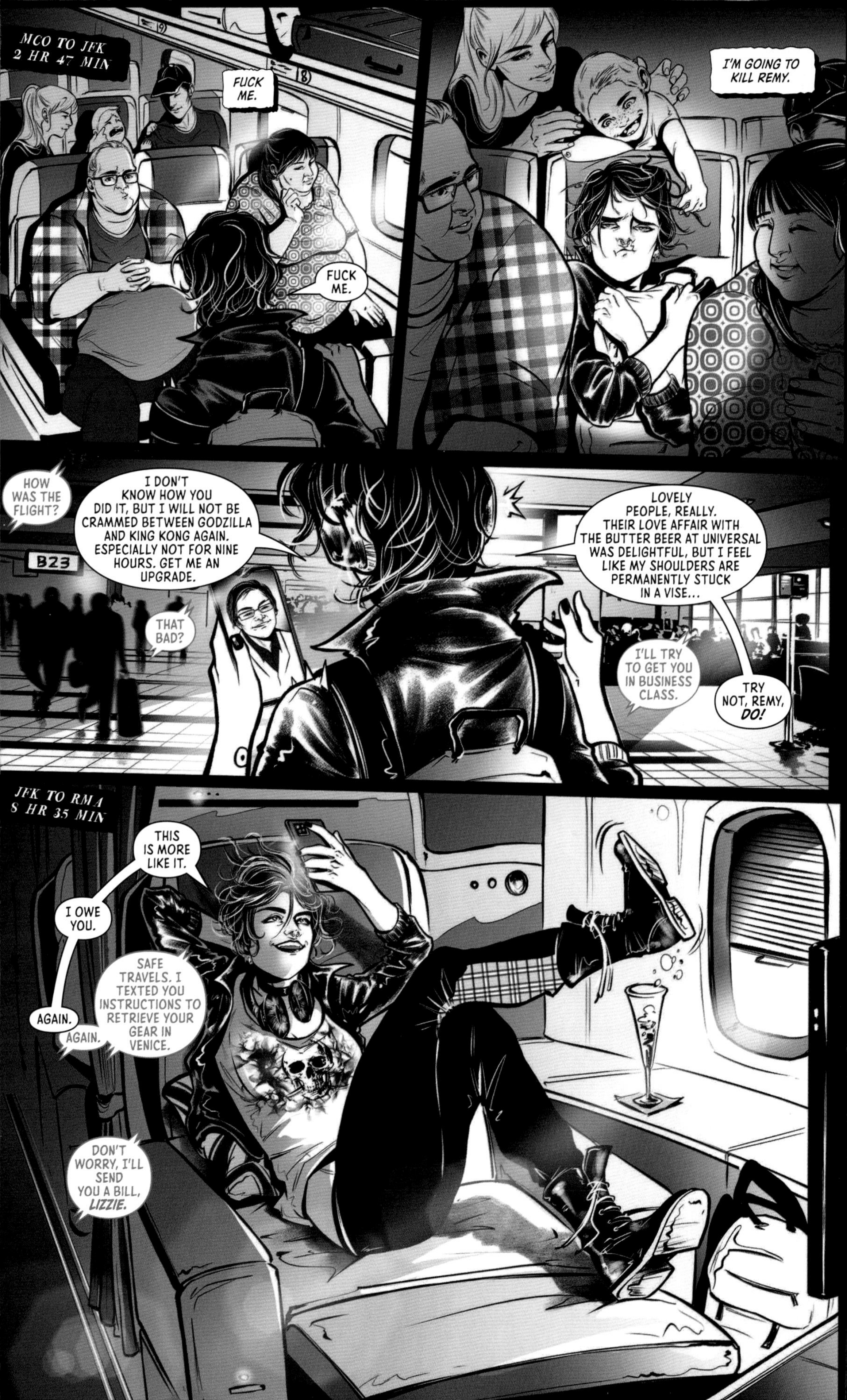

MCO TO JFK
2 HR 47 MIN
FUCK ME.
FUCK ME.
I'M GOING TO KILL REMY.
HOW WAS THE FLIGHT?
I DON'T KNOW HOW YOU DID IT, BUT I WILL NOT BE CRAMMED BETWEEN GODZILLA AND KING KONG AGAIN. ESPECIALLY NOT FOR NINE HOURS. GET ME AN UPGRADE.
B23
THAT BAD?
LOVELY PEOPLE, REALLY. THEIR LOVE AFFAIR WITH THE BUTTER BEER AT UNIVERSAL WAS DELIGHTFUL, BUT I FEEL LIKE MY SHOULDERS ARE PERMANENTLY STUCK IN A VISE...
I'LL TRY TO GET YOU IN BUSINESS CLASS.
TRY NOT, REMY, DO!
JFK TO RMA
8 HR 35 MIN
THIS IS MORE LIKE IT.
I OWE YOU.
SAFE TRAVELS. I TEXTED YOU INSTRUCTIONS TO RETRIEVE YOUR GEAR IN VENICE.
AGAIN.
AGAIN.
DON'T WORRY, I'LL SEND YOU A BILL, LIZZIE.

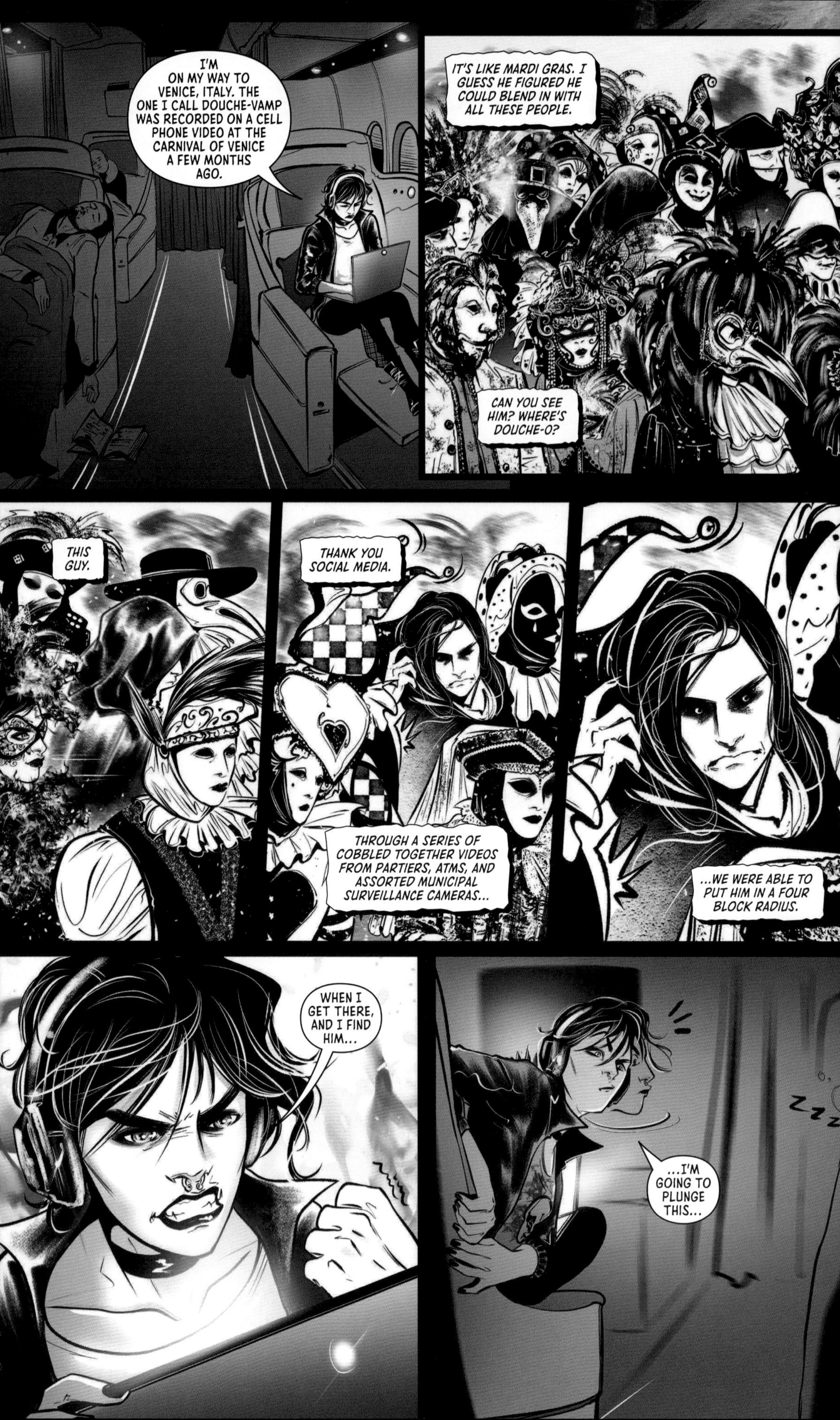
I'M ON MY WAY TO VENICE, ITALY. THE ONE I CALL DOUCHE-VAMP WAS RECORDED ON A CELL PHONE VIDEO AT THE CARNIVAL OF VENICE A FEW MONTHS AGO.
IT'S LIKE MARDI GRAS. I GUESS HE FIGURED HE COULD BLEND IN WITH ALL THESE PEOPLE.
CAN YOU SEE HIM? WHERE'S DOUCHE-O?
THIS GUY.
THANK YOU SOCIAL MEDIA.
THROUGH A SERIES OF COBBLED TOGETHER VIDEOS FROM PARTIERS, ATMS, AND ASSORTED MUNICIPAL SURVEILLANCE CAMERAS...
...WE WERE ABLE TO PUT HIM IN A FOUR BLOCK RADIUS.
WHEN I GET THERE, AND I FIND HIM...
...I'M GOING TO PLUNGE THIS...
Z Z Z

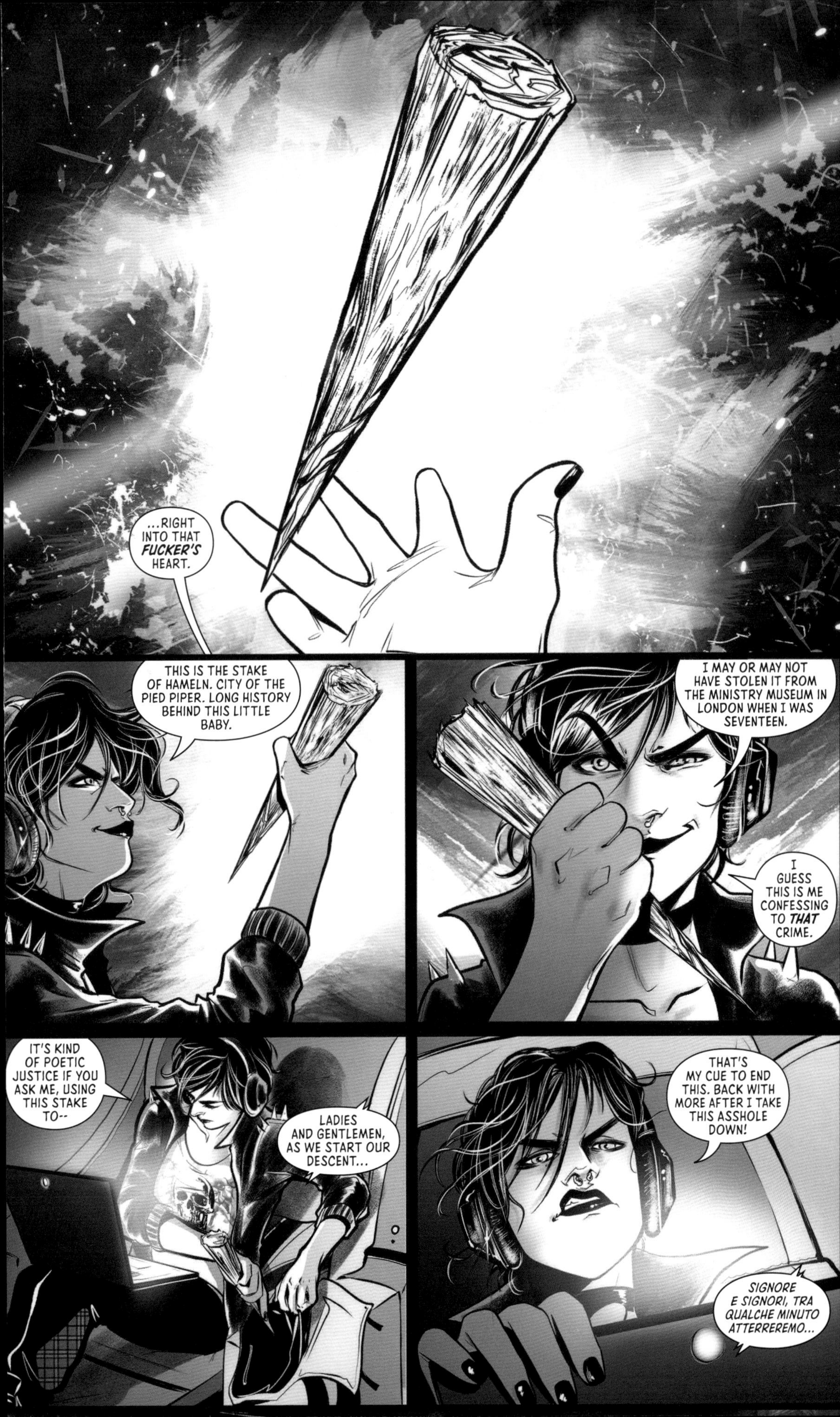
...RIGHT INTO THAT FUCKER'S HEART.
THIS IS THE STAKE OF HAMELN. CITY OF THE PIED PIPER. LONG HISTORY BEHIND THIS LITTLE BABY.
I MAY OR MAY NOT HAVE STOLEN IT FROM THE MINISTRY MUSEUM IN LONDON WHEN I WAS SEVENTEEN.
I GUESS THIS IS ME CONFESSING TO THAT CRIME.
IT'S KIND OF POETIC JUSTICE IF YOU ASK ME, USING THIS STAKE TO--
LADIES AND GENTLEMEN, AS WE START OUR DESCENT...
THAT'S MY CUE TO END THIS. BACK WITH MORE AFTER I TAKE THIS ASSHOLE DOWN!
SIGNORE E SIGNORI, TRA QUALCHE MINUTO ATTERREREMO...

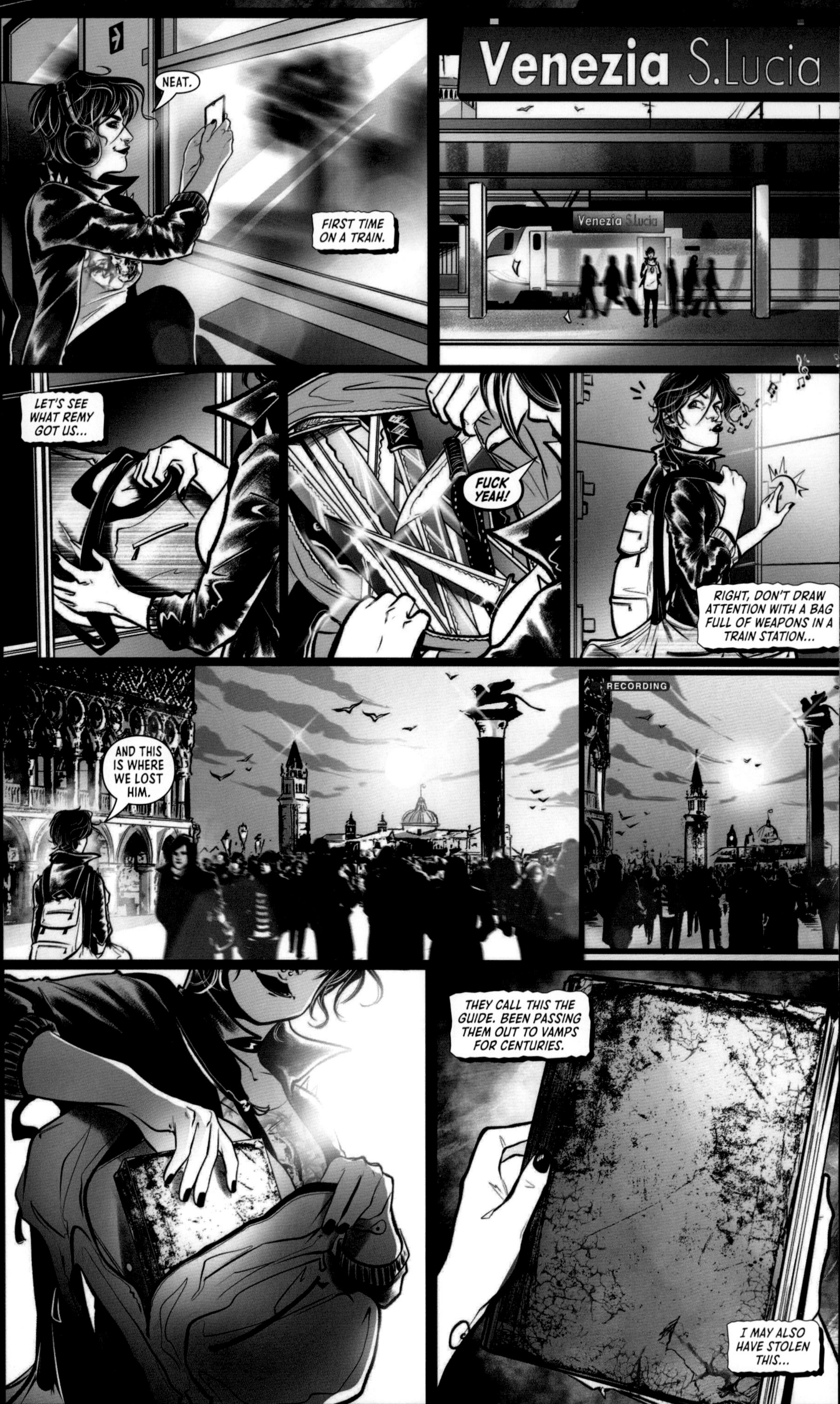
NEAT.
FIRST TIME ON A TRAIN.
Venezia S.Lucia
Venezia S.Lucia
LET'S SEE WHAT REMY GOT US...
FUCK YEAH!
RIGHT, DON'T DRAW ATTENTION WITH A BAG FULL OF WEAPONS IN A TRAIN STATION...
AND THIS IS WHERE WE LOST HIM.
RECORDING
THEY CALL THIS THE GUIDE. BEEN PASSING THEM OUT TO VAMPS FOR CENTURIES.
I MAY ALSO HAVE STOLEN THIS...

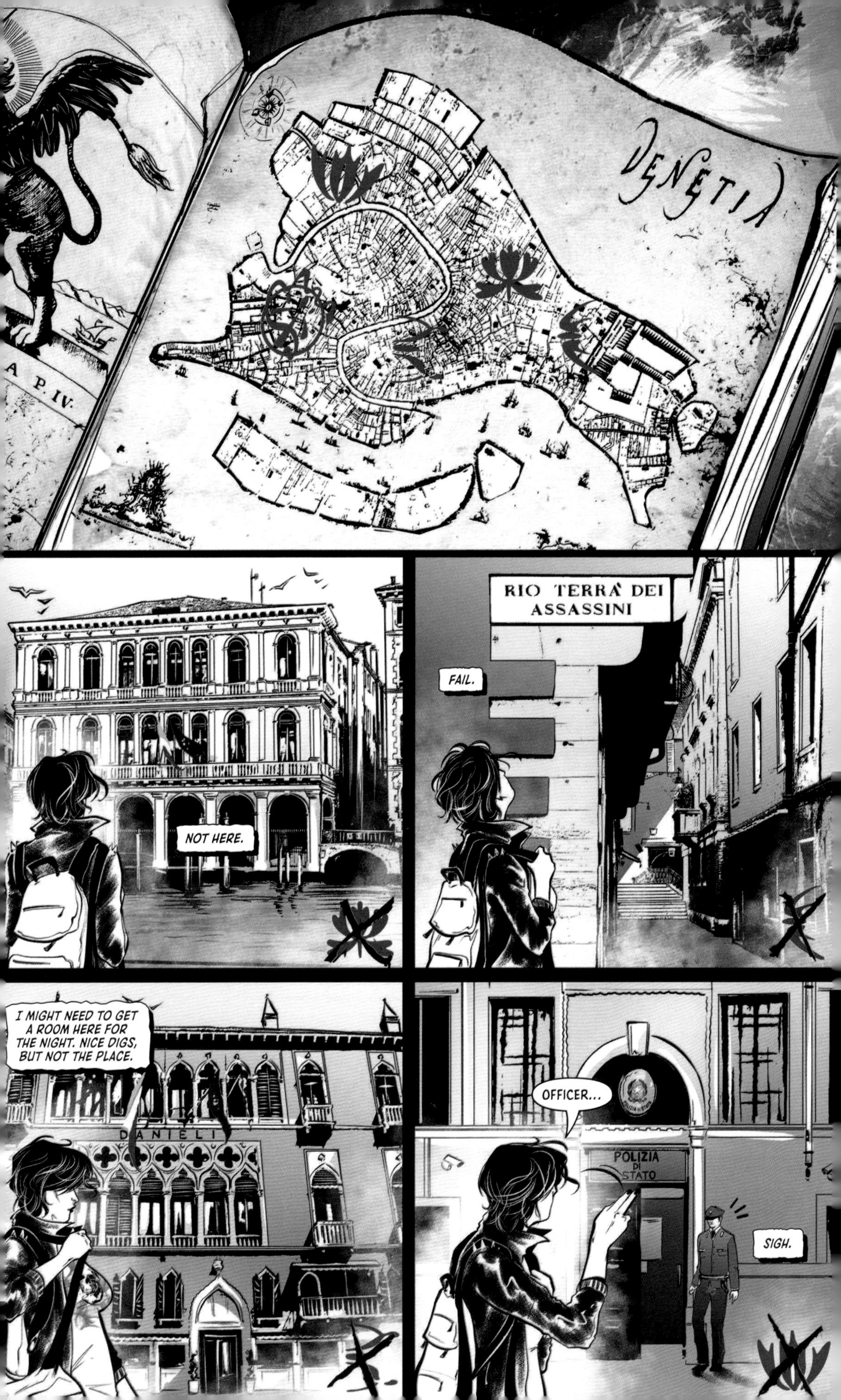
VENETIA
A P. IV
NOT HERE.
RIO TERRA' DEI
ASSASSINI
FAIL.
I MIGHT NEED TO GET A ROOM HERE FOR THE NIGHT. NICE DIGS, BUT NOT THE PLACE.
DANIELI
OFFICER...
POLIZIA DI STATO
SIGH.

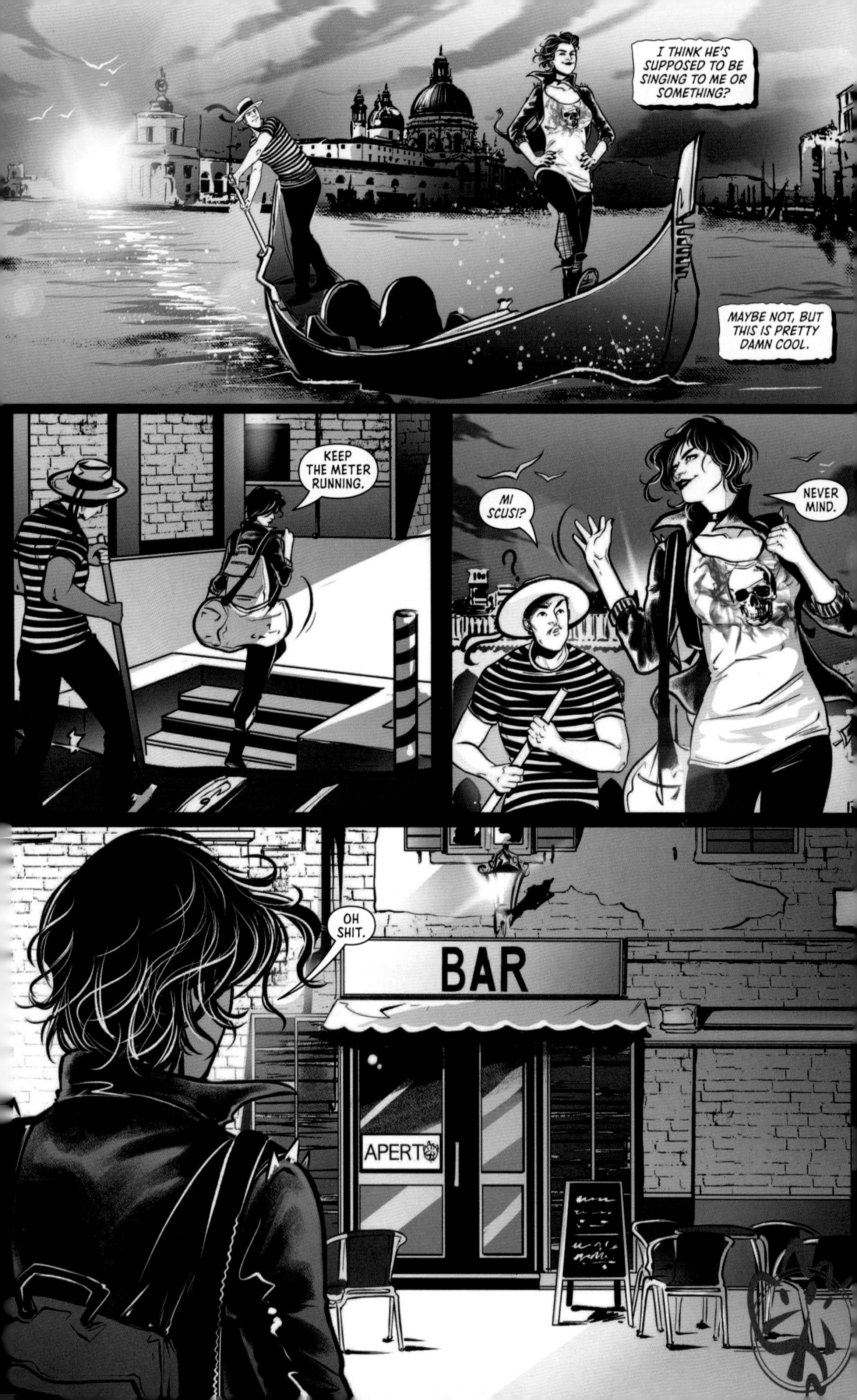
I THINK HE'S SUPPOSED TO BE SINGING TO ME OR SOMETHING?
MAYBE NOT, BUT THIS IS PRETTY DAMN COOL.
KEEP THE METER RUNNING.
MI SCUSI?
NEVER MIND.
OH SHIT.
BAR
APERTO

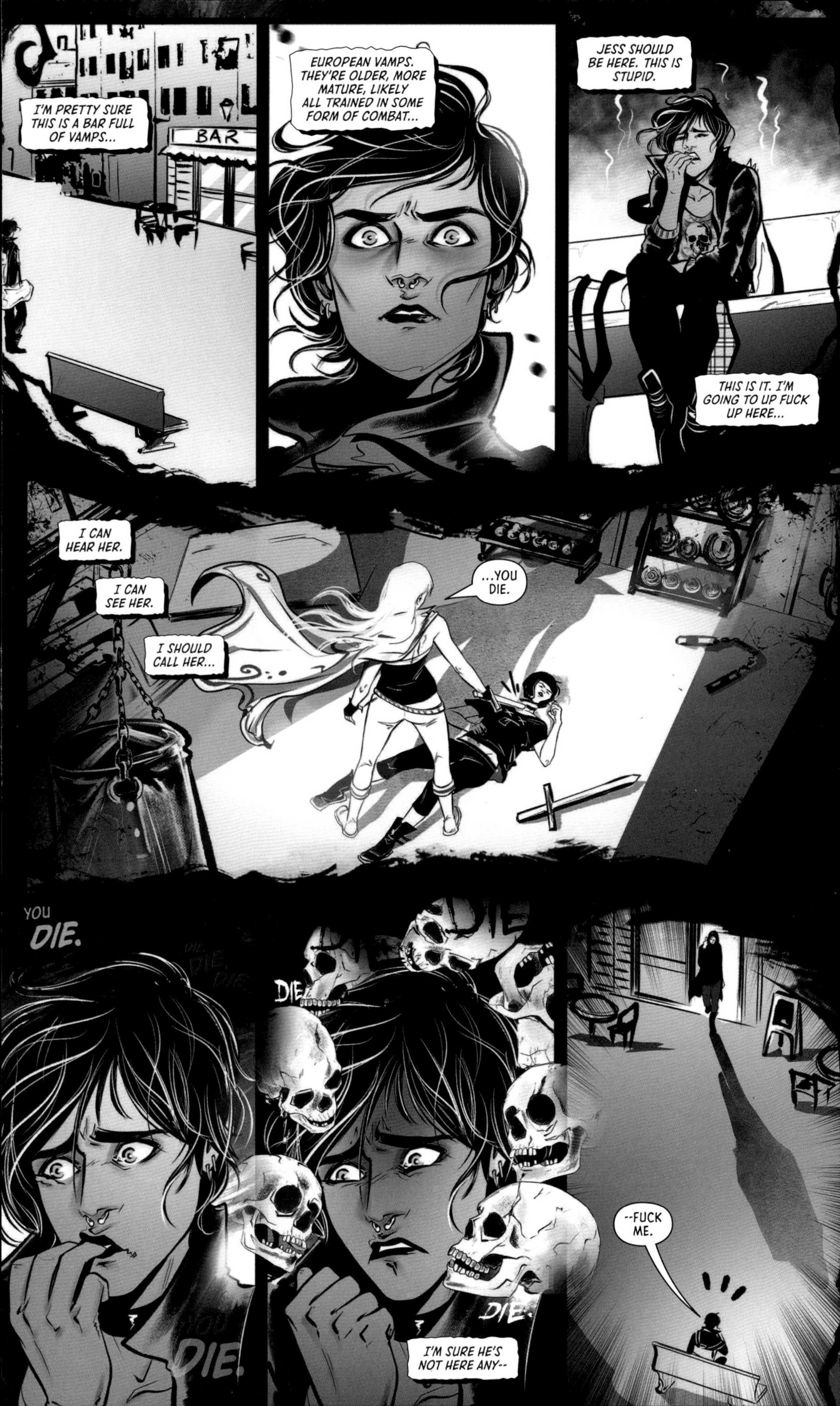
I'M PRETTY SURE THIS IS A BAR FULL OF VAMPS...
BAR
EUROPEAN VAMPS. THEY'RE OLDER, MORE MATURE, LIKELY ALL TRAINED IN SOME FORM OF COMBAT...
JESS SHOULD BE HERE. THIS IS STUPID.
THIS IS IT. I'M GOING TO UP FUCK UP HERE...
I CAN HEAR HER.
I CAN SEE HER.
I SHOULD CALL HER...
...YOU DIE.
YOU DIE.
DIE.
I'M SURE HE'S NOT HERE ANY--
--FUCK ME.

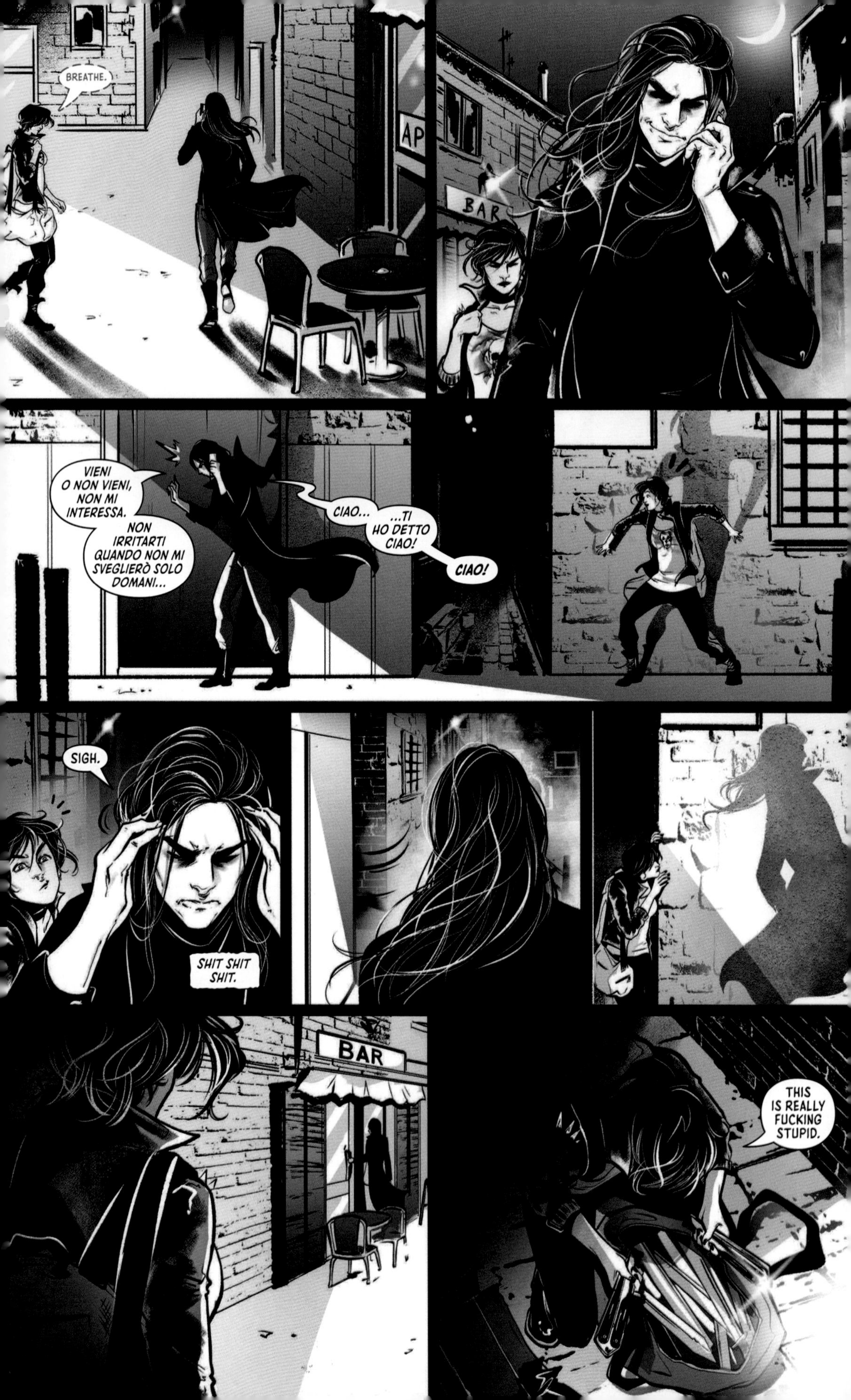
BREATHE.
VIENI O NON VIENI, NON MI INTERESSA.
NON IRRITARTI QUANDO NON MI SVEGLIERÒ SOLO DOMANI...
CIAO...
...TI HO DETTO CIAO!
CIAO!
SIGH.
SHIT SHIT SHIT.
THIS IS REALLY FUCKING STUPID.

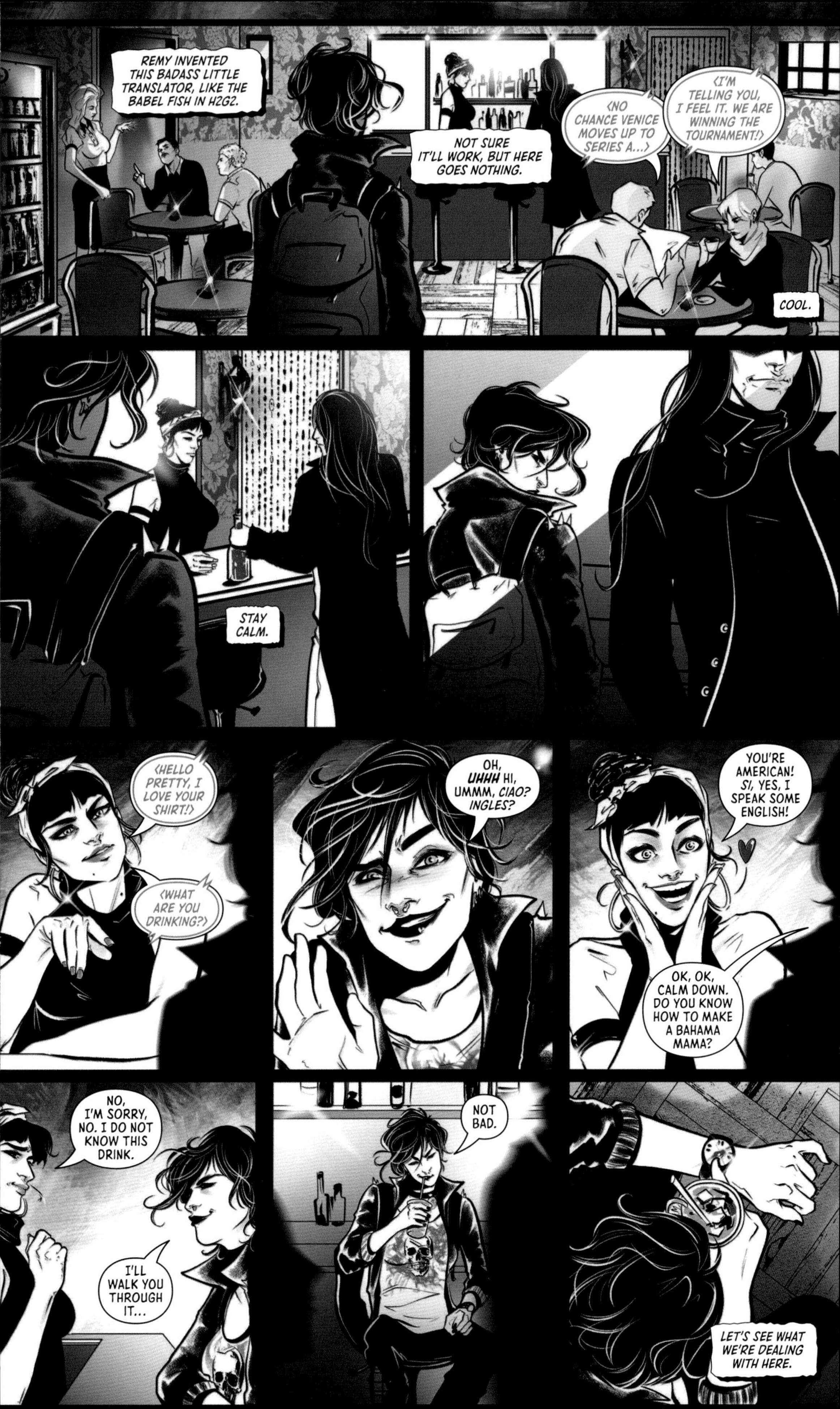
REMY INVENTED THIS BADASS LITTLE TRANSLATOR, LIKE THE BABEL FISH IN H2G2.
NOT SURE IT'LL WORK, BUT HERE GOES NOTHING.
‹NO CHANCE VENICE MOVES UP TO SERIES A...›
‹I'M TELLING YOU, I FEEL IT. WE ARE WINNING THE TOURNAMENT!›
COOL.
STAY CALM.
‹HELLO PRETTY, I LOVE YOUR SHIRT!›
‹WHAT ARE YOU DRINKING?›
OH, *UHHH* HI, UMMM, *CIAO? INGLES?*
YOU'RE AMERICAN! *SI*, YES, I SPEAK SOME ENGLISH!
OK, OK, CALM DOWN. DO YOU KNOW HOW TO MAKE A BAHAMA MAMA?
NO, I'M SORRY, NO. I DO NOT KNOW THIS DRINK.
I'LL WALK YOU THROUGH IT...
NOT BAD.
LET'S SEE WHAT WE'RE DEALING WITH HERE.

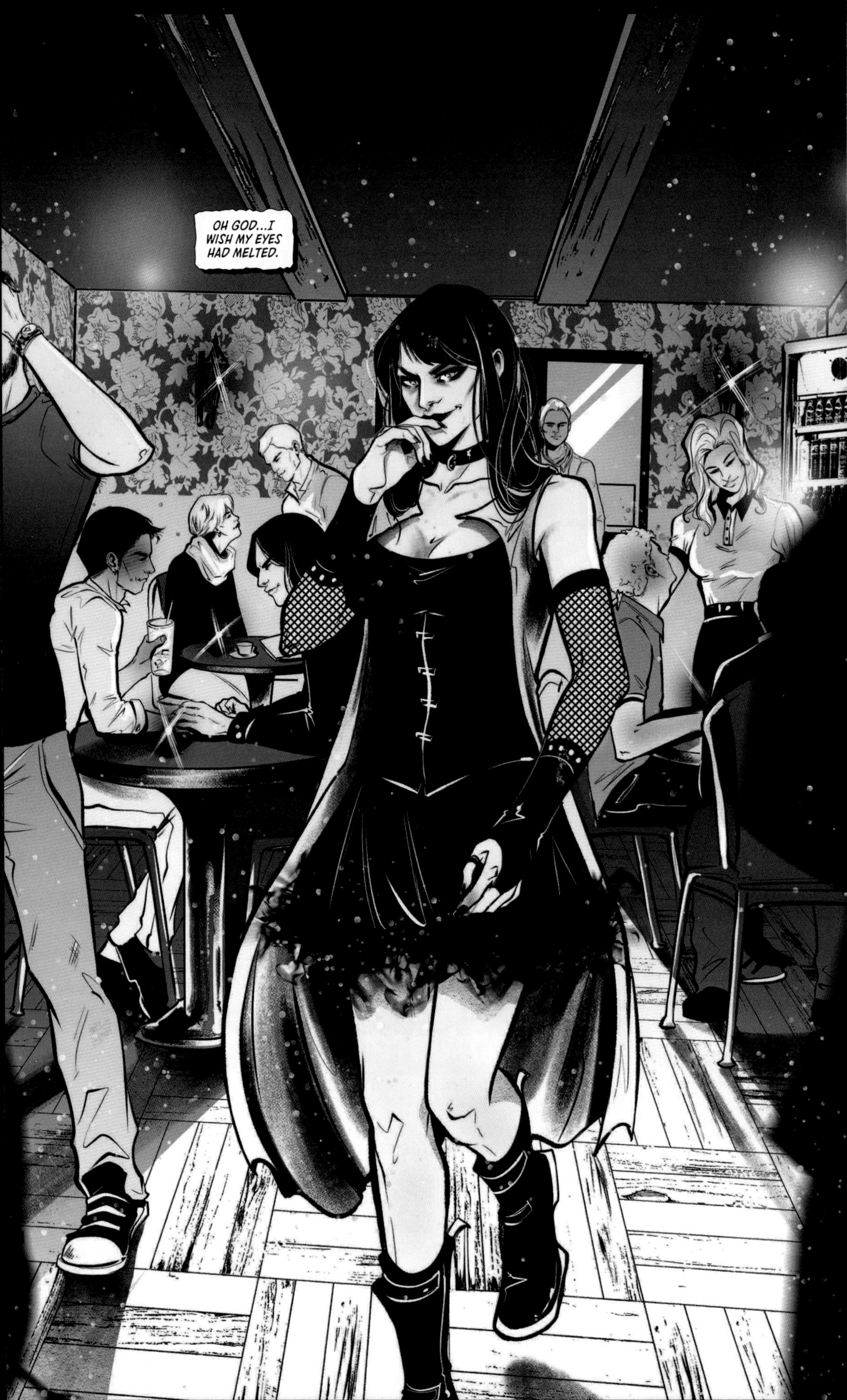
OH GOD...I WISH MY EYES HAD MELTED.

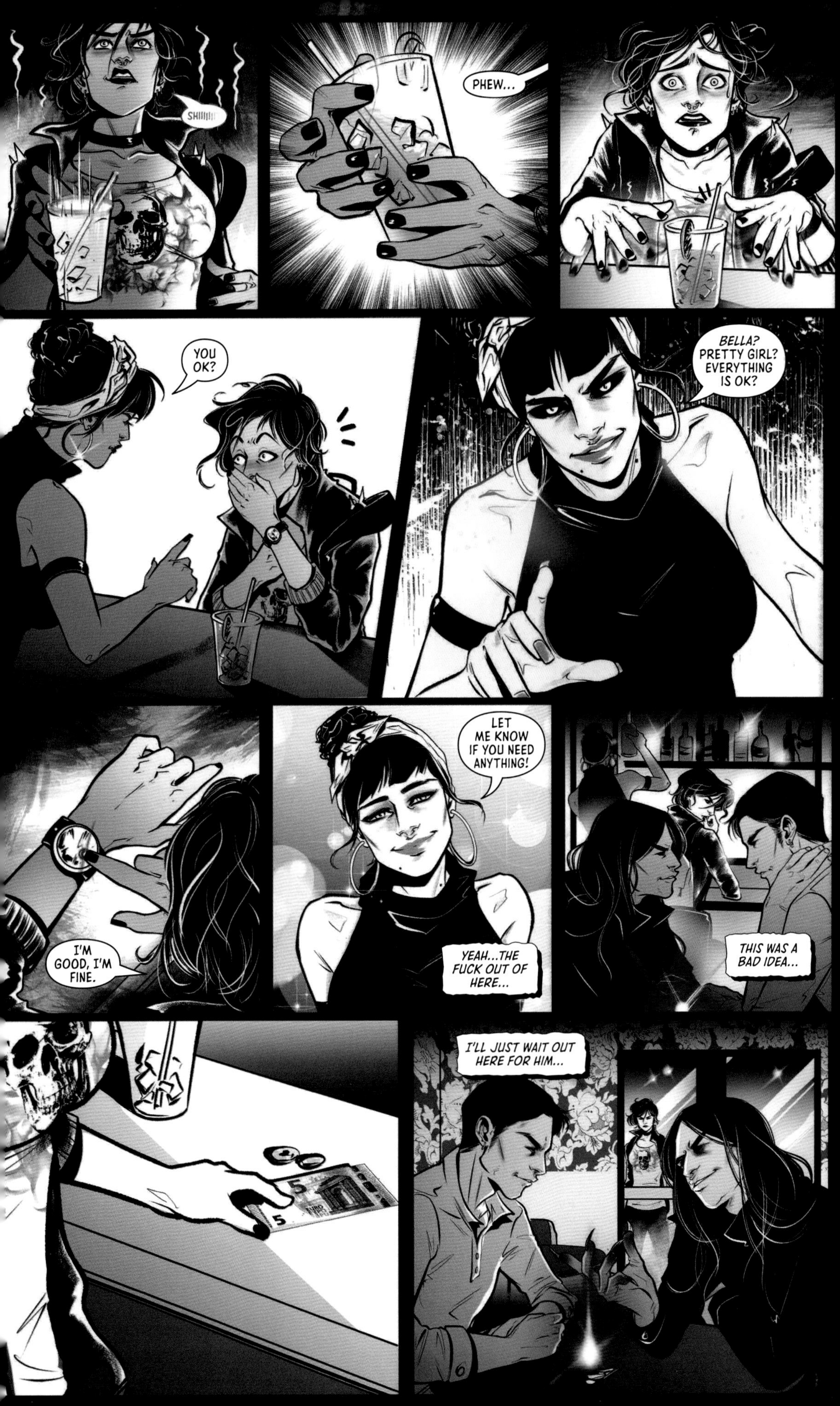
SHIIII!!!
PHEW...
YOU OK?
BELLA? PRETTY GIRL? EVERYTHING IS OK?
I'M GOOD, I'M FINE.
LET ME KNOW IF YOU NEED ANYTHING!
YEAH...THE FUCK OUT OF HERE...
THIS WAS A BAD IDEA...
I'LL JUST WAIT OUT HERE FOR HIM...

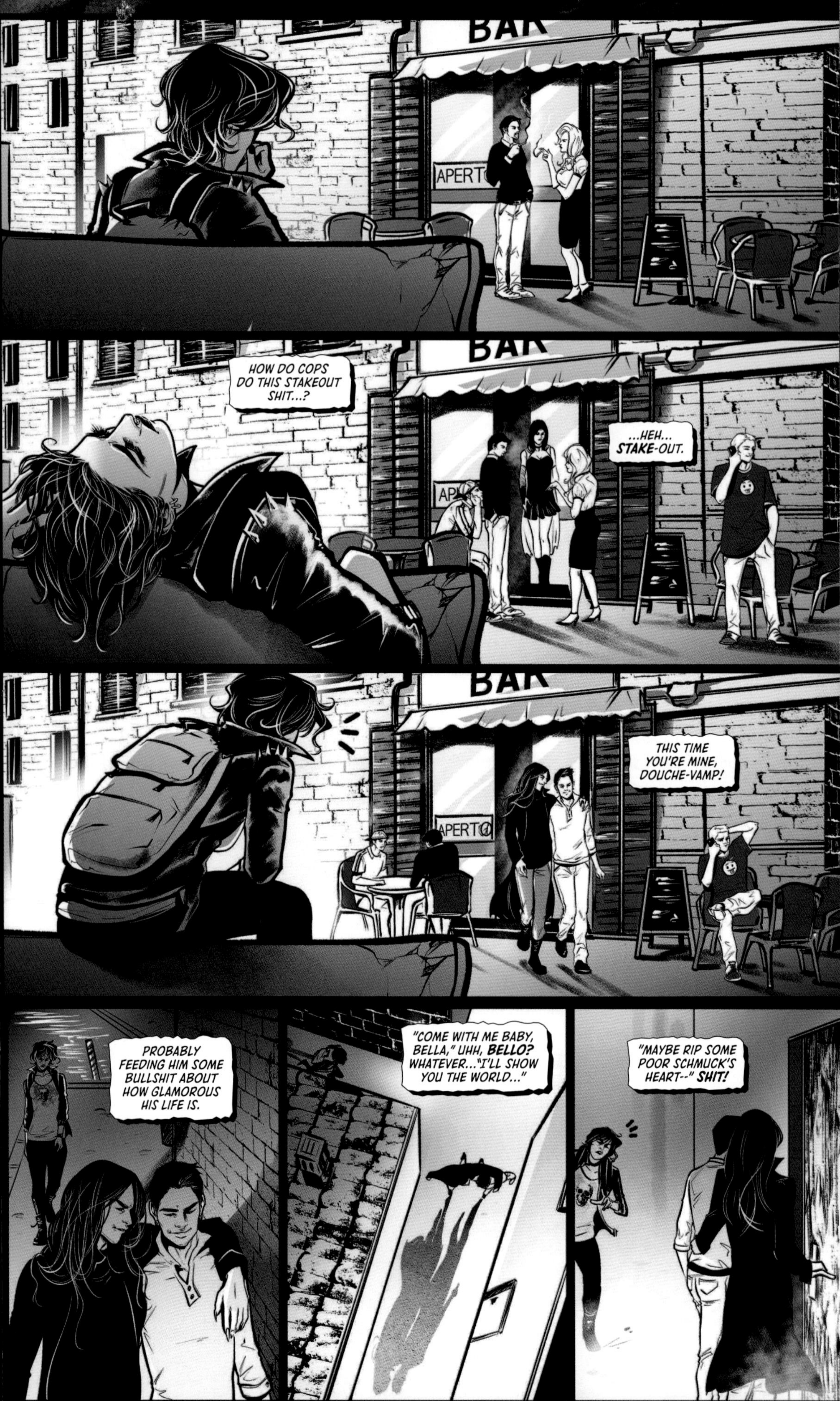
BAR
APERTO
HOW DO COPS DO THIS STAKEOUT SHIT...?
...HEH... STAKE-OUT.
THIS TIME YOU'RE MINE, DOUCHE-VAMP!
PROBABLY FEEDING HIM SOME BULLSHIT ABOUT HOW GLAMOROUS HIS LIFE IS.
"COME WITH ME BABY, BELLA," UHH, BELLO? WHATEVER..."I'LL SHOW YOU THE WORLD..."
"MAYBE RIP SOME POOR SCHMUCK'S HEART--" SHIT!

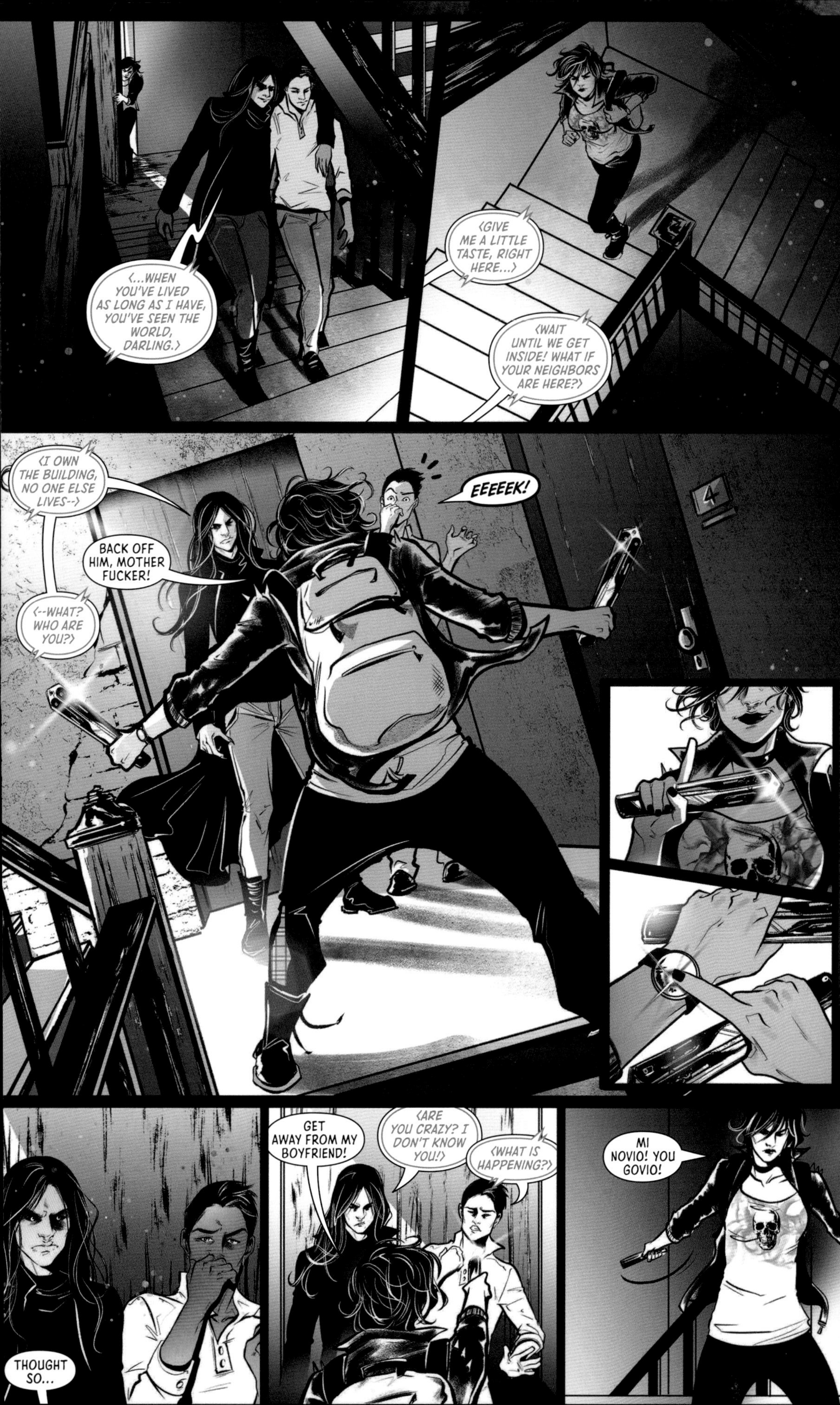
<...WHEN YOU'VE LIVED AS LONG AS I HAVE, YOU'VE SEEN THE WORLD, DARLING.>
<GIVE ME A LITTLE TASTE, RIGHT HERE...>
<WAIT UNTIL WE GET INSIDE! WHAT IF YOUR NEIGHBORS ARE HERE?>
<I OWN THE BUILDING, NO ONE ELSE LIVES-->
BACK OFF HIM, MOTHER FUCKER!
EEEEEK!
<--WHAT? WHO ARE YOU?>
4
THOUGHT SO...
GET AWAY FROM MY BOYFRIEND!
<ARE YOU CRAZY? I DON'T KNOW YOU!>
<WHAT IS HAPPENING?>
MI NOVIO! YOU GOVIO!

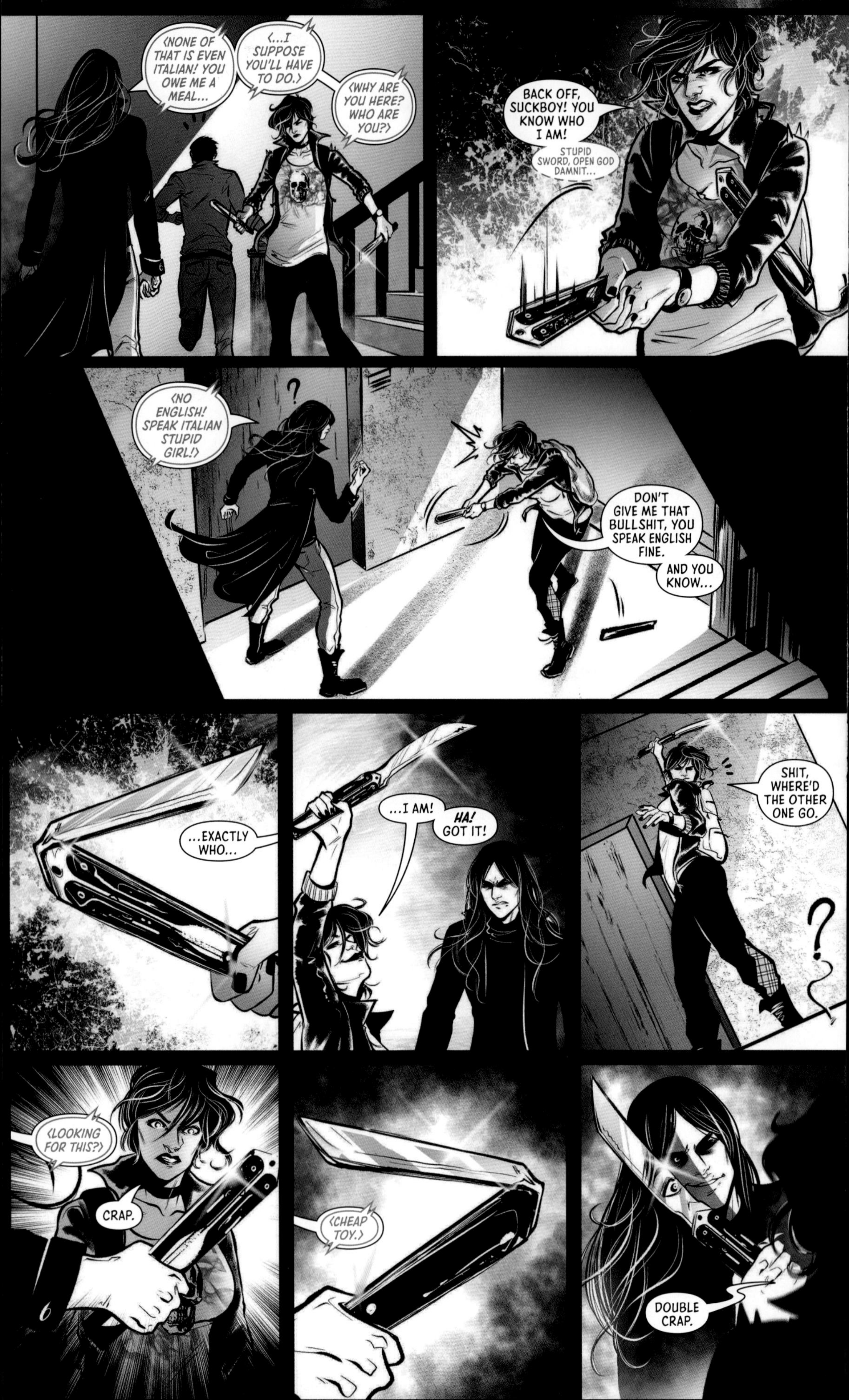
<NONE OF THAT IS EVEN ITALIAN! YOU OWE ME A MEAL...
<...I SUPPOSE YOU'LL HAVE TO DO.>
<WHY ARE YOU HERE? WHO ARE YOU?>
BACK OFF, SUCKBOY! YOU KNOW WHO I AM!
STUPID SWORD, OPEN GOD DAMNIT...
<NO ENGLISH! SPEAK ITALIAN STUPID GIRL!>
?
DON'T GIVE ME THAT BULLSHIT, YOU SPEAK ENGLISH FINE.
AND YOU KNOW...
...EXACTLY WHO...
...I AM!
HA! GOT IT!
SHIT, WHERE'D THE OTHER ONE GO.
?
<LOOKING FOR THIS?>
CRAP.
<CHEAP TOY.>
DOUBLE CRAP.

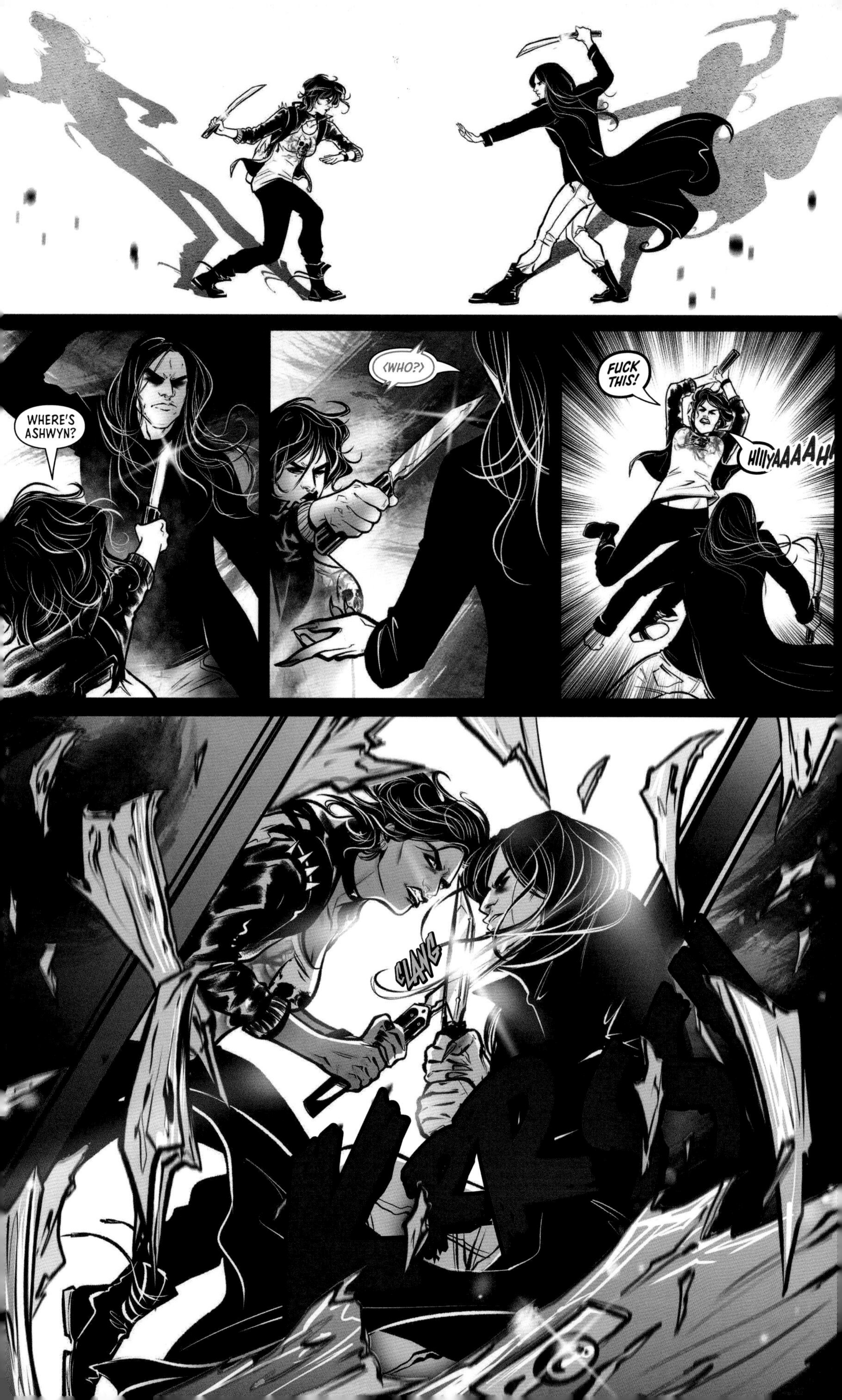
WHERE'S ASHWYN?
‹WHO?›
FUCK THIS!
HIIIYAAAAH!
CLANG

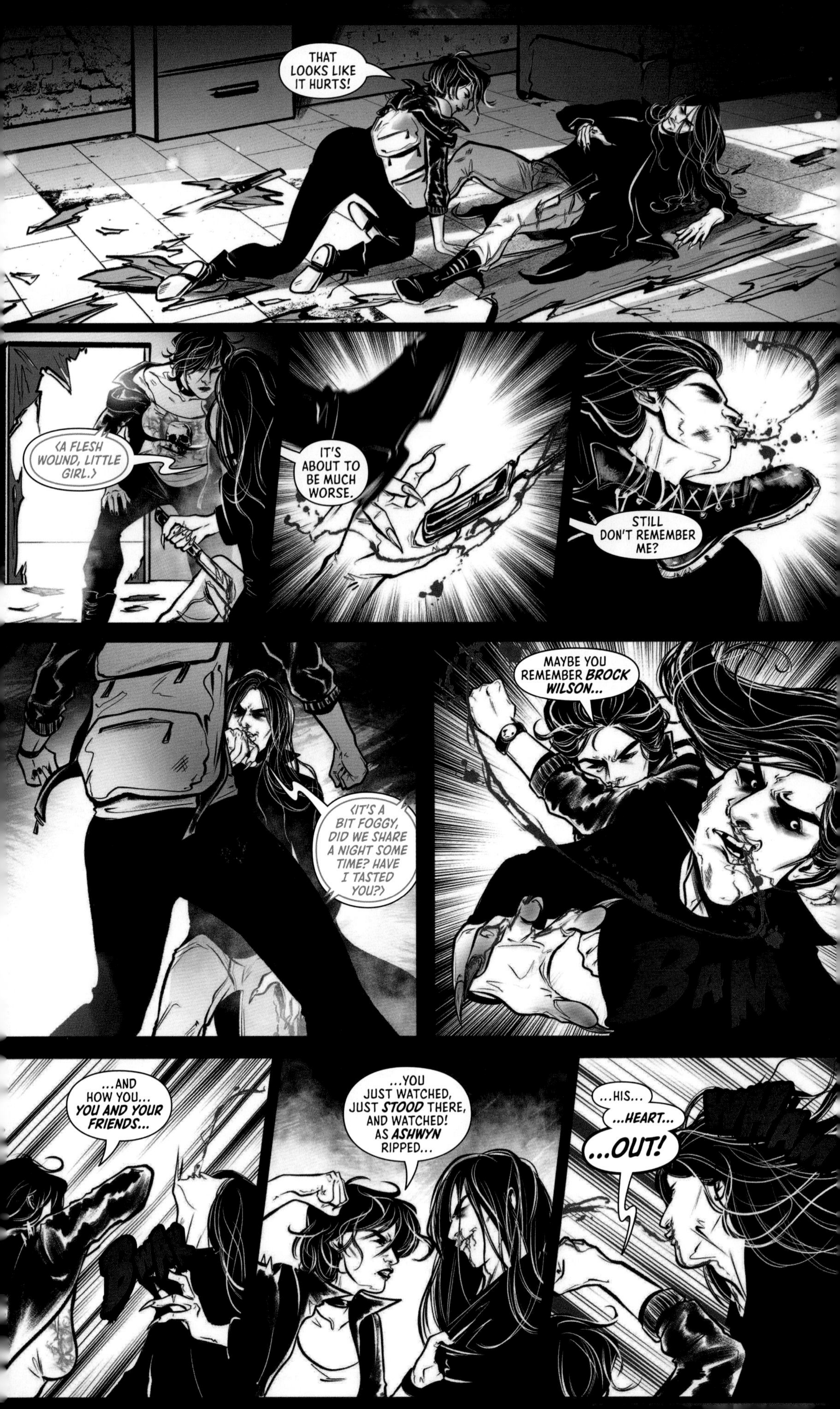

THAT LOOKS LIKE IT HURTS!
<A FLESH WOUND, LITTLE GIRL.>
IT'S ABOUT TO BE MUCH WORSE.
STILL DON'T REMEMBER ME?
<IT'S A BIT FOGGY, DID WE SHARE A NIGHT SOME TIME? HAVE I TASTED YOU?>
MAYBE YOU REMEMBER BROCK WILSON...
...AND HOW YOU... YOU AND YOUR FRIENDS...
...YOU JUST WATCHED, JUST STOOD THERE, AND WATCHED! AS ASHWYN RIPPED...
...HIS...
...HEART...
...OUT!

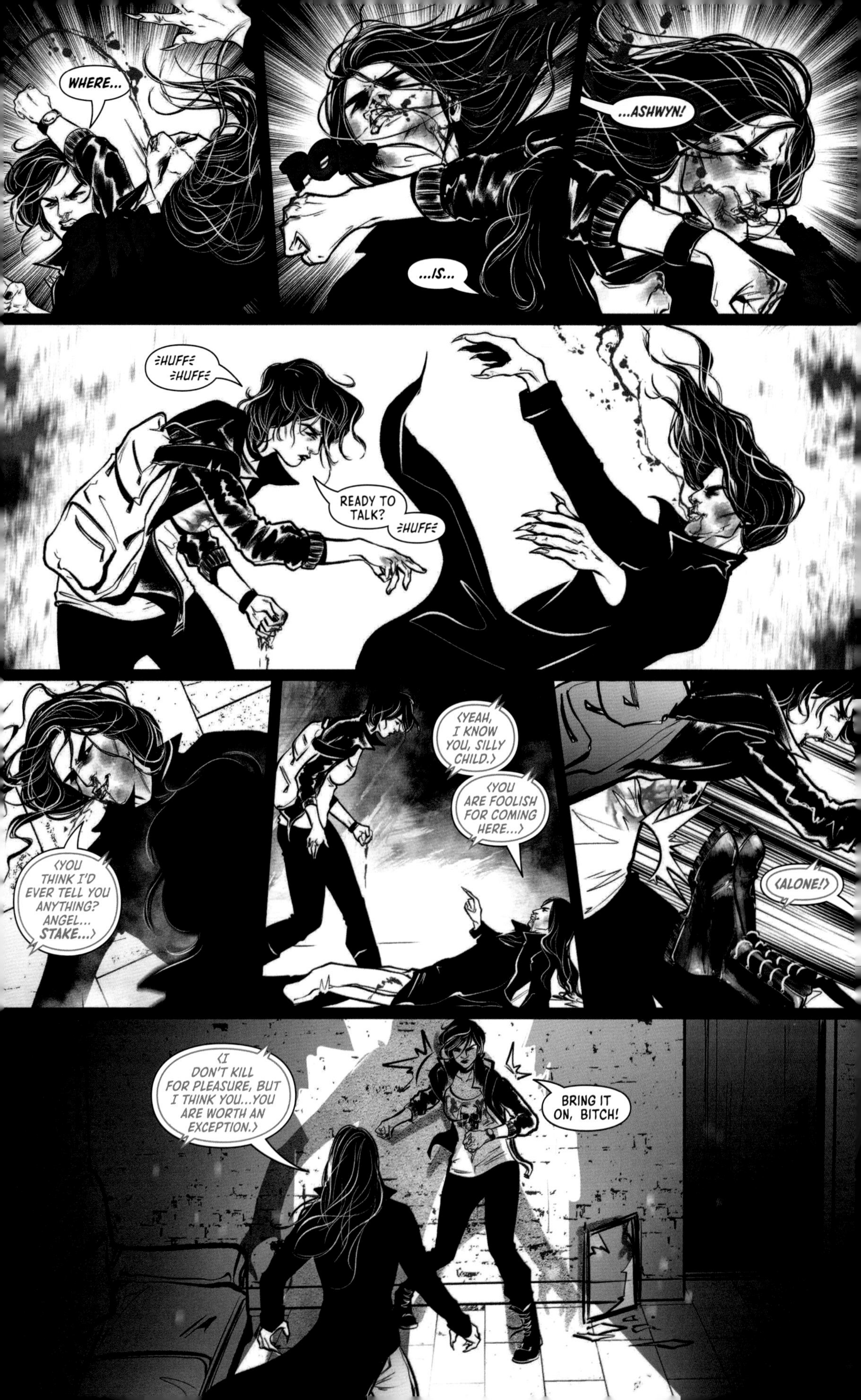

WHERE...
...IS...
...ASHWYN!
HUFF HUFF
READY TO TALK? HUFF
‹YOU THINK I'D EVER TELL YOU ANYTHING? ANGEL... STAKE...›
‹YEAH, I KNOW YOU, SILLY CHILD.›
‹YOU ARE FOOLISH FOR COMING HERE...›
‹ALONE!›
‹I DON'T KILL FOR PLEASURE, BUT I THINK YOU...YOU ARE WORTH AN EXCEPTION.›
BRING IT ON, BITCH!

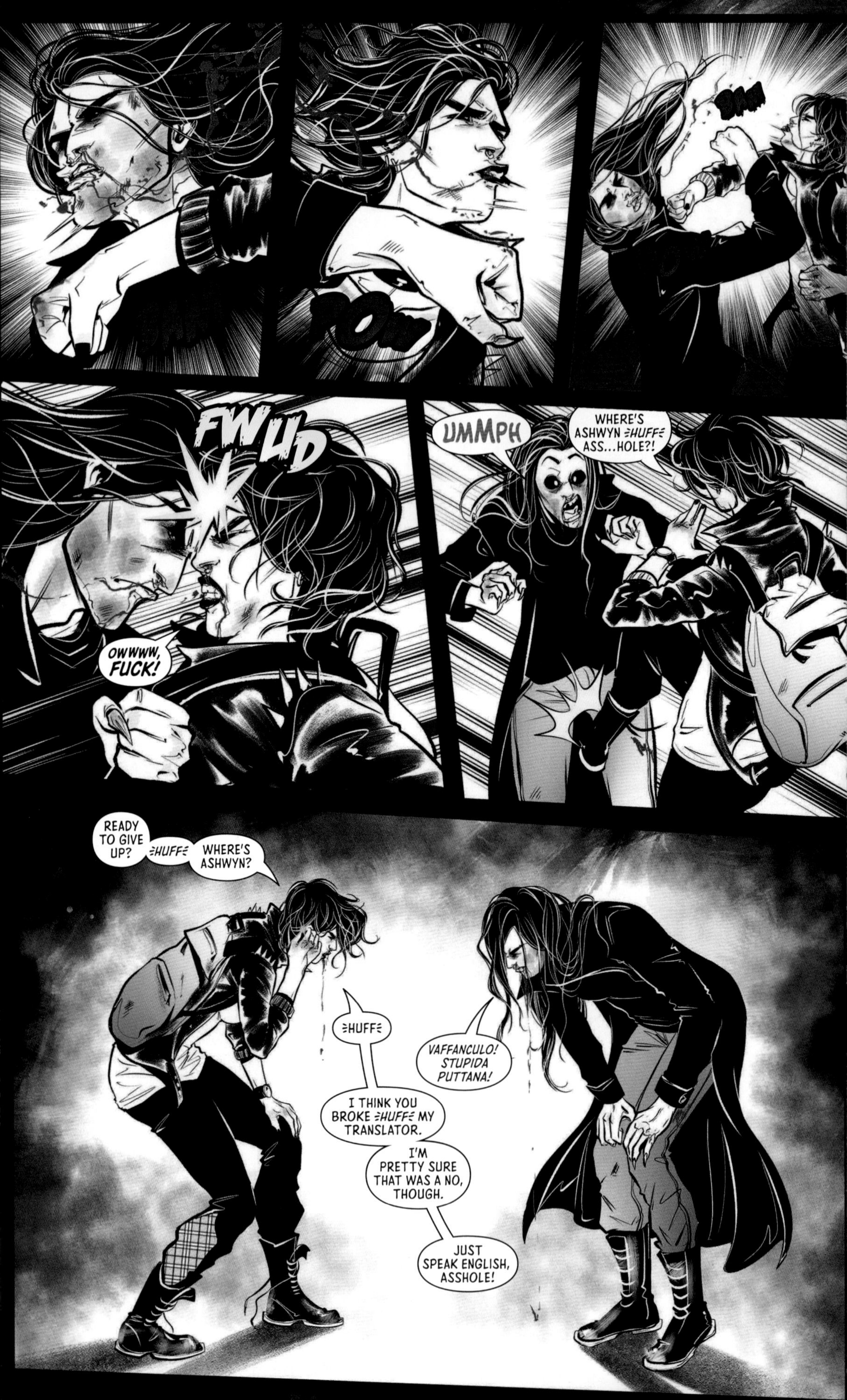

POW
FWUD
OWWWW, FUCK!
UMMPH
WHERE'S ASHWYN ≡HUFF≡ ASS...HOLE?!
READY TO GIVE UP?
≡HUFF≡
WHERE'S ASHWYN?
≡HUFF≡
VAFFANCULO! STUPIDA PUTTANA!
I THINK YOU BROKE ≡HUFF≡ MY TRANSLATOR.
I'M PRETTY SURE THAT WAS A NO, THOUGH.
JUST SPEAK ENGLISH, ASSHOLE!

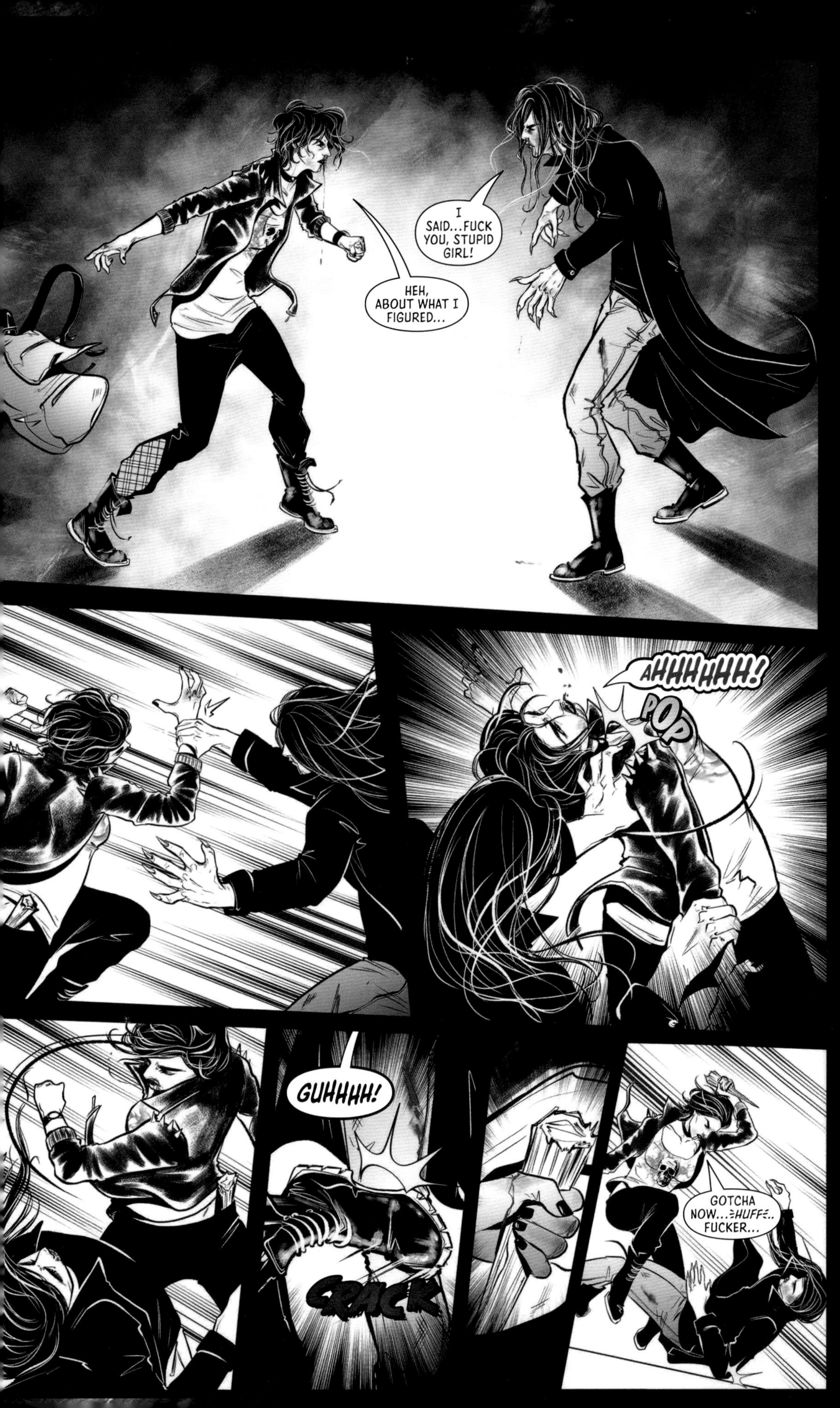
HEH, ABOUT WHAT I FIGURED...
I SAID...FUCK YOU, STUPID GIRL!
AHHHHHH!
POP
GUHHHH!
CRACK
GOTCHA NOW... HUFF.. FUCKER...

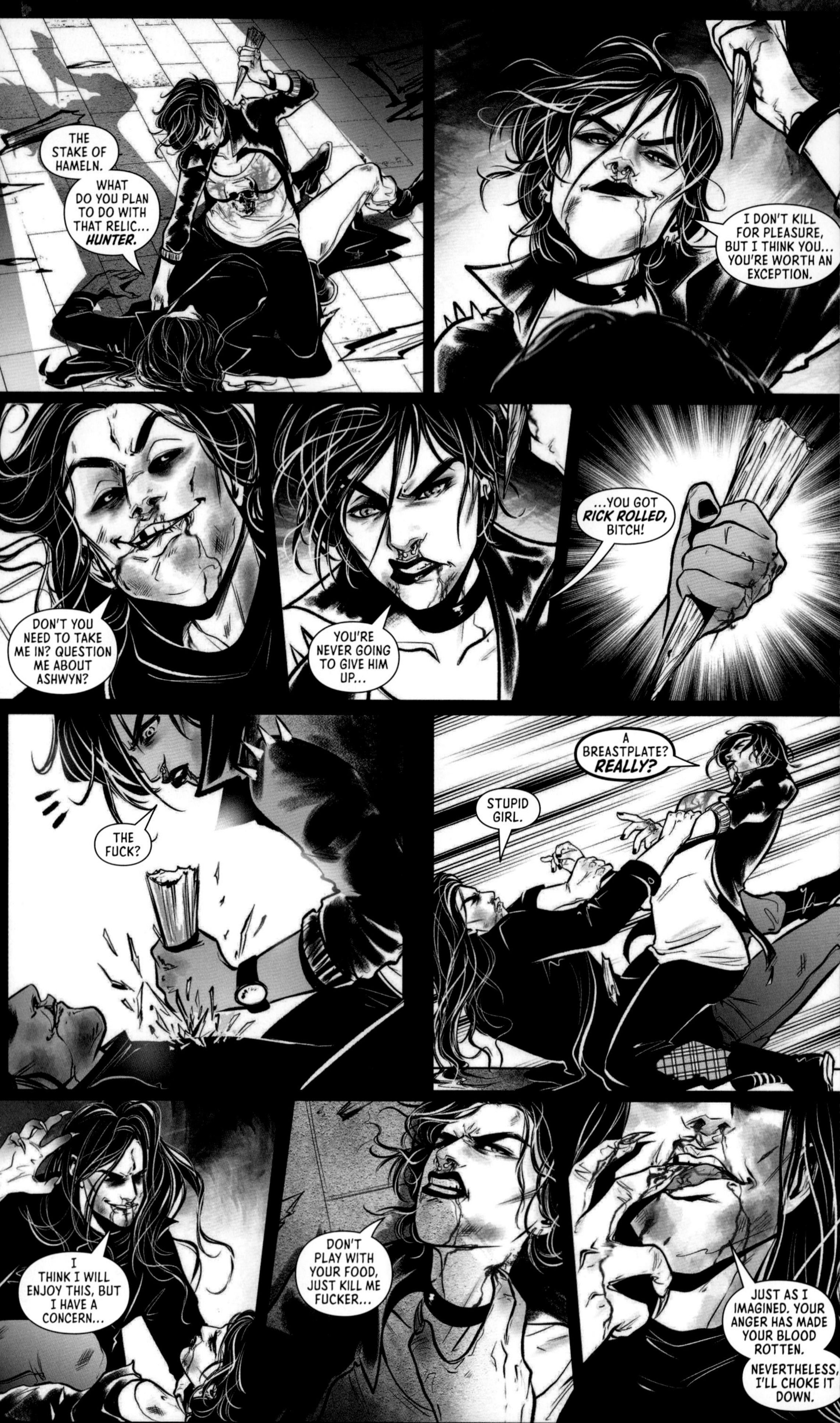
THE STAKE OF HAMELN.
WHAT DO YOU PLAN TO DO WITH THAT RELIC... ***HUNTER.***
I DON'T KILL FOR PLEASURE, BUT I THINK YOU... YOU'RE WORTH AN EXCEPTION.
DON'T YOU NEED TO TAKE ME IN? QUESTION ME ABOUT ASHWYN?
YOU'RE NEVER GOING TO GIVE HIM UP...
...YOU GOT ***RICK ROLLED,*** BITCH!
THE FUCK?
A BREASTPLATE? ***REALLY?***
STUPID GIRL.
I THINK I WILL ENJOY THIS, BUT I HAVE A CONCERN...
DON'T PLAY WITH YOUR FOOD, JUST KILL ME FUCKER...
JUST AS I IMAGINED. YOUR ANGER HAS MADE YOUR BLOOD ROTTEN.
NEVERTHELESS, I'LL CHOKE IT DOWN.

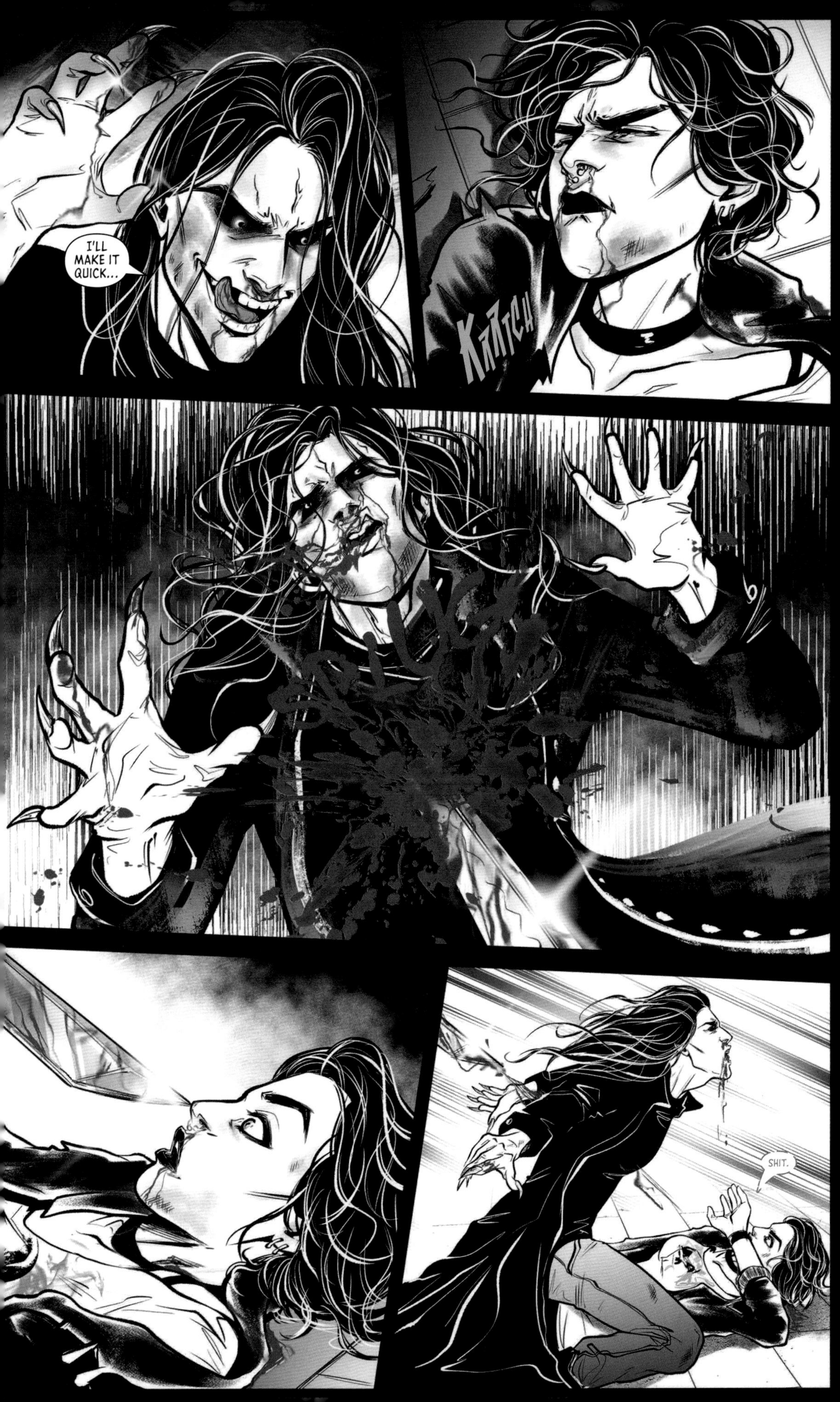

I'LL MAKE IT QUICK...
KRATCH
SHIT.

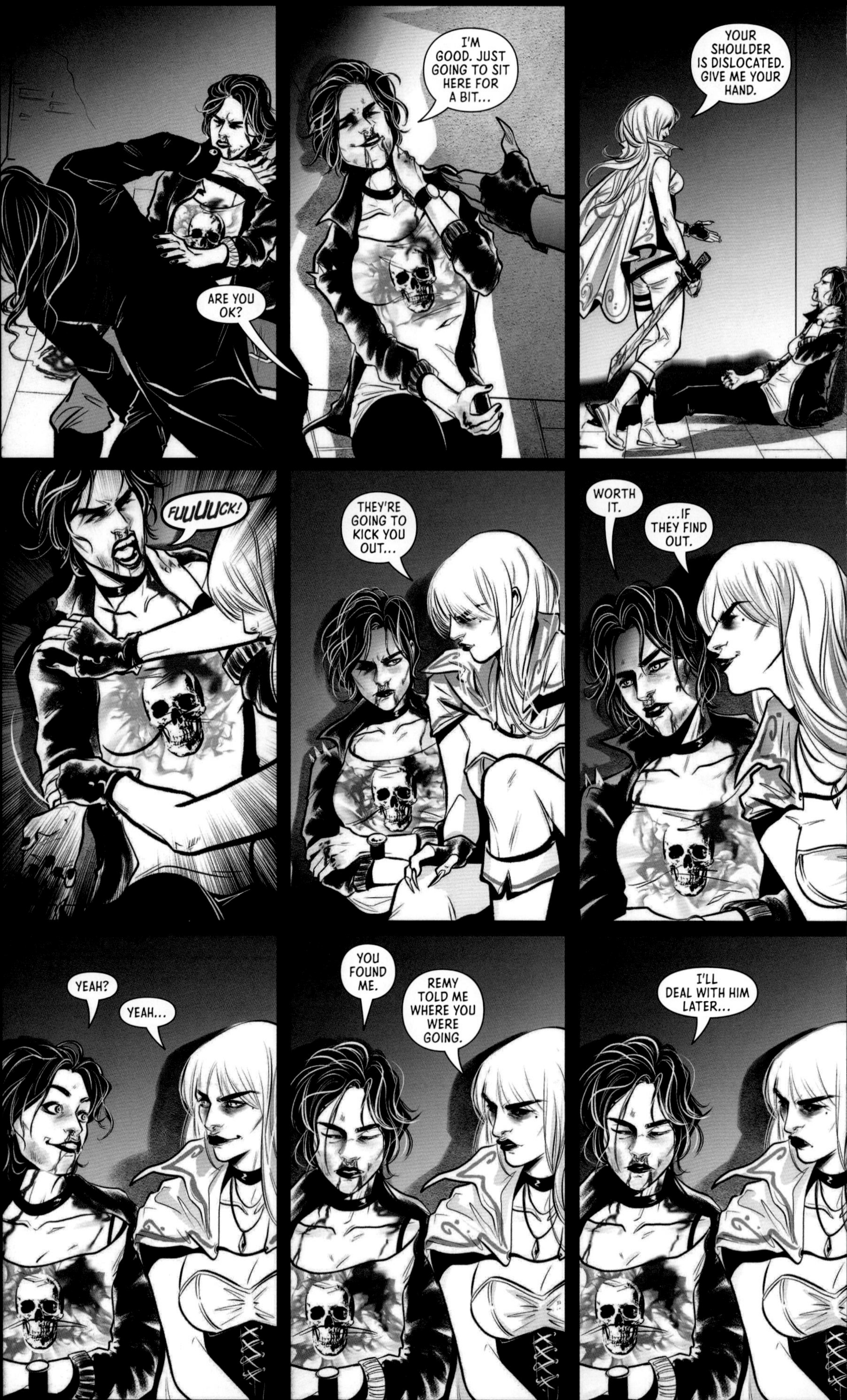
ARE YOU OK?
I'M GOOD. JUST GOING TO SIT HERE FOR A BIT...
YOUR SHOULDER IS DISLOCATED. GIVE ME YOUR HAND.
FUUUUCK!
THEY'RE GOING TO KICK YOU OUT...
WORTH IT.
...IF THEY FIND OUT.
YEAH?
YEAH...
YOU FOUND ME.
REMY TOLD ME WHERE YOU WERE GOING.
I'LL DEAL WITH HIM LATER...

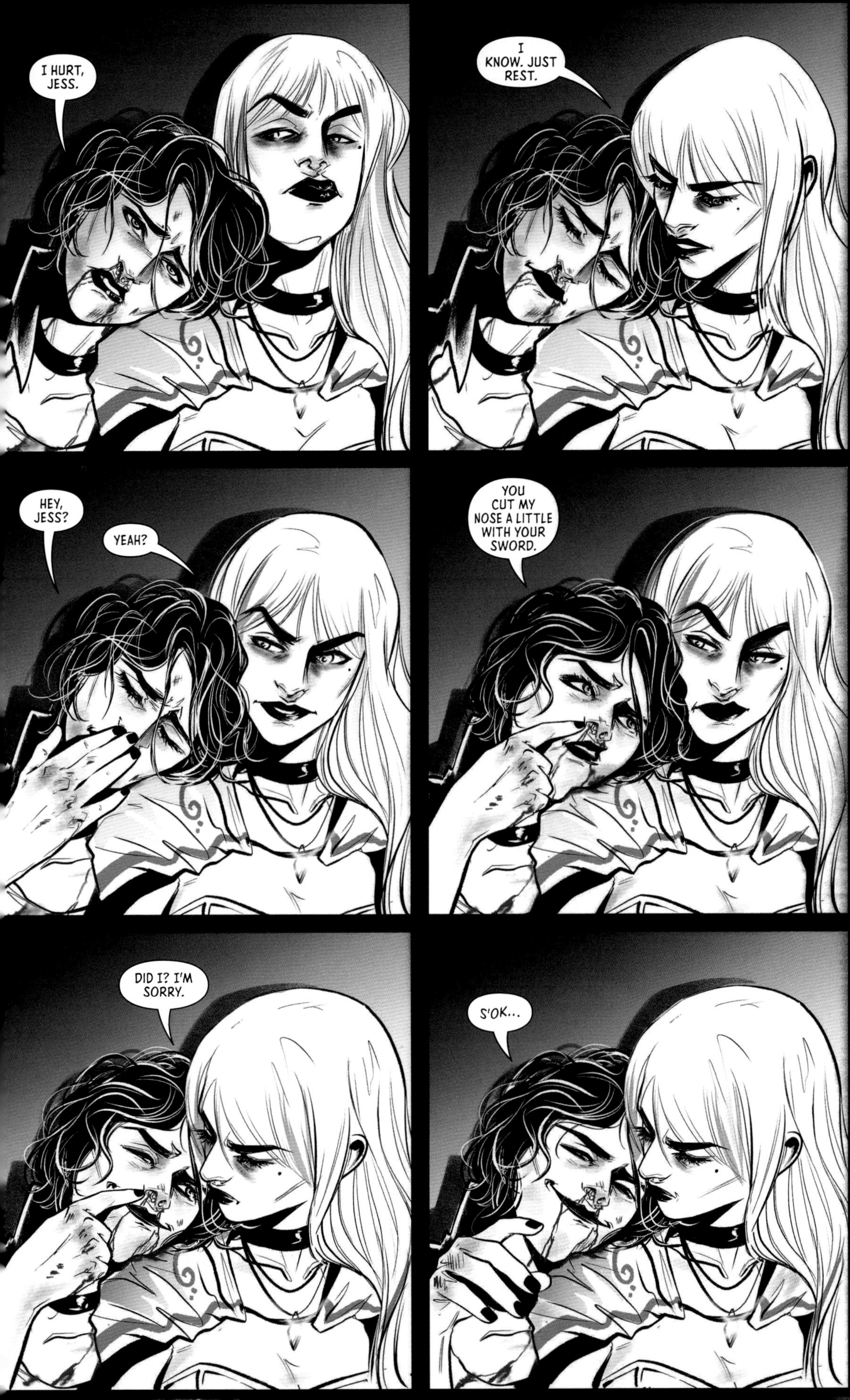
I HURT, JESS.
I KNOW. JUST REST.
HEY, JESS?
YEAH?
YOU CUT MY NOSE A LITTLE WITH YOUR SWORD.
DID I? I'M SORRY.
S'OK...

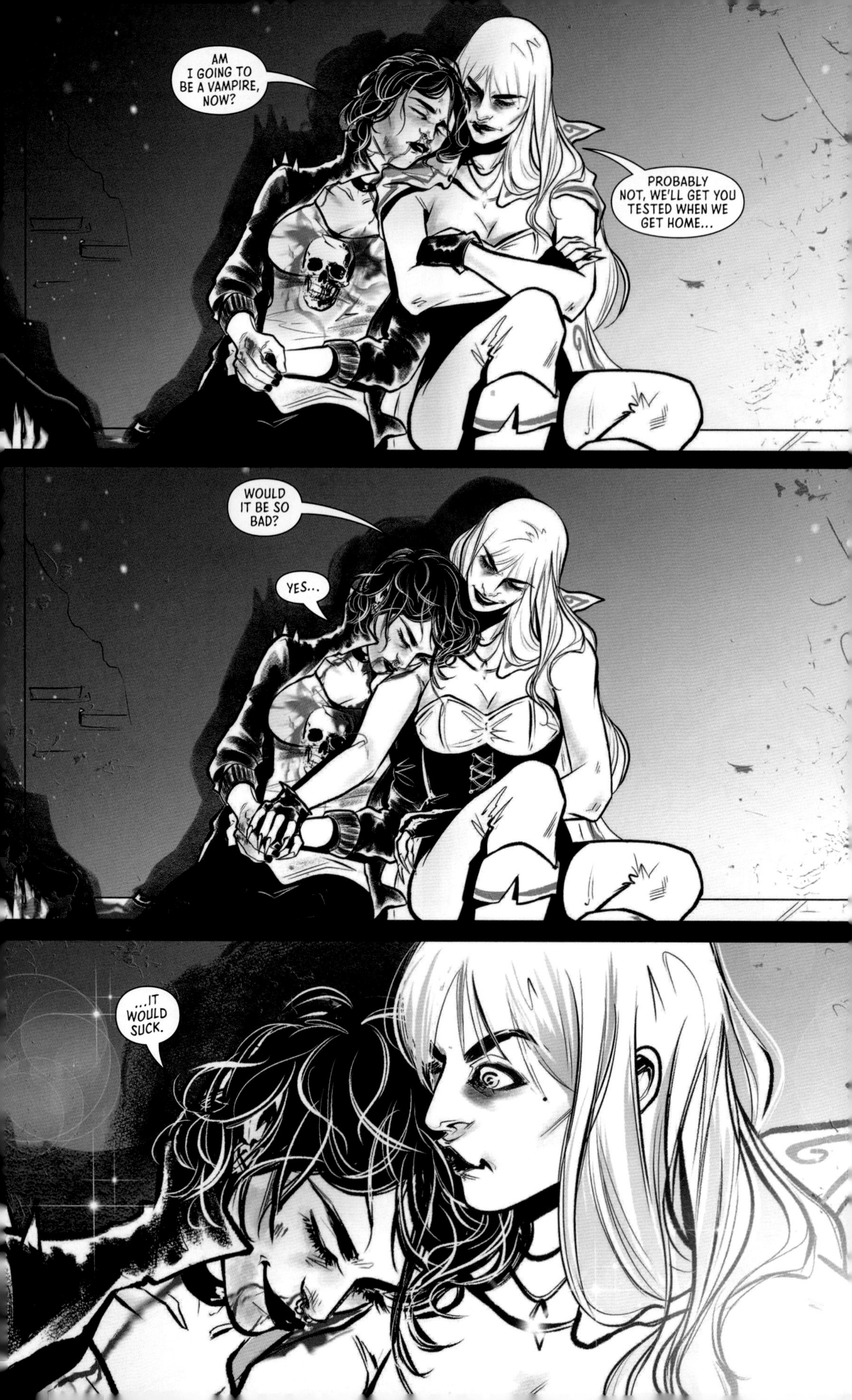
AM I GOING TO BE A VAMPIRE, NOW?
PROBABLY NOT, WE'LL GET YOU TESTED WHEN WE GET HOME...
WOULD IT BE SO BAD?
YES...
...IT WOULD SUCK.

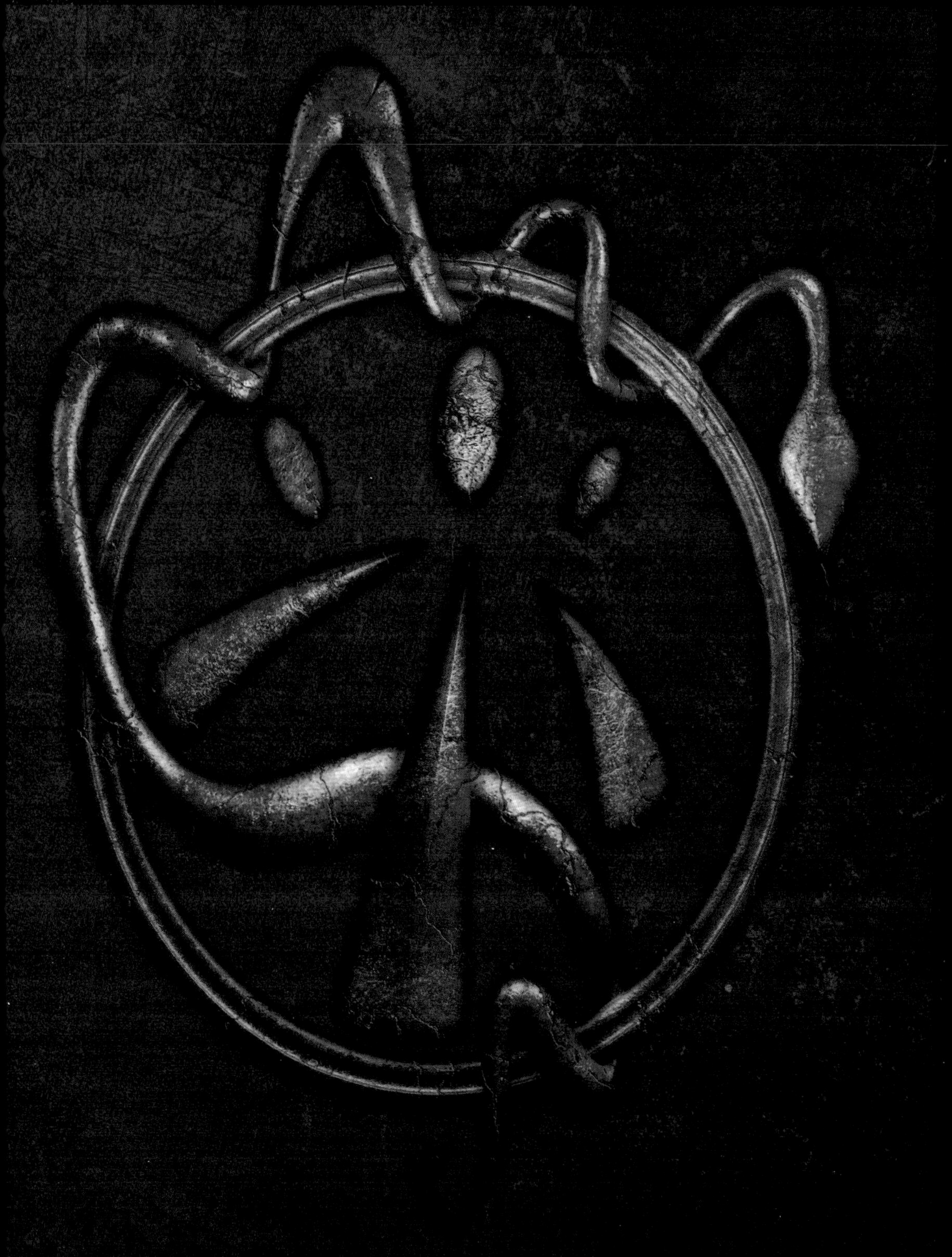

End Volume One

Joel Rodriguez

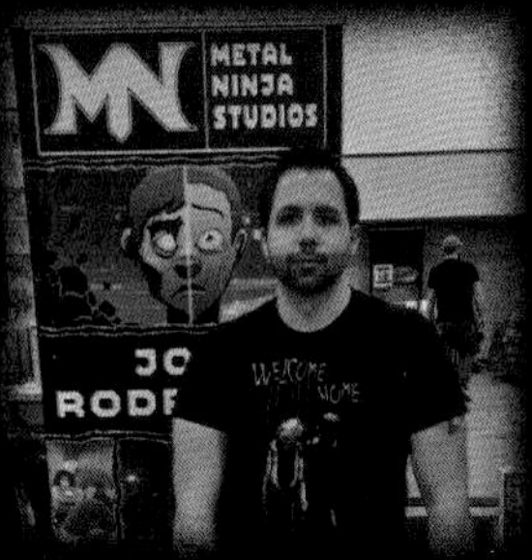
MN
METAL
NINJA
STUDIOS

JOEL RODRIGUEZ IS THE CO-CEO/OWNER OF BRINK OF REALITY PRODUCTIONS AND THE CO-FOUNDER OF METAL NINJA STUDIOS. HE HAS LETTERED MULTIPLE TITLES FOR SCOUT COMICS, BLACK CARAVAN, SCOOT!, ANTARCTIC PRESS, CALIBER COMICS, WANNABE PRESS, AND SEVERAL KICKSTARTED TITLES, INCLUDING HIS OWN SERIES: THE DUSK COUNTY CHRONICLES.

FIND JOEL ON FACEBOOK @METALNINJASTUDIOS.

The Creation of
STAKE

HEY STAKERS, DAVID HERE!

I CAN'T BELIEVE WE'RE FINALLY COLLECTING THE FIRST ARC OF STAKE! IT'S BEEN QUITE THE JOURNEY FROM ORIGINAL CONCEPT TO THIS TRADE PAPERBACK.

I CAME UP WITH THE IDEA FOR THIS SERIES BACK IN 2017, BUT DIDN'T REALLY DIG IN UNTIL THE SUMMER OF 2018. IT'S AN UNDERSTATEMENT TO SAY THAT IT HAS NOT BEEN A STRAIGHT PATH FROM CONCEPT TO RELEASE. THIS SERIES HAS HAD FOUR DIFFERENT ARTISTS ATTACHED WITH TWO SEPARATE VERSIONS OF ISSUE ONE COMPLETED BY TWO OF THEM.

THE ORIGINAL VERSION OF STAKE #1 WAS EXCLUSIVE TO KICKSTARTER AND FEATURED ART BY LUIS BERNARDINO. I BROUGHT FRANCESCA ON TO ILLUSTRATE A JESSAMY SPINOFF, AND WHEN LUIS COULDN'T CONTINUE ON THE BOOK, SHE STEPPED UP AND BECAME THE DEFINITIVE LOOK FOR THE ENTIRE SERIES.

IN THE FOLLOWING PAGES WE'RE GOING TO SHARE ORIGINAL CHARACTER DESIGNS AND A FEW SIDE BY SIDE COMPARISONS OF WHAT IT LOOKS LIKE WHEN YOU HAVE THE SAME ISSUE DRAWN TWICE. I HOPE YOU ENJOY THIS INSIDE LOOK AT STAKE!

THE CAST:

I ALWAYS HAD A VISION OF THE CHARACTERS AS I DEVELOPED THE STORY AND LUIS BREATHED THE ORIGINAL BREATH OF LIFE INTO THEIR DESIGNS:

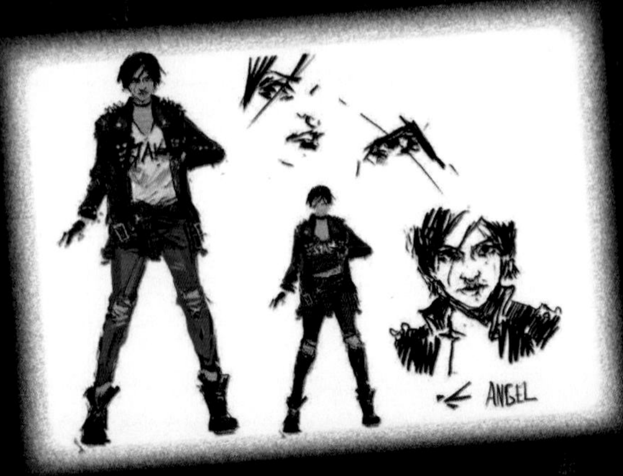
ANGEL

ANGEL "STAKE" BELTRAN STINSON

19, HISPANIC AND AFRICAN-AMERICAN, DARK HAIR, GREEN EYES. SHE'S TALLER, LIKE 5'10-5'11, LANKY, KIND OF A PUNK, SHORTER STYLISH HAIR, ALMOST LIKE A FRIZZY NATALIE IMBRUGLIA CUT.

WHEN WE FIRST SEE HER IN THE OPENING IMAGES, SHE'S ONLY 16.

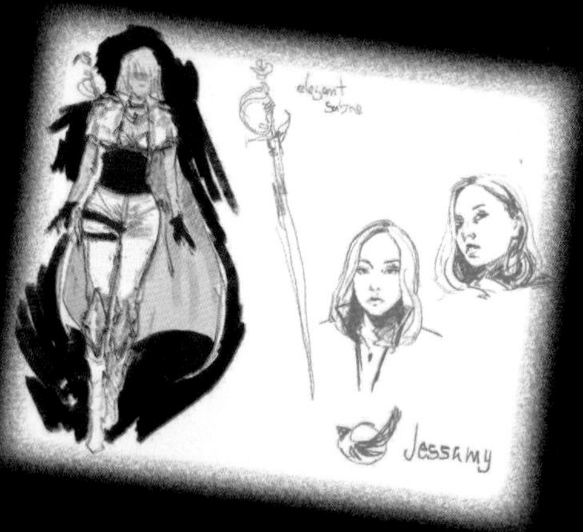
Jessamy

JESSAMY

REALLY OLD, BUT LOOKS LIKE MAYBE SHE'S IN HER LATE 20S-EARLY 30S. SHE'S PALE, WITH CRYSTAL BLUE EYES (FRANCESCA DECIDED THEY SHOULD BE YELLOW AND I DIG IT), AND SILVER HAIR. SHE DRESSES IN WHITE AND CARRIES A BIG SWORD. SHE'S SHORT.

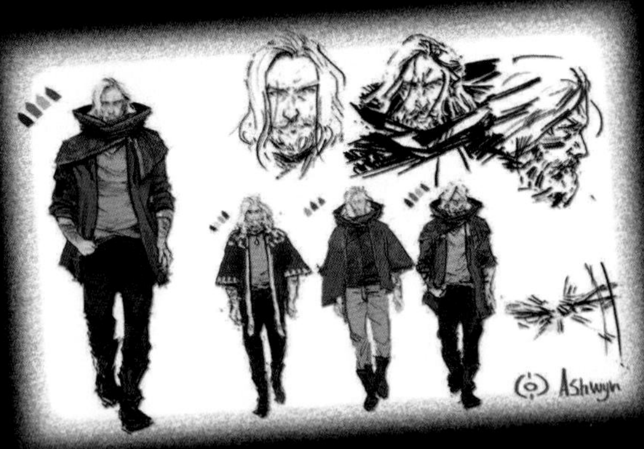
Ashwyn

ASHWYN

HE'S OLD, BUT DOESN'T LOOK IT, BELOW AVERAGE HEIGHT. AS A VAMPIRE HE'S SOMEWHAT PALE. HIS HAIR IS LONG, LIGHT COLORED, AND HIS EYES ARE LIGHT. HIS CLOTHES ARE MODERN, EUROPEAN (CIRCA 2015).

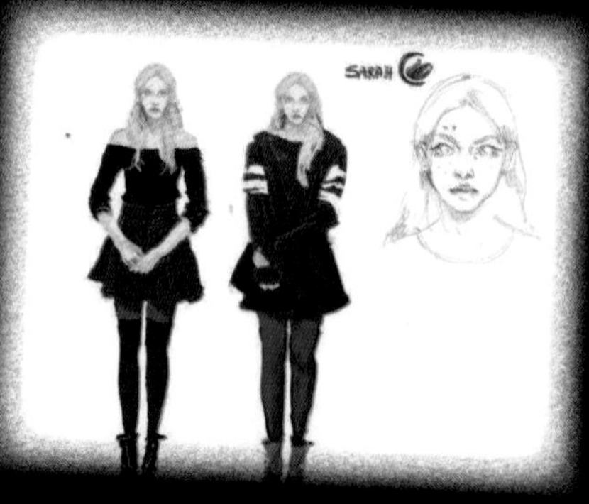
SARAH

SARAH SMITH

19, BLONDE HAIR, BLUE EYES. SHE'S A PRETTY, DOE-EYED VAMPIRE YOUNGLING, WHO DOESN'T KNOW SHE'S A VAMPIRE. SHE'S SHORTER THAN ANGEL.

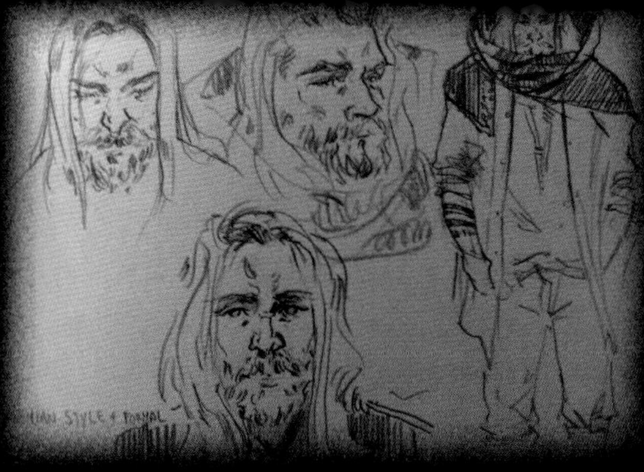

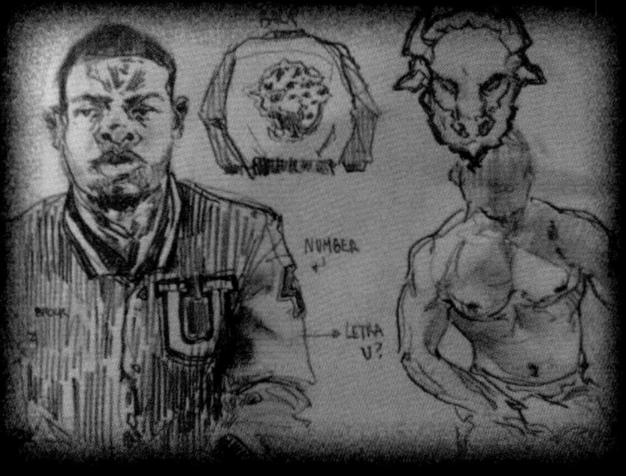
NUMBER
LETRA U?

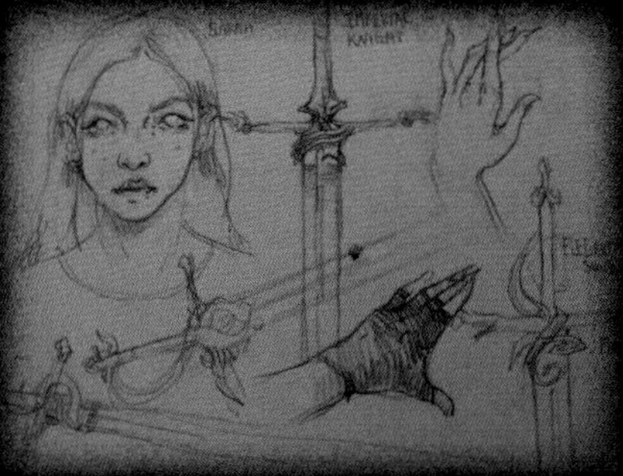

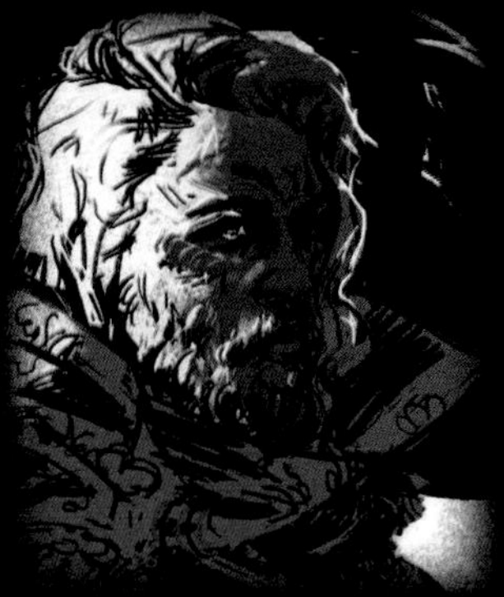

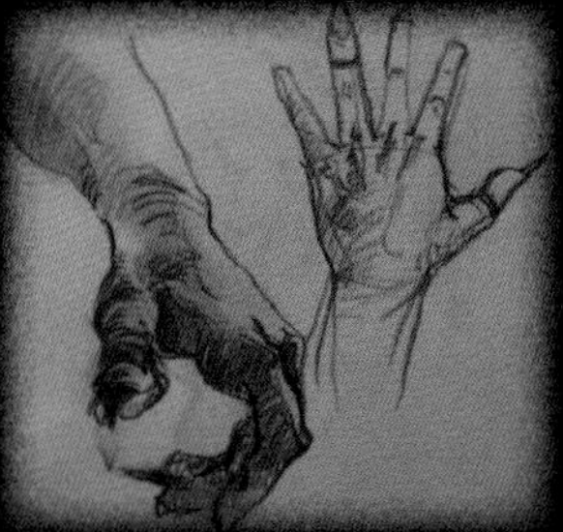

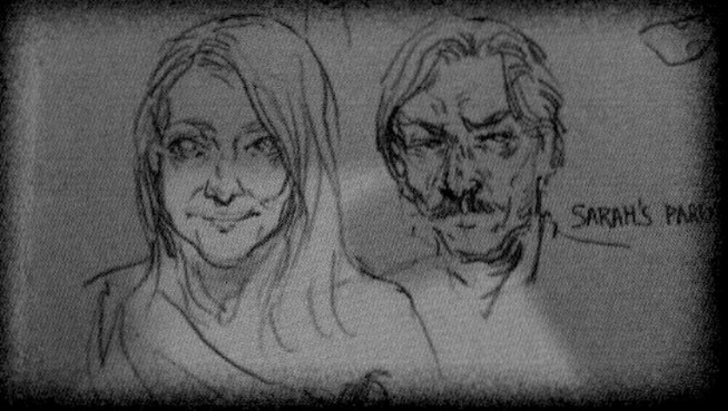

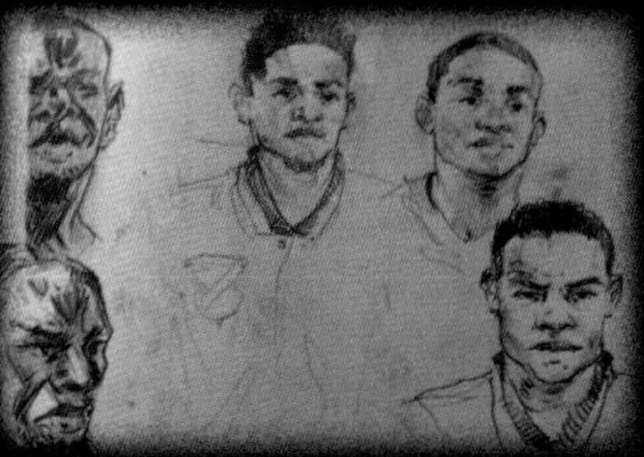

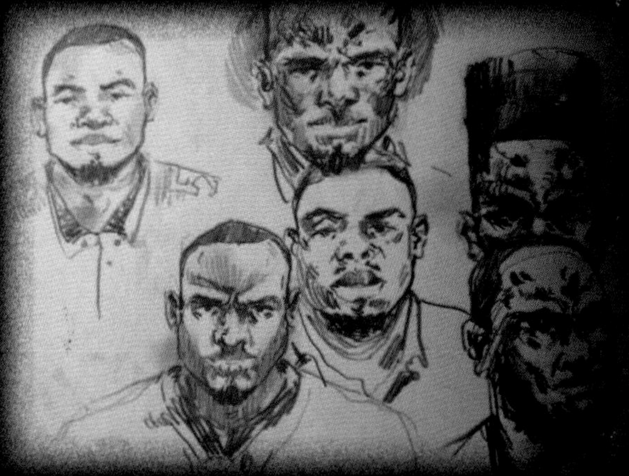

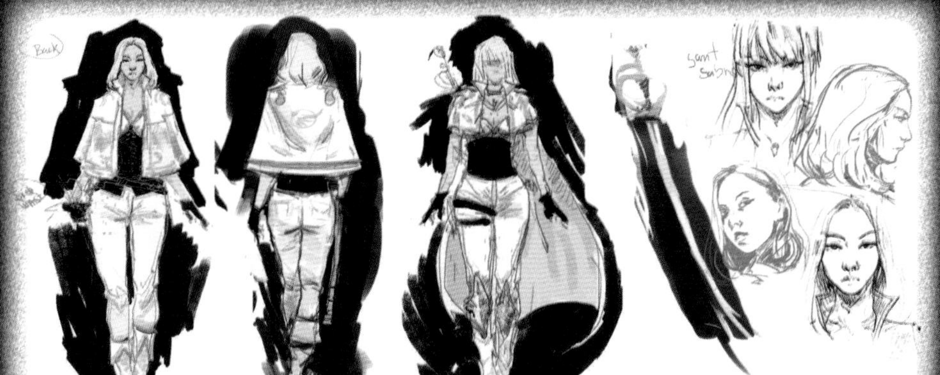
Back
Jessamy

We Got You Covered:

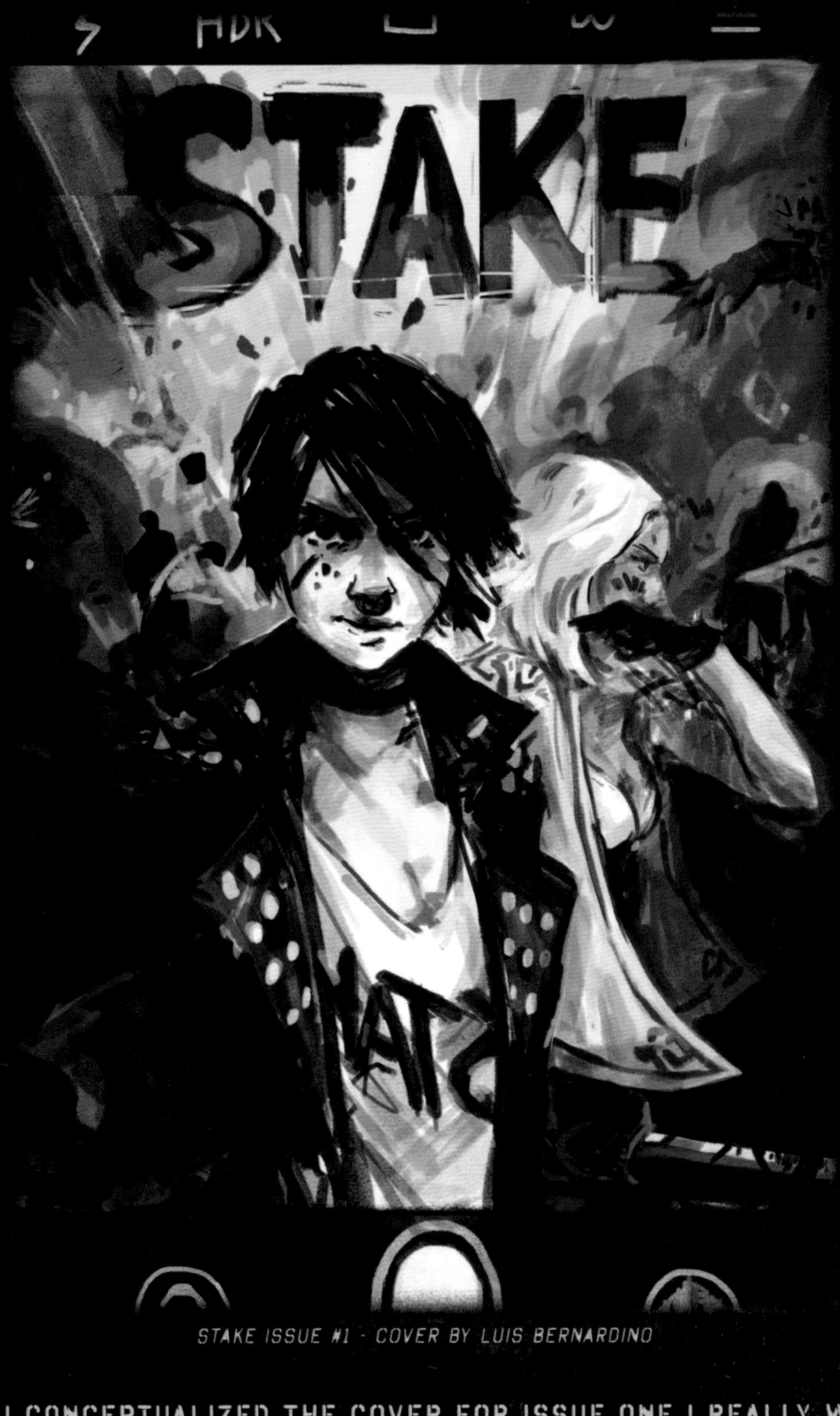
STAKE

STAKE ISSUE #1 - COVER BY LUIS BERNARDINO

WHEN I CONCEPTUALIZED THE COVER FOR ISSUE ONE I REALLY WANTED TO GET THE POINT ACROSS THAT ANGEL WAS A MODERN TEEN WHO ONE MIGHT EXPECT TO TAKE A SELFIE IN THE MIDDLE OF A BATTLE. AT THE SAME TIME, I WANTED TO CONVEY THE IDEA THAT JESSAMY IS THERE FOR HER, IS HER MENTOR, AND INEVITABLY WILL BAIL HER OUT WHEN NECESSARY. ULTIMATELY BOTH ARTISTS SET THE TONE FOR WHAT YOU CAN EXPECT FROM THEIR INTERIORS MASTERFULLY.

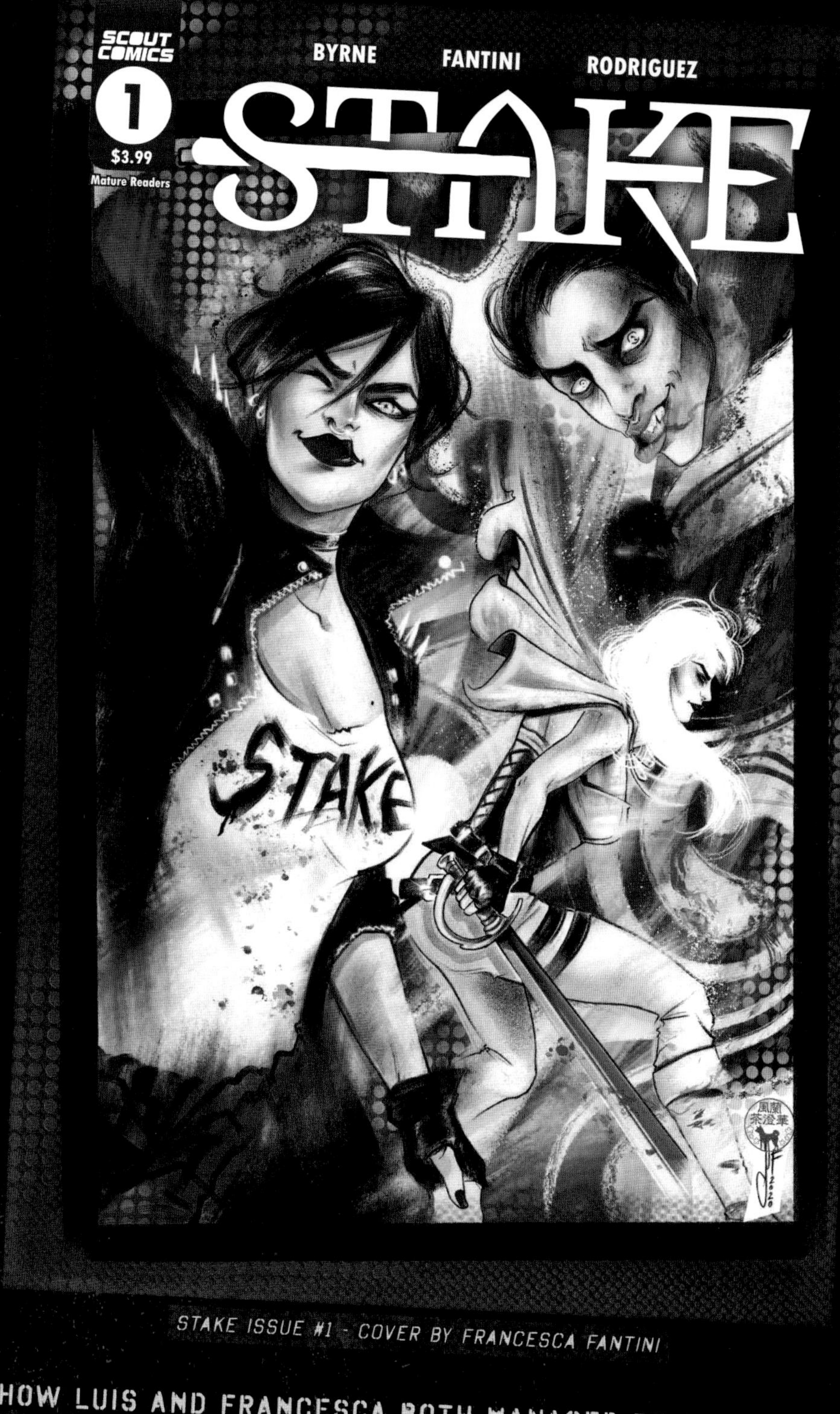
SCOUT COMICS
BYRNE
FANTINI
RODRIGUEZ
1
$3.99
Mature Readers
STAKE
STAKE

STAKE ISSUE #1 - COVER BY FRANCESCA FANTINI

I LOVE HOW LUIS AND FRANCESCA BOTH MANAGED TO CAPTURE THE CONCEPT I WAS LOOKING FOR BUT IN THEIR OWN UNIQUE STYLE. IT'S ALWAYS FUN TO SEE HOW ARTISTS WILL TAKE YOUR VISION AND RUN WITH THEM. IN THIS INSTANCE I LOVE BOTH VERSIONS; LUIS WITH HIS SCRATCHY BLACK AND WHITE STYLE WITH THAT GRIT AND DIRTY FEELING THAT REALLY GETS YOU INTO THE WORLD, AND FRANCESCA WITH HER VIBRANT LIVELY COLORS AND EMOTIONS THAT PERMEATE THE PAGES OF THE ENTIRE SERIES.

Tear My Heart Out:

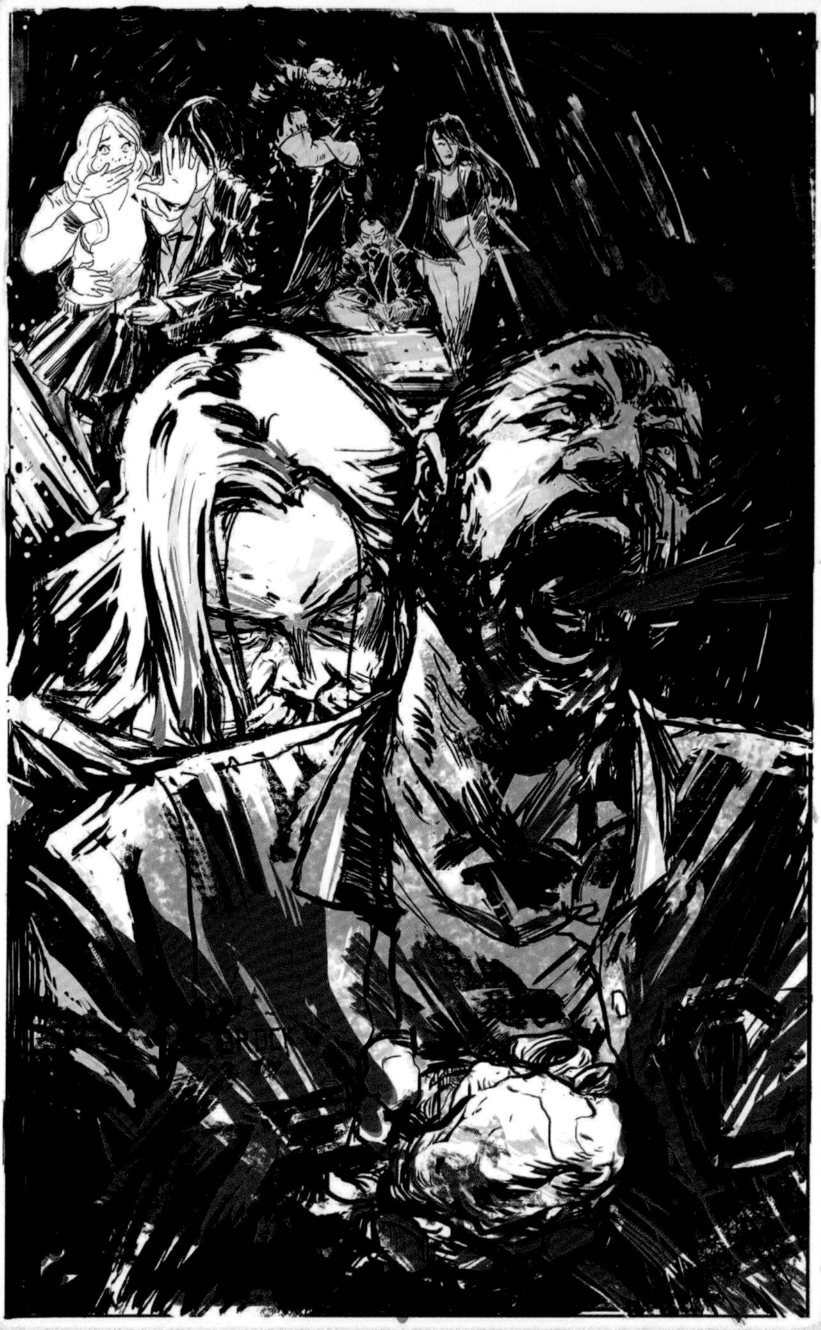

STAKE ISSUE #1 - PAGE 1 BY LUIS BERNARDINO

THIS PAGE WAS REALLY IMPORTANT TO ME. I WANTED TO ESTABLISH THE TONE FOR THE ENTIRE SERIES WITH ONE IMAGE AND GIVE A PREVIEW OF WHAT KIND OF WORLD WE WERE JUMPING INTO. THIS IS SOMETHING I TRIED TO DO IN EACH ISSUE OF STAKE - SET A TONE FOR AN ISSUE ON THE FIRST PAGE. BUT THIS ONE WAS MORE, THIS WAS THE CHANCE FOR THE READER TO START THE WHOLE SERIES OFF WITH A BANG.

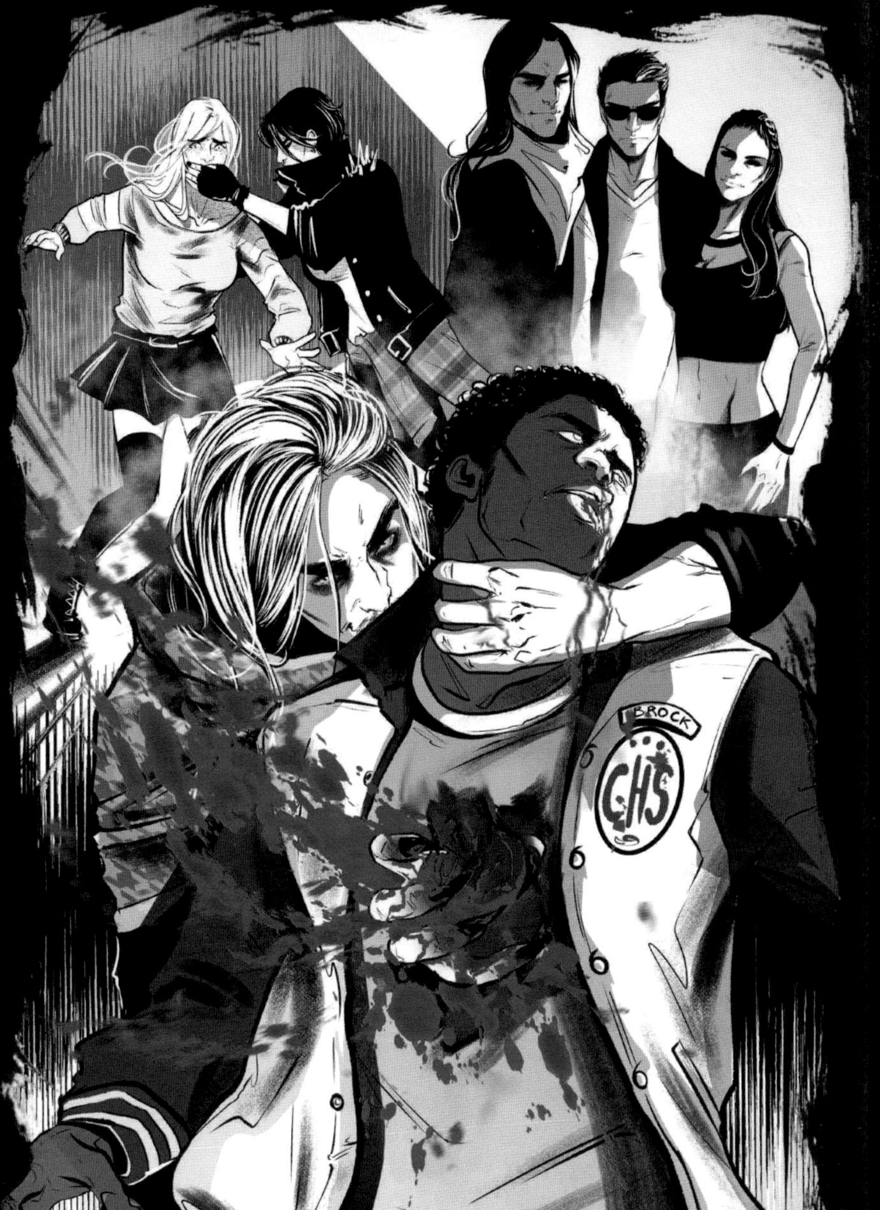
BROCK
CHS

STAKE ISSUE #1 - PAGE 1 BY FRANCESCA FANTINI

LUIS AND I WENT BACK AND FORTH ON EXACTLY HOW TO PRESENT THIS PAGE, FROM CHARACTER POSITIONING TO HOW MUCH WE SHOWED. IN THE END, THE DECISION WAS TO SHOW IT ALL - BROCK WILSON'S HEART WAS NOT JUST ASHWYN'S SHOWPIECE, IT WAS OURS. THIS MADE IT PETTY EASY FOR ME TO DIRECT FRANCESCA TO REPLICATE THE PAGE LAYOUT AND SHE NAILED IT WITH HER INTERPRETATION. *POOR BROCK...*

Monkey See, Monkey Do:

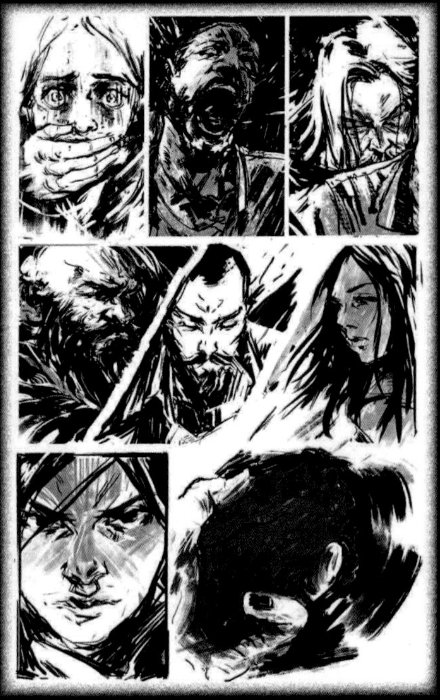

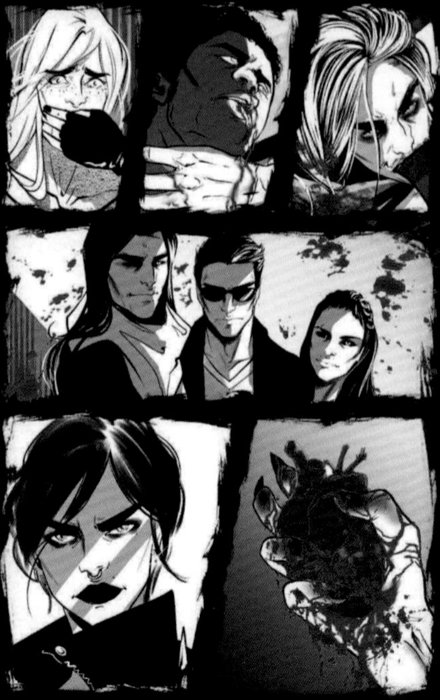

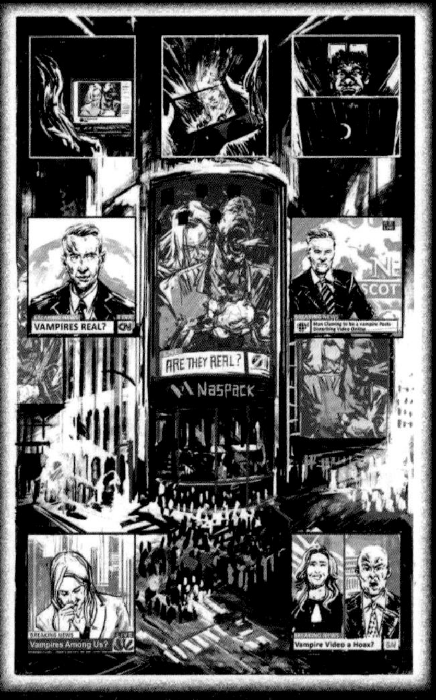
VAMPIRES REAL?
ARE THEY REAL?
Vampires Among Us?
Vampire Video a Hoax?

STAKE ISSUE #1 - PAGES 2-3
BY LUIS BERNARDINO

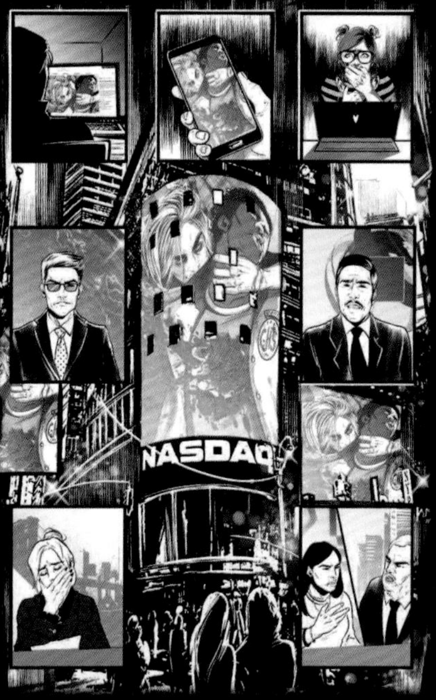
NASDAQ

STAKE ISSUE #1 - PAGES 2-3
BY FRANCESCA FANTINI

AS YOU CAN SEE HERE THE DIFFERENT VERSIONS OF STAKE ISSUE ONE HAD VERY...VERY SIMILAR LAYOUTS. LUIS AND I WENT TO GREAT LENGTHS TO GET THE EARLY PAGES OF THIS ISSUE JUST RIGHT. WHEN I HANDED ART DUTIES OVER TO FRANCESCA THE INSTRUCTIONS WERE SIMPLE, "DRAW THIS IN YOUR STYLE."

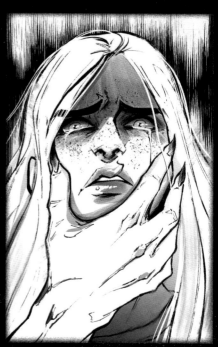

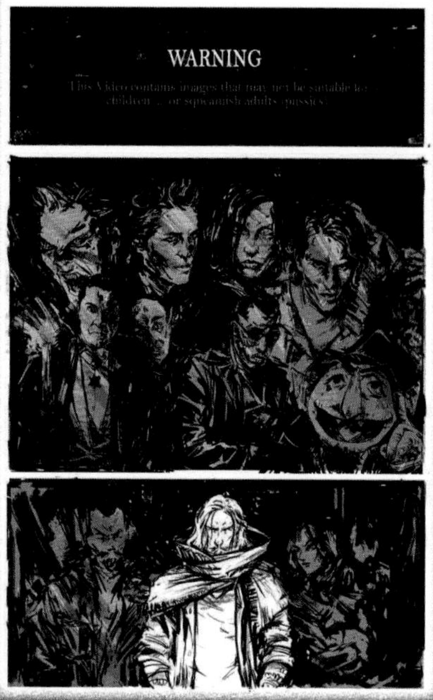
WARNING

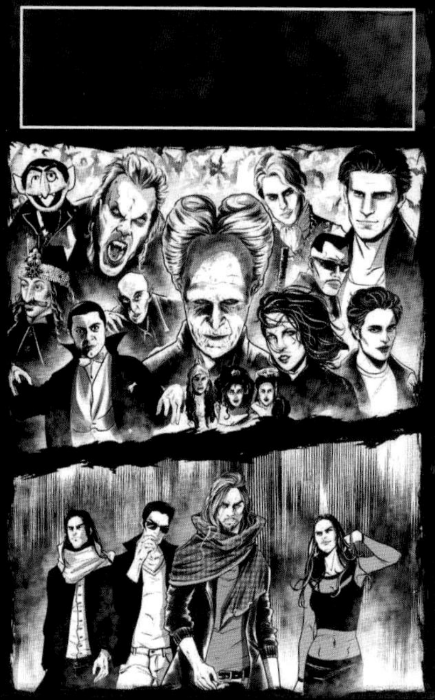

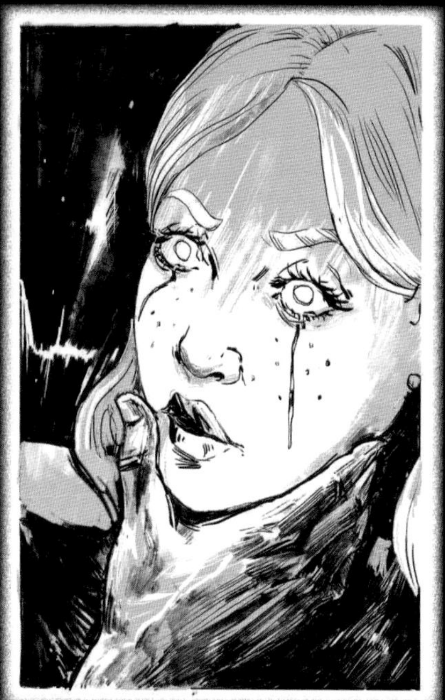

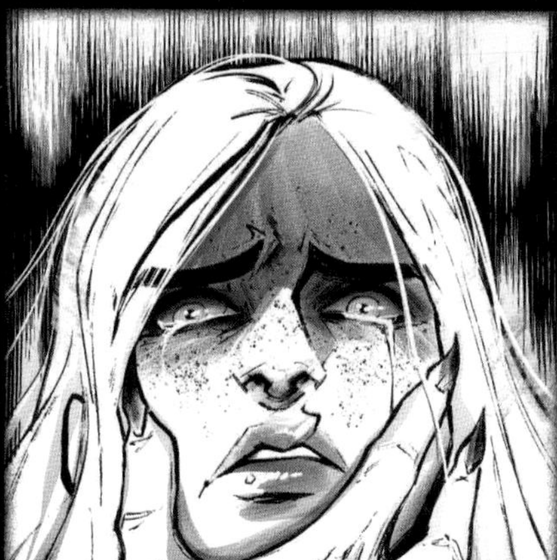

STAKE ISSUE #1 - PAGES 6 & 8
BY LUIS BERNARDINO

STAKE ISSUE #1 - PAGES 6 & 8
BY FRANCESCA FANTINI

THERE WAS NO WAY I COULDN'T INCLUDE BOTH VERSIONS OF ONE OF MY FAVORITE PAGES OF THE ENTIRE SERIES. PAGE SIX FEATURES A PANEL I CALL "THE VAMPY BUNCH." I LOVE HOW BOTH LUIS AND FRANCESCA PUT THEIR SPINS ON THE VAMPS WE ALL KNOW AND LOVE (OR LOATHE IN SOME CASES). AS FUN AS THAT PAGE IS, PAGE EIGHT IS AN EARLY LOOK AT THE EMOTIONS FRANCESCA INFUSED IN THE CHARACTERS FOR THE SIX ISSUES IN THIS EDITION.

He Said, She Said:

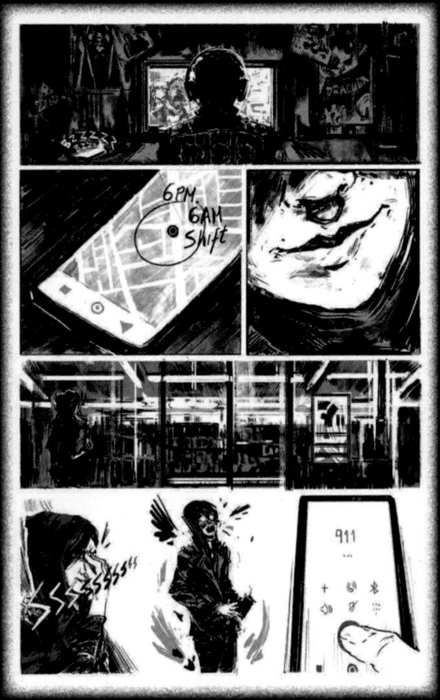
6PM.
6AM
Shift
911

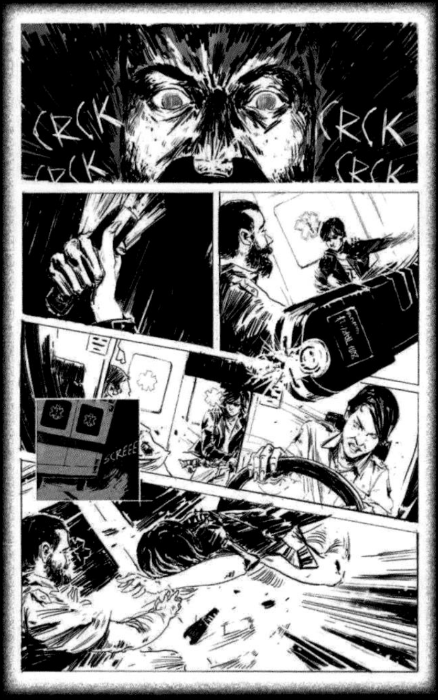
CRCK
CRCK
CRCK
CRCK
SCREEE

STAKE ISSUE #1 - PAGES 12 & 19
BY LUIS BERNARDINO

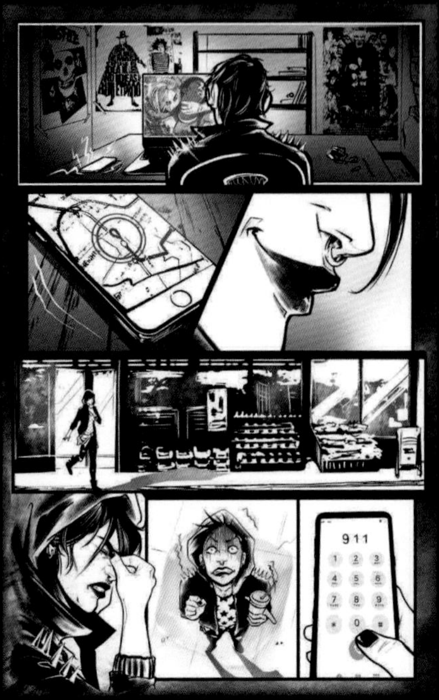
911

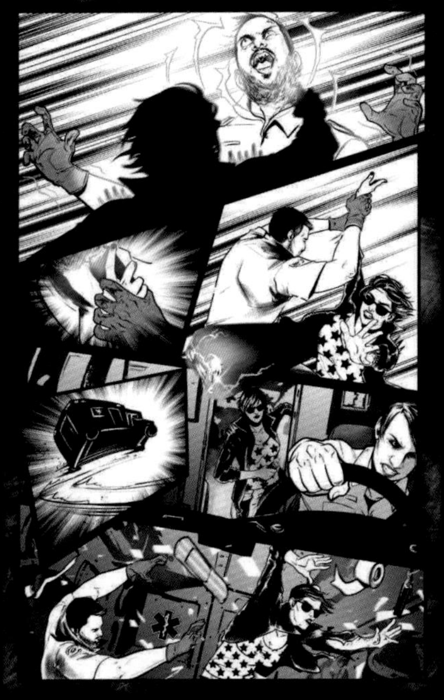

STAKE ISSUE #1 - PAGES 12 & 19
BY FRANCESCA FANTINI

ONCE WE HIT THE MIDDLE PORTION OF THE BOOK I TOOK THE REINS OFF AND FRANCESCA USED THE SCRIPT INSTEAD OF PREVIOUSLY DRAWN PAGES TO REALLY LEAVE HER MARK ON THE SERIES. YOU CAN SEE IN THESE PAGES HOW DIFFERENT THE STYLES WERE AND HOW DRASTICALLY DIFFERENTLY TWO ARTISTS CAN TELL THE SAME STORY.

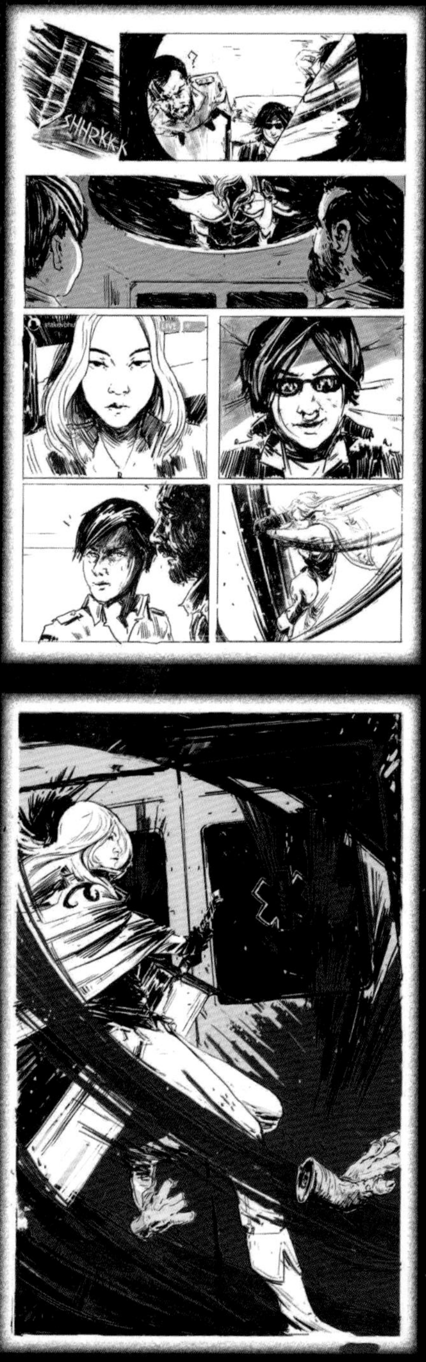
SHHRKKK

STAKE ISSUE #1 - PAGES 23 & 24
BY LUIS BERNARDINO

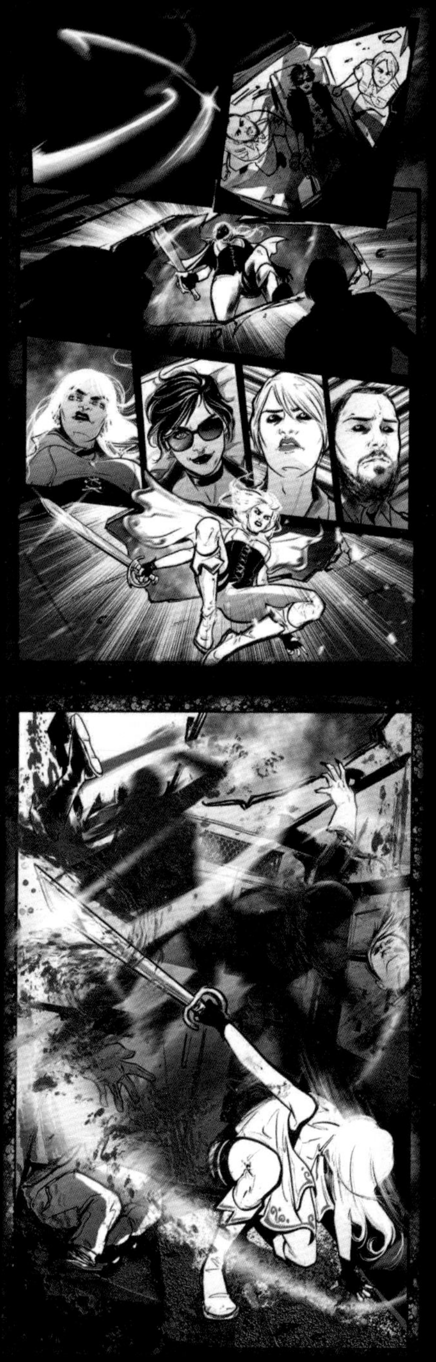

STAKE ISSUE #1 - PAGES 23 & 24
BY FRANCESCA FANTINI

YOU'VE MADE IT THIS FAR, SO LET ME TAKE THIS OPPORTUNITY TO THANK YOU ON BEHALF OF FRANCESCA, JOEL, AND MYSELF, FOR PICKING UP THIS TRADE AND GIVING OUR LITTLE STORY ABOUT A WORLD WHERE VAMPIRES ARE REAL A CHANCE. THERE'S LOTS MORE STAKE TO COME, SO KEEP YOUR EYES OPEN FOR FUTURES VOLUMES OF *STAKE* AND *STAKE PRESENTS!*

- DAVID